The Enemy Within

DONALD THOMAS

The Enemy Within

HUCKSTERS, RACKETEERS, DESERTERS &
CIVILIANS DURING THE SECOND WORLD WAR

NEW YORK UNIVERSITY PRESS
Washington Square, New York

NEW YORK UNIVERSITY PRESS
Washington Square
New York, NY 10003

First published in 2003 by John Murray (Publishers)
A division of Hodder Headline

Library of Congress Cataloging-in-Publication Data
Thomas, Donald Serrall.
[Underworld at war]
The enemy within : hucksters, racketeers, deserters,
and civilians during the Second World War / Donald Thomas.
p. cm.
Originally published under title:
An underworld at war. London : J. Murray, 2003.
Includes bibliographical references and index.
ISBN 0–8147–8286–8 (alk. paper)
1. Crime—Great Britian—History—20th century. 2. Criminals—
Great Britian—History—20th century. 3. World War,
1939–1945—Great Britian. 4. World War, 1939–1945—
Desertions—Great Britian. 5. Military deserters—Great Britian—
History—20th century. I. Title.
HV6957.T38 2004
364.1'06'094109044—dc22   2003066469

10 9 8 7 6 5 4 3 2 1

For Isabel, George, Kate, Graham, Ellie, David and Agnieszka

Contents

Illustrations

The author and publishers would like to thank the following for permission to reproduce illustrations: Plates 1, 10, 13, 14, 20 and 23, Hulton Archive; 2 Hulton-Deutsch Collection/CORBIS; 3 and 4, Public Record Office; 11, The Advertising Archive; 12 and 21, Topham Picturepoint; 22, the Estate of Osbert Lancaster with permission of John Murray.

Preface

It is not the intention of this book to suggest that the heroism or sacrifice of the British people in the Second World War was less than traditionally portrayed. Pitt the Younger's assertion, a century and a half earlier, that England had saved herself by her exertions and would save Europe by her example, was never more true than in the years 1939 to 1945. The purpose of the great majority of her people was to fulfil Pitt's promise.

The aim of the wartime underworld was equally direct, as the gang leader Billy Hill described it. By determined exploitation of shortages, the frontiers of crime would be extended throughout a thriving civilian black market. Men and women who might never have broken a law in peacetime would find themselves linked, distantly but inevitably, to the thief and the racketeer. Much was to be heard of racketeers. Before 1939 some had already acquired the status of gangsters, whilst others were merely envied for their success in business. War was to prove the great leveller of both classes. In many cases, those who had not previously been professional criminals showed themselves a lot brighter and able to do a lot better as wartime law-breakers than the boastful gangsters. For a Liverpool ship repairer to cheat the government of the modern equivalent of £20,000,000 in two years made Billy Hill's smash and grab raids on West End jewellers seem almost paltry.

The activities of its underworld were to feature little in histories of the war but a good deal in its fiction. Basil Seal's evacuee racket in Evelyn Waugh's *Put Out More Flags* (1942) had its parallel in reality. In Waugh's 'Sword of Honour' trilogy, *Men at Arms* (1952) recalls the sergeant-major's warning to young officers about the frauds practised on the Army by civilian contractors. Meantime, at the castle near Penkirk, the Pioneer Corps has made itself cosy throughout the winter by trading tools and supplies from the company stores for civilian comforts. *Officers and Gentlemen* (1955) adds a disturbing undertone to the war in the Middle East. An Egyptian taxi driver lies buried under the sand close to the camp with his throat cut. The camp police flush women from the company lines. The medical supplies are stolen by an Arab waiter. The NAAFI till is burgled as a matter of routine and there is news of wholesale pilfering of drink and tobacco on the railways in far-off England.

In *The Third Man*, which appeared in 1950, a year later than the film, Graham Greene's poetic portrayal of the black market in occupied Vienna is a muted echo of reality. In 1946 Fiorella La Guardia, who had been a popular Mayor of New York, was appointed head of the new United Nations Relief and Rehabilitation Administration, UNRRA. This organization's first ask was to prevent starvation in the lately defeated or liberated countries of Europe. La Guardia was dismayed to find that a modern equivalent of £80,000,000 of relief supplies every month was being stolen at the port of Trieste alone, for sale on the black market. An entire shipment of penicillin was among the supplies which had disappeared. Nor were such markets dependent solely on professional thieves. A friend of Graham Greene's went with two doctors to see *The Third Man*. The doctors were silent and subdued after the visit, then confessed to having been RAF medical officers in post-war Vienna and having sold penicillin without thinking of the consequences.

Waugh and Greene were giants of the fiction of war. Yet few documentary accounts of the political underworld could match F. L. Green's drama of a wounded IRA gunman on the run in *Odd Man Out* (1945) or John Mair's political thriller *Never Come Back* (1941) with its overtones of John Buchan. Patrick Hamilton's novel *The Slaves of Solitude* (1947) is a fine portrayal of wartime shortages and the resentments of residents at a Thames valley boarding-house, a disenchantment on which the black market thrived. To complement these, the short stories of Julian Maclaren Ross in *The Stuff to Give the Troops* (1944) and *Better Than a Kick in the Pants* (1945) form a sharply observed comedy of other ranks' manipulation of army routine.

Of subsequent studies of criminality, Edward Smithies' *Crime in Wartime* (1982) offers a skilful analysis and statistical categorization of crime, forming a well-documented social history of this aspect of the war. When the conflict ceased to be a British affair and became what Winston Churchill called a 'Grand Alliance' with the United States, there was already an American black market, though it had few contacts and much to learn in relation to its longer-established transatlantic cousin. However, M. B. Clinard's study of the American experience, *The Black Market* (1952), is a densely detailed account of wartime racketeering in the United States, and a reassuring reminder that such racketeering was not the business of any one nation alone.

For those of us to whom the war was a reality, it is increasingly a childhood vision. My earliest recollection is of a formation of grey aircraft, flying so low that the black crosses on their wings were plainly visible. No bombs had yet fallen on Weston-super-Mare and there was no sense that we might be their target. In the sunlit September lunch-time they had re-formed over the Bristol Channel after a low-level flight from northern France. While the RAF was fighting the Battle of Britain elsewhere, this formation was on its way to devastate the Bristol Aeroplane Works at Filton. Later, on a school walk, there was a field-gate, beyond which the long wooden huts of an army camp had sprouted. Some genial soldiers from South Wales presented our group with a technically illegal tin of corned beef. As far as black market groceries were concerned, I believe my parents were once invited to buy an extra pound of jam, because it was my birthday.

Air raids were synonymous with nights under the stairs. In scenes that might dismay the emergency services of a later age, bomb disposal was sometimes a matter of self-reliance. My father, as a Special Constable, had a couple of unexploded incendiary bombs pointed out to him by an anxious neighbour – a large number of them had failed to go off. He put these in his capacious saddlebag and wheeled them away to be dealt with at the police station. A Morrison shelter arrived, when it was no longer needed, occupying a third of the living room, its wire-mesh sides like an animal cage. Then, almost at the war's end, twiddling the radio tuning-knob I heard an English voice, far off among the whoops and gurgles of the airways. It promised us that though 'Jairmany' was collapsing, a new war would soon follow, now that Britain had spurned an alliance with the 'German legions'. It was puzzling to be told we should soon be at the mercy of our friends Uncle

Joe and his gallant Russian troops. This was the last, longest and most drunken of Lord Haw-Haw's harangues, in May 1945.

In describing the activities of a criminal underworld during those years, I have borne in mind that the memoirs of professional robbers should be taken with more than a pinch of salt. The value of stolen gold or gems, fur coats or the contents of post office safes is likely to be exaggerated. Indeed, it may also be exaggerated by the victims, who seldom understate the amount for the purpose of their insurance claims.

However, it seems worthwhile to give an approximate modern equivalent to the sums of money as expressed in thefts and fines, though this is to some extent subjective. Prices of articles do not rise uniformly but a general rate of increase since the war may be said to be by a factor of 35 times. Of course, inflation is not the whole story. The average weekly wage in 1939 was £4.45 and has multiplied a hundred times, though this income is spent on a wider range of modern comforts rather than in simply paying more for them. Allowing some weight to this, I have suggested that a multiple of 40 would give the reader a fair idea of equivalent values. I have included a modern approximation in brackets beside the sums as they were given at the time. Few people would now feel greatly inconvenienced by a fine of £20. They might hesitate to risk conviction if the penalty were £800. In real terms, property is now more expensive, while foreign travel and telephone calls are much cheaper. A commodity like butter, which was a luxury to many families in 1939, is no longer so.

It is a pleasure to acknowledge the help which I have received in writing this book, involving as it has done a wide variety of sources. Mrs Jenny Collis and her colleagues of the Bodleian Library Map Room have done much to make my work a great deal easier by their patience and helpfulness. The gathering of material has also been greatly assisted through the facilities provided by Professor David Skilton and the Cardiff University School of English, Communications and Philosophy. Ms Sue Anstey, Ms Sue Austin, Ms Sarah Bithell, Ms Helen D'Artillac-Brill, Mr Tom Dawkes, Mrs Chris Hennessy, Ms Nancy Hooper, Mrs Ann Lowery and Mrs Ann Thomas of the Information Services at Cardiff University have between them shortened the writing of the book by many months, by bringing to the desktop documents whose originals lay far off. They have, I fear, saved my time at the expense of a good deal of their own. Without the support of Cardiff and the Bodleian, the completion of this book would have been far distant.

To Major Ian Ambrose MBE of the Royal Corps of Military Police and to Mrs Sue Lines, Curator of the Royal Military Police Museum, I am most grateful for their kindness, hospitality, and an insight into the work of the Corps and of its Special Investigation Branch. It is good to be able to record the part played by the Corps and the Branch in final victory.

Friends and colleagues who have supplied me with information and material include Mr and Mrs Ben Bass of Greyne House Books, Mrs Kate Bradbury of the Cardiff Business School, Mrs Marie Elmer of Clifford Elmer Books, Mr Graeme Holmes, Mr and Mrs W. Shakespeare, Dr Linda Shakespeare. To all of them, I record my thanks.

Among libraries and institutions who have supplied material, I should like to acknowledge particularly the Bodleian Law Library and Modern Papers Room; Brighton and Hove Libraries; the British Library Document Supply Centre; the British Library Newspaper Division; Brixton Central Library; Cambridge University Library; Camden Reference Library; the City of Bristol Reference Library; Hackney Reference Library; Kensington Reference Library; Leeds City Libraries; Manchester City Libraries; the Public Record Office; Romford Reference Library; Tower Hamlets Local History Library and Archives; and the City of Westminster Archives.

I have greatly appreciated the encouragement of Mr Bill Hamilton of A. M. Heath Ltd, Mrs Caroline Knox of John Murray Ltd, and Dr Howard Gotlieb, Director of Special Collections, Boston University, Massachusetts. To them and to Mrs Gail Pirkis, Ms Caroline Westmore and Mr Howard Davies of John Murray I express my thanks. Finally, if this is, indeed, one of the last untold stories of the Second World War, my wife and my family will have done much to aid its telling.

To Mr Eric Zinner and Miss Emily Park, I express my thanks for their work in preparing the American edition of this book. 'Spiv', one of the most evocative English words of the 1940s, never made its way to the United States and has no easy synonym. However, the men described by it were common to many cultures. The fast-talking racecourse hustler, who became a supplier or curb side dealer in stolen or rationed goods, was an inevitable accompaniment to the age of shortages and austerity.

The criminal law thus proceeds upon the principle that it is
morally right to hate criminals.
– Sir James Fitzjames Stephen, *A History of the Criminal Law of
England* (1883)

'One farthing on all the policies . . . So what real harm have
we done?'
– Alec Guinness as 'Professor Marcus' in *The Ladykillers* (1955)

I

The Lost Peace

To most observers, the professional underworld of the later 1930s comprised three main areas of activity. There was a new type of motorized crime, increasingly in the form of smash and grab raids; there was prostitution on the street and in the international 'white slave trade'; and there were the protection rackets of horse racing and the dog tracks.

In the last years of peace, such crimes appeared more ambitious and therefore a good deal more threatening. On 23 July 1937, the *Evening Standard* reported that a new Scotland Yard was to be built, three times the size of the existing police headquarters. The modern criminal was said to be an entirely different proposition compared with his counterpart of ten years before. Few readers needed to be convinced. A new form of street theatre had been provided by smash and grab raids, Flying Squad chases, wage snatches, and robberies in which the public was able to participate by chasing or seizing criminals. In one such drama, on 28 October 1936, in what the placards reported as 'Flying Squad Chase Thrills', hundreds of bystanders lined the pavements and watched two high-powered squad cars race through the streets of Wandsworth in pursuit of a getaway vehicle. Pedestrians leapt clear and cyclists jumped for their lives. After a long chase, the fugitive car cut a corner, became airborne, turned two somersaults and crashed. The occupants were drawn from underneath the wreck. It was, the witnesses said, just like watching a gangster film. After dramas of this kind, they frequently added, 'It was a miracle that nobody was killed.'

Indeed, some people were killed. On 15 January 1938, for example, midnight fur robbers sped down East Ham High Street at seventy miles an hour, a police car just behind them. As the thieves' saloon braked to turn into Caulfield Road, the driver skidded on the greasy road surface and performed two complete circles. The police car hit the saloon at full speed, knocking it sixty feet up the street, head-on into a trolley-bus standard. Three men were found huddled in the wreck: two seriously injured, one dead.

Not all thieves needed to move at such speed. A man racing his engine at night might be a thoughtless motorist keeping the neighbourhood awake. He might also be a getaway driver or 'chauffeur' blanketing the detonations of a safe-blower at work.

The most common illegality seen on the streets was prostitution. For many individual prostitutes in this class, the criminal as pimp was an exception. Sheila Cousins, in her autobiography *To Beg I Am Ashamed* (1938), recalled only one man who had attempted to become a hanger-on. He was seen off with little difficulty.[1]

For the more fortunate there was a higher class of prostitution, in Mayfair and St James's, often run by women and sometimes as a form of cooperative. The first of two prominent cases in 1938 involved a house in Duke Street, St James's, run by a former dress designer. Police observation revealed a routine whereby a phone call from a regular client would be received by the dress designer, as if to make a request for a particular woman. After an outgoing phone call, a smartly dressed young woman would arrive, followed by an older and equally smartly dressed man. It seemed less a conventional brothel than what the Victorians knew as an 'introducing house'. Subsequently, in the so-called 'Vault of Vice' case that year, the location was Mayfair and the setting more elaborate. The house was managed by its madame, a six-foot Jamaican woman wearing only a pair of thigh boots, and the female staff was assertively middle class. This was an area of prostitution far removed either from the shadow of the pimp or from the dramas of white slavery.[2]

Though the so-called 'white slave' trade had become a novelist's cliché, parodied by Evelyn Waugh in *Decline and Fall* (1928), it was to make headlines in 1936. Albert Londres, in *The Road to Buenos Ayres* (1928), had distinguished it from simple prostitution, since its pimps or gangs ran an international traffic. Prostitutes from England were sent to France or South America, those from France or Belgium to England, as if to ensure that they worked in an unfamiliar country and were suitably dependent on their protectors.

In January 1936, the body of Max Kassel, 'Max the Red' from the colour of his hair, was found in a ditch near St Albans. Latvian by birth, he had lived in France, Venezuela and North America, supplying women to South American brothels. Now he posed as a diamond merchant, to cover his supervision of French girls working in Soho for a gang in Paris.

Three months later one of the French girls, Jeanette Cotton, was found strangled with her silk scarf at her flat in Lexington Street, Soho. Scotland Yard connected her death with that of Josephine Martin, 'French Fifi', strangled some months earlier. A month after Jeanette Cotton, a third girl, Leah Hines, 'Dutch Leah' or 'Stilts' from her very high heels, was found in her Old Compton Street room, copper wire tightly twisted round her throat.

The victims had been allowed by the gang to keep between £7 (£280) and £8 (£320) a week of their earnings. The balance was to be remitted to Paris. When they rebelled against this gangland tax, a warning was sent, to no effect. The first murder, that of Josephine Martin, was carried out and those who failed to profit by her example became the next victims. The killer in each case came to England on a forged passport. He was back in France, his identity unknown, before the crime was discovered. At the inquest on Leah Hines, the coroner concluded, 'I do not see any direct evidence against any person except a person unknown.'[3]

The third main area of pre-war gangland activity was that of protection in horse racing and on the dog tracks. Greyhound racing was still something of a novelty, having been introduced from the United States in 1926, whereas gangs associated with horse racing had been identifiable by the 1890s. After the First World War, criminals as 'protectors' of bookmakers became a matter for more serious concern. Soon after that war, gang members used firearms on the racecourse at Alexandra Park and later that day tried to throw police officers under trains at King's Cross underground station. It was rare for such violence to end in murder but it was not unknown. At Cardiff prison in January 1928, Edward Rowlands and another member of his gang, Danny Driscoll, were hanged for the murder of Dai Lewis who had challenged their monopoly of protection at the old Ely racecourse in the west of the city.[4]

As a rule, the gangs fought one another rather than the racing public. The most memorable pre-war incident was the fight on Lewes racecourse in 1936, adapted two years later by Graham Greene in *Brighton Rock*, as the fracas at Brighton races in which Pinkie and Spicer are 'carved'. Mr Colleoni in the novel was modelled on the elderly Darby Sabini, who had retired from the Clerkenwell gang to the hotel suites and crescents of Brighton.[5]

The supremacy or the Sabinis was challenged at Lewes on 8 June 1936 by fifty or sixty men, led by James Spinks of Hackney and Charles Spring or Upper Clapton. Hackney, Shoreditch and Bethnal Green took on Clerkenwell's 'Little Italy', beating up a Sabini bookmaker, Alf Solomons, his clerk, Mark Frater, and their 'protectors'. The challengers carried life-preservers or coshes, choppers, sawn-off car-handles with nails through the head, jemmies, knuckledusters and iron bars.

As in Greene's novel, the fight was broken up by 'bogies'. A warning had been received from a woman anxious to protect her lover, and plain-clothes police were concentrated by the five-shilling ring. Racegoers spoke of one of the fiercest fights for thirty years. Fifteen of the injured were left rolling on the ground in agony. Despite the intimidation of witnesses and with groups of gang members surrounding his court, Mr Justice Hilbery, at Lewes Assizes, passed sentences totalling forty-three years' hard labour or penal servitude on sixteen attackers. When *Brighton Rock* was serialized in the *Evening Standard* in the autumn of 1938, it was promoted as 'A Race-Gang Thriller'.[6]

The only case from the dog tracks whose publicity exceeded the notoriety of the Lewes fight was the Wandsworth Stadium murder of 1 September 1936. On that evening, before the first race, there was a flash of blades and a scuffle in the two-and-sixpenny ring. Two Colombo brothers from Clerkenwell were attacked by rivals from the same area. Massimino Colombo died from throat wounds in Balham Hospital, though his brother, Camillo, stabbed twice with a stiletto and slashed with a razor, survived.

The accused were Herbert Wilkins, described as a garment worker, and Papa Pasquale. Pasquale boxed professionally as 'Bert Marsh' and supervised bookmakers' pitches at the track. Both described the Colombo brothers as aggressors, not victims. Marsh had the good fortune to be defended by Sir Norman Birkett KC. Defence witnesses, after a period of collective amnesia when first questioned, swore in evidence that Massimino began the fight by attacking Wilkins. The jury acquitted both defendants of murder, though convicting them of manslaughter.

Camillo denounced dog-track intimidation to the court for denying justice to his dead brother. 'You can't get proper witnesses here because of the gang.' Asked why he had first said he did not know the attackers, he replied, 'Because in this racing gang, if you get hurt and rush to the police, you have a black mark against you. I thought that if my brother lived, I would not inform the police. My brother died and then I made a statement to the police.' But he spoke to a courtroom filled with friends of the men who had killed Massimino. When the acquittal of murder was announced, race-course frequenters and workers began to tic-tac congratulations to the smiling prisoners in the dock.[7]

The coming of war was to limit the scope for racecourse protection. Dog racing was restricted by the impossibility of lighting stadiums during the blackout. Racing was permitted on one afternoon a week at each stadium, usually on a Saturday. Its urban tracks were not open to the objection made in Parliament against horse racing, that petrol would be wasted by people travelling greater distances to courses. Horse racing was banned briefly in 1940 and subsequently restricted to six courses and a fifth of the pre-war meetings. The Derby was run at Newmarket when the Army requisitioned the course at Epsom.

Apart from these main areas of activity, a major difference between the pre-war underworld and its successors was the relative unimportance of drugs, which had not been fully criminalized until after the previous war. Marijuana or what was called 'Indian hemp', like cocaine and heroin, was generally seen as the preserve of bohemians or the night-club set. In 1936, the League of Nations publicly apologized for a report which suggested that there were 30,000 drug addicts in Britain. As the report was withdrawn, the Home Secretary confirmed that the correct number was not more than 2,000, and that 'most of those are known to the authorities'. Even this seemed an over-estimate, judging by the Home Office's own figures two years later. In 1938 it knew of only 519 drug addicts in the country, 246 men, 273 women.

Yet undercover officers of a Scotland Yard drugs squad were already at work. On Sunday 15 February 1938, Detective Constable Liddle posed as a 'student' trying to buy drugs in Paddington. He met an off-duty barman in the Edgware Road. They went to a pub and the barman said, 'Pal, I can get you anything you want. It is all snow but I know just the stuff for you.' The stuff was a 'heel-ball' pellet of opium to be smoked in a cigarette. The two men met again at a café in Commercial Road, Stepney. The barman handed a matchbox and a tin to Liddle under the tablecloth. 'Open them, pal, they are the goods.' The matchbox held ten black pellets, the tin seven more. The price was £7 (£280). The barman added, 'There is enough there to last for a month and they are the best we can get. When you take a few puffs, you will feel it go right through you and you will dream lovely dreams.' Liddle called a taxi and, when they were both inside, ordered the driver to take them to Paddington Green police station.[8]

It was rare for dealers to be caught but, in October 1937, a dance hostess was convicted for dealing in cocaine hydrochlorine, diamorphine hydrochloride and Indian hemp from her flat at Connaught Mews, Marble Arch. Others received short prison sentences for attempting to obtain drugs by forged prescriptions. The proprietor of the Brown Bomber Club in Foubert's Place, and his American business partner, were sent to hard labour for possession of heroin, supplied by registered post from Paris. At Hyde Park Corner, the regular customers of a matchseller, 'Long John Silver', gave him £1 and got what he called 'dope'. Wearing a sailor's blouse, and with the face of a friendly ruffian, he was a well-known figure in pre-war London, killed in 1939 while trying to save his dog from the traffic.[9]

At the outbreak of war, most London gangs were defined by geographical areas. Other cities contained such groups as Birmingham's 'Brummagem Boys', or Glasgow's 'Billy Boys'. Among the gangs of the capital, the Sabini family of Clerkenwell's 'Little Italy' had been pre-eminent in racecourse protection since 1918. Their closest rivals on the course were the Whites of Islington and King's Cross, who also controlled much of Soho, as well as the Hoxton 'boys', and the Kimbers from Birmingham. Billy Hill, who saw himself as a young contender in the 1930s, had established his gang at Kentish Town and thereby invited trouble from the neighbouring Whites. Hill also liked his men to be known as 'The Heavy Mob', despite the more general application of this to the Flying Squad. There was a Hackney gang and, south of the river, the Elephant Boys, a more loosely organized group. The Elephant Boys were more like freelance criminals in an extended family, while most of the other gangs relied on protection rackets at race tracks or in clubs.

Before the war and during it, the penalties that the gangster faced were severe by the standards of a later age. The death penalty for murder remained in force until 1964. Until the Criminal Justice Act of 1948, flogging might be imposed in addition to imprisonment where a crime had involved serious violence. There was also penal servitude, originally introduced in 1853 to replace transportation to a penal settlement overseas. Under its provisions a convicted prisoner might be sentenced to any term, including life imprisonment, but not to less than three years. In practice, it meant that he would be put away for as long as possible under the harshest available regime. Penal servitude as a particular form of imprisonment was also abolished by the act of 1948.

Perhaps the most controversial crime to be dealt with in wartime was looting during the aftermath of air attacks. In theory, looting was punishable by hanging, or by shooting in the event of martial law. Yet despite government threats during the autumn blitz of 1940, no death sentence was passed for this crime.

To many people by 1939, the war against crime was synonymous with the activities of Scotland Yard, which was itself often synonymous with the CID or the Flying Squad. Other squads came and went as they were needed. After the fight at Lewes Races in 1936, a Protection Squad was formed to work in partnership with the Jockey Club's own security force, a force manned largely by retired policemen. In January 1937, as part of a drive to clean up London before the coronation of George VI in May, the Yard set up an 'Anti-Vice' Squad, known officially and more prosaically as the Clubs Office. Its duties were principally the regulation and prosecution of clubs in and around Soho, as well as keeping prostitution and the sale of pornography out of public view. Similar duties had been performed by the Metropolitan Police before the Great Exhibition of 1851 and Victoria's jubilees, and even before her coronation. In June 1939 the former Drugs Squad was reconstituted, following reports that cannabis rolled in cigarettes was being sold to the young in the dance halls of Brixton, the Elephant and Castle, and Battersea.

The most famous of all these squads, the Flying Squad, had been created after the First World War and almost from the start had chosen to sacrifice solidity for speed. It had used a succession of high-powered cars, including Railtons and Bentley Invictas. The glamour of the chase was enhanced by news that some of the squad's super-charged sports models were tested and used for driver-training on the banked motor-racing circuit at Brooklands. Though the police also tried out an armoured car in 1936, its windows two inches thick with loopholes for guns, the preferred 'chasers' were the long low super-charged Invictas or Railtons.

The introduction of the '999' telephone service and the use of police radio were further advantages for the crime-fighters, but it was still only possible for radio cars to communicate by tapping messages in Morse code. By the outbreak of war, the balance swung again in favour of the fugitives. On 15 June 1939, Scotland Yard admitted that recent robberies had been carried out by criminals using an unnamed American car, unkindly headlined by the press as 'Car Police Cannot Catch'. It was capable of 130 miles an hour through London streets, leaving any pursuit far behind.

A number of Scotland Yard officers were already public names by 1939, while others already in the service were to be recognized during and after the war. Their ages divided them into those who had served in the earlier war and were now too old to be called up, and those young enough to be conscripted as the exemption of police officers from mili-tary service became more selective. Among the older officers, Chief Inspector George Hatherill was to draw up a plan for the creation of a Special Investigation Branch within the Corps of Military Police. Chief Inspector Edward Greeno, with almost twenty years' service by 1939 and an unrivalled knowledge of the racecourse, had served in the Flying Squad and later joined the 'murder rota' in October 1940. He was to lead the successful hunt for the 'Blackout Ripper' in 1942.

By the late 1940s, no Scotland Yard officer was better known than Superintendent Robert Fabian, 'Fabian of the Yard', whose cases were to form books of memoirs and an early television series. As the war began, Fabian was awarded the King's Medal for Gallantry by George VI, for single-handedly dismantling an IRA bomb in Piccadilly Circus. One of the most successful thief-takers, not least in dealing with black marketeers during the war, was Inspector John Capstick, whose skills earned him the rueful underworld nickname of 'Charley Artful'.

Of the younger men, Sergeant John Gosling in 1946 was to head the so-called 'Ghost Squad', an intelligence force whose aim was to penetrate the criminal underworld. Among specialists, Superintendent Fred Cherrill was unequalled in knowledge and practical experience of fingerprints. In the case of those corpses whose fingerprints could not otherwise be reproduced, he perfected the technique of removing the skin from the fingers of the cadaver, wearing it as stalls on his own fingers, and so recreating the prints. Civilian advisers to the police included Sir Bernard Spilsbury, who remained the great pathologist throughout the war, and Robert Churchill, gunsmith and owner of a famous shop near the Haymarket, an expert witness in firearms cases for over thirty years.

A number of Scotland Yard officers played a direct part in the war. Chief Inspector C. E. Campion became the first commander of the Special Investigation Branch of the Corps of Military Police, as Major Campion. Commander Leonard Burt was transferred to MI5, where some of his last duties included escorting William Joyce, 'Lord Haw-Haw', and then John Amery, from Germany to face trials for treason in England in 1945. One of Burt's junior officers in MI5, working in the safety of the cells in Wormwood Scrubs, was Reginald Spooner, later to make his name as the leader of the hunt for the murderer Neville Heath in 1946.

Chief Inspector William Salisbury, who remained at Scotland Yard during the war, specialized in penetrating the shadow world of dodgers and racketeers. Salisbury ran to earth the 'impersonation' racket, in which those who had failed army medical boards would attend them for others who were anxious to avoid military service. It was also Salisbury who cooperated with the Army's Special

Investigation Branch to follow up stories of doctors writing medical exemption certificates for money. In countering other forms of evasion, he listened in the scullery of a pub as a Ministry of Labour official in the adjoining kitchen blackmailed a client whom he had promised to save from military service by ensuring that his papers were 'lost'. In 1942, Salisbury was also the senior Scotland Yard officer in the Manchester clothing coupon forgery case, one of the biggest crimes of its type in the entire war.

Inevitably, senior officers and major criminals were well known to one another. A gang leader like Billy Hill and Flying Squad officers, including its earlier commander Peter Beveridge and his successor Ted Greeno, drank in the same bars and occasionally exchanged words. On Monday afternoons they found themselves in the same Soho club in Archer Street, where leading members of the gangs and their women paraded in a 4 p.m. ritual, 'like an Ascot of the underworld'. Drinking with Hill, Beveridge said philosophically, 'When I feel your collar, you're going to stay nicked for a long time.' Offered a drink by Hill, Greeno replied more abrasively, 'I don't want your drink, I want your body.'[10]

Crime and law enforcement alike were soon to be embroiled in a wartime world of registration and conscription, rationing and regulations. In September 1939, the National Service (Armed Forces) Act imposed conscription on all men between the ages of eighteen and forty-one. There were, however, reserved occupations in which men were exempt from call-up. Even within some of these professions, age limits were imposed so that younger men might be called up and the older ones left in their jobs. The regulation of conscription, like rationing, varied throughout the war. When the manpower shortage became serious, the rules for reserved occupations were revised and in December 1941 the call-up was extended to single women between twenty and thirty, as non-combatants.

Conscription on this scale included many thousands of unwilling recruits. It was perhaps not surprising that the number of deserters from all the armed forces should have passed 20,000. Those who were caught could expect to be sent to a civil or military prison for a few months and then returned to their units. However, they consoled themselves by believing that there was a good chance that their units might regard them as more trouble than they were worth. Having served their sentences they would perhaps be dishonourably discharged to civilian life.

Until a 1953 amnesty, wartime deserters were being caught, usually as a matter of accident, and were now receiving harsher sentences than some of those imposed during the war. On 13 February 1950, an RAF man from Blackfriars who had deserted in 1941 to protect his mother from his father's violence, was sentenced to nine months' detention – one month for every year of his absence. Three months later, a soldier who had deserted in 1944 was sent to prison for two years. By April 1950, when those who had no identity cards could still not draw the new issue of ration books for the year, stolen books were said to be changing hands at several times the price of some books during the war. So great was the official apprehension over major thefts of the new books that, on Friday 14 April, a twenty-four-hour weekend guard was announced on all London food offices, from which the books were due to be issued on the following Monday. Yet in the following month, a man was arrested, having deserted from the Lancashire Fusiliers ten years earlier. He had survived simply by applying regularly for emergency ration cards on a variety of plausible pretexts.[11]

The huge majority of deserters evaded capture, while some were caught as a matter of chance and some through over-confidence. A soldier who had deserted in 1941 made his way to the United States. Five years had passed since the end of the war when he returned and was arrested as he left the liner, though he appeared as an American, dressed in American sports jacket, slacks and silk tie. 'I admit it,' he told the court and was handed over to a military escort for detention at the Royal Artillery barracks in Winchester.[12]

Though desertion was more common in a theatre of war, the figures were generally lower when the fighting was intense and higher when there was a lull on the battlefront. The reasons for desertion were more often boredom or family troubles than a reluctance to fight. Over 10,000 men deserted from the British D-Day invasion forces between 6 June 1944 and 31 March 1945. Once again, the majority did so during winter inactivity, rather than when the fighting was at its peak. Similarly, the number of deserters rose after the war, among those men impatient to be demobbed.[13]

On 29 March 1950 Emanuel Shinwell, as Minister of Defence, told the House of Commons that there were still 19,477 absentees, some 5,000 less than at the worst: 1,267 were from the Royal Navy, 13,884 from the Army and 4,366 from the RAF. However, he called this a 'nominal' figure because it included an estimated 10,000 men from the Irish Republic. These Irishmen had chivalrously joined the fight against Hitler with none but a moral obligation to do so. When the war was over and servicemen were told that they must now wait a year or more to be demobbed, it seemed hard indeed on these generous volunteers. Taking matters into their own hands, the Irishmen had quietly and reasonably gone home. More than a thousand men had similarly returned to European countries. By 1950, however, there was a further steady desertion rate of 200 a month among the new generation of post-war National Servicemen.

Deserters were a shifting population. Many gave themselves up within a few weeks, having no money nor even a ration book, but were then replaced by new absentees. Those who knew how to steal military supplies or civilian property for the black market, or even to drive goods vehicles, might remain at large indefinitely. Their value to the criminal underworld, whether in London, Paris or Brussels, was self-evident. If they needed identity or ration documents, that underworld was well placed to supply them.

Identity cards were first issued in September 1939 and ration books in December. Ration books came with extra pages of coupons. These extra coupons were not valid for any commodity rationed at the time of issue but were to be kept until the holders were told what to do with them. In due course, they would be used for further items whose rationing might be announced during the annual currency of the book. Throughout the war, the raising or lowering of the ration, whether of clothes or individual items of food, was commonplace. The small allowance of petrol for the private motorist in September 1939 was abolished completely in the summer of 1942 and not restored until 1945 at a level of about ninety miles a month.

During nine post-war years, before all rationing ended, there were complaints that the new Labour government had a political fondness for such controls. Though Clement Attlee, as prime minister, denied and resented this, there was at one point in 1949 more meat at the docks than the ration could consume. At the same time a glut of rationed margarine was caused by a small increase in the butter ration. More than ten years after petrol rationing had begun, the weakness of sterling and the consequent 'dollar gap' still made it impossible for the country to buy adequate supplies. Winston Churchill, speaking at Plymouth in February 1950 during the general election campaign, could only hope that petrol rationing would be abolished by a Conservative government, but he could not promise it. On 20 March when the Labour government was asked in the House of Commons why motorists were worse treated than in any other country, Philip Noel-Baker for the Ministry of Fuel could only reply, 'It is really a question of dollars.' In the event, petrol rationing ended on 27 May, to be followed swiftly by a steep increase in fuel tax.

So long as the war lasted, every shipload of imports that could be saved was one less target for the waiting U-boats as well as one less demand on the nation's dwindling financial reserves. In addition to formal rationing, manufacturing regulations were imposed by the Board of Trade, which had power to vary them at any point. In the immediate aftermath of Dunkirk, the Limitation of Supplies Order 1940 imposed restrictions on the quantity of materials available to manufacturers of a wide range of products. Once again, the government was free to vary the materials listed or the quotas permitted, as circumstances required. Two years later, the Board of Trade enforced Utility designs upon clothes and, within a few months, upon furniture and other household equipment.

In the case of clothes, the size of lapels and the number of pockets were regulated, while men's trouser turn-ups and frills on women's underwear were banned. Books were not rationed but the supply of paper was strictly controlled and its quality reduced to 'War Economy Standard'. Newspapers shrank to a four-page broadsheet or an eight-page tabloid. In 1945, the publishers of F. L. Green's *Odd Man Out*, Michael Joseph, inserted a prefatory note in the first edition, explaining that their paper allocation had compelled them to set the novel in uncomfortably small type, reducing 418 pages to 224.

Such was the wartime world. Yet until the last moment in the summer of 1939, the nation appeared to turn its back on the approaching shadows and, if the polls were to be believed, thought war much less likely than it had been during the Munich crises of the previous year. Like so many summers preceding a war, this was to be remembered as a season of sunlit frivolity. Police manpower was currently devoted to such easygoing projects as the suppression of cafés, not brothels, in the City of London, where the tired businessman on his way home could purchase a kiss and a cuddle from one of the waitresses, provided he paid 2s. 6d. (£5) for his cup of tea and left a tip for a similar amount, about fifty times the cost of tea elsewhere. Plain-clothes officers who spent afternoons as dutiful customers of such establishments testified to sounds of 'petting' from behind screens. When asked to describe the precise sound of petting, they were unable to do so.

By contrast with the horrors already evident in Germany and in her conquered territories, it was difficult to deny a certain charm to these furtive and illicit amusements of the dying peace. On Hampstead Heath in the last Whitsun holiday before the battle, 'Price's Continental Show' folded its tent among a collective imposition of fines. Its amateur fan-dancer had 'moved about, smiled and winked' at the audience, which contained its regulation sprinkling of plain-clothes policemen. One of them testified that he had sat through the entire performance three times running, in the discharge of his duty, before intervening at last.

This case against Arthur Price of Salford, who toured the country with his 'Show', was heard on 30 May 1939. He was fined £5 (£200). His elderly mother, who assisted at the tent, was also fined £5. The smiling dancer, Betty Ross, was let off with ten shillings (£20), and the barker who had stood outside shouting at the passers-by, 'It is impossible to believe unless you see it!' was fined £1 (£40). Old Mrs Price said sadly, 'They do worse than this in the West End. I have seen it.'[14]

They were doing worse all over Europe. The innocent holiday world of the fairground fan-dance with its smiling and winking performer was swept away as the Continent moved towards armed conflict. Neville Chamberlain warned Hitler on 23 August that

Britain would stand by her guarantee to come to the aid of Poland. Parliament passed an Emergency Powers Bill, ready for war, on the next day. Within the week, a general evacuation of women and children from London and other major cities had begun. Before daylight on the next morning, 1 September, German forces invaded Poland.

2

'Don't You Know There's a War On?'

When the war was over, the Chairman of the Mile End Conservative Association reminded his audience at a large open-air meeting that there were 'more criminals to the thousand now than at any time in our history'. They were culprits of a new kind, decent men and women, 'all sorts of people in all walks of life . . . brought before the courts for all manner of offences which never before were considered as such'. Most of these lawbreakers had contravened one or more of the complex regulations issued since September 1939. As Sir Harold Scott, Commissioner of the Metropolitan Police, put it more urbanely, crime rose in wartime because there were, quite simply, more laws to break.[1]

Long before the war ended, other protestors turned to abuse rather than complaint. In April 1944, an outraged small trader wrote to the Chancellor of the Exchequer, who indiscreetly passed the letter to an MP, who even more indiscreetly gave it to the press.

> The government has governed my business until I do not know who the bloody hell owns it. I am suspected, inspected, examined, informed, required and commanded so that I do not know who the hell I am and where I am, or why I am here at all . . . The only reason I am clinging to life at all is to see what the Bloody Hell is going to happen next.[2]

Even in peacetime certain frontiers of crime had been ill-defined. Now, with the assistance of the authorities, wartime criminality was to snare men and women who had thought of themselves as instinctively law-abiding. It would fulfil the underworld's ambition of linking them, however distantly, with professional villains and racketeers. A peacetime gangster had seen his future in a West End jeweller's window or in blowing a post office safe on a quiet Sunday. Yet even before Dunkirk, war would make worthwhile the 'jump-up' theft of an unattended lorry carrying such previously unappealing

16

products as margarine or dried egg powder. Before long, a petty criminal might turn his talents to the home-made manufacture of cheap and insanitary cosmetics. Petrol, in almost any quantity, caught his eye. More skilfully, underground printing presses, which in peace had provided fake tote tickets or the narratives and images of pornography, now rivalled those of the government in turning out the drab little designs of ration coupons or identity cards.

So far as a thief or racketeer dealt in such contraband, he was the end of that chain linking vice to virtue. It led from the racketeer to the quick-witted wholesaler, the obliging local grocer, the ambivalent stallholder, and finally to the loyal 'regular' customer grateful for 'a little extra' to feed the family. Yet not until many months of what was more like phoney peace than phoney war, was that supply line fully active.

'They have made criminals of us all' – the Conservative chairman's post-war cry at Mile End might seem a caricature of reality, yet professional crime had infected Middle England. When the Bishop of Liverpool, Dr Albert David, wanted a theme for his address to a diocesan conference in 1942, he chose 'Public Dishonesty in Wartime'.

> We have been confronted by an outbreak of self-seeking, carried far beyond the limits of ordinary honesty. Men in a big way of business, some of them leaders in public life, have been abusing public confidence in the perpetration of reckless frauds. Lower down the scale we see the same shameless spirit in pilfering and shoplifting, in wanton and senseless damage, and in falsifying time-sheets. There is abundant evidence of dishonest work. I know quite well what can be truly said in explanation of some of the slackness and idling in factories and on the docks . . . But there can be no doubt that what I have described is a great and growing evil.[3]

In the late summer of 1939, a great majority of Parliament and people had welcomed strong and autocratic legislation in the face of international terror. These measures, after two years of uncertainty and national dishonour, showed a will to face the war and win it. Parliament was recalled on 22 August, as that day's Cabinet statement explained, 'to meet on Thursday next [24 August], when the Government proposes to invite both Houses to pass through all its stages the Emergency Powers (Defence) Bill. The effect of this will be to place the Government in a position to take any necessary measures without delay should the situation require it.' Within hours of the statement, Nazi Germany and the Soviet Union concluded their twenty-five-year non-aggression treaty, opening the way for the annihilation of Poland.

At Westminster, the Commons passed the bill by 457 votes to 11, after Sir Samuel Hoare, as Home Secretary, undertook that its powers would never be used in peacetime. Authority was transferred wholesale from Parliament to ministers and civil servants. The nation would be ruled by Defence Regulations rather than Acts of Parliament. The regulations were the greatest transfer of power to government since the Bill of Rights had laid the foundation of constitutional government in 1689. They would secure 'public safety, the defence of the Realm, the maintenance of public order, and the efficient prosecution of any war in which his Majesty may be engaged'.

In theory, all existing laws, even the safeguard of habeas corpus, were set aside by authority delegated to the Cabinet and its bureaucrats. Ministers and departments would issue new regulations, as Orders in Council, on matters great and small. 'A defence regulation is effective, notwithstanding anything inconsistent in any other enactment.' The new law also authorized the government to prosecute and punish offenders, detaining indefinitely and without trial those whose detention 'appears expedient'. It gave unlimited power to take possession or control of any property or undertaking, and to acquire any property other than land. It authorized immediate entry and search of any premises. It gave power to suspend or alter existing law. The first list of Defence Regulations issued on 28 August 1939 extended from the safety of the state and public order, down to the control of family cameras and permits for pigeon-owners. If military conscription was not included, that was because a subsequent bill had already been drafted to impose the measure.

Any infringement of a regulation was a strict liability offence. An honest mistake, or misunderstanding of tortuous Civil Service prose, or ignorance that a regulation existed was no excuse. In *Fruin v. Linton* (1941), a touring actor forgot his ration book on leaving his lodgings. The landlady's daughter picked it up with the others and went to buy provisions. Neither she nor her mother knew the book was still in the bundle. Though mother and daughter acted in complete innocence, their convictions were upheld on appeal. The new world of regulations coupled innocent and guilty intentions without ceremony.[4]

The Civil Service, alleged to have recruited the best brains, proved to have some of the dullest minds when putting matters of urgency into a prose that ordinary people could understand. In *Meadow Dairy Co. Ltd v. Cottle* (1942), Lord Chief Justice Caldecote attacked the new blackout restrictions, in the Lighting (Restrictions) Order 1940. This order, addressed to every member of the public, ran to what Caldecote described as 'some thirty-three articles and innumerable sub-paragraphs which everybody concerned with lighting in its various forms is required to understand . . . I find it impossible to believe that the regulations could not have been in a simpler and more intelligible form.' Mr Justice Humphreys, sitting with him, also condemned 'the confused and confusing regulations'.[5]

Many defence regulations did away with any burden of proof on the prosecution. The accused was guilty as charged unless he could prove his innocence. In the case of *R. v. Oliver* (1944) the defendant had been convicted at Middlesex Sessions under the Sugar (Control) Order 1940 of supplying sugar without a licence. He had been sent to penal servitude for three years and fined the draconian sum of £8,500 (£340,000) with £150 costs. Believing that the prosecution had not discharged the 'onus of proof', he appealed. He was told that there was no onus of proof on the prosecution and that his appeal was 'without merit'.[6]

All the same, a versatile defendant charged with a strict liability offence might still seek a loophole in the prosecution case. John Lindsay, who lived at the Selsden Park Hotel in Surrey, was charged in August 1941 with the attempted black market sale of more than 18,000 tins of fruit, 394 cases of canned pears, peaches and apricots. Tinned fruit had become a luxury and the price demanded was £1,876 (£75,000). This was three times the maximum permitted price under the Defence Regulations.

Lindsay and his accomplices had approached one of the major wholesale grocery firms, Allied Suppliers Ltd. Thomas Langdon of that firm agreed to buy the tinned fruit at the black market price and take further delivery of tins of sardines and figs, all warehoused at the Standard Wharf, Wapping High Street. Langdon arrived to conclude the deal, bringing his cashier. As the deal reached completion, the cashier revealed himself as Detective Sergeant Glander of Scotland Yard.

The three conspirators followed the old lags' policy of never pleading guilty. At Bow Street, however, the case looked unpromising. Mr Lindsay thereupon performed a neat sideways move. He withdrew his plea of 'not guilty' to the charge of selling black market groceries and pleaded insanity. If successful, this was a complete defence, even under strict liability.

He called a psychiatrist, Dr Joseph Geoghean, who said vaguely that he had treated the defendant 'on and off' during six years and could say that 'Lindsay is suffering from a mild form of insanity. He is never quite normal.' Unfortunately Dr Geoghean spoilt this by agreeing in cross-examination that Lindsay knew the difference between right and wrong. This at once deprived his patient of the defence of insanity under the M'Naghten Rules, which since 1843 had governed the legal definition of madness.

The Bow Street magistrate decided that Lindsay was not insane, merely 'a weak character', and sent him to prison for six weeks. Though not mad, he then behaved with considerable stupidity by appealing against the most lenient sentence likely to be imposed. At London Sessions in December, his prison term was increased from six weeks to three months, the maximum on summary conviction.[7]

Similar ingenuity was shown by two thieves in January 1945, charged with looting parcels from the railway. They admitted that one loaded a barrow while the other kept a lookout. They argued, however, that they were incapably drunk at the time and unable to form an intent to steal. Therefore they could not be convicted of the offence. They had no more luck than John Lindsay.[8]

When the new regulatory system was devised in 1939, the sole constitutional safeguard was that every Order in Council containing Defence Regulations must be laid before Parliament as soon as possible. If either House, in the twenty-eight days when it sat, following the order being laid before it, resolved that the order be annulled, it would cease to have effect. As an item of wartime legislation, the

Emergency Powers Act itself was only to remain in force for one year. However, like the Army Act, it would be renewed on an annual basis, as long as Parliament thought necessary. It was unthinkable that Parliament would do away with it so long as the war continued.

Despite its wide powers, the regulatory system in 1939 was neither so complex nor so extensive as it became in the next two years. Petrol was rationed soon after the war began, but there was no rationing of food until January 1940, and then only of bacon, butter and sugar. Clothes rationing did not begin until June 1941. In Germany, by contrast, clothes were rationed on 15 November 1939. A ban in Britain on petrol for private use was delayed until the summer of 1942, when the Japanese invasion of Malaya further reduced the supply of petrol and of rubber for vehicle tyres.

Within the framework of Defence Regulations, rationing and control were imposed step by step, by the Board of Trade, the Ministry of Food and the Ministry of Supply. Pre-war views on Britain's chances of starvation or survival against blockade had varied. The majority view was expressed by J. R. Clynes, Food Controller in 1918–19, who in a *Daily Express* article in 1937, 'Could We Be Starved Out?', wrote that only coordination and the rationing powers of a Food Ministry would save the nation. Sir Herbert Matthews, a senior official of the Ministry of Food in the earlier war, warned his readers in June 1939 that the position was a good deal worse than in 1914. The policy must be 'fair shares for all'.

New wartime crimes were quickly identified. The wholehearted peacetime drive for profitability in business became the offence of 'profiteering', punishable during a preliminary 'warning period' by fines of £500 (£20,000) in each instance. The warning period ended on 23 September 1939. Prosecutions and more detailed legislation were prepared. The government itself would fix prices and committees would watch for any breach of regulations. In early October, shop assistants in Cardiff reported through their union that shops and stores in the city were hiding away items which would fetch better prices when the shortages began.

It seemed just the sort of case the government had in mind but the informants were told that no official action could be taken under existing regulations. Later in the war, however, 'hoarding' was added to the list of criminal offences. At present, profiteering remained the target. Under the Prices of Goods Bill, introduced on 12 October, profiteers faced a fine of £100 (£4,000), three months in prison, or both, for each offence of exceeding the maximum price. Next day, the government announced that three months in prison and a ban on trading would be added to existing fines. Such were the penalties imposed on commercial activities that had been normal, even laudable, six weeks earlier.

At the end of November, an enforcer hailed by the press as the 'Profiteers' Enemy' was named, one of innumerable stern-faced men and women whose wartime appointment promised a relentless tracking down and bringing to book of dodgers and racketeers. Raymond Evershed KC, Chairman of the Central Price Regulation Committee, would deal with complaints from no less than sixteen subordinate committees. In theory, by making it illegal to charge more than a controlled price for butter or bacon, the black market would be strangled at birth. By the end of February 1940 a hundred London shopkeepers had been formally warned. Yet when the government extended price controls to further items in January, it was not fair shares but fear of inflation and wage claims which had made profiteering unacceptable. On 18 July 1940, price controls were announced on all foodstuffs.

It seemed remarkable how easily an old-fashioned Conservative administration had taken to 'war socialism'. In October 1939, income tax was fixed at an almost confiscatory level of 7s. 6d. or 37.5 per cent in the pound. This was later raised to 50 per cent, while super tax reached 95 per cent. In July 1940, after Dunkirk, a system of purchase tax, first used in the 1914–18 war, was also imposed on purchases of clothes or goods regarded as 'luxuries'.

How did the public react to this early wartime regime and its apologists? The *News Chronicle* reported at the beginning of December 1939 that after three months the BBC, as the mouthpiece of authority, had attracted more hatred in the war than even Hitler himself. Of those questioned, 49 per cent were satisfied with the BBC against 34 per cent who were dissatisfied, whilst 10 per cent never listened anyway. The star of the airwaves appeared to be Lord Haw-Haw, not yet identified as William Joyce, whose English-language propaganda broadcasts from Berlin were listened to by 40 per cent of high income earners, 49 per cent of middle income earners, and 54 per cent of low income earners. Despite its later zeal for self-congratulation, the BBC did not stand high with those men on active service who suggested that its initials stood for 'Bloody Baptist Cant'. Yet it provided certain moments of high comedy, as when on 11 November 1941 its programmes broadcast loyal birthday greetings to the King of Italy, with whose country Britain had already been at war for almost eighteen months.[9]

The news from such polls was mixed. On 29 December 1939, Neville Chamberlain's popularity, which had stood at 50 per cent after the Munich agreement and 55 per cent at the outbreak of war, was reported by the *News Chronicle* to have risen to 68 per cent. On 13 December, it had reported the results of a survey in which respondents registered their views on the conduct of the war: 61 per cent were reported as satisfied, 18 per cent dissatisfied, and 10 per cent as uncertain. The remaining 11 per cent insisted on answering a question they had not been asked. They thought the war should be ended altogether and at once.

The 29 per cent who were dissatisfied with the conduct of the war or thought it should be ended anticipated the result of the Kettering by-election in March 1940. By wartime convention, the government candidate, in this case John Profumo, should have been unopposed. However, a Workers and Pensioners Anti-War candidate stood against him and polled 27 per cent of the vote, the figures for the two contenders being 17,914 and 6,616. For an independent anti-war candidate to attract so many votes was scarcely a boost to government morale.

Any criminal contemplating a career in the black market might draw comfort from these figures, so far as they revealed the number of his potential customers. It seemed that some three million adult citizens thought the war was pointless and should be ended, while a further five million thought that even if it had some point, it was being badly directed. Did disaffection, in either form, represent a willingness to ignore regulations and government propaganda? If so, even before the rationing of food and clothing, there appeared to be an attentive market of some eight million customers for illegally supplied goods.

The privations of war did not come with the speed expected. Cinemas and theatres, closed on the outbreak of hostilities, reopened six days later. Enemy bombers failed to appear. Films were to end by 10 p.m., though shows would continue if the sirens sounded. German machine-gunning of the streets of cities that were bombed made it safer for audiences to remain under cover.

By 11 October, there was still no sign of aerial bombardment. A decision was taken to close some of the West End air raid shelters at night. In Paris, the capital of England's sole European ally in arms, there was not even a full blackout. On 31 October, Jerome Willis, correspondent of the Beaverbrook press, published his weekly report under the title, 'It's Hard to Believe in Paris there is a War on'. The same was true of Britain's trade. After three months of war at sea, Oliver Stanley, President of the Board of Trade, told the House of Commons on 7 December that Britain's exports were again at pre-war levels. As yet the German U-boat fleet had no naval base for an Atlantic campaign, nor had industrial production in Britain been disrupted by conscription or aerial attacks.

As for rationing, on which the main hope of a black market depended, many people, including the Labour opposition, wondered when, if ever, it would be introduced. Five days after war was declared, the government had assured the nation that food supplies and prices were steady, though it encouraged customers to complain if shopkeepers overcharged them.

The aim of rationing was reassuringly explained at a press conference on 9 September 1939 by the Minister of Food, W. S. Morrison. There were no present shortages and no need of rationing of any kind for at least three or four weeks. Bacon and butter might be 'a little short'. The idea of food rationing did not imply a scarcity of food. It would simply ensure that 'everyone gets his fair share of what is going, and there is no dislocation, shortage, food queues, or anything of that character'.

Sugar and petrol were the most sensitive commodities. On the day of the press conference, the government commandeered sugar stocks, though it did not ration them. It also requisitioned imported meat, and issued new regulations to control the food supply. On 16 September it announced that there was enough petrol to supply everyone's needs and rationing was postponed. It was rationed soon afterwards but for almost three years there was a basic allowance for so-called 'pleasure' motoring. Those who could show they needed extra fuel for business or professional purposes would get a 'supplementary' allowance. Sometimes there was a bonus. Easter 1940 saw an extra allowance of three gallons for private motoring over the weekend holiday.

In the autumn months of 1939, the coming of rationing seemed as elusive as the expected air raids or the opening of a campaign on the Western Front. At the end of September it was decided that there should be no food rationing but that price controls should be imposed on bread, eggs and fish. It had been an unpromising month for the racketeers. Next it seemed that bacon and butter were to be rationed, though no one quite knew when.

After the discussion had dragged on a further month, over such issues as meat rations for vegetarians, the Labour opposition began a stop-the-ration-muddle campaign in November. It complained that the dates for rationing bacon and butter had already been delayed by two months.

Rationing, as the convenient phrase had it, would be a guarantee of fair shares. Later still, in July 1940, the press interviewed a woman who had tried to buy eggs in London. They were not rationed at this point but she gave up after nine shops had refused to serve her. Retailers imposed unofficial rationing, by which they would sell only to 'regular customers'. Given the new mobility of the population it was not easy for some people to have been regular customers, the definition of the term being in any case at the whim of the grocer or butcher.

Rationing by law was plainly preferable to rationing by retailer. On 20 November 1939, according to the *News Chronicle* 60 per cent now thought that rationing was necessary and should be introduced, 28 per cent thought it unnecessary and 12 per cent did not know. Ten days later it was announced that rationing of bacon and butter would start on 8 January 1940. Sugar would not be rationed yet but customers must register with a grocer for their supply, restricted to 1lb a week. It was generally expected that meat, as well as sugar, would be rationed in the near future. Meals in cafés and restaurants would generally be available without coupons. Hotel residents must hand over their ration cards for stays of more than a few days. The brewing trade made a helpful intervention on 13 December, assuring the public that barley stocks were ample. There was no question of rationing beer.

When 8 January 1940 came, sugar as well as bacon and butter went 'on the ration'. In some cases, proprietary brands of food began to disappear, to be replaced by such products as 'National Butter', blended from various sources, which went on sale on 1 February at 1s. 7d. (£3) a pound.

The anomalies of the system were soon evident. Of the items now rationed, many people could not afford butter and had not been in the habit of eating it. The same was true of bacon. On 24 January 1939, for example, a report had been presented to the National Tribunal for Railway Staff, pointing out that to railwaymen and their families fresh fruit was a luxury, while bacon, butter, cheese, jam and syrup were rarely seen on their tables.

After three weeks of rationing, there was a surplus of butter and talk of doubling the ration for those who could afford it. For those who could not, there was margarine at half or a third the price. Margarine was later rationed but at present the government's 'Pool' margarine, made of whale oil with added vitamins A and D, was 6d. (£1) a pound. The cost was less than in the 1914–18 war because the government had bought large quantities of whale oil and oil seed at peacetime prices.

Rationing brought a glut of ham and bacon, for similar reasons, and in these cases the rations were temporarily doubled. By April, there was still plenty of 'extra' butter. Eggs were plentiful at 1s. 9d (£3.50) a dozen. Meat rationing on 11 March was imposed by price at 1s. 10d. (£3.60) a week. The pretext for its introduction was that imported meat took up too much shipping space in wartime. In vain, the butchers protested that the shops were filled with home-killed meat and that rationing was not necessary. Sugar, however, remained a major import and was running short. By May 1940, even before Dunkirk, it was suggested that saccharin would take its place for the duration of the war.

The true anomaly was that the effects of rationing could not be universally restrictive. Not all forms of meat were rationed nor, when the time came, were all forms of cheese. Butter, milk and eggs were casually accessible to many country-dwellers. Wherever poultry was kept, it was impossible to control the supply of eggs and meat. In towns and cities, where such opportunities were lacking, the black market was the means of supplementary supply. It was in Stepney and its neighbours, rather than in the villages of England, that the black market in food was described in court as 'absolutely rampant down here'.[10]

With the implementation of rationing orders in January 1940, each customer was required to register with a grocer and a butcher. Food rationing was then progressive until 1941. In the meantime, the unofficial weekly ration imposed by London shops on each customer included two ounces of cheese, two eggs and two sausages. Most of those who applied to register with another grocer or butcher were refused outright. Short of moving house, which the billeting system and the duties of civil defence might prevent, a change of registration was only possible by appealing to a Local Food Committee. Thousands of disgruntled customers who were turned down by these committees extended the natural constituency of the racketeers.

Food Office undercover men and women were soon at work. In April 1940, prosecutions for food offences in London, which had totalled only 135 for the first complete five months of the war, had now passed 200 a month. There was a new determination on the part of officials and their plain-clothes enforcers that public examples should be made quickly. So, on 11 April 1940, a kindly and impressionable grocer, Henry Sitwell, found himself facing Aldershot magistrates on charges of selling half a pound of butter without coupons. D. Llewellyn Griffiths, local Food Control Officer, had instructed his daughter to go to Mr Sitwell's shop and see if she could wheedle a packet of butter out of him without surrendering any coupons.

The shopkeeper succumbed at length to her persuasion, saying, 'You won't let anyone know, will you, or you will get into trouble as well as myself?' Under cross-examination, Mr Griffiths explained that he disliked 'decoys', as he called them, 'but we have to use them'. Why a decoy should be used to persuade a hitherto law-abiding grocer to break the regulations was not a matter for the court. This was a strict liability offence and there was no way for the magistrates to show their disapproval of the methods used, other than by fining Mr Sitwell the lenient sum of £2 (£80).

It was one of the earliest cases in which Food Office officials went incognito into shops to ask the owner to break rationing orders or visited cafés and restaurants to see if they could persuade the staff to serve them a meal larger than the permitted number of courses. They were, of course, obliged to eat and charge for such meals in the course of their duties. Unsurprisingly, as the war merged into the years of austerity, there was increasing distaste for the figure of the 'snoop'.

In the face of these tactics, shopkeepers learnt to become more devious than Mr Sitwell. When Walter Edwin Tarrant of Wimborne Road, Bournemouth, was tried in August 1942 for selling shoes without coupons, the court heard that those who wanted the shoes had first to know the password: 'A little firewatcher told me to come.'[11]

Rationing anomalies encouraged a subversive refrain that the rich were doing all right in wartime – as in peacetime – or at any rate were doing a lot less badly than anyone else. After cheese rationing had begun, it was revealed that some types of cheese had never been rationed and never would be. This was news to most people who thought of cheese as 'mousetrap' cheddar. In June 1941 there was still an unrationed supply of 'Gruyère-type' and 'Roquefort-type' cheese imported from South America, and sold by high-class grocers at four times the price of rationed cheddar, which was controlled at 1s. 1d. (£2) per pound.

To make matters worse, the Ministry of Food had derationed expensive cheeses in May 1941, including 'soft cheese, curd cheese, blue-veined cheese, processed cheese, and cheese made from milk other than cow's milk'. One leading manufacturer of processed cheese admitted that production was still running at 50 per cent of the pre-war total. The press noted that it was generally sold under the counter and most housewives never saw it. The Ministry of Food insisted that supplies were 'very small', as were the number of those who could afford the prices. Rationing was intended to impose fairness and to ensure that no one need starve. An attempt to enforce equality, even with the existing army of 35,000 Food Office functionaries, would have seemed absurd.[12]

To offset such revelations, the authorities showed that the mighty were offered no favours if they broke the law. Woolworths and Sainsbury, D. H. Evans, J. Lyons, Swan & Edgar, Odeon Theatres, Grosvenor House, the Savoy Hotel and the East India Club were a handful of famous names who found themselves in court. Prominent individuals with American interests were prosecuted over currency regulations. Noël Coward was convicted of the new offence of failing to offer dollar holdings for sale to the Treasury. George Black the impresario pleaded guilty to using illegally obtained lawn hangings. The Anglo-American film star George Arliss was fined £4,500 (£180,000) under the Defence (Finance) Regulations for neglecting to register United States and Canadian securities valued at £13,160 (£526,400). Ivor Novello went to prison for misusing petrol. The band-leader Victor Silvester was convicted of smuggling with the aid of US service personnel, who allowed him to collect duty-free goods, which they were entitled to import, from an address in Old Quebec Street. For those who suffered this form of wartime justice there was satisfaction when in May 1943 Sir Peter Laurie, Provost Marshal of the nation's Military Police, was convicted of rationing offences at the Old Bailey.[13]

Despite such examples, the feeling persisted that the rich and the richer members of the middle class did not share the privations of others. At Easter 1940, those who could afford it were allowed to stay in a hotel for four days without handing over their ration books. In general, there was no limit to the number of meals that might be eaten in restaurants and cafés by those with money, though the number of courses might be limited. It was alleged that a couple could dine at a single restaurant by eating their hors d'oeuvres and fish, paying the bill, then coming back and sitting at another table to order the next two courses. On Sunday 2 March 1941, the Brighton No. 3 Branch of the National Union of Railwaymen passed unanimously the motion that

This branch of the NUR, conscious from personal observation of the inequality produced by the present system of rationing, protests against the continuance of a system whereby workers and their families are kept short while persons possessed of the means are able to eat in restaurants or to purchase luxury foods.

Such sentiments were common in the union movement all over the country.

In the first summer after Dunkirk, J. B. Priestley visited Bournemouth and published his report in *Picture Post* on 21 June 1941. The accompanying photographs of well-stocked foodshop windows with asparagus to the fore confirmed the resort's reputation as a place where, in the catchphrase of the day, 'they hardly know there's a war on'. Priestley concluded that no one could call it a bad war in Bournemouth. Of course, men in uniform mingled with the seaside civilians. Air raid warnings sounded from time to time. The town was, after all, no more than eighty miles from German-occupied France. Yet those with money enjoyed comfortable hotels, three theatres, two orchestras, super cinemas, tea dances at the Pavilion and dinner dances after dark. Bournemouth in the second summer of the war was a haven of azaleas, scented pines, cocktail bars, salmon and lobster.

Priestley was no killjoy. His objection was that self-evacuated people spent all their lives in Bournemouth, while thousands were never to leave the bomb-damaged wastes of industrial Warrington or Wolverhampton. Just along the coast, advertisements for Torquay and the 'English Riviera' promised 'a roaring good time' to those who could afford it, but not to the homeless and shell-shocked of the Plymouth blitz forty miles away, nor to that city's doctors and air raid wardens dropping with fatigue.

James Langdale Hodson, journalist and narrator of one of the war's outstanding documentary films, *Desert Victory* (1943), made a number of pilgrimages through the country, reporting for the BBC and summing up his findings in a series of books on the people at war. After being taken to lunch at the Connaught Hotel in Mayfair on 5 May 1942, he confirmed Priestley's findings that 'if you have the brass, as they say in Lancashire', it was possible to live very well in the third year of global conflict.[14]

The distinction appeared in other ways. In October 1939, when members of the Auxiliary Fire Service in Manchester expressed a grievance over their rates of pay, they were paraded by the Chief Constable and threatened with imprisonment. Within a few days, the Civil Service asked for higher rates of pay to compensate for the strain of working in wartime. They were heard with patience and sympathy.

From time to time, the authorities faced strong public hostility in such matters. On 6 October 1942, Ellen Wilkinson, Parliamentary Secretary to Herbert Morrison, Home Secretary and Minister of Home Security, travelled to Liverpool. She was to warn her audience that an order compelling women in the city to become fire-watchers, in the absence of volunteers, 'must go through'. She was quite unprepared for the shouts of 'Let Morrison come and do it!' Hecklers threw back at her the government transport slogan of the day, 'Is your journey really necessary?'

Worst of all, she appeared to exonerate the more affluent citizens who caught the so-called 'Funk Express' from Liverpool every night, slept in the safety of the countryside, and returned to their offices in the morning, while others watched the fires and faced the bombs. She caused fury among the crowd by insisting that she did not blame those who caught the train out of Liverpool on six nights of the week, provided they fire-watched on the seventh.

There had been official dismay over the apathy of younger women in 1941, during such morale drives as War Work Week, and over the discovery in November that year that 'girls were dodging the call-up' by the simple expedient of not registering for it. A National Service Bill was thereupon introduced in the following month, which lowered the call-up age for men from nineteen to eighteen and a half, and made single women between the ages of twenty and thirty liable to military service. Those who could not understand why any man or woman should be a shirker, slacker or dodger might have been enlightened by the reply of an industrial worker in Coventry. Memories of near-starvation in the slump of the 1930s died hard. 'You didn't want us then and now you want us – and you can go to Hell.'[15]

Despite such responses and the numbers who listened to Lord Haw-Haw 'for a laugh', there was almost universal hostility to Germany. Yet those who fell foul of the police or the courts sometimes invoked Hitler and a German victory as the means by which they would be revenged. On 25 May 1940, Sylvester Fahey, a booking clerk, was gaoled at Croydon, having failed to answer a summons for 'an unobscured light'. When arrested in the street, he called the police

'English swine', spat in their faces, became violent, and said, 'Hitler will soon be here, and a jolly good job.' He was gaoled for one month for the unobscured light, and two months for assaulting the police.[16]

Similarly, at Brighton in February 1941, a boy of sixteen convicted of shopbreaking was sent to an approved school by the juvenile court. His mother burst into tears, the boy threw his arms round her, and the father shouted at the Chairman, 'When the invasion comes, I hope they bomb your house first!' At North London magistrates court, the sister of a man convicted of receiving stolen coupons and identity cards smiled at him. The magistrate ordered her to be removed for this 'damned impertinence'. She was manhandled from the court shouting, 'I hope the Germans bomb the lot of you', and there was a sound of breaking glass outside. Similarly, when a ship's greaser, Harold Allibone, was sent to prison for six months by Liverpool magistrates in February 1942 for running a card-playing swindle in the docks, he was removed shouting, 'The sooner the Gestapo gets here the better!'[17]

Elsewhere it was the British authorities who were likened to the Gestapo. In June 1944 the Chairman of the West Riding Education Committee made the comparison when he was fined £30 (£1,200) at Leeds for driving 800 yards out of his way to work. A retail furrier denounced a Board of Trade officer in court for having 'ransacked his place like a Gestapo agent'. Once the war was over, the term was freely thrown about in the years of austerity that followed. The Borrowing (Control and Guarantees) Bill, which gave the government power to examine bank accounts, was denounced as a 'snoop' or 'Gestapo' bill. 'We will cut its ugly throat,' Brendan Bracken promised on behalf of the Conservative opposition. 'Meal-snooping' in restaurants by Ministry of Food officers to ensure that customers were not served extra portions was denounced by the *Evening Standard* as a 'Gestapo' measure.[18]

Most abuse was an instinctive response to authoritarianism, to the 'jack-in-office' raised to personal power by wartime conditions, and to some of those conditions themselves: what were seen as pointless regulations and inequalities of suffering. Only in a handful of cases did bloody-mindedness indicate the least sympathy for Germany, let alone for Hitler. London prisoners unwillingly transferred to provincial gaols in the early months of the war were so riotous that in the disturbances at Horfield Prison, Bristol, their chants of 'We want to go back to London!' 'We want better food!' and 'Fetch Hitler!' were heard almost a quarter of a mile away. They were on a par with 1941 suggestions that the only competent British general had been Booth of the Salvation Army or that it was time to ask the Germans to quote Rommel's transfer fee.

To most people, the weakness of regulations lay in the too frequent mean-mindedness and absurdity of their enforcement rather than in the regulations themselves which were seen to be well-intentioned. They turned bureaucrats, it was said, into 'little Hitlers'. It was also hard to accept that normal activities were now illegal. In the aftermath of Dunkirk, for much of the war until D-Day, exclusion zones stretching twenty miles inland from the Kent and Sussex coast made it a crime for a non-resident to travel there. One defendant was fined for coming to visit a grave and another for having gone to the seaside on an impulse. In November 1942, a Brighton colonel who was entitled to live there was fined for inviting an actress from London. Later on, men and women were sent to prison for these offences.

In such 'front-line' towns as Brighton, a 10 p.m. curfew was imposed on areas near the sea. Walking on the fortified promenade at any time required the permission of the local military commander. In June 1941, a middle-aged Brighton reveller, who confessed to the police that he had been to see 'a nice lady' in Palmeira Square and had drunk six whiskies and soda, was found in the area after curfew. Fearing the appearance of a court report at the foot of a local newspaper column, perhaps to be noted by wife or family, he tried to bribe the arresting policeman with a £1 note. The bribe was refused and the unfortunate defendant, instead of having his indiscretion tucked away at the foot of a column listing local magistrates court cases, became a headline of the week on charges of attempted corruption. His adventure with the 'nice lady' was reported prominently by the local press when he was dealt with at Lewes Assizes.[19]

Exclusion zones were later as closely guarded to conceal preparations for an invasion of France, as they had previously been to guard against an invasion of England. From time to time, all pedestrians and drivers were stopped by civil or military police and identity cards demanded. There were 'swoops' at frequent intervals. On 31 October 1942, the police made Saturday afternoon and evening raids in Brighton on dance halls, football grounds, the Greyhound Racing Stadium at Hove, pubs and restaurants. At the greyhound stadium alone, 121 people were detained for having no identity cards. On 12 May 1944, when military and civilian police carried out a mass check of identity cards in Brighton, the railway station and Western Road shopping parades were cordoned off. Those within the areas were checked in groups of twenty at a time. Traffic was stopped. A military funeral cortège was halted on the seafront until the mourners had proved their identities.

Restrictions on movement had other causes. With full petrol rationing, only official use of cars was permitted and only when essential. A driver might be fined for using a car when he could have gone by bus, even if there was an urgent reason for the journey. Offenders were caught at times of great embarrassment. Jack Barnes, scrap metal dealer of Hove, claimed he had driven from work to Brighton police station to report the loss of his fountain pen. PC Archdeacon, who was watching him, saw Mr Barnes stop on his way, outside a shop in East Street where a lady got out and went into the premises. Barnes was still waiting there with his car when the policeman approached him.

The suspect claimed never to have seen the lady in his life before. He had only given her a lift from a bus stop, as drivers were encouraged to do. PC Archdeacon then saw her come out of the shop. Barnes signalled to her agitatedly and when the policeman went up to her, pushed in front of him and said to the total stranger, 'I wasn't going to pick you up here, was I?' 'Why, what is the matter, Jack?' she asked. When questioned in court as to this deliberate lie, he said uneasily, 'I didn't want the lady's name to come into anything. It was an error on my part.'[20]

Police surveillance of those travelling from Hove during the Brighton lunch hour was unremitting. A tailor was fined in 1943 for making an 887-yard deviation from his business route. His shadow, PC Sweetman, saw him stop in Steine Street and park outside a restaurant. He had a lady with him. They went in at 12.15 and came back to the car at 12.40 to find the policeman waiting. The tailor was fined £5 (£200) which, as the press pointed out with heavy humour, made it an expensive lunch.[21]

By contrast, it seemed harsh that a motorist should have been fined in the bitter February of 1942 for wasting fuel because he left his engine running briefly while the vehicle was stationary, knowing that otherwise it might not start again. Waste, however, was the crime of the season. Next month the Paper Order became law, making it a criminal offence, punishable by a fine of £100 (£4,000) or three months in prison, to throw away or destroy a used bus ticket or cigarette packet. Waste of food was the worst offence of this kind, made punishable in August 1940 by imprisonment for three months on summary conviction or two years on indictment. J. Lyons Ltd seemed to be unique in being prosecuted for wasting food on the grounds that they had allowed mice to eat it during a persistent infestation in their kitchens at Cadby Hall.[22]

Despite the embarrassment caused to a curfew-breaker on an indiscreet visit or to a businessman keeping an intimate lunch appointment, regulations were generally respected and kept. As the war went on, however, prohibitions had more than a touch of bureaucratic lunacy. Some provoked a strong reaction. Among these was the Transportation of Flowers Order in 1943. A new Defence Regulation, on 16 February, made it illegal to send or take cut flowers by rail, but not by road. No action was taken when flowers arrived at Covent Garden by lorry, depleting the nation's petrol or diesel resources. However, the effect of a rail ban on Cornish flower-growers was ruinous. In two days, six men had been arrested on the Penzance to Paddington train, one having a carton and a suitcase containing the new season's first flowers from Cornwall. The case was heard at Marylebone magistrates court. It was a strict liability charge with no defence and the men were fined £105 (£4,200).[23]

Authority had the bit between its teeth. Even as a reduction in police manpower was announced, it drafted in Metropolitan police and railway police to Paddington. They were to wait for trains from Cornwall, watch for 'flower smugglers', question travellers and order them to open their luggage for inspection.

Among more accusations of 'Gestapo' tactics, the matter was raised in Parliament, where Captain McEwen, Lord of the Treasury, insisted the order could not be relaxed, even for consignments of flowers worth less than £1. A fortnight passed, during which press and public opinion made the government increasingly ridiculous. At last, without fuss, the Transportation of Flowers Order was quietly killed on 18 March.

From the first, lighting restrictions were enforced with improbable severity. On 22 November 1940, a Naval Reserve officer was fined at Yarmouth for striking matches in a telephone kiosk so that a woman could see the dial. At Eastbourne, Ernest Walls was fined for striking a match to light his pipe. Elsewhere a man was arrested because his cigar glowed alternately brighter and dimmer, so that he might be signalling to a German aircraft. A woman was prosecuted for running into a room, where her baby was having a fit, and turning on the light without first securing the blackout curtains.[24]

The Lighting (Restrictions) Order 1940 was notorious for the absurdities it spawned. In *Blackshaw v. Chambers* (1943) strict liability was applied to a cyclist who feared he might be killed in the blackout because the tiny 2.5 volt torch-bulb on his bike would not be seen. Having fastened a second lamp to his machine, he was convicted of flouting the order on the grounds that German bombers flying high above him might see the glimmer of his torch, though traffic a few feet away might not.

'Unobscured lights' were by no means the only cause of offence when bombing began. In one of the odder cases, in December 1941, fifty-three-year-old George Hall was sent to prison on the grounds that 'he did wilfully disturb other persons in the proper use of an air raid shelter contrary to Rule 3(a) made by the Ministry of Home Security under Regulation 23 (A-B) of the Defence Regulations 1939.' In plain words, Mr Hall snored during an air raid. He was woken by those around him, mumbled his apologies, went back to sleep, snored, was woken repeatedly, until he began to use 'abusive language' to the devils – as he saw the matter – who would not let him sleep. The shelter marshal was called. He ordered Mr Hall to stop snoring, whereupon Mr Hall threatened to hit him. By this time a policeman was in attendance and arrest followed. 'I can't help what I do when I'm asleep,' said the defendant wearily, as he was led away to begin a fourteen-day prison sentence.[25]

Sleeping was also the crime of Thomas Mackworth Lucas, a sixty-seven-year-old accountant from Dulwich whose destination in May 1944 was Kent. He nodded off, slept more soundly than he had intended, and woke up when the train stopped at Hastings, well within the forbidden 'exclusion zone'. To make matters worse, his wife had left him in December 1943 and, intending to make his life as difficult as possible, had thrown away his identity card before she went. He had tried without success to get a replacement. The court first remanded him in custody and then sent him to prison for a month. At the same time, two girls who had travelled without authority to see their American army boyfriends in Bournemouth were also sent to prison.[26]

For every person who felt that such findings and sentences were absurd, there was another who saw the nation's peril and insisted that laws were made with good reason and were to be obeyed. Even before a single bomb had fallen on London, an angry crowd gathered outside the MIL Furnishing Company at Clapton Common, when a faulty time-switch turned on the display lights which had not been used since the outbreak of war. Police broke in and turned them off. The owner was fined £50 (£2,000) with the option of two months in prison.[27]

Improbably, one of the largest and angriest mobs gathered outside the London premises of the Church Missionary Trust in Salisbury Square, early in November 1940. Constable Hammond arrived at midnight to find 'a hostile crowd' in front of the building, shouting and hurling bricks at the windows. Light was showing from seven of the windows, which were all unscreened. Hammond tried to get into the building, then called out an air raid warden, and finally the fire brigade who smashed their way in through the back and turned the lights out. The basement of the building was used as a public air raid shelter and it seemed that a shelterer had got into the upper floors and turned the lights on. This being a strict liability offence, however, the Church Missionary Trust was prosecuted and fined at the Mansion House Court.[28]

Not all defendants submitted tamely to the notion of strict liability regardless of moral guilt. The secretary of the Enfield Riding Club chose to go to prison rather than pay a blackout fine, on the

37

grounds that there was as much light showing from Enfield police station as from his premises. 'I am a man of principle. I would sooner do ten years than pay a penny for this offence.' Among other cases were many resembling that of the girl who made herself up to go to the cinema and forgot to turn off the light in the room before leaving. Turning lights on before dark and accidentally leaving them was a common offence. An elderly survivor of the Oscar Wilde scandal, Lord Alfred Douglas, was fined for it at Hove in June 1944. George Lovell of Amersham was also fined because he had put up his black-out curtains and had then gone outside to make sure they were effective. A policeman was already there and arrested him for the crack of light still showing. Albert Bachelor was fined at Great Missenden for having a car headlamp that was too bright. It was no defence that his radiator had just burst and the hot water had washed off the black paint with which he had masked the lamp.[29]

There was no definable moment when resentment of authority began, in the minds of many people, to overtake a sense of national emergency. However, in *The Slaves of Solitude* (1947) Patrick Hamilton was to sum up this mood, as it had developed by 1943. His Fascist-hating and, indeed, German-hating, heroine Miss Roach is worn down by the 'lecturing and nagging' tone of government propaganda, with its constant reminders not to waste food or use fuel, not to leave litter and to telephone briefly, if at all, not to travel unless absolutely necessary and not to spend her own money when she could put it into government savings. In her case, the hectoring and nagging are aggravated by the absence of stockings, shampoo, scent, nail varnish, hairpins, scissors, darning wool and other common feminine necessities.[30]

That there was growing dislike of the methods employed by officialdom, when the threat of invasion receded and the possibility of a German victory vanished with the arrival of American troops, is beyond question. Later, as war passed into peace and restrictions continued, resentment became outright hostility. It was one thing to suffer deprivation in a crusade against the evils of the Third Reich, quite another to suffer more acutely in order to close a 'dollar gap' in the peacetime balance of payments. As for the methods of enforcement, first the malcontents themselves invoked Hitler and the

Gestapo. At length it was the courts which condemned the application of the law by such means.

The police too often took to the new measures and methods with unwholesome enthusiasm. When it was suspected that the See-Saw Club in Western Road, Hove, was serving drinks out of hours, three plain-clothes officers were dispatched to get on friendly terms with the two women who owned the club. One policeman rapidly ingratiated himself as a dashing RAF hero.

The owners, Margery Moss and Elizabeth Daphne Morgan, were completely deceived and suspected no malevolent intention when their admirers invited them out to dinner. On their return to the club, the women wanted to show appreciation for the meal and offered the men a drink. There was no question of payment being made but, in the strictest sense, the act of kindness amounted to serving drinks after hours. As soon as the men had their drinks, the mask of amiability dropped. They announced themselves as police and arrested Mrs Moss and Mrs Morgan.

When the case came to court, Mrs Moss was fined the substantial sum of £115 (£4,600) with £20 16s. (£832) costs and Mrs Morgan was fined £10 (£400). Far worse, the women were put out of business, since their club was also struck off. Their solicitor, Bruce Dutton Briant, attacked the police for having behaved in 'a most un-English manner' but the magistrates in this case were unimpressed. In time of war they were inclined to support the police unless some flagrant impropriety could be shown. Moreover, the defence solicitor was unpopular for other reasons. The year before, there had been a by-election in Brighton. Contrary to the all-party agreement that elections should be uncontested during the war, giving the government candidate a clear run, Mr Dutton Briant had not only stood as an Independent against the government's candidate but had almost beaten him.[31]

Far more common were traps set for shopkeepers by local officials of the Ministry of Food. As meat rationing took full effect in 1940, council food inspectors were busy in areas like Stepney, which had an impressive record of black marketeering. The inspectors would soon have been recognized so when it was decided to target East End butchers at the end of that year, volunteers were needed. The usual tactic was to ask other council workers to act as decoys. Mrs Isabella Tompsett, a Stepney Borough Council charlady, was employed. On the instructions of Herbert Ansom, the food inspector, she went the rounds of butchers' shops on 14 December, attempting to buy meat, until she came to those where the meat was supplied without coupons taken or questions asked as to whether she was registered with the shop. By the end of the afternoon she had found three shops, all of them in Salmons Lane, Limehouse, where regulations were entirely disregarded.

In sentencing the chief culprit, Richard Webster, the magistrate described the offences as 'extremely serious . . . It has got to be stopped and I am going to do all in my power to stop it.' He fined Mr Webster £15 (£600) and the other two defendants £10 (£400). Compared with other cases, the sentences were lenient and when Mrs Thompsett confessed in cross-examination that her role was to try and make the butchers break the law, the magistrate admitted, 'One doesn't like it. It's Continental.' It was, however, thought necessary.[32]

Sometimes it seemed worse than Continental. At Lambeth, in November 1942, evidence was given in two prosecutions against Ministry of Food officials for taking bribes from a Brixton butcher in order to close down a case against him. Evidence of character, given on behalf of one of the officials by his superior, was solely a tribute to the amount of money he had brought in from fines, by hook or by crook. 'Appointed in 1940, he is an excellent officer who has been very successful with prosecutions. The fines and costs in cases brought by him since his appointment amount to over £3,000 [£120,000].'[33]

As powers of enforcement grew, investigations spread to private homes under the Acquisition of Food (Excessive Quantities) Order. The pre-war virtues of saving and storing now became the crime of hoarding. With the advent of general food rationing in 1941, the public was reminded that 'food officials' had absolute power to enter and inspect larders. If there was more than a week's rations, an amount sometimes counted in ounces, a prosecution might follow. The only concession was for those who could not shop every week. The first prosecution of this sort was brought in July 1941 against James Garrett of Glasgow.

According to the President of the Board of Trade, Hugh Dalton, in the House of Commons on 8 September 1942, strict rules had been laid down for undercover enforcement officers of his department in their dealings with shopkeepers. They were not to hold any conversation with the trader about coupons, nor make any comment 'calculated to arouse the trader's sympathy'. So far as possible, they should avoid making purchases from young assistants who might make an honest mistake.

How far this was disregarded appeared in such cases as the prosecution of Sydney Goodman in Manchester for selling clothing material above the regulation price. Two female Board of Trade inspectors went to his shop and pretended to be customers with no coupons. He sold them ten yards of the cloth without coupons but charged more than the regulation price. The magistrate, Alderman Harry Lord, asked what would happen to members of the public if they had behaved in the same manner as the two *agents provocateurs* by pretending to have no coupons but agreeing to pay more than the permitted price. The solicitor for the Board of Trade told him that they would be prosecuted. 'I thought so,' said Alderman Lord, adding that employees of the Board of Trade 'should not be differently treated to any ordinary person'. Sydney Goodman was discharged.[34]

On such occasions, the courts were acting against both the letter and the spirit of the Defence Regulations. That they did so was some indication of a growing distaste for undercover enforcement officers – 'stooges', 'narks' and 'snoops' – once the immediate dangers of invasion seemed to recede, with German involvement on the Russian Front, in the Mediterranean and in North Africa. The most contentious area of activity was in supervising café or restaurant meals. Many of the austerity regulations were scarcely enforceable. When it was announced that the serving of bread at lunchtime was to be banned, the public was warned that obedience would be ensured by a near-farcical scheme in which enforcement officers would raid such premises and peer into the plates of the customers.

The preferred method was for enforcement teams to treat themselves to a meal and see if they could get more than their entitlement. Often they acted on information from a concerned member of the public. In November 1942 a woman having lunch in the café of the Astoria Cinema, Streatham, noticed two other women being served with fish and then meat. To serve fish and meat at a single sitting was a criminal offence. She tipped off the local Food Office who at once 'arranged a test'. A 'test' was the euphemism for an official having a meal at suspect premises in order to attempt to get illegal portions. In the Astoria case, the test proved positive. Odeon Theatres were fined, the manageress was fined, even the two waitresses who had carried the trays were fined for 'aiding and abetting' the offence of serving both meat and fish to an assistant enforcement officer.[35]

So long as hostilities in Europe continued, courts were generally willing to respect regulations – with a few well-publicized exceptions. At the Mansion House, in the spring of 1945, a prosecution was brought against the New Corn Exchange Restaurant in Mark Lane for allowing customers to consume more than five shillings' worth of food. Two 'food spies' had gone there on 15 March and persuaded the staff to serve food to a total value of 12s. 6d., rather than ten shillings, the maximum for two people. The magistrate, Sir Harry Twyford, checked the evidence and saw from the day's bills that no other customer had been served beyond the legal limit. If the two spies had not gone there to 'test' the system, no offence would have been committed. The restaurant was crowded and the two 'enforcers' were therefore served in the snack bar with hors d'oeuvres, fish, two vegetables and sweet. It was far more difficult, in the snack bar, to check the amount that customers had been served.

Sir Harry asked one enforcer, John Hawkins, 'Why could you not have said plainly, "I am not entitled to any more?"' Hawkins replied, 'I definitely could not do that. I am sent there to do my job, not to provoke an offence but to see whether one is committed.' Sir Harry was not impressed. 'Then I don't envy you your job. And I don't think much of a system which requires that people should be sent round spying on restaurants to see whether the law is broken.' Alarmed by this, the Board of Trade solicitor, B. M. Stephenson, got up. 'I can't see how these orders can possibly be carried out unless the officials of the Ministry can go round and make test purchases.' He was too late. The magistrate ignored the regulation and dismissed the case. 'These people employed in restaurants are short-staffed and during the rush hour, as everybody knows, it must be most difficult to see what food each customer is consuming.'[36]

As war passed into austerity, there was animosity against men and women who had spent the years of peril 'testing' how much food they could get in restaurants at the taxpayer's expense, while the rest of the country lived on its rations. Malcontents and black marketeers might hint at justification for their own activities in the absurdities and hypocrisies of such a system.

Attacks on the regulations were widespread and varied. By November 1939, in the opening months of the war, there were proposals to abandon or modify the blackout as a scheme which had achieved nothing except to add to road accident figures. It was decided to impose a blackout speed limit of twenty miles an hour. This would be enforced by police cars travelling at twenty miles an hour, waiting to be overtaken. If this happened, officers would lean out of the windows with paper-covered torches and wave them up and down to attract the offender's attention and bring him to a halt. It was in keeping with the surreal ritual that the first man to be convicted should have been travelling at thirty-four miles an hour, and that he was driving a hearse.[37]

Was an absolute blackout, rather than the 'dim-out' which served Paris, necessary at all in that autumn of 1939? The first air attack had been on ships in the Firth of Forth with no bomb falling on the mainland for more than three months. As the casualties from road accidents mounted, the King's surgeon wrote an article on 'panic' for the *British Medical Journal*. He pointed out that by frightening the nation into blackout regulations, the Luftwaffe was able to kill 600 British citizens a month without ever taking to the air, 'at a cost to itself of exactly nothing'.[38]

By no means all injuries were accidental. A combination of the blackout and a reduction in police manpower made the effective policing of the worst areas for violence and street robbery almost impossible. Before the war, the MP for North Camberwell, C. G. Ammon, had warned the Home Secretary that 'in South London, citizens had had to form bands to protect traders against gangs who smashed up snack bars and cafés.'

One area known for youthful violence was outside the Elephant and Castle tube station with its coffee stall and King's Head public house. In response, Inspector Frank Beavis had taught his men to fight thugs 'in their own style with fist and truncheon'. As one resident said after the inspector's wartime transfer to Stepney, 'There was only one man the gangsters were really scared of and that was Beavis. The Southwark police are a good crowd of fellows but it needed the inspector to scare the toughs.'[39]

The menace of blackout gangs reached the headlines with the Skipton Street murder of seventeen-year-old James Bolitho Harvey, on Saturday 21 March 1942. Harvey and his younger brother had come out of the Elephant and Castle station at midnight on their way home from a West End show. They went to the coffee stall and then towards the stop for the Brixton tram. Almost at once, they were set upon in the dark by a gang seeming to consist of seven men, though only three were caught. Both boys were robbed, Harvey was beaten to death with a lead-weighted cosh, his fifteen-year-old brother kicked into semi-consciousness. Witnesses at the coffee stall heard their screams but assumed that it was yet another 'drunken squabble such as we often hear around here'. 'I'll never forgive myself for not going,' said one of the men at the stall. A woman on her way home from work at the King's Head heard cries and sobbing, then shouts of 'Shine your torch! For God's sake shine your torch.' She saw the face of the dead brother, 'head and eyes covered with blood'.

A combined hunt by civil and military police led to the arrest of a labourer, a barrow boy and a naval deserter from the area, their ages between nineteen and twenty-two. There was dismay in Southwark when it was realized that the three would not face the death penalty, since their pleas of guilty to manslaughter had been accepted, despite the callousness of the crime. They were sentenced to three years, eighteen months and twelve months respectively. All had previous convictions, including three for assault by the nineteen-year-old ringleader James Essex. The effect of leniency on the blackout gangs of South London was summed up by a local resident. 'They say now that it is worth taking chances in burglary and strong-arm work with only the possibility of a sentence of a year or two rather than take the risk of fighting for their country.'[40]

An assessment of such dangers posed by the blackout had been made long before in a memorandum written on 20 November 1939. The writer suggested that a complete blackout, as opposed to a dim-out which left visibility at six hundred yards, was serving no useful purpose. He cited the fear and reality of criminal assault but also the demoralizing effect of 'vexatious prosecutions for minor infractions'. He quoted the case of the man who was prosecuted for smoking a cigarette too brightly and of the woman who had been fined for turning on the light when her baby had a fit. The writer was certainly a man with a reputation for subversion and trouble-making. This memorandum had been addressed to Neville Chamberlain and his cabinet. Its author was the First Lord of the Admiralty, Winston Churchill.[41]

3

Running for Cover:
The Dodgers and the Dealers

Despite the celluloid myth of *Casablanca*, a gangster who rallied to his country's cause, exercising his antisocial talents on the enemy, was a rarity. The first instinct of the criminal underworld was to escape military service at all costs.

The easiest way to avoid conscription was by not being conscripted in the first place, usually by disregarding the summons to register for National Service. An alternative was to register, obtain a certificate, then ignore further instructions to attend a medical board. Despite official propaganda, which portrayed the resolute hunting-down of defaulters and their departure under escort to meet military justice, this threat was truly effective only with the law-abiding.

John George Haigh registered for military service in 1941. When called for his medical, he ignored the command and eluded the authorities with little difficulty. In 1945 his file, like thousands of others at the end of the war, was marked 'No further action'. He was one of many, though better documented because he was convicted and hanged in 1949 as the notorious 'Acid Bath Murderer', who killed at least six of his dupes for financial gain and dissolved their bodies at his 'factory' in Sussex.[1]

There was greater risk in the solitary evasion of military service, and paid helpers were soon at hand. In the weeks before Dunkirk, Scotland Yard was on the trail of at least four schemes operating in London, whereby a man who had failed his medical would hire himself out, for a fee, to impersonate others. A simpler alternative was the forging or stealing of medical discharge certificates – 'green forms' – and the stamps to validate them. Before Dunkirk, the cruder method of impersonation seemed adequate.[2]

In May 1940 Inspector William Salisbury was leading Scotland Yard's investigation into medical impersonations, which he described as a well-organized racket, prevalent in the East End of London. In one case £70 (£2,800) had been charged for the service. This was soon the cheaper end of the market. Prices for skilled tradesmen and professionals might be several times higher. They stood to gain much by remaining in civilian occupations for the foreseeable future, with the bonus of not being killed or wounded.

To most people, impersonation seemed one of the rumours or myths of war, until the arrest of a principal performer. Jack Brack of Brick Lane appeared in the dock with eight of his clients. He had been examined at Whipps Cross in 1939 and rejected as Class IV, unfit for service, because of an enlarged heart. He was twenty and had only done casual work. Soon afterwards he was approached while playing snooker at the Carlton Club in Brick Lane. Maurice Kravis, twenty-three, had received his call-up papers. He invited Brack to impersonate him at the medical board in exchange for £20 (£800) and a cigar.

Brack agreed. He was driven to the medical centre and failed on behalf of Kravis. From this small beginning the invalid's profession became a well-organized enterprise. According to the police, it prospered sufficiently for Louis Cohen, *alias* 'Buster Collins', to become Brack's 'business manager'. Brack was ultimately able to command such fees as £200 (£8,000) for impersonating a master tailor.

The growing demand for his services may be gauged by the geographical spread of his co-defendants: Brighton, Hackney, West Acton, Stamford Hill, Stepney, Stoke Newington, Lewisham and Forest Gate. Unfortunately, his usefulness was advertised by word of mouth, and one mouth whispered it to Inspector Salisbury. Brack was shadowed, usually to race meetings and bookmakers. He was eventually caught, doing one of his impersonations. At Bow Street, he submitted that his health was far too delicate for him to be remanded in custody. Salisbury retorted that it was not too delicate for him to travel to race meetings 'in various parts of the country'. Indeed, he was considered healthy enough to go to Borstal for three years.[3]

Brack's case was by no means unique, though impersonation was sometimes an act of friendship for which no money changed hands. More remarkable were cases in which doctors gave false certificates.

There was enough evidence by the autumn of 1942 for the General Medical Council to order an inquiry. By then, Inspector Salisbury's investigations also required a special squad at Scotland Yard to check on cases of medical rejects for the armed forces.

In November 1942, a Teddington doctor was struck off by the GMC for giving false certificates to three men 'to enable them to evade their liabilities under the National Service (Armed Forces) Act'. Two days later a doctor from Brick Lane was struck off for 'infamous conduct' of this kind. It seemed that he was working a more ambitious system. Men wishing to avoid conscription contacted him through a woman known only as 'Miss Brown' or her 'mother'. His prices were higher than Jack Brack's, one man having paid £367 10s. (£14,700) for his certificate. On the other hand, his services were more sophisticated. After all, his clients might still have to face a medical board. Eight of them described how they were taught to feign epilepsy, either at their boards or, in the case of those already in the services, to ensure their discharge on medical grounds.[4]

William Salisbury, promoted to Chief Inspector, and Stanley Baker, his sergeant, had worked during the autumn of 1942 with the Special Investigation Branch of the Military Police. Servicemen could get certificates exempting them from duty and extending their leave by paying a fee to Dr William St John Sutton of Sutton Street, Stepney. 'It was common knowledge in East End public houses,' Salisbury added. Dr Sutton did not examine the patient but merely sold him a certificate. To ensure that the certificates were not immediately traceable to him, they were printed on official blue paper of 'Bluegate Hospital'; it was better for the document to come from a hospital rather than a private address. Dr Sutton had seven hundred of these certificates printed for him in Commercial Road, Stepney, using paper which was obtainable only for this purpose.

To test these stories overheard in public houses, a military policeman, Sergeant William Henderson of the SIB, went to Dr Sutton's surgery on 20 November 1942 in the uniform of a private in the Royal Army Service Corps. He complained of 'a touch of flu' and said, 'I don't feel like going back to my unit tomorrow. Can you help get me an extension for a couple of days?' 'Certainly I'll give you a certificate,' Dr Sutton said. Without examining Henderson or asking any questions except name, rank and number, the doctor wrote a certificate saying that the patient was suffering from influenza and catarrh, and was unfit to travel. He sold the certificate to Henderson for half a crown. Three more men were sent by SIB, all as fit as Henderson had been. Each bought a certificate with as little difficulty.

On 13 January 1943, Dr Sutton appeared at the Old Bailey, where he was sent to prison for nine months and ordered to pay £50 towards the prosecution's costs. Christmas Humphreys, for the Crown, told the Recorder that Dr Sutton wished to have fifty other cases taken into consideration. A curiosity was that Dr Sutton had obliged his clients for such small sums and that he failed to take precautions against the virtual certainty of being caught.[5]

As well as being exempted from military service by virtue of poor health, it was possible to escape conscription by having a 'reserved' occupation, making the holder too valuable to be spared for soldiering. The possibilities for manipulating the system were evident in cases like the so-called 'Liverpool Call-Up Evasion Conspiracy' of 1941–2. This ended with a Liverpool city councillor, David Rowan, being sent to prison for seven years and fined £2,000 (£80,000) on charges of false pretences, forgery, and inciting others to destroy or falsify documents. As managing director of David Rowan (Vidro) Ltd, he had committed what Mr Justice Oliver described as 'almost every kind of fraud your ingenuity could conceive' to prevent the call-up of his employees.[6]

Early in 1944, a similar case came to trial in London, where it was alleged that two haulage contractors had conspired with three of their employees to keep employees out of military service by false statements which would classify them as being in 'reserved' occupations and therefore not liable to be called up. One of the owners was also charged with having arranged for another man to impersonate him at his medical board.[7]

A safer method was to find a corrupt civil servant who would provide a complete cover. Maurice Miels of Palmers Green, an official of the Walthamstow Labour Exchange, was sent to prison for four months and fined £50 (£2,000) in November 1940. He had charged £25 (£1,000) for altering the classification of Harold Green from 'managing director', which was not automatically a reserved

occupation, to 'tailor and cutter', which had become one. Harold
Green, owner of a firm of gown-makers, had had no need to find the
corrupt official, it was Miels who came to him. The sum asked
seemed small but the work amounted to no more than making an
error on a form, untraceable except by Miels himself.

A question in this case, as in all such prosecutions during the war,
was how the defendant came to hold a position of responsibility. Five
years earlier Miels had been convicted on six charges of fraudulent
conversion. Two years before the war, he had also served a month's
hard labour for receiving stolen goods. The prosecution, confronted
with this in the present case, could only say, 'The man had good references when he was appointed at the Labour Exchange.'[8]

An even simpler, though somewhat more expensive, means of
avoiding conscription through the agency of a helpful official was by
mislaying papers. In December 1942, Wilfred Bailey of the Ministry
of Labour was sent to prison for six months at Clerkenwell, having
charged a client £200 (£8,000) for getting rid of documents in this
way. He had assured the man that anyone whose papers were mislaid
would be dead, so far as the Ministry and the call-up system were
concerned. There were, however, stories of dupes who had later been
blackmailed with the threat that their papers would be 'found' again
unless further payments were made. The dupe was in no strong position to complain to the police.[9]

On the day following Wilfred Bailey's trial, Albert Dummett, a
forty-three-year-old clerk from Kentish Town, appeared in court. He
worked at the Employment Exchange in Medina Road, Holloway,
and preferred the safer method of destroying rather than mislaying
the papers of his clients. Having tempered his friendly services with
a little amateur blackmail, he was sent to hard labour for a year.

Chief Inspector Salisbury and Sergeant Baker had gone to the
Fonthill Tavern in Finsbury Park, following a tip-off from the land-
lord, Charles Sage. They gave Sage two marked £1 notes and a ten
shilling note, then hid in the scullery to listen to his conversation with
Dummett. When Dummett came in, Sage said, 'Now, look here, Jack.
If I give you fifty bob will you blackmail me any more?' 'No, Charlie,'
replied Dummett amiably, 'I have not blackmailed Bill any more, have
I?' Sage then asked, 'What will happen to my papers if I give you the

money?' Dummett said, 'I will destroy them. You may get a paper some time or other, and if you do, bring them to me, and I will destroy them.'

Once the two CID officers had heard enough, they emerged from the scullery, arrested Dummett and cautioned him. When they made him turn out his pockets, his hip pocket yielded Sage's call-up paper – Form 442, as it was known – and seven other Armed Forces Registration Cards. Dummett had been destroying call-up documents systematically for some time before he misjudged the character of Charles Sage, whom he approached, saying, 'I can get you out of the Home Guard for fifty bob. Your papers will be destroyed.' Home Guard duties would certainly have interfered with the running of the Fonthill Tavern. However, Charles Sage was the only one of Dummett's contacts to report the matter to the police. At the trial, the defendant's other activities came to light. He had 'obtained money from a number of men' about to be summoned for military service. Had he not been caught on this occasion, 'it would have been impossible to trace them'.[10]

With so many schemes on offer, it was remarkable that men like Billy Hill, the youthful 'Boss of Britain's Underworld', should have thought they were in danger of being conscripted. Hill enjoyed a further safeguard: the armed services wanted him and his kind as little as he wanted them.

From time to time, an officer giving evidence at the civilian trial of a serviceman would be asked whether the forces would take the man back if he were convicted of the offence or if he were sent to prison. The usual answer was that he would not be wanted back. This offered an escape to men conscripted before they had time to avoid it. The trial of two Brighton burglars was typical of its kind.

In April 1941 Brian Williams, a soldier, and his brother Patrick, a sailor, walked into Brighton police station and confessed to breaking into the Gloucester Hotel, Brighton, more than three years earlier, on 23 January 1938. They had stolen cigarettes and money. Since then, however, the world situation had changed and the police hesitated. Brian Williams said hopefully 'We have done a number of jobs in Brighton and Hove.' There was little the police could do except prosecute the pair.

At their trial, an army officer gave character evidence of Brian Williams as 'an insubordinate and dirty soldier'. If he was convicted, the Army would not want him back, 'unless it is absolutely necessary'. He was sent to Borstal for three months, the threat of soldiering removed. Three months in Borstal was a holiday compared with several years in the Army, much of it probably spent in a military prison. Patrick Williams was less fortunate. The Royal Navy was prepared to take him back, so long as the court bound him over without a criminal conviction. The court bound him over and he went back to sea.[11]

Many servicemen trying to escape by this route were entirely candid. In January 1942, a private of the RAOC was described by his commanding officer as 'my worst soldier in twenty-nine years'. The soldier, on trial in a civilian court for stealing money from a telephone kiosk, had sixteen military convictions by the age of twenty, including a year's military detention imposed the month before. As for the theft from the phone kiosk, 'I did it to see if I could get out of the Army,' the defendant explained. He was sent to prison for six months with hard labour.[12]

A few months in prison and a return to civilian life seemed far preferable to years of military service. When a former engineer's clerk deserted in March 1942, he survived on the run until December with an identity card which he had stolen from a wallet in a post office. Arrested at last, he hastily announced that he had become a conscientious objector. There was no mistaking his horror when the kindly magistrate asked, 'If I let you return to the Army are you willing to go back and try again?' 'No, sir!' said the deserter with alarm, 'I would rather go to prison.' He went to hard labour for nine months, coming out to civilian life when his contemporaries faced another two or three years in uniform.[13]

For those who had no sympathetic doctor or invalid friend, no anxious employer and no criminal record bad enough to make them unacceptable, there was little beyond the hit-or-miss method of not registering for National Service. From time to time, as in July 1942, these 'dodgers' were warned they were being given one last chance to register. The 'one last chance' offer, like the bizarre proposal in March 1942 to forgive black marketeers all their past offences if they 'owned up', and promised to be good, was taken to mean that the authorities were at their wits' end in the matter.

The 'last chance' warning of July 1942 had been somewhat undermined by a report that a round-up of 'dodgers' had begun six months earlier in collaboration with the Ministry of Labour. During this exercise, it was admitted, 'many more escaped than were caught'. In July, however, the enforcers threatened that addresses of those failing to register would be obtained from Ministry of Food records and by these means they would be tracked down. Unfortunately, this information gave the dodgers time to take evasive action, by for example purchasing a black market ration book, which Billy Hill was buying in quantity at £2 (£80) each and selling on for £3 (£120).[14]

Even police 'swoops' and 'check-ups' had uncertain results. On the night of 27 June 1941, military and civilian police targeted the King's Cross area of London 'to catch army dodgers and deserters', only to discover that all those who waited to be found had identity cards. When police raided a Plymouth funfair on 31 October 1942, however, almost two-thirds of civilians checked as well as some service personnel had no identity cards at all. It was impossible to inquire further because at that point someone let off a stolen smoke bomb and the premises had to be evacuated.

By February 1944, when Scotland Yard investigated open-air markets and the liquor trade, the primary aim was no longer to round up dodgers but to find the source of a thriving trade in stolen identity cards, which had made dodging so much easier. This was coupled with a stricter check on all identity cards in the security-conscious exclusion zones adjacent to the South Coast, where preparations for the invasion of France were in progress.

There were some incidental successes in rounding up fugitives, as when police raided an illegal gaming party at the Cleveland Club in Whitechapel Road during January 1942. A number of men of military age had been hiding there, their evasion of duty described as 'monstrous' by the magistrate at Thames police court. Military escorts were waiting to take them in charge after the gaming charges against them had been dealt with.[15]

In March 1942, Bow Street magistrates heard how the police had broken up a West End 'dodgers' hideout'. This was a common gaming-house between the rear of the Palace Theatre and Leicester Square. The club entrance was covered by a steel security gate, a type used to protect safe deposits. Police kept watch through a peephole on the men at the tables as they threw dice. It was alleged that they gambled with the proceeds of stolen goods brought to the club and sold. After watching for some time through their peephole in an oak door, dividing the club from the next premises, the police removed the door and carried out their raid. Of the twenty-nine men at the tables, sixteen were known as having convictions for burglary, house-breaking, receiving, smash and grab, and wounding. They were certainly dodgers but how many of them would be wanted by the Army under any circumstances was questionable. There were also six deserters. One was dealing in petrol coupons and another had a road fund licence stolen in Piccadilly less than two hours before.[16]

Even a petty criminal dodging the call-up would take the trouble to equip himself with a forged or stolen identity card and, if necessary, a ration book. So would deserters. As soon as a man deserted, as over 20,000 servicemen did from the British forces, supplemented by those from the Canadian and United States services, he was without a legal form of identity or a means of buying food. The underworld could provide whatever he needed, so long as he was worth it or could make his own way.

As the authorities were to discover, the forging of their rather crudely designed ration books and identity cards was child's play compared with reproducing banknotes. It was scarcely worth doing in the early days of food rationing, when it was easier to steal food in the first place, but as clothes and petrol were added to the ration, the secret presses became busy. Similarly, to burgle a Food Office or Petroleum Office by night for blank ration cards or books was infinitely easier than tackling a bank or even a post office. Their safes were seldom large enough for the millions of sheets of coupons, which were often left on desks or tables. Moreover, though nightwatchmen were eventually employed, they were no match for organized gangs and were countered by those officials who were not only prepared to assist in the thefts but sometimes perpetrated them on their own account.

*

Many of the 'dodgers', even when their milieu was criminal, were not far removed from those civilian offenders who evaded conscription or combined the traditions of honest trading with a little black market opportunism. At another level, professional criminals who were well established before the war continued to pursue their careers. Among these was the Sabini family, whose history of race-course protection and grievous bodily harm stretched back twenty years. However, the Sabinis found that war added a new hazard to their profession. When Italy became a belligerent in June 1940, the criminal members of the family and many smaller fry, including 'Bert Marsh' of the 1936 Wandsworth Stadium murder, were rounded up and interned under the Defence Regulations.

Darby Sabini had been an old man living quietly in Brighton. His retirement was interrupted when he was sent to prison for handling stolen goods. During this sentence, his son, an RAF pilot, was killed while flying. Darby's brother Harry 'Harryboy' Sabini was also detained in June 1940. Like his relatives, he protested unavailingly that he was not Italian and had never been to Italy. But the Sabinis were subject to a general contempt for Italians, as a nation who had waited until the fallen had irretrievably fallen before stabbing them in the back.

With Italy's declaration of war, police patrolled Soho in pairs to control angry crowds. In vain did Italian-sounding cafés and businesses display notices on their doors, 'We are Swiss' or 'This is a British firm'. In such circumstances, Harry Sabini got short shrift from his judges when he appealed against his internment as an enemy alien. He was described as a 'violent and dangerous criminal of the gangster type'. Mr Justice Humphreys, who sat with the Lord Chief Justice, also denounced him for 'deliberate perjury intended to deceive the court', and sent him to prison for this offence.[17]

Native-born criminals were more fortunate. Many prisoners were given early release, in some cases to make them available for military service, in others to save prison manpower. The early surrender of so much of the Italian army also obliged the government to house some of these captives in civilian prisons.

Billy Hill, then twenty-eight years old, was freed from Chelmsford Gaol in 1939 and celebrated his first evening of freedom with his gangland cronies, Franny the Spaniel, Horrible Harry, Bear's Breath, Soapy Harry, Tony the Wop, Square Georgie and a cast of extras. Though he later protested he had never intended to dodge the war or 'go on the trot' as a deserter, he put himself down for what he thought would be the easier life of the RAF, where one might fly or drive, rather than marching with the 'Kate Carney'.[18]

By the time the Army or the RAF might have wanted him, Hill was no longer available. To provide for the necessities of war by a few big jobs in 1939 and 1940, he first kept watch on two Hatton Garden messengers. By his own account he waited until the third morning to be sure of their routine. Then he and his accomplice coshed them and carried what he claimed to be £5,000 (£200,000) in bullion to a waiting car. In a series of West End smash and grab raids during the first year of the war, Hill was a frequent suspect. He boasted of the raids as a defeat for the police but never confessed to taking part.[19]

Smash and grab, like safe-blowing, was a headline crime of the 1930s. There was no evidence that it had gone out of fashion in 1940. Between December 1939 and June 1940, jewel raids remained the most visible evidence of criminals at work. By day, they staged hit and run attacks on jewellers' windows. At night they worked through the blackout, and later through the blitz, shinning up pipes, crossing roofs, patiently boring through walls from next-door premises to reach a safe in Mayfair or Piccadilly.

In preparation for Christmas 1939, teams of London thieves made some of their greatest hauls. Ernest Lowe, a prestigious Mayfair jeweller in North Audley Street, had his window smashed and emptied by three men with a car on the morning of 4 December. Four days later, another West End jeweller, Longman & Strongitharm, was robbed of its entire stock during a night raid. Four days after that, a gang worked its way by night into a large jeweller's shop in Dover Street. They began by attacking a door at the back of adjoining premises, under cover of the moonless blackout. By drilling through this door, which guarded nothing of particular value and was therefore not reinforced, they were able to remove the interior bolts and enter the building. They dug their way through an internal wall to the jeweller's and emptied the safe of its gold, silver and watches. Eight days later, another gang carried out five Mayfair jewel robberies in a single night, four of them by the use of patiently crafted master keys. The fifth was a theft of jewels valued at £600 (£24,000) from Lady Queensberry's house in Charles Street, where there was no sign of how the thieves had entered. Then it was time for Christmas.

As 1939 ended, the Western Front remained inactive. In November, Queen Wilhelmina of Holland and King Leopold of the Belgians, as neutrals, had tried unsuccessfully to start peace talks between Germany and Britain. On land, the most dramatic news came from a quite separate conflict, in which the Soviet Union had invaded Finland over territorial disputes, only to be driven back. At sea, the battleship *Royal Oak* had been torpedo'd in Scapa Flow. The aircraft carrier HMS *Courageous* and an auxiliary carrier had also been sunk. The Germans had lost their battleship *Graf Spee* in the Battle of the River Plate, and ten U-boats in other operations. Of the all-important air war, there was little sign. In this season of relative peace, the government relaxed lighting restrictions sufficiently for passengers to read on buses.

The blackout was 'a present from Hitler' to gangs who could travel to and from their work with little risk of recognition. They attacked unoccupied premises, whose owners were forbidden to let any light from the building be seen outside. In such circumstances, almost the entire Bond Street stock of Ciro's Pearls Ltd was removed on the night of 1 February 1940. Waiting until the coast seemed clear in the blacked-out street, the intruders forced the lock of a metal grille protecting the shopfront, then burst open the door. Protected from view by blackout screens over every window or glass door, they were able to empty the display windows which in peacetime would have been lit and on view, as well as ransacking the showcases, the drawers and the cash box. They were in the shop for some hours, sorting the booty and discarding items of lesser value, which were not worth the risk of fencing. They were, said the manager ruefully the next day, 'experts'.

They were not the only ones. On the following day, Mrs Erskine Gwynne, whose home was in Paris and who was a close friend of the Duchess of Windsor and a relative of the Vanderbilts, returned to her London flat in Arlington House, Piccadilly. Carefully selected jewels worth £6,000 (£240,000) had been taken. They were not insured.

Thieves of this calibre worked with care, entering unguarded premises at night and seldom leaving clues. Yet the biggest and quickest money was still in smash and grab. So were the biggest risks. However, smash and grab raiders benefited from petrol rationing, which reduced the traffic in city streets, leaving escape routes open. The robbers were not inconvenienced by rationing because, as a precaution against identification, the cars used in such raids were stolen anyway.

The Goldsmiths' and Silversmiths' Association in Piccadilly, a target that a jewel robber might dream of, had learnt the lesson of the night raid on Ciro's Pearls. It offered fewer items but each of considerable value. At night the diamond rings, bracelets and brooches were removed from the windows and locked in a safe which was a burglar's despair. When the shop opened on the morning of 24 February 1940, the staff unlocked the safe as usual, brought out the stock, and laid the items in the window. A few minutes later, a car drew up with four men in it. Two of them left the car, ran across the pavement, and one of the pair smashed the window with what looked like a heavy stick.

The manager and his assistant ran from the shop, by which time the most valuable items in the window had been grabbed and the men were running back to the car. The manager tried to trip the first man, who was carrying most of the jewellery. His assistant tried to hold the thief who had broken the window and who now hit out at him with the stout stick. Both robbers broke free and ran a good deal faster than the shopmen. The pavements were almost empty early in the day, when the rush hour was over and few shoppers had arrived. It was a favourite time for smash and grab.

Piccadilly was clear of traffic at such an hour. There was little the witnesses could do as the car accelerated, though a man threw his umbrella at the windscreen and several ill-advised pedestrians ran into the road to stop the robbers. To intercept a moving car required more than good intentions. The getaway was easy. In a matter of seconds the robbers had made a clean sweep of the window, taking jewellery worth between £15,000 (£600,000) and £20,000 (£800,000). Two bracelets alone were worth £1,000 (£40,000) each.

When Scotland Yard decided to concentrate its resources on the West End, robbers turned their attention to jewellers' shops in the suburbs. On 6 April, a gang attacked Sanders & Co. in Balham High

Street in a scene 'like a gangster film', as one witness described it. Shopping crowds watched motionless, like a cinema audience, while two men from a car smashed the glass with an iron weight and emptied the window. A motorist tried to swing across the path of the getaway car but the robbers' driver swerved round him and escaped. Three weeks later, a masked gang attacked F. Hinds in Denmark Hill, even while another raid was taking place on J. H. Shakespeare in the High Road, Leytonstone.

Because raids were so fast, they were seldom violent. The most aggressive took place on James Walker's premises in Streatham High Road on 29 May. It was carried out by four masked men, wearing scarves or handkerchiefs over the lower part of their faces. Although the street was busy, two of them held back a crowd of shoppers by brandishing iron bars, while a third man with a bar stood over the counter staff, threatening to cosh anyone who touched the telephone. As the robbers drove off, their car smashed into a tramcar and almost overturned. A traffic policeman chased them, but before he could catch up they reversed and vanished down a narrow road towards Norbury, the wing of the car smashed in.

As the 'phoney war' became the 'Battle of France', Billy Hill continued his own attacks on West End jewellers. In one blackout robbery, he and four accomplices had just wrenched the padlocks from a steel window-grille on a shop in Belgravia when two policemen on the beat approached and took up duty on the opposite pavement. Hill and the others had withdrawn at the sight of them. Though the thieves waited, the policemen remained in view.

Hill went to the nearest phone box and called the fire brigade, assuring them that a huge blaze had broken out near by. A few minutes later the fire engines converged on an area just out of sight and the policemen ran towards it. The din was such that the robbers were able to work unheard until, in a moment of silence, one of them shattered a large glass shelf. Even so, they reached their car, drove up the one-way street against the traffic to frustrate any pursuit, crossed a roundabout, and reached safety with £800 (£32,000) in gold.

Hill was arrested soon afterwards for a robbery at Carrington's in Regent Street. At 10 a.m. on 20 March 1940, a small maroon car was driven over the pavement and into the doorway of the shop, blocking the entrance so completely that no one could get in or out of the premises. With the jeweller's staff trapped in the building, a black saloon car drew up. A man got out, carrying a car-jack, with which he smashed both the display window and the inner showcase. In a matter of seconds he had taken gold rings worth £6,000 (£240,000) and driven off. Hill was a prime suspect and was put on an identity parade at Vine Street police station. He was not picked out.

Identification was seldom easy and could be made more difficult. A suspect whose solicitor or friend provided a copy of the evening paper to read might carry it in his pocket. A witness walking down the line would see the paper and think that this could not be the man. He was obviously a volunteer for the parade who had been out on the streets a few minutes earlier, as the paper showed, and not in a police interview room or cell.

Superintendent Beveridge, Inspector Greeno and the Flying Squad had little doubt that Hill was behind the smash and grab raids carried out in the spring of 1940, probably as one of the team but at least as the 'putter-up'. He was paraded again on 21 May, when raiders drove their car on to the pavement in Wardour Street, scattering pedestrians who assumed the vehicle had gone out of control. The car moved on slowly but without stopping, while the man in the passenger seat stood up and leant through the sunshine roof, robbing the broken display window as he passed. With its new wartime spirit, the public was too prone to take action against robbers. This method of using the open car roof had been devised by Hill. Standing on the passenger seat, he could smash the glass and scoop up jewellery out of reach of a policeman or vigilante.

The same method was used soon afterwards to rob Phillips's in New Bond Street of tiaras worth £11,000 (£440,000), the car sweeping along the pavement as far as Grosvenor Street and round the corner, before a second stolen car drew up behind it, aslant the street, and blocked any pursuit. The second car blocking the way bore the false number plate MUG 999. Once again, Hill was not picked out from the suspects on parade nor for a raid on a Cornhill jewellers in the City of London.

His last smash and grab raid was on 26 June 1940, the day after an armistice granted by Germany recognized the collapse of France.

With Harry Bryan, an Islington bookmaker who had featured in the Clerkenwell bullion robbery of 1936, and 'Square Georgie' Ball, a Euston coal-porter, Hill reconnoitred Hemmings & Co. in Conduit Street, running between Regent Street and Bond Street. The others stole a pair of cars, while Hill provided the plan. Bryan at the wheel would take the corner from Bond Street into Conduit Street, driving on the pavement, level with the jewellers' window. Hill would stand up, shoulders above the open sunshine roof. With room to use a sledgehammer on the shop window, he would grab whatever jewellery he could reach. Bryan and he would drive off, leaving Ball with the second car to block any pursuit. If anything went wrong with the first car, Hill and Bryan would use the second as their getaway.

The raid started unpromisingly when Bryan drove his car erratically round the corner from Bond Street and almost knocked down a policeman. Following orders, he swerved on to the pavement, which was crowded in the summer morning. Hill leaned from the open roof and raised the sledgehammer. At that moment, Bryan at the wheel of the car shouted, 'Bill! I've caught the front bumper or something. I can't move her.' By now a police whistle had blown and passers-by were running towards them. Hill slid down the roof of the car to the ground. With no chance to snatch any jewellery, he shouted, 'Get over to Georgie's drag, fast.'

Hill and Bryan ran for the second car, clambering in as the pursuit closed on them. Ball let in the clutch and headed straight for a crowd of people on the corner of Bond Street. PC Higgs, running past the jewellers, saw the second car moving towards Bond Street and threw his truncheon at the windscreen. 'This seemed to scare them,' he told the court. The windscreen had shattered and, as Hill tried to clear the glass, 'Square Georgie' stalled the car. Hill shouted, 'Make your own ways, boys,' and jumped out. PC Higgs seized one man left behind and the crowd held the other.

Hill sprinted across Bond Street and down Bruton Street with most of the crowd and two policemen in pursuit. He turned into the first doorway and ran up the stairs, past the offices, coming out on the roof. When he looked down into the street, several hundred faces seemed to be looking back at him. From one roof, he got to the next, and went down the stairs of a neighbouring building. As he opened the door, a policeman was standing outside. 'Quick, he's in here,' Hill said hopefully. By that time, however, the crowd was pointing and shouting, 'That's him!'

Bryan and Ball pleaded guilty to stealing and receiving the two cars. Each was gaoled for three years. Hill pleaded guilty to conspiracy. He went down for two years. The question of which armed service to join was, temporarily at least, irrelevant.[20]

The risks of smash and grab remained high, yet it had been a successful form of crime in the new 'motor age' of the 1930s. It continued to be so during the first months of the war, which still appeared more like peacetime than war as the country would soon know it. Then, in a few weeks of April and May 1940, Germany conquered Denmark, Norway, Holland, Belgium and France. The British Army escaped from Dunkirk with the loss of all its equipment. On 7 May, as Norway fell, Neville Chamberlain and his government resigned, to be replaced by Winston Churchill. This crisis in the nation's affairs had a direct effect upon the criminal underworld. In the total war that was to come, there were safer ways than smash and grab for the professional crook to prosper.

Small-scale organizations exploiting shortages or the rationing system had begun to appear soon after the outbreak of war. In November 1939, there were warnings of forged petrol coupons. These were 'clever copies' being circulated in Hampshire, though apparently by people who did not live there. Presses to produce counterfeit petrol coupons were also set up in the Irish Republic. One method of smuggling the counterfeits into Britain was by concealing them in food parcels. Two men were sent to prison at Bow Street in July 1940 for hiding them in consignments of sugar from Eire. Their coupons had been discovered during a random check by the postal censorship.[21]

In November 1939, the first thefts of coupons from a government department were brought to trial. Stanley Swann, a thief who marketed stolen coupons by posing as the Secretary of the Regional Petroleum Board, went to prison. He had sold some of them to the licensee of Pond House, Reading, who first agreed to the deal, then thought better of it and reported the matter.[22]

Stanley Swann was not a peacetime criminal, rather an illustration of the way in which war had altered the frontiers of the underworld. He was somewhere between the smash and grab raiders and the amateur petrol racketeers reported in January 1940, who would pay for petrol and race off without handing over coupons, or would drop the coupons as if by accident, and drive off while the pump attendant was picking them up and before he could find out that there were too few.

An alternative source of petrol was by stealing it from the armed services who were naturally well supplied. To counter this, it was announced in May 1940 that such petrol was to be dyed and that random checks would easily show its use by any unauthorized person. The dye would not harm any engine that used it.

Counterfeiting petrol coupons was not difficult but obviously remunerative. Food coupons were scarcely worth the bother. Replacement ration books were readily issued after hundreds of the first batch were 'lost in the post'. There were also home visits by officials of the 'Food Control Office'. An error had occurred in certain books, now being collected for return to the food office. Replacements were on their way. The bogus callers then disappeared with the ration books. In the blitz of September 1940, applications for the replacement of missing ration books multiplied. In Battersea alone, they totalled over 2,000. 'Enemy action' was the cause of loss: in most cases true, in some not.

The underworld adapted readily. In the small hours of 8 December 1939, there occurred what the press called the first 'anti-ration' robbery, though food rationing of any kind was not imposed for a further month. The break-in was at a chain store in Old Oak Common Lane, East Acton. The haul included eight sides of bacon and a hundred pounds of butter, commodities already announced as 'to be rationed', as well as seventy-five pounds of tea and a quantity of cooking fat. Pre-war security had not been increased and the lorry, heard driving away from the rear of the building at 5 a.m., had been loaded without attracting attention. In another raid at Acton, involving thefts of bacon from a warehouse, two men were charged. The bacon had been found in the garage of Antonio Esposito, who had a ready, if too familiar, defence. 'I only took over the garage on Monday and I can't help it if someone else put the stuff in it.'[23]

Sugar was thought to be the scarcest commodity. The first major case of theft was heard on 18 March 1940. A master baker of High Street, Poplar, was convicted of receiving three lorryloads of sugar delivered to his shop after dark, knowing it to be stolen. He had already begun supplying the neighbourhood when he was caught. Detective Sergeant John Gosling of Scotland Yard assured the court that the Commissioner of Police took 'a very serious view of larcenies of rationed commodities'.[24]

Scotland Yard was certainly prepared to use undercover officers in trapping wartime criminals. Of six men involved in robbing Bontex Ltd, Wembley, of thirty-seven rolls of artificial silk in March 1940, the 'receiver' was Detective Sergeant Jordan. He went on the raid with five Harlesden men, helping them to load the silk outside the premises they had robbed. Then he asked them to come to the top of the road, out of earshot of the getaway driver, so that he could pay them. As they followed him in the dark, they were set upon by waiting plain-clothes officers and, after a scuffle and a chase, were arrested.[25]

In the early weeks of 1940, as rationing of butter, bacon and sugar was implemented, criminal gangs began to target food lorries leaving London in the blackout. The lorries were trailed by car until they were left briefly unattended while the driver took a rest. If the lorry was in working order, which was almost always the case, it was easy for a carload of criminals to carry out a 'jump-up' theft, driving away the vehicle with its contents. So began a form of crime that would have seemed scarcely worthwhile to major criminals a year before.

An even more promising wartime enterprise was cigarette robbery. Cigarettes had not yet assumed the importance that they would do in 1944, as the unofficial currency of liberated Europe, but they were one of the most portable and valuable of restricted commodities. The government declined to ration cigarettes but at times of particular shortage, from 1940 onwards, some control was improvised at the counter by allowing customers to buy only a limited number on any one occasion, sometimes as few as five. Even before the fall of France, cigarette supplies to the Army were a natural target for thieves. One of the first such thefts, in the small hours of 11 April 1940, was of two lorryloads of cigarettes from a Maidstone warehouse. The darkness which should have concealed the robbers from the police, in this case concealed from the robbers the fire brigade that was watching them.

The firemen phoned the police, who arrived just as the two lorries were driving off. One of the lorries escaped. The policemen threw their truncheons to shatter the windscreen of the second, while a fireman jumped on to the running board to overpower the driver. Two men, from Silvertown and Canning Town, were arrested.

When a consignment of cigarettes was stolen by night from a Brentford warehouse in July 1940, it was thought to be the work of a gang carrying out a series of daylight robberies. The thieves would follow a tobacco lorry as it made deliveries. When the lorry driver stopped, took a carton from the lorry and carried it into the recipient's premises, the car would reverse up to the tailboard, the thieves taking as much as possible as quickly as possible, making off before the driver's return. Substantial robberies of this kind had occurred at both Purley and West Wickham High Road in the week before the Brentford warehouse theft.

By the time Billy Hill came out of prison, the casual dealing of early 1940 had become full-fledged racketeering. Hill had been dismissive of the black market, rather as major criminals were of pimping; it provided no more than what he called 'pocket money', when compared with the proceeds of fur robberies or jewel raids. By the end of 1941, however, it was the single great opportunity brought him by the war. 'I did not merely make use of the black market, I fed it,' he said later. With his growing influence in the underworld he was well placed to be one of the big dealers. 'So that big, wide, handsome, and oh, so highly profitable black market walked into our ever open arms.'[26]

Such trading was a natural extension of robbery, though without the glamour of Mayfair jewellery. Hill found an army bedding store that could be robbed with no more effort than driving a lorry down to the West Country and loading it. The quality was excellent, sheets that he claimed would sell on the black market at £5 (£200) a pair. There were thousands, and storing them was such a headache that he was glad to get rid of them for £1 (£40) a pair. Fur coats were a problem, when he emptied an entire warehouse. To avoid storing the evidence on his premises, he sold them for £6 (£240) each, unaware that the continuing war would make them unobtainable luxuries.

Most of those whom he called trivial villains cashed in on such enterprises as the drink trade. They manufactured their own spirits, likely to cause brain damage or blindness, and put proprietary brand labels on them. Hill was prepared to sell black market whisky to the trade by the barrel. Under his own peculiar law of economics, he also sold sausage skins to butchers at the same rate as whisky, that being the price the shortage dictated.

If war was a leveller of social classes, the black market levelled criminality. At its extremes it made common cause between the regular customer, who got a little extra on the ration, and a scar-faced jewel robber who provided sheets or a fur coat at knock-down prices.

4

The Bomb Lark

In May 1941, the Australian statesman, Robert Menzies, returned home from London. Exiles had once tried to be worthy of an English ancestral home. Now he cited the nobler example of 'Bermondsey, Shoreditch and the London Docks, the people of Britain under deliberate and indiscriminate bombing'. Those dismayed by German victories should remember their example. 'They are the world's princes.' Not least, the blitz had proved that the women of Britain were 'among the great soldiers of the war'.[1]

For an increasing number of Britons, 'war' meant the blitz, as the indiscriminate bombing of London was followed in 1941 by targeting of such industrial and commercial cities as Bristol and Coventry, Liverpool and Glasgow, Manchester and Birmingham. Yet defeat seemed more likely to result from a German U-boat victory in the Atlantic and the end of American supplies. On land, the Italian army was routed in its African colonies and rescued by Rommel's Afrika Korps. British troops in Crete and mainland Greece supported that nation's small but valiant army. Greece fell but its humiliation of Mussolini's invasion, and a fighting retreat in the face of the Wehrmacht, impeded Hitler's attack on the Soviet Union for two months, turning his summer campaign into a winter war.

During the blitz of 1940–41, it was calculated that 190,000 bombs were dropped, 43,677 civilians killed and 50,387 wounded. The intensity of the fires round London docks set light to the roadways themselves. Pepper from bombed warehouses filled the air with burning particles so that firemen and rescue workers in the streets felt they were breathing flame. Plagues of black flies and rats swarmed from the blazing grain warehouses. Barrels of rum burst into chains of fire like further sticks of bombs.

Heroes were everywhere – the man sixty feet up on a gasometer, calmly repairing a flaming splinter-hole in the roof, with millions of cubic feet of explosive vapour under him; the shelter marshals in Newcastle who held a collapsing concrete street-shelter roof on their arched backs until the people trapped inside had got out and the structure gave way. After the heaviest night raid on London docks not a job was unmanned next morning. Foremost among these heroes were men and women of the National Fire Service and men of the heavy rescue squads who crawled through the falling wreckage of shattered buildings, among the dead, the dismembered and the dying, carrying morphia and medical supplies. As in bomb disposal squads, these firemen and rescuers included many conscientious objectors to military service.

War, in the familiar cliché, mingled horror and farce in generous proportions. One rescue squad clambered through a wrecked house in St James's Place, in search of survivors, and found three naked women in the back room. The wrecked premises were a brothel run by a notorious pimp, Gino Messina, where Marthe Watts and two companions had escaped death by having gone through to the back room just before the bomb destroyed the front of the building.[2]

Despite the presence of medical auxiliaries and even doctors in the medical posts of larger shelters, medical aid was still a matter of improvisation. In September 1940, when a 'torpedo' bomb destroyed houses in South-West London, a doctor crawled into the wreckage to give morphia to an injured man and woman in a subterranean flooded crater, while a Flying Squad officer at the scene swam across the crater, using his own body to shield the doctor and the couple from falling debris and the danger of the wall's collapse.[3]

At the worst, a neighbourhood might be bombed when all the rescue squads were fully committed. When this happened in one East End street, the survivors told the firemen stoically, 'That's all right. We can look after our own.' They turned to dismantle the debris of houses with their hands. They were still searching when the night ended and the rescue squads arrived.[4]

Through the nightly blitz, the life of the capital continued in large public shelters or leaky 'Andersons' dug into back gardens. Street shelters, brick oblongs with concrete roofs, had been hastily erected as war approached. Underground tube stations became improvised communal refuges, the pre-war government having decided that purpose-built 'deep' shelters could not be provided. On 21 October 1940, the Home Secretary, Herbert Morrison, announced that tickets would be issued for public shelters, though not for tube shelters, so that there would be no queues in the street during an air raid. Bunks would be provided for ticket-holders. Shelters in one form or another could hold about half the population of London. All the same, a Stepney shelter for 2,500 people was said usually to hold 10,000. The so-called Tilbury shelter, improvised under the Tilbury railway arches in Stepney, was intended to hold 3,000 people, and despite poor ventilation and sanitation frequently accommodated an overflow of several times that number. Fights and rowdyism among its multicultural population were common. In 1940, when the journalist and broadcaster J. L. Hodson visited a shelter allocated to 7,000 but which held 12,000, the conditions were appalling, the sanitation minimal, so that some shelterers and their bedding were lying in urine. 'One thing about the blitz,' said an elderly Glaswegian, 'it certainly takes your mind off the war.'

Eight deep shelters were later to be built in central London, far below ground and with adequate facilities for 8,000 people in each, but this was after the main blitz was over. Elsewhere in London there were 'shelter disasters' which had nothing to do with enemy action. In 1943, at Bethnal Green tube station, 178 people were suffocated in what was variously described as an accident or a stampede. As they were streaming past the booking hall after the air raid siren had sounded, some at the top of the stone stairs appeared to lose their balance. A woman and child fell, a bald-headed man fell on top of them. 'It was so quick,' said an eyewitness, 'and in a moment or two there were dozens of people falling.' Those on the platform below heard shouting and screaming from the staircase. 'We tried to pull some out – it could not be done. We could not move them, they were so inextricably mixed up.' Crammed in the underground stairway with scores of others falling on them, the victims, according to the pathologist's evidence, suffocated within a minute or two. In 1944, the occupants of a purpose-built shelter in London were drowned when it was 'filled to the brim' by a burst water main.[5]

Some men and women were doing well out of the 'shelter business'.

Shelterers and bedding were to be off the premises by 8 a.m. Those going to work had nowhere to keep their bundles. Other were obliged to carry them home and back next night. Entrepreneurs living near the shelters set up a daytime 'minding' service for bundles at 7s. 6d. (£15) a week. The health hazards of soiled bedding stored indiscriminately were reported to Stepney Council as being likely to lead to 'a very serious epidemic'. It was one of many risks to health from shelter living.[6]

The government had set up a Shelter Hygiene Committee under the chairmanship of Lord Horder. Horder had been Extra Physician to both George V and George VI and was regarded as the leading clinician of his day. He was also Medical Adviser to London Transport and had been directly involved in the creation of tube shelters. On 19 November 1940, his committee urged that shelterers should be issued with health masks. Two days later they were 'strongly urged' to wear them, and were promised that two designs were being tested. What was called a 'new-type' mosquito with a 'dangerous bite' had been identified in tube shelters. That same month, surface shelters in Hammersmith acquired the ominous nickname of 'brick coffins' because of poor construction and inability to withstand bomb blasts. By Christmas, the Enfield Medical Officer of Health was warning his audience that shelters were a major cause of diphtheria. In December 1942, the Wimbledon magistrates were informed that their £30,000 (£1,200,000) underground shelters were 'damp, foul, evil-smelling, and unhealthy'.[7]

Not surprisingly, many people preferred to take the chance of being killed in their own beds. By the end of 1940, there were rumours of shoddy building and racketeering by contractors. Hammersmith had experienced the reality of 'brick coffins'. In the autumn of 1940, a 500lb bomb had dropped in the area, not with maximum effect. A tractor parked next to it was scarcely damaged. Thirty yards away, the Macfarlane Road communal shelter collapsed on its occupants with fatal results.

The ruined shelter was built of sub-standard material. Payments had been made to the contractors because the clerk of works at Hammersmith Town Hall certified the building as satisfactory. He was one of those now arrested and charged. Far worse, 120 shelters had been built in this manner and might disintegrate if a bomb dropped anywhere near. The clerk of works and the builder were indicted on a specimen charge of 'conspiring with other persons unknown to defraud the Hammersmith Borough Council of £25,119 [£1,004,760] by divers false pretences and fraudulent contrivances'. Later there were charges of manslaughter against the clerk of works and the contractor.[8]

On 23 April 1941 the government was taken to task over such cases in the House of Commons. Ellen Wilkinson, for the Home Office, explained that it had been necessary to relax certain building conditions but that the contractors had relaxed them still further. Instructions were now given for the shelters to be closed while the Home Office considered what to do with the builders. Examination of surviving shelters revealed steel reinforcement made of light metal lathing suitable only for ordinary ceilings. There were spaces with no reinforcement, which could not have 'withstood the shock of falling debris'. An extra row of bricks had been added to the tops of the walls, almost halving the thickness of the concrete roofs. In another case, the space at the tops of the walls was filled in with old cement bags. Though the defendants had been charged with the manslaughter of those killed in the Macfarlane Road shelter, their convictions and prison sentences were for the lesser offence of conspiring to effect a public mischief. Following the Hammersmith incident, 120 shelters were rebuilt at a cost of £17,674 (£710,560).[9]

Members of the public had done their bit to make shelters ineffective. In June 1940, the Borough of Lewisham appealed against 'thefts from air raid shelters', pilfering of metal and bricks, wanton damage to the structures. Escape ladders and metal covers for escape and ventilation holes had also been stolen.

Shelter life in the autumn and winter of 1940–41 stimulated defiance of the Germans. It also stimulated defiance of law and order, even as bombs exploded above. Those without tickets who were turned away were known to fight shelter marshals and the police. A Saturday-night brawl broke out in Tilbury shelter on 10 October 1940, when a drunken Dunkirk veteran knifed a market porter in an argument over stolen bedding. On 4 January 1941, there was a Saturday-night fight at Tilbury as a group of 'foreigners' chanted, 'England is no good', and Stepney replied with 'We want bloody Hitler here to deal with you bastards!' The fight, which had begun in blacked-out Commercial Road, was broken up by the police, but continued in the shelter. When the police arrested the Stepney leader, two women urged the crowd to rescue him. 'Let's get them bastards,' shouted Mrs Agnes Squibbs, referring of course to the police, not to the Germans.[10]

Even as this drama ended in Leman Street police station, two plain-clothes officers trailed a wanted man into Tilbury shelter at 11.15 p.m., as he made for the bunks. Unfortunately the two policemen were recognized by a group of youths, beaten up and clubbed with a bottle, while the wanted man escaped. The two officers got clear, the less injured leading his colleague to the first aid post. Even in the blitz, it seemed, the principal risks to life and limb in Tilbury shelter were not presented by the Luftwaffe. Before the month was over, the shelter marshal had been beaten up on 28 January by a woman who arrived with no ticket. Shelterers fought marshals for many reasons but Eleonora Hardingham appears unique in having done so, in December 1940, because she was not allowed to take her monkey into the shelter with her.[11]

Those with a grievance against the way the shelters were run made their feelings plain. On the afternoon of 20 October 1940, 200 protesters, led by a woman of twenty-one, marched on Stepney ARP Control Centre, demanding to see the officer in charge. When a War Reserve policeman saw the size of the crowd and its mood, he slammed the gates. Their leader still demanded to see the controller. The policeman outside asked her to wait, at which point he was punched in the face and his helmet knocked off, as she shouted to her followers to rush the gates. The gates were forced and, when ARP workers inside confronted the crowd, fights broke out among shouts of 'Come on! Let's get at the yellow bastards!' At this moment the air raid siren sounded and the Luftwaffe's arrival restored civil order.[12]

Sexual promiscuity among the young in public shelters became an issue in December 1940, though the authorities felt this was a subject to be avoided. Watkin Boyce, probation officer for Southwark Juvenile Court, bluntly denounced the shelters of South-East London. 'There are few boys and girls of 17 and 18 living huddled together in public shelters for whose chastity I would care to vouch.

I have seen youngsters in their teens, of mixed sexes, making up their beds together on the floors of public shelters, even under their parents' eyes.' Nor was this confined to quietly illicit conduct. A prosecution in Hammersmith involved youths fighting over girls in the shelters, among small children trying to sleep.[13]

The ARP denied suggestions of anything going on under the blankets. There were cases of 'bad behaviour' in the early days of the raids, but these had been 'speedily dealt with'. London Transport assured the public of constant supervision in the tubes by 'shelter marshals, police, and our own officials'. The truth was known only under the blankets. However, Herbert Morrison issued a 'code' to clean up shelters in December 1940, including plans for women police, in response to Public Morality Council concerns over health and decency. What was called 'The Girl Protection Patrol' would consist of an inspector, eight sergeants and thirty-one constables.

A squad of plain-clothes police was already on duty to deal with shelter crime. One problem was the use of empty shelters by criminals during daylight, either as a rendezvous or to hide stolen goods. Gambling and card sharps were a further threat. When the marshal at the Hermitage shelter, Wapping, tried to interrupt an all-night card school on 9 November 1940, he was knocked unconscious with such force that he did not come round until attended by hospital medical students.

The scourge of gambling and the violence against those who tried to prevent it was a frequent complaint. Gambling was an offence in itself. Two youths who organized pontoon in a Bromley shelter on an improvised table were prosecuted and convicted in November 1940. Gangs of card sharps were reported travelling from shelter to shelter, spending two nights in each. A dupe was allowed to win a little on the first night and was then cheated of every penny on the second.[14]

A different threat to authority in East End shelters was presented by Communist 'agitators'. Since Hitler and Stalin were still allies, the duty of a party member was to persuade the public that the war was an imperialist venture not worth fighting. By December 1940, some Communists had managed to become shelter marshals and to control the distribution of defeatist propaganda. On 1 February 1941, London Transport responded by prohibiting the distribution of all leaflets in the shelters 'for fear of passing on subversive propaganda'. When there was a disturbance in the Tilbury shelter in March 1941, it was caused by a group led by Israel Panner of Commercial Road, 'who had been attending shelters and making a nuisance of himself on numerous occasions. He had a quantity of Communist literature upon him.'[15]

Communists or criminals had a captive audience but in June 1941, as Hitler struck at the Soviet Union, the faithful prepared to change sides. In England, the Clothes Rationing Order, signed on 29 May, came into force. Communist agitators were replaced in the shelters by touts who went round inviting the poor to sell their newly-issued clothing coupons.

As early as October 1940, the first stories of 'gang rule' in shelters were gaining ground. M. K. Leigh had a large private shelter for 300 workers in his office block. At night he made it available for those who lived in what was described as a very crowded area of the city. Mattresses and tea were provided. At first all went well. 'Then a mob of what can only be described as "gangsters" came along. Everybody who uses the shelter is terrified of them – so frightened that they will not even tell me the names of these men.' The volunteers who ran the shelter were attacked. Mr Leigh appealed to the police and was told they could not intervene on private premises. Herbert Morrison asked for 'particulars of the difficulties'. By December, shelter marshals had also asked for legal powers to evict 'unruly shelterers'.[16]

Early in 1941, 'shelter gangs' went to work, robbing those who had sought refuge for the night. In 1940, there had already been individual cases of thieves stealing handbags or suitcases, a crime that had more significance as shelterers began to take their valuables with them. 'A disgustingly mean theft,' as the Thames magistrate said, sending a workman to hard labour for six months. In another case, the victim was said to have been robbed by the defendant of 'every penny' in a Liverpool Street shelter, her entire wealth being in the stolen handbag. A woman in Tottenham who took her £3,000 (£120,000) life savings to the shelter every night in an attaché case was robbed by a man whom she knew as a friend of her sons. Few victims had the good fortune of Gerrit Bentvelsen, whose clothes were stolen one night in Tilbury shelter and who met a man wearing them three days later.[17]

By January 1941, however, organized gangs infested the crowded tube shelters. Their method was to target bags in which shelterers carried their valuables. When the chosen victims settled down to sleep, the thieves found a space near by. They would edge the bags further away, little by little, while the owners and others around them slept, and then carry them off as if they were their own. Pickpockets were also at work as sirens sounded, jostling those who crowded down into the tube.

Though the police increased patrols in the shelters, there was not the manpower to make the operation effective. Yet some shelter gangs were caught. These were not full-time criminals as a rule but people who had jobs during the day and were not averse to pilfering at night. One gang of two men and two women consisted of a soldier, an office boy and two female chromium-platers. Feeling against them was savage. 'People take their belongings to public shelters to get sleep and then you are cad enough to steal from them,' Colonel Henriques told a Borstal fugitive whom he sentenced. 'I wish we had the power to order you to be thrashed. When you can be as cruel as this to innocent people, then it is up to us to be cruel to you.'[18]

There were cases of stealing by finding. A woman accidentally put her shopping bag with her life savings in it on a pram belonging to a nearby couple. The couple wheeled it off. Another woman went to a Fulham shelter with her 'family jewels' in an attaché case, which she forgot after the air raid. Two brothers, trying their luck, made off with the contents. By day shelters became a natural refuge not only for criminals but for army deserters who were sometimes harboured there. The first court case occurred in December 1940, when the shelter marshal himself was convicted of harbouring Canadian deserters on his premises.[19]

An alternative to shelter theft was burgling the houses of those who had gone to the shelters. When a fifteen-year-old was convicted of rifling the gas meter of an unoccupied house, Colonel Henriques told him, 'A crime almost as serious, if not as serious, as looting is going round to houses of evacuated people or people who are taking shelter and stealing. It is becoming more and more common. It is just playing dirty in wartime.'[20]

On the night of 22 May 1941, after eight months of the blitz, all

Britain was briefly raid-free. Shelter life was over, for the present. Even as the refugees emerged, the first ARP warden to be shot had been unfortunate enough to interrupt a smash and grab raid on a Wealdstone tobacconist. While shelterers had snatched at sleep or sung through the night, crime had been going on above them, as if war had never been declared. They went home, knowing they might find their houses or businesses damaged or destroyed by the bombs. They might also find that they had been looted.

Some criminals of military age were in hiding from conscription and some had been caught by it. Soho boasted 'The Dead End Kids', a gang created by a generation too young to be called up. It named itself after the 1937 Humphrey Bogart film *Dead End*, which made famous a New York gang of the same name. For gangs of all ages, there was satisfaction on 21 September 1940, when West End Central police station was partially destroyed by a parachute bomb which fell in the street outside it.

At the conclusion of Leeds Assizes, on 5 March 1941, Mr Justice Charles took the unusual measure of issuing a public statement.

> More than two whole days have been occupied in dealing with cases of looting which have occurred in one city [Sheffield] . . . When a great city is attacked by bombs on a heavy scale, numbers of houses and their contents are left exposed and deprived of their natural defences. Necessarily these are the homes of comparatively poor people, since they are by far the most numerous.
>
> In many cases these looters have operated on a wholesale scale. There were actually two men who had abandoned well-paid positions, one of them earning £7 [£280] to £9 [£360] a week, and work of public importance, and who abandoned it to take up the obviously more remunerative occupation of looting. The task of guarding shattered houses from prowling thieves, especially during the blackout, is obviously beyond the capacity of any police force. In view of the fact and having regard to the cowardly, abominable nature of the crime the perpetrators of which are preying upon the property of poor folk rendered homeless and often killed, the Legislature has provided that those found guilty of looting from premises damaged or vacated by reason of attacks by the

enemy are on conviction liable to suffer death or penal servitude for life. Thus the law puts looters into the category of murderers, and the day may well be approaching when they will be treated as such.

There were few more emotive subjects in the course of the war than looting. It seemed the most evil and mean-minded preying upon the poor and the unfortunate. Sometimes it showed the tragedy of a life ruined by a moment of greed, in which the greater victim might be the perpetrator. At its worst, it was well organized by pre-war pickpockets, members of race gangs, and minor West End criminals. By 18 October 1940, apart from numerous cases at magistrates courts, there had been ten cases serious enough to be tried at the Old Bailey. In the last of these, the ARP defendants were sent to prison for a year for stealing £12 (£480).

In all, 390 cases of looting were reported in the first eight weeks of the London blitz, to the end of November 1940, though others would come to light in due course. At the Mansion House, the Lord Mayor suggested that notices should be posted throughout the city, reminding the population that looting was punishable by hanging or shooting. Sentences increased sharply and one Auxiliary Fireman received five years' penal servitude for carrying two buckets of food from a bombed grocer's shop, though this was quashed on appeal in February. On 9 November, of fifty cases to be heard at the Old Bailey, twenty involved looting. Ten concerned members of the Auxiliary Fire Service.

As the CID gave increasing time to the offence with 300 of its officers now forming an anti-looting squad, professional looters formed 'out of town' gangs to operate in other blitzed areas. There was priority evacuation, for example, from bomb-damaged Dover, which was within range of German artillery bombardment and ten minutes' flying-time from enemy airfields. Many inhabitants did not return until 1942, when Anglo-American air power held control of the straits. In some cases, returning evacuees opened their front doors to find nothing left in the houses except blackout curtains at the windows. A statement issued by Chief Inspector Percy Datlen of the Dover CID on 17 April 1942 revealed that, in some streets, whole rows of houses had been stripped.

In cases where there are several houses bombed out in one street, the looters have systematically gone through the lot. Carpets have been stripped from the floors, stair carpets have been removed: they have even taken away heavy mangles, bedsteads and complete suites of furniture . . . We believe it is the greatest organized looting that has yet taken place and many front line citizens who have returned to their homes to carry on their essential jobs there are facing severe financial difficulties as a result of the work of the gang.

There was little doubt that this was the work of a London gang, large enough to dispose of such quantities at a time when the underground market in second-hand domestic goods was most active. To import timber for furniture-making in the circumstances of 1940–41 was unthinkable and the supply to the trade had ended in July 1940. Though Utility furniture was to be made with hardboard and veneer, plus a small allowance of domestic timber, pre-war items were at a premium on the illegal market supplied by thieves and looters. Yet how had so much transport entered a Defence Zone unchallenged when all unidentified vehicles were liable to be stopped? Dover CID heard that the vans had arrived in the town painted in the livery of local firms and with the names of those traders upon them. They came and went without suspicion.

Every officer of Dover CID was put on the case and a search was begun for vans with unfamiliar registration plates. It was far too late. Not only were the looters long gone, but Southend-on-Sea had now suffered a similar fate. At Southend, however, the police had been more successful and thirty cases of robbery from houses of evacuees were brought to trial.[21]

Professional gangs were undeterred by anti-looting squads or by the hazards of the blitz. They looted or robbed while the bombs fell and the police were fully engaged. 'Barrage gangs' carried out raids in the small hours of the morning, the sound of breaking glass or gelignite blowing open a safe lost in the din of the anti-aircraft barrage. Though the Flying Squad mounted patrols, it was a time when even they were wary of shell-casings from the big guns, which rained on the streets with lethal effect. Conventional cracksmen worked alongside looters. When the post office safe in Grove Park

Road, Kingston, was robbed in mid-November 1940, it was the latest of thirty such crimes in six weeks. Thousands of pounds in securities and the government's War Savings scheme had been taken in that time by the blackout gangs.

Intrepid opportunists patrolled the streets for sounds of a bomb followed by the fall of shattered glass in Regent Street or Piccadilly. From ladies hats to clocks and wristwatches, everything in the West End was fair game in the moments after an explosion. On 23 October 1940, admitting that 'thieves risk the bombs to be first', the Metropolitan Police invited members of the public to act as looter-spotters during air raids. Thieves who specialized in looting were said to be young and to travel about both East End and West End, the booty in the west being more valuable than near home. Next month, Scotland Yard promoted a 'radio squad' to trap looters but this did little to halt the crime and perhaps not much to reassure the public.[22]

Large-scale looting was sometimes the work of soldiers, though few military looters matched the activities of the thirty-three defendants, including their NCOs and a scrap metal merchant, who filled the Old Bailey in February 1941. They were Royal Engineers, brought in by truck to clear debris after air raids and to assist in the demolition of unsafe ruins. The lorries and the drivers waited to take the men back to camp at night. Sergeant George Gallon first noticed the amount of lead on the roofs of bombed buildings and became the instigator of the crime.

Gallon approached the drivers of the trucks that brought the men to work, and found them amenable. These Royal Engineers then made contact with Averell Thomas Jackson, a scrap metal merchant of Merton. The soldiers stripped the lead from the roofs, nine tons of it in the first case, and used the Army's lorries to deliver it to Mr Jackson's yard. With a sense of fair play, they agreed that the money from the sale of the lead should be pooled and equally divided. They kept deliveries going from 16 January to 3 February 1941, when so many military transports in Mr Jackson's yard attracted suspicion and the attention of both civil police and the Army's Special Investigation Branch.

When the trial began, the defendants were so numerous that they were obliged to wear numbers pinned to their battledress. Though they followed the old sweat's policy of never pleading guilty, most had no defence. However, four were acquitted. The recorder, Sir Gerald Dodson, passed prison sentences on the rest totalling seventeen years. Sergeant Gallon drew the longest term of three years' penal servitude for 'conspiring to loot'. At sixty-three, it was all too much for Mr Jackson, the scrap metal dealer, who collapsed and was carried weeping from the dock to begin a sentence of fifteen months for receiving.[23]

A month later, another party of Royal Engineers and their lance corporal were arrested for looting from a bombed house where they were working. The police had insufficient transport for them all and they were driven to the cells in their army lorry.[24]

Sentences passed by the civil courts on soldiers who looted became more severe. In June 1942, sixteen men were convicted of looting from houses in Kent. Mr Justice Humphreys handed down terms ranging from five years' penal servitude to eight years' hard labour. Sergeant Gallon who got away with three years for shifting tons of lead at a time was to prove fortunate. Judges began to see soldiers as natural looters. In December 1942, when Alfred Burton of the Pioneer Corps pleaded guilty to looting property worth £12 (£480) at Dover, he explained that he did not realize the seriousness of the crime. 'If you don't appreciate the seriousness of these charges,' said Mr Justice Croom-Johnson grimly, 'it is not for want of serving soldiers being told.'[25]

Quite as alarming as military looting was the increase in theft from the railways. Railways were a natural target for pilfering, when so many goods were being transported with minimal surveillance. But on 16 November 1940 Harry Ricketts, on behalf of the railway companies, claimed that under cover of enemy raids, pilfering had assumed the proportions of looting. 'While the bombs fall and everybody is taking cover, wholesale looting is going on upon every railway . . . Railway police are facing risks they ought not to be obliged to, every night, to stop wholesale looting.'[26]

Looting in transit was not confined to the railway system. By 1943, the Toronto Board of Control heard that only 60 per cent of the cigarettes destined for Canadian troops who had been shipped to Britain ever reached them. If capital punishment were to be imposed on looters, it was presumably crimes on this scale which the advocates had in mind. Yet the greatest anger was reserved for those who robbed such people as Mrs Mary May of Sandgate Street, Camberwell, bombed out in the 1940 blitz and evacuated to stay with friends. By the time she returned, her neighbour had looted her damaged house comprehensively, including the piano, the sewing machine and the armchairs. 'I am ashamed that an Englishman should behave in such a way,' said the magistrate who sent him to prison.[27]

Looters were routinely executed in Germany. In England, on 25 September 1940, the Chief Metropolitan Magistrate, Sir Robert Dummett, demanded to know why cases of thefts during air raids were brought before him as 'theft', rather than 'looting, which can be punished with penal servitude for life or even death'. Offenders were repeatedly reminded by magistrates and judges that they could be shot or hanged. Looting was a capital offence under the Defence of the Realm Act, though magistrates could only send an offender to prison for three months or remit the case to a higher court. A new Defence Regulation increased the maximum in the magistrates courts to twelve months. In the Commons, in November 1940, Osbert Peake, Under-Secretary of State for Home Affairs, promised that the government would prescribe the death penalty if looting increased.[28]

The problem of deciding which cases should carry the death penalty seemed insurmountable, though some appeared prepared to surmount it. When Walter Williams was fined £1 for taking cups and saucers from a bombed bungalow at Southend, his wife having informed on him, the police inspector helpfully advised the court that 'The extreme penalty for this offence is death.'[29]

Many instances of looting were trivial and brought disgrace out of all proportion to the offence. In an early case of August 1940, a man took some tablets of soap from a bomb-damaged factory in Croydon after two men working in the yard told him he could have them. In the press, he soared to notoriety as 'The Air Raid Looter'. Another defendant was told by a magistrate that he had committed 'a capital offence' in September 1940, by taking two shoes from a damaged lock-up shop. On 2 January 1941, two women and a man in search of coal were caught raking through the debris of St Mark's Church, Holloway, which had been destroyed by German bombs. The coal in their sacks was worth two shillings and they had been told they could take it. They were charged with looting under the Defence Regulations, though one of them protested, 'Everyone has been taking it for almost a week.'

These defendants were discharged but in a similar case three female 'coal looters' were sent to prison for three months, reduced on appeal to one month because of previous good characters and the lesson the case had taught them. In another case, a fifty-five-year-old widow from South London was fined because, after the house next door was destroyed, her feet had worn a path into its back garden, where she helped herself to abandoned coal.[30]

There was oddity in the items which some opportunists coveted. George Daly of Liverpool went looting exclusively for cough mixture and hair cream. When caught and confronted, he pleaded he was drunk at the time. The court bound him over for two years. Even the sternest advocate of capital punishment could scarcely have intended that Mr Daly and his kind should end their days before a firing squad or at the end of the hangman's rope.

The same might have been said, in January 1941, of James Martin of Islington. He looted what he believed to be clothing material valued at £3 (£120) from bomb-damaged premises so that his wife could make clothes for their children. As he walked home, he was stopped by the police and ordered to open the parcel. It contained burial clothing. 'I had no idea what the parcel contained,' he said plaintively. 'If I had known I would never have taken it.'[31]

Many looters were too young to be shot or hanged. In December 1940, East London Juvenile Court considered the looting of toys by children from a bomb-damaged warehouse. The boys were truants who had not been to school for a year. In order to steal from bomb-damaged premises in Southwark in January 1941 another enterprising pair disguised themselves as adult ARP wardens. The courts suggested that the Home Secretary should allow young looters to be flogged but the suggestion was rejected. So far as the young were concerned, a pertinent comment was made by Basil Henriques, Chairman of the East London Juvenile Court, in March 1941, when he pointed out that the way in which abandoned goods were left 'lying about' and apparently unwanted might be a strong temptation to many law-abiding children.[32]

The misery of those who returned to find damaged homes looted could hardly be overstated. Yet there was tragedy in the brave and dedicated who fell prey to temptation or thoughtlessness. In October 1940, a defendant was sent to prison and disgrace for stealing a three-quarters-empty bottle of gin. The charge had been looting but a sense of humanity altered this. Leonard Watson was leader of a Heavy Rescue Squad, the heroes of the blitz when the raids were at their worst. The scenes of hell on earth, as he and his men dug or crawled through collapsing ruins in search of survivors, needed no embellishment. A public house had been bombed and Watson's squad searched the ruins for those who were trapped. Afterwards, he noticed the unfinished bottle of gin lying on the ground. 'I thought the men needed a drink,' he said, 'but I picked it up, so I must plead guilty, I suppose.' The value of the quarter-full bottle of gin was put at 4s. 3d. (£8.50), which seemed to set a high price on it.[33]

In the same month, three sappers and a lance corporal from a bomb disposal squad, which had saved St Paul's Cathedral from the unexploded bomb threatening it, were sent to prison after pleading guilty to taking shaving brushes from a bomb-damaged shop during the operation. Their section commander who had worked on the bomb with them stood bail. 'I am awfully sorry,' said the magistrate who sentenced them, suggesting that the Home Secretary should advise the King to order their release.[34]

Such stories were frequent. There was the 'one second's folly' of the London Transport official who looted two tins of sweets worth 2s. 8d. (£5.32) from the window of a bombed sweet shop and was sentenced to twelve months' hard labour. Subsequently, the prison sentence was quashed and a fine of £5 (£200) imposed but by then he had already served three weeks. In January 1941 two men from the Auxiliary Fire Service were each sent to hard labour for four months for the theft of boxes from bomb-damaged premises. The boxes were lying wet in the yard and the men did not think they were worth anything. A week later, a case involved a young policeman on duty in Highbury, guarding the area where an RAF fighter had crashed into a photographer's shop. The young man's crime, on seeing a small camera lying in the road, was to pick it up, which he should have done, and keep it, which he should not.[35]

Some looters relieved a victim of items he ought not to have had anyway. In February 1941, two members of a rescue squad went to prison for nine months and four for six months, after looting a wrecked house in which there was half a ton of food, which the owner held illegally. Unfortunately, the owner had been killed and was not answerable. The magistrate thereupon informed those convicted that 'It is an appalling thing to find a body of men so callous as to rob the dead in this way.'[36]

It was impossible to say whether those who were caught and brought before the courts were unrepresentative or unfortunate. Some naturally thought it was their misfortune. When another auxiliary fireman appeared at the Old Bailey in October 1940, to be sentenced to six months in prison for stealing three lighters and a pipe from bomb-damaged premises, he was said to have told the police, 'I am unlucky, they are all doing it.'

Though there were few excuses for those convicted, the righteous did not escape blame for leaving property on view and unattended. In a case of looting of furniture and linen from bombed premises, the West London magistrate, Sir Gervase Rentoul, remarked, 'I should have thought it would have been the duty of some authority to take steps right away to put it in a place of safety or to cover it up as a protection against the weather.'[37]

At the Mansion House, a demolition worker with 'an excellent character' was convicted of looting two bottles of wine. His foreman had views on bureaucratic incompetence.

> At this site there have been lying about for months hundreds of thousands of tins of fruit, no end of wine and other valuable property. I have communicated with the Board of Trade, and they have promised to clear the stuff away. I have heard no more about it. I have a perfectly awful time of it because I don't even now know what food and other valuables are just lying about unclaimed.[38]

As the blitz subsided and Britain became less subject to air raids, the incidence of looting decreased. On 26 June 1941, in the House of Commons, the Member of Parliament for Marylebone, Captain Cunningham Reid, announcing that the final number of cases of looting in 1940 were 4,584 in London alone, asked whether the government should not appoint a 'Director of Anti-Looting'. Herbert Morrison disagreed: the police must remain ultimately responsible. In any case, he added, the incidence of looting had fallen sharply. By 22 February 1941, there were only three cases waiting to be heard at the Old Bailey.

Perhaps the precept had prevailed that, as Morrison put it, 'It should be the sacred instinct of the citizen after enemy action that he must not touch other people's property.' Looting was not a problem again until the rocket attacks of the German 'doodle-bugs' in the second half of 1944.

Looting carried the stigma of an offence against the people. 'The Bomb Lark' was perpetrated by people against an impersonal system. The 'lark', its practitioners argued, hurt no one.

The Bomb Lark thrived in London's East End and the authorities took it very seriously. Its less successful exponents began to appear at the Old Bailey early in 1941. It was a simple trick, though not foolproof. The 'larker' would go to the National Assistance office after a raid and claim to have been 'bombed out'. Payment for the necessities of life was made and, with destruction all around, it was impossible for officials to examine every building beforehand, or check the name and address of every applicant. For good measure, the 'victim's' identity card and ration book would have been 'destroyed by enemy action', and new ones might be claimed.

A particular recommendation of the Bomb Lark was that the same individual could repeat claims for different addresses without too much risk. When Walter Handy was sent to penal servitude for three years in February 1941, he had been 'bombed out' nineteen times in five months, more or less once a week. Such frauds also had the advantage that there was a good chance of the offices of the Assistance Board and all its documentation being blown to pieces by the next bomb to fall in the area. However, three years' penal servitude was an exemplary punishment. In six other cases at the Old Bailey on the same day, defendants were sent to prison for periods ranging between twelve and eighteen months.[39]

When a further batch of cases was dealt with in March, the 'Bomb Lark' had been further refined. Claims were now being made on the basis of forged identity cards, an early instance of just how easy such forgeries were to make or come by. Yet greed sometimes failed to pay. In 1942, Bromley magistrates sent a man to hard labour for six months when he claimed for a second bomb-damaged house. It was not the house that betrayed him but the three-piece suite, which was recognized as having been damaged beyond repair in the first incident and then moved, like a stage prop, from one scene of the 'Bomb Lark' to another.[40]

A variant of the Bomb Lark was the Billeting Lark. The billeting of evacuees, servicemen, or those homeless in the blitz, on other people was a common experience of war. Allowances were paid by the government to the 'host' and, in the case of the lark, drawn for weeks or months after the evacuees had left. One of those sent to prison for six months at the Old Bailey in 1941 had drawn allowances for sixteen weeks after his lodger had left. He was well placed to commit the fraud being an accountant currently employed as a clerk by Islington Borough Council. The council seemed not to know that he had six previous convictions for burglary, larceny and receiving. A variant form of the fraud was to steal blank billeting forms and fill them in, so that allowances were drawn for non-existent people without the inconvenience of a lodger on the premises. The idea caught on and, in 1942, council officials elsewhere were sent to prison for forging these vouchers on their own behalf.[41]

Those who owned their houses and lost them in the blitz were made to wait until after the war for 'value payment', as compensation was called, but might claim an advance of up to £500 (£20,000) with £50 (£2,000) for furniture and £20 (£800) for clothes. The shortage of official property assessors, as men were called up for the services, led to severe delays for even the most modest claims. At this point the tricksters appeared. They visited the claimants and offered to advance the money at once in exchange for the victim signing away an extortionate 'commission'. Sometimes, they offered a document for signature, which authorized them to push through a claim in exchange for immediate legal expenses and an eventual percentage of the compensation paid.

Swindles of this sort were not the prerogative of the working class. Before the first bombs fell, fear of a blitz offered rich opportunities to the criminal entrepreneur. 'Eustace Hamilton Hargreaves', *alias* Frederick James White, was an experienced trickster. The coming of war gave him a chance to anticipate the evacuee frauds of Basil Seal in Evelyn Waugh's *Put Out More Flags*.

As crisis moved to conflict, 'Hargreaves' assumed his long-practised pose of a wealthy landowner, now in government service. He had been impressed by the unseemly scramble of the wealthy to get themselves and their possessions out of London and into the safety of the countryside. Promoting himself to the rank of a senior Civil Defence official, he became 'Chief Area Controller of Reservations'. As such, he was able to introduce the anxious rich to a little-known government department, 'ARP Crisis Evacuations'.

If the worst should come, this scheme guaranteed comfortable accommodation in the heart of the countryside for the nation's elite, at public expense, in exchange for a handsome registration fee as a confirmation of status and guarantee of solvency. The applicants were then offered details of substantial properties and given plentiful reassurance. In due course, when the worst came in 1940, his clients discovered that neither 'Eustace Hamilton Hargreaves' nor 'Frederick James White' was known to the ARP or to the Civil Defence authorities, although both names were well documented in the Criminal Records Office. The rural properties were not his nor theirs and the money paid as registration fees was gone. Moreover, the trickster was by this time in prison, which was to be his own personal 'Crisis Evacuation' centre for the rest of the war.

Swindles of this kind fed on public anxiety. On 5 April 1941 one of 'Hargreaves's' competitors, Arthur Pennock, was convicted of fraud and sent to prison for eighteen months at Middlesex Sessions for taking subscriptions from unwary Londoners to secure places in 'deep' air raid shelters. Pennock's shelters were non-existent but the government's refusal to dig deep under London, or into its own pockets, had driven people to seek their own refuges. The reputation of surface shelters had suffered after the discovery that some would collapse on the shelterers if a bomb dropped in the area.

Tricksters flourished at the moments of the nation's greatest peril. In the last days of Dunkirk, an opportunist gang recognized promising victims in the large number of aliens in London. The conmen would arrive at a house, posing as Scotland Yard officers sent to detain the occupants. The occupants had half expected something of the kind, following the defeat of the British Army in France and the threat of a German invasion. After driving them around for some time, those who had arrested them would leave them at a tea shop or some such rendezvous with instructions to wait there and not to move, on pain of being shot on sight, until they were collected in half an hour. The 'Scotland Yard men' did not return but when the victims at last suspected a trick and went home, they found their houses ransacked.

In contrast to the heroism of so many who endured the blitz, a minority culture of petty dishonesty seemed endemic. The stretcher-bearer who went absent to work as a tic-tac man, the warden who signed off sick not to miss the dog racing, represented what the Thames magistrate, John Harris, described on 1 November 1941 as 'cases of which there are far too many'. In March 1941, one London firm reported that its employees were refusing to take turns at fire-watching unless they were paid fifteen shillings (£30) a night or allowed a day off in lieu. This was given short shrift. Four days later, an employee of a firm in Finsbury, who had failed to turn up for duty as a fire-watcher, was informed by the Clerkenwell magistrate that employees who shirked such duties would be sent to prison.[42]

Yet still the disgruntled members of society remained unimpressed. They stripped lead, iron and other materials from 'emergency homes' – houses due for demolition before the war but now kept empty for those whose own homes were bombed. They stole hurricane lamps used in the blackout to mark obstructions, traffic junctions and pedestrian 'refuges', two hundred disappearing from the North London borough of Edmonton alone. With rather more polish, a well-spoken middle-aged man was visiting wardens in April 1941 with documentation purporting to show him as an official inspector of air raid shelters 'for damp', on behalf of the borough council. He would call at the home of the ARP warden and collect the key for the shelter, returning it later. After he had gone on his way, the shelter was found to have lost every item of portable and saleable equipment.

*

The blitz had no precise ending. In 1941, German attacks were borne increasingly by provincial cities. In 1942 came the so-called 'Baedeker Raids' on such historic towns as Bath and on coastal resorts. Yet the reinforcement of the RAF by the USAAF during 1942, followed by the invasion of Europe in June 1944, put an end to all but hit-and-run raids by individual German bombers. In September 1944, the black-out was at last replaced by a dim-out. Yet in June 1944, a week after D-Day and like a bolt from the blue, the first V-1 rocket bomb carrying 1,800lb of explosive fell on London and a savage coda to the air war began. A new evacuation of the capital was organized as 8,000 'doodle-bugs', or 'flying bombs', were aimed at it.

The deep shelters, little used except as accommodation for servicemen on leave, were now occupied in earnest. By mid-July it was necessary to issue tickets of admission. With bunks, canteens, medical posts and air conditioning, they were a civilized improvement on the shelters of 1940. Though by early September anti-aircraft guns and Fighter Command claimed to be shooting down 80 per cent of the V-1 rockets, on 8 September supersonic V-2s began to arrive. These were too fast to be shot down. The rockets cost 2,724 dead and 6,467 seriously injured before the Allied advance into Germany put London beyond their range.

Within a week of the first V-1, a jewel robbery was carried out by two men entering a block of flats minutes after it was hit by the bomb. A policeman's attention was caught by the packets of cigarettes in their pockets, as they hurried from the shattered building. At first, they claimed to have found the packets lying on the ground. When searched, their pockets also produced nine rings, two bracelets, three brooches, five necklaces and three watches. As one of them looked at the haul, he said gloomily, 'That's done it.'[43]

A certain amount of looting had continued between 1941 and 1944. For example, gas cookers had been taken from damaged houses in the East End during 1942, when domestic goods were in short supply. Thanks to the flying bombs there were now thousands of blast-damaged houses offering an easy source of black market goods, especially in South London where so many of the rockets fell. Camberwell, Herne Hill and adjacent areas were particularly favoured by the robbers late in 1944 and in the opening months of

1945. As at Dover in 1941, furniture vans in imitation livery were used. Thieves loaded these with furniture, carpets, clocks and china, though leaving behind items that were in need of repair.

Once it was known that a house was unoccupied, it became a thieves' priority. The arrival of a van was not in itself suspicious. With the new evacuation, it was hardly surprising to see vehicles being loaded with furniture for store. At one house in Herne Hill, the intruders loaded their van, made themselves a meal and washed up the dishes so that they might take these as well. The house had just been evacuated, and when they found the family's rations they added these to their haul. They drove away unchallenged.

The government added its pennyworth to the misery of the victims who were first blitzed, then looted. Its circular was quoted by the *South London Press* in an 'Open Letter to a Looter' on 11 August 1944. The War Damage Chattels Office, which dealt with claims for loss of household items through enemy action, wrote to tell the victims that 'it would appear that the goods for which you wish to make a claim were looted and therefore are not covered under the provisions of the War Damage Act.'

Looting often took place after dark but, in September 1944, the blackout had been inconveniently lightened to a 'dim-out'. By December the furniture thieves had moved out to the less well-lit suburbs. There was no organizing gang, rather individual entrepreneurs sure of a quick sale and a good price for domestic goods. Some were caught and, as in 1940, warnings from the bench reminded them that looters were liable to be shot. Such retribution seemed unlikely at this stage of the war. When a bricklayer from Brighton made off with a lorryload of goods from a house he was repairing in Upper Norwood in September 1944, he was sent to prison for fifteen months. A tiler caught in the same case went to prison for nine months.[44]

By early August, some councils in South London set up a scheme to guard bombed-out furniture by allowing victims to fill in forms for their possessions to be collected and stored. Yet it was beyond the resources of a council to ensure that this was done for everyone. The rocket attack had come at one of the worst seasons, making thousands of houses uninhabitable in the face of winter and, at the same time, easy to loot. Lambeth Council alone had 2,400 people in urgent need of accommodation, when the first temporary and prefabricated 'Portals', as these new emergency metal bungalows were called, could not be supplied until July 1945. In response, the council decided to erect 600 huts with communal bath-huts wherever there was space in the borough, including the edges of the parks. On 10 November, it announced that it hoped to have the first huts ready in a fortnight. But by then, as the press complained, there were only two of them, which was scarcely encouraging.

Repairs to damaged buildings were a priority. Since the blitz of 1940–41, the Ministry of Works had been recruiting volunteer building workers from all over the country, who were to be billeted in London hostels. By November 1944, however, trades unions found it necessary to rebut 'the many rash statements being made that building trade workers are not doing their share'. Current prosecutions brought against them in the rocket-bomb attacks had begun on 17 July, when a 'flying squad' repair worker from Liverpool was convicted of looting patients' jewellery at a damaged hospital. He was sent to prison for six months on 31 July, having told the police that he was 'not the only one' and that he had no intention of taking the blame for the whole gang. Two women and an RAF man had also been sent to prison at Lewes for looting, the man for four years.[45]

On 16 August, Herbert Morrison assured the House of Commons that looting in the Metropolitan Police district was running at only half the monthly average of 1940–41, and at less than a third of the peak rate for that period. Yet some areas reported the day before that bomb-damaged premises were being protected by Home Guards with loaded rifles. The reaction of the *South London Press* was unequivocal, insisting that the Home Guard who shot the first person discovered looting the property of those unfortunate enough to have lost their homes would win the gratitude of all decent men and women in Southern England. Despite the looting of absentees' premises, greater contempt was reserved for such offenders as the repair worker who was near by when a flying bomb landed on a council estate. He found an attaché case and helped himself to £333 (£13,320) in notes, leaving the owner of the case injured on the ground and his wife dead.[46]

Some of the 'flying squad' of repair workers, seizing the chance of a good time in London at public expense, proved more trouble than they were worth. Though they might be a minority, they got the majority of the publicity. Some were organizers of Sunday afternoon games of crown and anchor for hundreds of onlookers near their billets in the Kensington squares. Others got drunk and made a nuisance of themselves in South Kensington tube station shelter. At Ladbroke Grove station, a detective sergeant escaped death by inches as drunken Glaswegians of the repair squad staggered along the electrified track in the path of an approaching train. The sergeant jumped down, struck one man in the face to stun him and threw him on to the platform, then grabbed another round the waist and leapt to safety with him just as the train entered the station.[47]

As in the cases of the bricklayer and the tiler at Upper Norwood, repair squad workers did their share of the looting, if only because they had the easiest access to the householders' possessions. They also helped themselves in the accommodation provided for them. One Kensington hostel had lost a thousand blankets by the end of the year. The extent of this pilfering emerged when one of the blanket thieves was sent to prison for a quite different crime of looting at Balham in January 1945.

It was not until 27 March 1945, only six weeks before the unconditional surrender of Germany, that the last V-2 rocket fell on London. The blitz was over after four and a half years and the sirens fell silent. Now the Ministry of Works faced a different threat. Looting became a far more cheery business during London's VE-Day celebrations of 8 May. The happy crowds seized scaffolding boards, ladders, wooden barrows and timber of every kind from houses under repair to fuel the Victory bonfires. On 14 August, the government urged the population not to repeat this performance in celebrating the defeat of Japan. It had delayed urgent repairs to damaged buildings by several weeks. By that time, however, purloining of such items was not called 'looting' but 'liberating', an ironic tribute to the setting free of Europe from German occupation.

5

Deeds of Darkness

In the world above the shelters, the night sky was red with the glow of fires, turning streets to ribbons of fire where incendiaries were left to burn on roadways, pavements and in gutters where they could do no harm. Most were dropped in iron baskets by the bombers. The basket turned over as it fell and the bombs were scattered widespread. Some, falling through roofs and setting buildings on fire, were dealt with. Most others were left. In the light of the flames, ambulances with bells ringing and, inevitably, a hearse or two went on their way. It might have been some comfort to know that the burden of the hearse was black market sugar for delivery or that the ambulance contained nothing more alarming than a post office safe.

In the first three months of 1941, according to Scotland Yard on 7 April, gangs of safe-breakers had stolen £20,000 (£800,000) during the blitz, while posing as the emergency services. One gang was working in North London and another in the East End. Their vehicles were motor vans repainted to resemble ARP ambulances and, in some cases, fitted with stretchers. One gang destroyed all documents and took only currency. The other retained postal orders, cashed with tradesmen by 'women confederates'.

The thieves worked by using a 'spotter', a 'fitter' and, if necessary, a 'creeper'. The spotter paid a visit to the post office in the ordinary course of business. He memorized details of the interior, the position and make of safe. He would also note the type of lock on the main door, the size and position of windows and fanlights. This information would be passed to the 'fitter', who would pay a night visit to take a wax impression of the door lock so that a duplicate key could be filed. Sometimes the position of the door made it difficult to do this unobserved. In that case, a 'creeper' would find a way into the post office from adjoining premises. The spotter, fitter and creeper usually took no part in the raid, which was carried out by four other men. Two would enter the post office, a third would drive the van, and a fourth would be in ARP uniform, as if guarding the premises.

For preference, the robbery was carried out on a moonless night. The uniformed lookout would be posted so that any inquisitive citizen who wondered about the ambulance could be deterred by a warning of damaged walls in danger of collapsing or an unexploded landmine in the area. The ambulance was equipped not only with mock stretchers but also with a safe-carrier, on which safes weighing a quarter of a ton or more could be trundled out and loaded. As a rule the arrival of the ambulance coincided with the emergence of the safe on its trolley. It was driven to a shed, garage or some other 'run-in' and loaded into another van, in case the police had been alerted to an ARP ambulance that seemed 'not quite right'. Its final journey was to a warehouse in the City of London, where it could be opened at leisure. Older safes were dealt with by a hacksaw or metal-cutter to open the back. More modern ones were drilled so that the bolts could be forced.

The use of a hearse to deliver stolen sugar in Bermondsey was discovered and reported by a police informer. There was no proof that the local undertaker knew his vehicle was being used for this. However, the hearse was spacious enough to accommodate four hundredweight of sugar, in addition to a coffin, and could also make deliveries on the way back from the cemetery without inviting questions about extra mileage.[1]

Chief Superintendent Peter Beveridge, as commander of the Flying Squad, ensured that the pursuit of crime continued through the blitz, though manpower was diverted to anti-looting patrols and to helping heavy rescue squads in recovering trapped victims and the administration of first aid. Nonetheless, mobile patrols confronted criminals in a continuing feud in which the Luftwaffe had no part.

As the war went on, food thefts and even post office raids were often eclipsed by cigarette robberies, soon to reach a million cigarettes at a time. Cigarettes were portable and valuable for their weight. By the second year of the war they were also in short supply. Pipe smokers were encouraged to reuse half-smoked tobacco by adding a small slice of dried apple to make it palatable. Later, when the liberation of Europe began, cigarettes were to form the currency of the black market and to establish an unofficial rate of exchange.

In blacked-out streets, those who often seemed too timid or ill-equipped to be professional criminals felt tempted to try their luck as armed robbers. On 17 October 1940, Gwendolyn Louisa Wehrman was working behind the off-licence counter at the Alexandra Park Tavern in Wood Green. There was a pint glass above her containing eight £1 notes and she was chatting to the barmaid. At 9.15 a youth in a green pork-pie hat came in and asked for a packet of Players Weights. 'Sorry, no Weights, only Woodbines,' Mrs Wehrman replied.

The youth went out, then came back again with two of his friends but with a cloth over the lower part of his face. It was hard to take seriously a masked villain who had first shown himself to the witnesses and then put a mask on. While his two companions blocked the doorway, the youth said, 'Put your hands up.' Mrs Wehrman was not impressed and, perhaps in play, moved to slap the youth's wrist with a beer bottle. The automatic fired a single shot and Mrs Wehrman fell dead with a bullet through her chest.

The three youths scrambled out, empty-handed, and got into an American saloon car, which left so quickly that one of them was riding on the running-board. Scotland Yard's informers suggested a teenage gang in North London, one of whom was known to be armed. Inspector Greeno traced a second victim, Ernst Israel Altmann, to whom the four young men had given a lift in the black-out. He had then been robbed at gunpoint by the driver, who wore a scarf over the lower part of his face. According to Greeno's informant, a youth had boasted in an Edmonton café of picking people up in his car, taking them down a side turning, and robbing them with a gun. He had produced the gun to prove it.

Greeno traced three eighteen-year-old labourers and a nineteen-year-old clerk who formed the gang. It was scarcely the world of Al Capone or Bugsy Siegel. On the night of the killing, they were drinking. Someone suggested robbing the off-licence where Mrs Wehrman worked. After killing her with a Luger automatic pistol, they had recovered their composure and robbed an electrical shop in Silver

Street, Edmonton, of twenty-two radio sets. They had already robbed Mr Altmann of his wristwatch and wallet.

The four were soon caught and charged with murder. Their incompetence would have made them a liability to any professional gang but there was little doubt that they would be convicted and executed as a warning to other blackout robbers. Yet, by forensic good fortune, it was proved that there had been a metallic impact as Mrs Wehrman brought the beer bottle down. It was quite possible that this had been a contact between the bottle and the automatic, which caused the gun to go off, reducing the charges of murder to manslaughter.

The easy availability of guns made such small-time blackout thieves 'think big'. It was hard not to sense the disappointment of the police and the courts that they were unable to make a public example in the case of Mrs Wehrman. This was remedied in 1942 when a seventy-one-year-old pawnbroker, Leonard Moules, of Hackney Road, was robbed and died as the result of blows to his head from a revolver butt.

Once again, there was no immediate clue as to the identity of the assailant. Superintendent Fred Cherrill of Scotland Yard's Fingerprint Department found only a palm print with no match in the criminal record files. A professional gunman need only lie low and keep his mouth shut to escape capture. Inspector Greeno thought such a man might come from East End streets within the area of Hackney Road, Kingsland Road and Bethnal Green Road.

Yet detection was scarcely needed. The two men who committed the crime produced the gun in a café and began to display it. They might as well have signed a confession. A plain-clothes detective listening to conversations in cafés and bars not only heard of the display of the gun but even the names of the killers. 'It was George and Sam,' said one man, 'I will bet anything they did it.'

George Silverosa and Samuel Dashwood were incompetent petty offenders to whom any professional would have given a wide berth. Dashwood, at twenty-two, was the owner of the gun. He had been discharged from the Army on the grounds of 100 per cent incapacity due to mental deficiency. Silverosa, when arrested, at once made a statement admitting that Dashwood had shown him the gun as 'enough to frighten anyone'. They had agreed to go to the pawnbroker's shop to get some money, just as the old man was putting the shutters up. 'All right,' Silverosa had said, 'but no violence.' Unfortunately for him, it was his palm print on the safe.

Though they ran a 'cut-throat' defence, each man accusing the other of committing the murder, it was plain that while Silverosa was in the other room with the safe Dashwood struck Mr Moules the blows from which he died. Silverosa was what little 'brains' there were behind the robbery with Dashwood as the 'muscle'. Both were guilty of leaving Mr Moules dying on the floor of the shop as they made off with their booty. 'I gave Sammy £20,' said Silverosa. 'Sammy kept the rings, which he sold, and I had my wages left out of it – about £50 or £60.'

As so often, a gangster hunt caught men who, however repellent, had been unspectacular criminals. Their trial was less than satisfactory. Dashwood discovered that his counsel proposed to call evidence from army witnesses to prove his insanity. He thereupon dismissed his legal representatives and conducted his own defence. In the event both men were convicted and hanged.[2]

In the world of the blackout, Scotland Yard not only cooperated in policing tens of thousands of British troops on leave or in transit. Thousands of Canadian front-line troops had also begun to arrive in December 1939. For the most part, the Canadians had been too late for the Battle of France in May and June 1940. An initial agreement for their use in Europe precluded them from the North African campaign. They were left with little to do in London or in the South Coast towns near which many were encamped. From time to time, they rampaged through the blacked-out centre of Brighton, smashing windows of department stores and fighting the police, as in their New Year celebrations of 1942. Assault, rape and murder cases were heard by the civil courts. In Brighton, there was armed robbery of a café in Marlborough Place, while Canadian soldiers in a jeep held up a Kemp Town post office with sten guns – 'Don't move, sisters!' – then hijacked an ammunition lorry equipped with a mounted machine-gun.[3]

In London, Scotland Yard was grateful for the assistance of Canadian Military Police, who arrived in full force by January 1941.

The difficulty of policing blackout violence was well illustrated when Morrie Scholman, manager of the Coach and Horses Tavern in Wellington Street, Covent Garden, was shot dead during December 1941. A soldier with a muffler was seen by market porters running from the scene. That was the extent of the evidence. There were hundreds of British and Canadian troops in the area, many in transit, who would be far away and unavailable for questioning within a few hours.

Inspector John Capstick was roused from his billet on the top floor of the Charing Cross Hotel and given charge of the case. In an operation as much military as civilian, he called the Provost Corps of Military Police at Great Scotland Yard and asked them to round up every soldier within a mile of Bow Street. This included railway stations at Charing Cross and Waterloo, as well as the Union Jack Club, the overnight refuge for servicemen in London, on the south side of Waterloo Bridge.

Capstick then went to the headquarters of the Canadian Provost Corps in Henrietta Street, on the fringe of Covent Garden. This incorporated a detention centre for Canadian troops arrested in the West End and had a full staff of Military Police. With the assistance of the Canadian Provost Marshal, all British and Canadian troops were arrested by armed military police, in every pub in the area, every servicemen's club and every platform and refreshment room of the railway stations. They were brought by truck to Bow Street police station.

When the police station was full, 200 more soldiers were packed into the yard behind it. Even with the assistance of the Canadians, questioning seemed likely to take days. It was pure luck that a Canadian Provost Sergeant recorded an absentee from the hostel in Tavistock Square and heard that the man had a 'floozy' in Craven Street, behind the Strand.

Capstick and the Provost Sergeant went to Craven Street, an area of cheap wartime hotels. Having no address, they searched, building by building, until they found the soldier in bed with the woman but wearing a field dressing on his arm. He confessed that she had persuaded him to rob the Coach and Horses at opening time before there was anyone else around. He had threatened the manager with his gun, there was a struggle during which the gun went off, the bullet passing through the soldier's wrist and into the manager's head. Though convicted and condemned to death at the Old Bailey, his sentence was commuted to life imprisonment. Yet the complexities of such manhunts threw doubt on how effectively wartime crime could be policed.[4]

In most of their misdemeanours, individual Canadians were amiable. Sergeant John Worthington had nowhere to sleep in Brighton but was given the key to her flat by the absentee manageress of the Red Shield Club. Feeling lonely, he collected three elderly Home Guards, just going on duty to man coastal observation posts, on watch for a German attack. The four men ate dinner and drank six bottles of champagne. The Home Guards were found next morning 'in a drunken sleep' at their posts. Sergeant Worthington was in possession of a table lighter and a gold bangle, purloined before leaving the club. An enlightened magistracy decided he was too drunk to form a criminal intent and discharged him. By the time of his trial, whatever disruption the Canadian presence had caused in London or South-East England was eclipsed by their bravery and their losses in the ill-fated assault on Dieppe in August 1942. Of the attacking force of 6,000 men – 5,000 of them Canadian – half were either killed or taken prisoner in the attempted landing.[5]

Subsequent history selected two cases as the most atrocious blackout crimes, though they resembled offences which might also have happened in peacetime. They were personal, in the sense that the black market or safe-breaking was not, but circumstances and opportunities distinguished them.

As a fire-watcher, Harry Dobkin knew that the number of people being killed in the air raids made it impossible to carry out a post-mortem in every case. Once the remains of a victim had been identified, which was not always possible, they were released to the next of kin for burial. It must have crossed the minds of many who dreamt of doing away with their near relations, or rivals in love or business, that now was the time to do it. Deeds impossible to conceal before the war might pass unnoticed. An extra body found under the rubble of a building or charred to anonymity at the scene of an incendiary-bomb blast would warrant only a glance.

Statistics could not be drawn up for such a crime as Dobkin contemplated because, unlike successful robberies, those who got away with such murders would not be known to have committed them. Only the failures became statistics. Even a suspicious death might get perfunctory attention. In the small hours of 29 December 1942, the body of a bank official was found on a bomb site at North Street, Weston-super-Mare. He had died of head injuries and there was a trail of blood on shop windows leading back to the seafront. Whether he had been attacked, injured in a road accident or fatally wounded by some descending fragment of the air war seemed to be anyone's guess.

Harry and Rachel Dobkin had been married at Bethnal Green Synagogue in 1920. 'The marriage', he recalled, 'was arranged in the Jewish fashion by a marriage broker.' It was 'a failure from the start'. The couple parted after three days, Mr Dobkin going home to his parents and his wife being awarded a maintenance order for £1 a week. From time to time she quarrelled with him because the money was not paid and he accused her of upsetting his parents. Before the war, he had various jobs in the tailoring trade and as a ship's steward or cook. From 3 April 1941, at the age of forty, he was a fire-watcher to a firm of solicitors in Kennington Lane.

On 12 April 1941, Mrs Dobkin was reported missing by her sister. A good many people were missing at the time and the report was not in itself sinister. Mr Dobkin was still living in Kennington Lane, guarding the solicitors' premises. At the rear of the building stood Oswald's Place Baptist Chapel, badly damaged by bomb blast in 1940 and no longer used. On the night of 14 April, two days after Mrs Dobkin's disappearance, the chapel was further damaged by fire. There was no obvious reason for this but fires during air raids were too frequent for comment.

Dobkin remained a fire-watcher at the solicitors' offices for just over a year, until 20 May 1942, soon after which the firm moved to other accommodation. In July, the remains of Oswald's Place Baptist Chapel were demolished. During this, the workers came to a cellar under the vestry. When a two-foot pile of debris was removed from a slab of stone on the cellar floor, and the stone was lifted, they found a human body, little more than a skeleton.

The position of the body caused suspicion. Forensic examination showed that the head and the limbs had been severed from the trunk. Dr Keith Simpson, Home Office pathologist, concluded that the remains had been there from twelve to eighteen months. The injury to a bone in the throat was consistent only with manual strangulation. The height of the deceased was that of Mrs Dobkin. A photograph of Mrs Dobkin superimposed on that of the skull showed an exact match. Worse still for Harry Dobkin, forensic dentistry showed another exact match between the teeth of Mrs Dobkin and the skull. The body had been deliberately coated with builders' lime. The murderer had heard that lime would destroy a body. He did not know the difference between quicklime and builders' lime, which had actually helped to preserve it.

Harry Dobkin was convicted and hanged. He had hidden the body where it would be linked to him and would inevitably be found sooner or later. By dismembering it, he attracted immediate suspicion. By using lime, he helped to preserve evidence against himself. When the fire brigade came belatedly to deal with the blaze he had started, he pointed at the flames and said, 'I didn't do it.' Though it was a cliché to say that a murderer had put the rope round his neck, it was seldom more apt.

There was considerable coverage of this relatively minor case, which was treated as though it had been one of the great crimes of the Second World War. It struck a chord in the minds of readers who wondered how many other Mrs Dobkins might be lying, unsuspected, under the rubble of bomb-scorched buildings or might now be resting in one of the great necropoli of outer London without questions being asked. Harry Dobkin's case did not prove that it was impossible to get away with such a crime but merely that he had gone about it in an exceptionally clumsy manner.[6]

Between the disappearance of Mrs Dobkin and Harry Dobkin's day of reckoning, the 'Blackout Ripper' came and went. He was scarcely a match for his Victorian predecessor or, indeed, for those psychopaths who were to succeed him in the later 1940s. Curiously, his career occupied only a single week in February 1942.

In the early hours of 9 February, the body of Mrs Evelyn Hamilton, a forty-year-old chemist's assistant, was found in a surface air raid shelter in Montagu Place, Marylebone, between Baker Street and the Edgware Road. She had been strangled, the motive apparently being the theft of £80 (£3,200) from her handbag.

On the morning of 10 February, a more gruesome but apparently unrelated discovery was made of the body of Evelyn Oatley, former actress and Windmill girl, in her Wardour Street flat. She had been strangled but also mutilated with a tin-opener. Superintendent Fred Cherrill, with long experience as head of Scotland Yard's Fingerprint Department, noted that whoever used the tin-opener was left-handed. He had also noticed that when Evelyn Hamilton's body was discovered in the air raid shelter, the marks on her throat were those of a left hand.

Three days later, when the daughter of a Soho prostitute, Margaret Lowe, came to visit her mother in Gosfield Street, off Tottenham Court Road, there was no answer to her knock. The girl then went to a neighbour who phoned Tottenham Court Road police station. Her call was taken by Inspector Robert Higgins. Soho was his territory and he knew Margaret Lowe. Going to the house in Gosfield Street, he jemmied open the door and found her on the divan, strangled and mutilated. She had been dead since the previous evening.

Ted Greeno, now a detective chief inspector, was given what was reported as 'The Blackout Ripper' case. While he was with Sir Bernard Spilsbury, the pathologist, at Gosfield Street, a dispatch rider dismounted with a message. The body of a fourth woman, Doris Jouannet, a part-time prostitute and wife of a hotel manager, had been found at their flat in Sussex Gardens. She had been murdered and mutilated in a similar manner.

It was hard to imagine farce mingling with such horrors. However, Greeno hurried to South London to gather information in a pub from one of his informers. He came out to find that his Austin police car had been stolen. His criminal acquaintances apologized but blamed him for having changed from a high-powered Wolseley or Railton to an Austin without giving them notice.

The coolest head was Cherrill's, as he worked patiently on the evidence of fingerprints. None matched criminal records. However, he had left-hand prints from the tin-opener in Evelyn Oatley's room and a thumbprint from her handbag mirror. In Margaret Lowe's room a candle had been wrenched from a candlestick. Prints on the stick were right-handed, suggesting a left-handed killer who used his left hand to free the candle. The prints did not link the two crimes yet, being from different hands.

By Saturday 14 February, newspaper placards proclaimed a 'West End Search for Mad Killer'. It was not to last long. On 12 February, within hours of the deaths of Margaret Lowe and Doris Jouannet, a young woman was having a drink and a sandwich at the Trocadero with an RAF officer cadet, whom she had met in Piccadilly. Afterwards, as they walked down the Haymarket, he offered her money to sleep with him. She refused and hurried on into the darkness. He caught her up, pushed her into a doorway and said, 'You must let me kiss you goodnight.' Putting down his gas-mask case, as if to fold his arms round her, he gripped her throat and began to choke her. When she lost consciousness, he rifled her handbag until interrupted by a delivery boy taking drink to the Captain's Cabin. The attacker then ran into the darkness, leaving behind his gas mask in its case. The delivery boy called the police. Inside the gas-mask case was a service number, which identified Gordon Frederick Cummins, twenty-eight years old, billeted with other cadets in St John's Wood.

Cummins did not return to his billet. He picked up a prostitute in Regent Street, went to her flat in Paddington and gave her £5 (£200). As he did so, the electricity went off and his hands were round her throat. The young woman fought, struggled free of the grip on her throat and began to scream. Cummins seemed to come to his senses, pressed another £5 into her hand, and fled.

Greeno confronted his suspect next day but was met by a flawless alibi. The billet passbook, signed by cadets as they reported, showed that Cummins had been back every night of the week before the murders could have taken place. As for the gas-mask case, people were always taking one another's. Next day, Sunday 16 September, the alibi disintegrated. The cadets had a system for signing one another in and, in any case, it was easy to get out by the fire escape. Cummins was arrested and charged a week after his first crime.

It was a short career for a serial killer but the evidence against him was conclusive. His fingerprints were in Evelyn Oatley's flat and

Margaret Lowe's. His pockets contained a Swan fountain pen with Doris Jouannet's initials and a cigarette case belonging to Margaret Lowe. Evelyn Oatley's cigarette case was found at the billet. Items belonging to Evelyn Hamilton were in the billet dustbin. The young woman he attacked in the Haymarket picked him out at once from an identity parade. For good measure, when Cummins signed the fingerprint form, Cherrill noticed that he did so with his left hand.

At the Old Bailey in April 1942 Cummins was tried for the murder of Evelyn Oatley, since English law allowed an accused to be tried for only one murder at a time. When the jury was inadvertently shown photographs of fingerprints from Margaret Lowe's flat, the trial had to be stopped. It was no surprise at the second hearing that a new jury found him guilty. Though Cummins thought he would be reprieved, he was executed on 25 June, apparently with the distinction of being the only murderer to be hanged during an air raid.

There was no leisure to inquire why Cummins became a nine-day psychopathic wonder. Unlike Heath, Haigh or Christie and their kind, he had no criminal record nor any history of violence. He was well educated, had worked in a laboratory and was married to the secretary of a theatrical producer. He was selected for aircrew training and a commission in the RAF. Some comrades later said he put on 'airs'. They nicknamed him 'The Duke'. He fancied himself a ladies' man with a natural charm. Scotland Yard judged that his prime motive was theft. Yet it was a quantum psychic leap from puerile vanity to murdering four people in a week and attempting to murder two more – four crimes on the same night. As for theft, a thief would surely have found easier and safer ways. But a beleaguered nation had more important matters to attend to and soon Cummins was no longer around to answer questions. Scotland Yard credited him with two earlier blackout murders. In October 1941 Maple Church was found strangled in a bombed house in the Hampstead Road, while Edith Humphries was the victim of a brutal but apparently motiveless murder in her home near by.[7]

It was not surprising that even a 'Blackout Ripper' failed to hold the headlines in the second week of February 1942. On the day that Cummins murdered two women and attacked two others, the German battleships *Scharnhorst* and *Gneisenau* with the heavy cruiser *Prinz Eugen*, an escort of five destroyers and thirteen motor torpedo boats, forced the Straits of Dover, attempting a dash from Brest to Norway, shooting down fifteen RAF bombers and seventeen fighters who tried to stop them. The week also saw the last British resistance in Malaya crushed and General Percival's unconditional surrender of Singapore to the Japanese invaders on the day before Cummins was arrested and charged. With the entry of the United States into the war, it seemed impossible that it could be lost by the Allies, but El Alamein and the first victories lay some months in the future. In the face of present reverses, even a 'Blackout Ripper' rated little more than a few column inches.

6

Opportunity Knocks: The Civilians

Few people in positions of industrial or financial power chose to profit deliberately by the nation's peril. The challenge was to draw a frontier between permissible self-interest and moral treachery. Some of the wealthiest culprits concealed from the Treasury those dollars vital to financing the war. In industry, if some workers pilfered from shipyards or factories, some owners or custodians saw a chance to profit at the nation's expense. In dealing with defaulters, the government showed that in a war on behalf of the people no privilege of rank or name would be allowed.

Military power had long been dependent on civilian contractors. Racketeering by firms in time of war was no novelty in 1939. Even the 'hard-faced men' who did well in 1914–18 were relative late-comers to wartime profiteering. Sixty years earlier, army provisions sent to the Crimea had provoked the Victorian pleasantry that one man's potted meat is another man's poison. Pilfering of footwear persuaded the commissariat to dispatch to Balaclava separate consignments of winter boots for the left or right foot, a precaution still being used in the Second World War.

Dishonest contractors were to cause the government particular concern during the blitz. In May 1941 it secured the imprisonment of a Kensington builder, a repairer of bomb damage, who claimed from the council the union rate of pay, while paying his workforce 15 per cent less. In 1942, it brought prosecutions and secured convictions of builders in Birmingham who had similarly cheated the city council over bomb-damage repairs. Nor were tube shelters exempt from criticism. In a legal action which followed the death by suffocation of 176 shelterers at Bethnal Green underground station in 1943, Mr Justice Singleton described the structure of their refuge as 'in the nature of a trap'.[1]

The conduct of some ordinary members of the building trade was without question criminal. In February 1941, however, the government received a report from the Petroleum Board which referred to 'an organized conspiracy' to defeat the Fuel Rationing Order, involving two of the country's large construction firms, Sir Lindsay Parkinson & Co., and Sir Alexander Gibbs & Co., at a factory site in Lancashire. These firms and their subcontractors were said to be acquiring petrol to which they had no right and supplying it to others who certainly had no right to it.

The investigation and report were the work of Arthur Fox, Chief Petroleum Inspector for the North-West and major cog in the fuel rationing machine. They resulted in 299 charges being brought against the defendants in respect of 145,000 gallons of black market petrol, and contraventions of the Motor Fuel Rationing Order. The charges were reduced to 281 at the trial because some individual defendants had died since the investigation began.

The firms had an ingenious and simple answer. They were contractors for the Ministry of Supply, therefore they were agents of the Crown. Petrol rationing did not apply to them. The legal tag that 'the King can do no wrong' was nowadays to be taken as applying to 'officers of the Crown'. As contractors and agents for the Ministry of Supply, the firms had become officers by proxy. They could do no wrong in such matters as the petrol ration.

This argument was swept aside. As counsel for the Crown insisted, it was absurd to suggest that a humble office-cleaner in a government department might become a black marketeer and when arrested say, 'You cannot touch me, I am an agent of the Crown.' After that, the conviction of the defendants was a formality. However, the issue of black market petrol was soon eclipsed by questions regarding the principal witness for the Crown, Arthur Fox, Chief Petroleum Inspector for the North-West of England, the stern-faced man who had hunted the offenders and written the report.

When cross-examined about his profession Mr Fox admitted he was not a career civil servant. Until the war he had been, however improbably, a theatrical agent and had been in business with his wife as the International Theatrical Corporation. It was suggested to him that he had not been a mere theatrical agent but he insisted upon the fact. He was then asked if he had ever stood in the witness box before and he denied it. The cross-examiner rephrased the question and Mr Fox admitted reluctantly that he had been in court before, though not in the witness box. Indeed, he had stood in the dock not long before the war, charged and convicted of running an unlicensed and illegal theatrical agency.

That was not the worst. It was alleged by witnesses at this earlier trial that he had tried to entice young girls to go to Brazil, while earnestly advising them not to say anything to the consular authorities about the nature of their journey. Mr Fox explained that he had not gone into the witness box to deny these accusations because his counsel had advised him not to. Not only had the accusations been made in court. By November 1938, the London County Council was so concerned over the white slave potential of such companies as Mr Fox's that it had introduced by-laws to curb these bogus theatrical agencies.

At Newton-le-Willows in 1941, the Crown listened with dismay to these revelations by a senior official of its petrol rationing hierarchy. There was more to follow. Mr Fox admitted that he held bank accounts in several false names, that he welshed on bookmakers, and had been managing director of 'The International Oil Company' in Manchester, which had gone conveniently bankrupt several years earlier. He did not mention the white slave accusations or any of his other 'difficulties', as he described them, when appointed to the Petroleum Board.

And still that was not quite all. It was scarcely encouraging for the Board of Trade to hear Mr Fox admit further that a large number of documents in another current prosecution of his had gone missing, and that some of them had been stolen.

The petrol prosecution had been intended to show the government's determination to deal severely with the mightiest firms in the land. Instead, by March 1941, the Board of Trade's first major petrol trial was foundering among the shoals of 'white slavery' headlines. It was not a good beginning. The public was regaled as much by the incompetence of the Board and the government as by the criminality of the accused. 'This is a case which should never have been brought,' said Mr St John Hutchinson for the defence, 'a prosecution misconceived by a government department and run by a man who should never have been employed by a government department.' Hutchinson described Fox as

> a miserable underling who has been mixed up with bankrupt concerns and unpleasant police court proceedings . . . When this case opened we thought that Mr Fox was only some over-zealous red-tape worm, but now that we have learned something of his past I suggest it is a matter of great public importance that a man in his position should have a speckless past, and should be a person who can be trusted.

Contravention of the Motor Fuel Rationing Order was a strict liability offence, so that there was no way in which the firms and individuals prosecuted in this case could escape conviction, once their claim to Crown immunity had failed. However, they were fined more leniently than they could have hoped, £297 (£11,880) in respect of 158 offences, and the firm abandoned their appeal. Their counsel demanded that the court should comment on the 'people involved' in the Board of Trade's case. Mr Fox was sacked next day as Chief Petroleum Inspector for the North-West.

Geoffrey Lloyd, Parliamentary Secretary to the Petroleum Board, was tight-lipped in the House of Commons when challenged over the appointment of his chief inspector. He had no reason to suspect Arthur Fox's past. Fox had been 'recruited through the usual channel of the Ministry of Labour for temporary government employment'. The Labour Exchange had sent him. He had three references as to character and abilities, one from a man who knew nothing about his 'difficulties' and, more surprisingly, two from men who knew about them but still thought him the right man to be a Chief Inspector of Petroleum.[2]

The case was not easily forgotten. In the House of Commons on 2 June 1942 the Labour member for Maryhill, J. J. Davidson, questioned the Joint Parliamentary Secretary to the Ministry of Works. He asked about the department's employment of 'important officials from such firms as Lindsay Parkinson & Co., and Wimpeys – men who have been convicted in the courts for serious petrol offences'. He noted that the first firm owned Oddenino's, a well-known restaurant in Regent Street. Now that its officials were to have ministerial employment, would 'meetings or functions that are arranged' take place in Oddenino's?

It might be thought that Arthur Fox's appointment was an isolated error of judgement. Yet, as the war went on, it became evident that in the rush to recruit staff, government departments had taken on professional criminals, some with impressive prison records. Indeed, on 25 February 1942 the NAAFI admitted that it had been obliged to recruit many more staff after Dunkirk and that members of criminal gangs had taken jobs which put them in the best position to rob NAAFI stores. A month earlier, the scandalous increase in theft from the railways had been attributed to gangs placing members among railway staff.

A year after Arthur Fox, and only a few miles away, another senior official appeared in court. This time he was in the dock. The Admiralty had needed an area storekeeper, in charge of its storage depots in the North of England. It chose Vincent Furlong, forty-five years old and apparently well qualified. After a while, equipment began to disappear and finally 15,000 batteries valued at £3,000 (£120,000) went missing from a store in the North-West.

A police investigation revealed that the batteries had been sold by Vincent Furlong to two transport managers and a lorry driver, who was to collect and deliver the booty. The wholesale thefts which he committed in the naval stores were not really surprising. Furlong had only been out of prison two months when the Admiralty appointed him to the custodianship of this Aladdin's Cave.

In December 1942, Furlong was sent back to prison, to penal servitude for five years. Two of his customers went to penal servitude for three years and one to prison for eighteen months. Mr Justice Oliver wondered aloud, in Furlong's case, how a man with 'a disgraceful record of convictions for dishonesty' was given charge of 'storehouses protecting millions of pounds' worth of government property . . . Isn't it up to someone to inform the Admiralty of a man's character?' It was a sentiment echoed by judges and magistrates in a variety of cases before the war was over. On this occasion, Inspector Whittingham, who had led the investigation, could only say that the police had written to the Admiralty asking if they had made inquiries about Furlong before he was appointed, but the

Admiralty had not replied. 'It does not exactly help the war,' the judge said gloomily.[3]

This question of how such a man could be appointed was often asked elsewhere. In the call-up blackmail case of November 1940, how had Maurice Miels, a man with convictions for fraudulent conversion and receiving, been given a responsible job at the Ministry of Labour? At Clerkenwell magistrates court on 14 October 1942, a firm dong work for the Admiralty demanded to know why the Labour Exchange was sending them workers with no warning that the men had criminal records. For that matter, why did the Metropolitan Police recruit as a wartime policeman and plain-clothes officer John Reginald Halliday Christie, future serial killer of Rillington Place? A glance at their records would have told them that he had convictions and prison sentences for theft, false pretences and malicious wounding, stretching back to 1921. It was under the cover of his police uniform in 1943 that Christie turned from lesser crimes to the murder of his first young woman.

To civilian racketeers, the Admiralty had long appeared an easy target. Civilian and naval partnership in wartime had a particularly unhappy history. In 1808 Nelson's fleet, two-thirds built by private contractors, had brought 'a stink of corruption' to the nostrils of the First Lord of the Admiralty, Lord St Vincent. On launching, only the visible heads of expensive copper bolts secured the hulls of many wooden warships, built for a third of the price claimed from the government by the contractors. Among such casualties during the Napoleonic wars, HMS *York* and HMS *Blenheim* disintegrated on the high seas with the loss of their crews. Victualling the ships was equally lucrative. In India, food put ashore as 'condemned provisions' was repackaged by vendors. Landed and sold repeatedly, these rotting cargoes sailed the seas 'at the expense of the public', as the official report put it.[4]

In the dockyards and ship repair yards of such cities as Liverpool during the Second World War, this odour of corruption lingered. On the night of 30 January 1942 Frederick William Porter, of F. H. Porter Ltd, ship's scalers of Liverpool, shot himself. That afternoon his company's books had been examined by an Admiralty accountant. Porter, a man from whom it was said there emanated 'radiations of treachery, treason, false pretence and conspiracy', was described as 'a master mind in crime'. After his suicide, CID officers investigating suggestions of corrupt practices in his firm at once began a search of 'lakeland strongrooms', the vaults of banks in towns and villages of the Lake District. Dispersed among small branches of banks in the area they found deed-boxes with Porter's name on them. Inside were banknotes, many in small denominations but in very large sums, to a total value of £308,000 – or rather more than £12,000,000 by present values.

The police were still checking the contents of boxes when the case came to the magistrates court and had not had time to finish counting the quantity of currency found. They had reason to think that the notes counted were less than two-thirds of the total which Mr Porter had stored since the beginning of the war. They had yet to discover how he had probably made, by present values, some £20,000,000 in a couple of years, unknown to the authorities. Mr Porter was no longer available for questioning, but the officers believed that he had deposited even larger sums of money in places where they might never be found. He could have financed the building of a warship out of his own pocket.

Those arrested in the case soon included a Liverpool city councillor who was also a director and manager of F. H. Porter, a woman who was the company secretary, a Royal Navy commander, a marine superintendent, the Senior Naval Inspecting Officer for the Ministry of War Transport, the Admiralty Recorder of Plymouth Dockyard, and the assistant secretary of Liverpool Football Club, who also represented the Merseyside Ship Repairers' Federation.

This fraud had grown from modest beginnings, in which timber was stolen from Grayson Rollo and Clover Docks Ltd, ship repairers, to make good the marine superintendent's bomb damage. It also built the naval commander a luxurious underground air raid shelter in his basement, and provided new gates for Woolton Golf Club. Part of the stolen timber was stored at the club, on the pretext that it had been moved from the ship repairers' during an air raid 'for safety'. Labour and other materials were also supplied unwittingly by Grayson Rollo and charged for as work being done on behalf of the Admiralty. In a parallel case, F. H. Porter Ltd were accused of providing members of the conspiracy with ration-free petrol for private motoring.

From this scheme, a fraud developed which was variously called 'colossal', 'astonishing' and 'stupendous'. The officer from the Ministry of War Transport directed work to the firm. Frederick Porter then charged for the wages of two thousand men to work on ships urgently needed for convoy duty, while paying only eight hundred. He was thus able to embezzle some £5,000 (£200,000) a week, the wages of a non-existent workforce. In this he had the assistance of his fellow director, the company secretary, the representative of the federation and the two naval officials. The direct victims of the scheme were the Admiralty itself and Grayson Rollo, the ship repairers. This was 'money which belonged to the nation . . . Mr Porter is known to have changed small notes into notes of larger denominations, packed them in deed-boxes, and stored them in strongrooms of banks in the Lake District.' He was seen leaving his office at the end of the week bowed under the weight of a large suitcase containing the unissued pay packets. Neither his son nor his daughter-in-law knew the details of the scheme. When he showed them the strongrooms in which some of the deed-boxes were kept, he maintained that he was afraid of a German invasion and that they would now know where to find money if that should happen.

The conspiracy was aided by the urgency and to some extent the confusion of getting ships ready in time to join their convoys by the appointed date of sailing. The city councillor, who was also managing director, had told the foreman to send insufficient men to various jobs in order to 'kill' the work and prolong the task, so that the Admiralty paid for even more phantom workers to be taken on.

The case was of great complexity, running in tandem with prosecutions for illegal use of petrol. There were a hundred witnesses for the Crown and it was almost a year after Porter's suicide before it was concluded. Full details were given when the company secretary admitted her part, accusing herself of having stolen £5,000 (£200,000) in a subsidiary operation. She admitted there were two sets of wage sheets, one fictitious and one genuine, and that Mr Porter pocketed the difference.

There was no ingenious defence in this case, indeed no defence at all. In November 1942, the Liverpool city councillor was sent to penal servitude for nine years with a fine of £10,000 (£400,000), the senior naval official for three years, while the less important figures went to prison for periods of nine to eighteen months.[5]

To claim money from the government for a non-existent work-force, or in the armed forces to claim for non-existent personnel, was an obvious white-collar fraud. In a South Wales case in July 1941, the accused were said to have refined the technique somewhat by listing genuine names for payment by the War Office Contracts Depart-ment. On investigation, these were names of people who were dead. Very often, the firm as well as the government was cheated by its employees. On other occasions, the firm might attempt to bribe departmental officials, sometimes in very small sums. When James Keighley, a Ministry of Supply inspector, inspected army battle-dresses made by H. Berg Ltd in Stepney, on 9 January 1941, the owner and his sister tried to persuade him to pass sub-standard uniforms by pressing a ten-shilling note into his hand as he was leaving and adding, 'We hope you will take it, but do not say anything about it.' Another official alleged that after he had left the Gilpin Electric and Radio Factory, he found £45 (£1,800) in his notebook.[6]

In Liverpool, the troubles of Grayson Rollo and Clover Docks Ltd were not over. Eight months after the leaders of the war contracts conspiracy went to prison, another 'Colossal War Fraud' appeared in the headlines in July 1943. Timekeepers at the ship repairer were alleged to have collected tens of thousands of pounds by entering sums as wages, though these were never paid. By 1944, a subsidiary racket, code-named 'the minesweeper', was discovered. Drillers working on the ships were invited to donate two shillings and six-pence to certain officials, in return for which they would be entered as having worked after they had gone home or before they arrived. If they refused to pay this money, they were sent to another of the firm's docks, known to them as 'the concentration camp', where they were only paid for the time they worked. This scheme was revealed when John Plaistow, who refused to join it, alleged that he had left his job because the organizer of the swindle told the rest of the workers that he was 'the main one responsible for giving the show away'.[7]

The victims of frauds were often major firms. A number of 'big names' were targeted in other fields, as when Hydro Dividers Ltd, subcontractors to the Air Ministry, extracted £25,000 (£1,000,000) by false pretences from both the Bristol Aeroplane Co. and Rootes Motors Ltd, as a result of which both the managing director and the works manager of Hydro Dividers went to prison in October 1944.[8]

In some cases, a reputable firm might be compromised by the criminality of its employees rather than by senior management. In March 1940, for example, Mrs Yvonne Reekie of Bovingdon was detained while driving through Watford in her Rolls-Royce with enough sugar to provide rations for 140 people. This hundredweight of sugar had been sold to her by the branch manager of John Kay Ltd in Watford, a well-known grocery chain with 125 branches, its headquarters in the City of London. 'This company is not a tinpot concern trying to make quick money or trying to skip round the regulations,' its counsel protested. Unfortunately the Watford branch had also sold an illegal quantity of sugar to an importunate customer, Mr J. W. Shirley, who subsequently proved to be a Ministry of Food inspector. The firm was fined £175 (£7,000) and Mrs Reekie £75 (£3,000).[9]

Branch managers or subordinates engaged in black marketeering unknown to their head office or directors. They sometimes traded in goods obtained from other premises. It would not have occurred to most people in the autumn of 1941, however, that the place to buy black market raincoats and other garments without coupons was Lloyds Bank in Gracechurch Street. Sir Maurice Jenks, at the Mansion House hearing, confessed himself 'amazed'. Not only were these garments black market, they had been stolen in the first place from S. W. Silver & Co., a firm of outfitters in Eastcheap. One of the clerks at Gracechurch Street said candidly, 'I have seen all sorts of clothing offered for sale in the bank. It was done quite openly.' He had bought his own clothes from a bank official who was one of the three men prosecuted.[10]

Some employees exploited their places of work, others accepted punishment on behalf of their firm in return for the favours it might show them in future. There was considerable interest when Grosvenor House, Park Lane, was prosecuted in May 1943. In February, the restaurant had obtained almost six times its quota of fish, much of it high quality and including an extra ton and a half of salmon, which it sold to its more favoured customers. It was clear to the Marlborough Street magistrate that, though the buyer and the assistant catering manager appeared in the dock, they were being sacrificed on behalf of the firm. 'This is a scandalous case. If I could send a company to prison, I would send Grosvenor House. The ordinary citizen is lucky if he gets any fish at all, and the sort he does get is frequently of a sort not considered fit for human food before the war.'

Unfortunately, Mr Sandbach could do no more than fine Grosvenor House £500 (£20,000). The buyer went to prison for six weeks and the assistant catering manager for a month. Mr Sandbach was left to mutter his suspicions from the bench.

> There seems to be general agreement that whoever is to blame Grosvenor House is not. I think they are the worst offenders of the lot. Major Black, the managing director, allows the blame to be thrown on Smith and Abbott who, I am told, make nothing out of it. But they stand well with Grosvenor House if they make their departments pay.[11]

The prosecutions of well-known firms and individuals remained an inflexible strategy of the people's war. Two Cities Films, makers of such classics as *In Which We Serve*, *Odd Man Out* and *Henry V*, were tried and convicted in January 1941 for making improper use of £2 worth of petrol in an emergency, while filming for the Ministry of Information. Before the year was over, J. Sainsbury had been convicted of selling meat without coupons, ten West End stores including such famous names as D. H. Evans and Swan & Edgar had been prosecuted for taking loose coupons rather than cutting them from ration books. Woolworths was subsequently convicted of breaking price regulations for various articles in its Bond Street store.[12]

The most famous name in language-teaching by post, Linguaphone, was one of several companies convicted of the awesome-sounding offence of trading with the enemy. The Linguaphone Institute Ltd was fined £1,000 (£40,000) and its managing director £500 (£20,000) for having sent gramophone records to New York in 1940 for sale to Norway and Sweden. Following the German occupation of Norway, these had found their way to the markets of the enemy. The managing director of Linguaphone did not know that there would be any breach of regulations in sending the records to the United States but, once again, this was a strict liability offence and no excuses could be accepted.[13]

In similar circumstances, Carters Ltd, well-established City of London merchants, were convicted because goods sold to Paraguay were resold to the enemy. Another major case in January and February 1941 depended on whether the directors realized that by supplying rubber to their Swedish subsidiary, they might be aiding the German war effort. In the end the jury acquitted the defendants on three counts. It could not agree on the remainder.[14]

While such prosecutions reminded the public that the war was a serious matter, those which drew most publicity were trials of famous faces for 'currency racketeering' and similar offences. In the autumn of 1941 public attention was turned upon two of the most renowned names of the inter-war stage and screen, George Arliss and Noël Coward. Both were prosecuted under the Defence (Finance) Regulations.

Arliss was seventy-two and, born in England, had spent his screen career in Hollywood before retiring to London. His crime was to have held a number of United States and Canadian securities valued at £13,160 (£526,400) without registering them when war began. Dollars, vital in financing the supply of arms and food from the United States, were to be offered for the Treasury to purchase. It was pointless for Arliss to plead that he had never intended to break the law and did not realize he had done so. At the Mansion House court, before the Lord Mayor, he pleaded 'guilty subject to mitigating circumstances', and was fined £4,500 (£180,000), more than a third of his investments.[15]

No offender was more famous than Noël Coward. His latest play *Blithe Spirit* was a current West End hit, while he was writing, directing and starring in a film *In Which We Serve* which *Newsweek* described as 'One of the screen's proudest achievements at any time and in any country'. Coward was to win an Academy Award for his portrayal of Lord Louis Mountbatten, whose destroyer, the *Kelly*, was sunk under him. Of the charges against Coward, one was for failing to offer to the Treasury dollars brought back from a visit to the United States made on behalf of the government. Coward had been an unofficial ambassador, using his influence with individuals to reinforce the blockade on Vichy France and to check the activities of German sympathizers in San Francisco. For this currency offence he was fined £200 (£8,000).

By careful reading of Coward's autobiography *Present Indicative*, a Bank of England clerk also gleaned details of the author's American investments, made before the war. The bank's investigations showed that no such investments had been notified to it since 1939. When confronted with this, Coward confessed his incompetence in financial affairs. His London office had been 'blitzed' in 1941 and his papers reduced to chaos. However, as soon as he realized he was in breach of the new financial regulations, he had put the matter right. He made to the court what he called a plea of moral innocence, which was accepted. Though he was liable to a further fine of £22,000 (£880,000), the penalty imposed was £1,600 (£64,000).[16]

It was possible to believe in Noël Coward's pose of the unworldy artist. Elsewhere, currency violations were dealt with as major crimes. A month later, Charles Lennard of Hampstead was fined £40,000 (£1,600,000) at Bow Street for failing to offer $112,387 for sale to the Treasury. In November 1942, a fine of £100,000 (£4,000,000) and a month's imprisonment was imposed on Ellis Kahn, who had failed to offer $135,593 for sale. This fine was reduced on appeal to £50,000 (£2,000,000) but the prison sentence was confirmed.[17]

In Noël Coward's case, the Treasury might well have been eager to make a similar example of him. However with 'Lord Haw-Haw' and his associates riding the Berlin airwaves, it was not in the public interest to destroy the hero of a splendid British propaganda film even before it was released.

If Noël Coward had a rival on the West End stage in the 1930s, as playwright, composer of musical comedies and actor in his own right, it was Ivor Novello. In 1944, Novello's crime was not a breach of financial regulations but the misuse of his Rolls-Royce, which he had patriotically converted to a 'gas-producing' car to avoid the use of petrol. Yet though it carried a gasbag on its roof, a small amount of petrol was needed to prime the system. In 1943, when appearing in his musical *The Dancing Years* in the West End, he applied for a licence to use the car to travel home at weekends, so that he might work there. He was still recovering from pneumonia at the time. The application was refused.

A young woman who had been a fan – and a friend – for some years suggested that he should transfer ownership of the car to the firm for which she worked. The firm could apply for a licence to use petrol while he continued to use the car. This was done, though it seemed that no one else in the firm knew what was going on and that the application she made was fraudulent. Whether or not Novello was a party to dishonesty or remained ignorant of the truth was the point of the case. On occasion, he certainly continued to use the car, which was still driven by his chauffeur.

When the arrangement was discovered, he was prosecuted, convicted and sentenced to eight weeks' imprisonment. He appealed against conviction and sentence. The conviction was upheld in May 1944 but the sentence was reduced to four weeks, after character evidence had been heard from Lewis Casson, Dame Sybil Thorndike and Sir Edward Marsh, a former prime ministerial secretary. Though Novello was the only famous name of his kind to go to prison, it seemed doubtful that this had the effect his prosecutors hoped. Because his guilt was far from plain, the case generated as much sympathy as condemnation, a feeling that it had been incited by spite rather than a zeal for justice. On his release, he was received with an ovation by the audience at the next performance of *The Dancing Years*.[18]

Those who suffered the penalty of the law in this way derived particular satisfaction from the downfall of their adversaries. In August 1942, Sir William Jowitt, who as Solicitor-General had been the grim-faced prosecutor of morally innocent but technical offenders guilty of 'trading with the enemy', was himself prosecuted for purchasing animal feed without coupons for his farm in Kent. In the witness box he protested that he 'had not the smallest knowledge that that breach of the regulations was being committed' – an excuse which he had sternly informed other defendants was no defence at all. Then, rather huffily, he added that he had employed a bailiff to run the farm and that 'I have always been taught that it is a very bad policy to keep a dog and bark yourself.' Though these were strict liability offences, the prosecution promised obsequiously that it would not ask for penalties, as Sir William and his co-defendants were 'persons of the highest respectability'.[19]

The most significant name in such prosecutions was a nonentity by contrast with Noël Coward or Ivor Novello. Yet Major-General Sir Percy Laurie, who appeared at Bow Street in 1943, charged with rationing offences, was Provost Marshal of Great Britain, former Assistant Commissioner of the Metropolitan Police and brother of Dr John Laurie, a former Lord Mayor of London. Those who tracked him down as well as those who had been investigated by him felt a certain satisfaction at this turn of events.

The charge was that he held two ration books, one army and one civilian, conduct more often associated with a black marketeer in Stepney or Brixton. Sir Percy had fallen out with a friend whose London flat he had shared. This man, Dennis Capron, later found the two ration books, became 'very excited' and told his secretary, 'I am going to smash Sir Percy. He is drawing two lots of rations.'

Patriotism was no less effective when activated by a dash of malice. Capron did not take the ration books to the police but to a left-wing Labour MP, D. N. Pritt QC. Capron also told Pritt that Sir Percy had mentioned getting his servant, Corporal Hodge, out of the country, so that he should not be able to make trouble over the matter or give evidence. Even before the prosecution began, Mr Pritt had a chance in Parliament to air the sins of the mighty, in this case the gross misconduct of the commander of the nation's Military Police.

The solicitor for the Ministry of Food insisted that when Sir Percy applied for a second ration book, 'There was clear evidence that he knew the statement he was making was false.' His explanation that he thought he was meant to use a civilian book when he was at home and an army one when travelling was unbelievable. 'Where the court has a person in a high position in the Army whose duty it is to see that other people do not break the law, this becomes a graver matter than for an ordinary individual.'

Five days later, the Bow Street magistrate refused to accept that Sir Percy had made 'an honest mistake' and fined him £550 (£22,000) for rationing offences. Sir Percy appealed to London Sessions, where one conviction was quashed and the sentences on the other two reduced to nominal fines. However, those convictions remained. Like so many defendants, he insisted that he 'had not the slightest idea that he had done anything wrong'. Unfortunately, this was no more a defence for the Provost Marshal than for a man selling coupon-free stockings in Berwick Street market. It was announced that his future was being considered but, in any case, his tour of duty as Provost Marshal came to an end in 1943.[20]

Headlines were made by the courtroom martyrdom of important people or by Frederick Porter's fortune lying in strongrooms in the Lake District. Yet such cases were comparative rarities. Week after week in the magistrates courts, and month by month at assizes or quarter sessions, the ordinary people of Britain were represented by more or less ambitious pilferers and dishonest employees. Grayson Rollo, the Bristol Aeroplane Company, the Admiralty, the War Office and the Air Ministry were all victims of financial swindles, which might operate in much the same way in peace as during war.

While Sir Lindsay Parkinson & Co. were dealing illegally in petrol, the firm itself was being systematically robbed by part of its workforce, engaged in building a large army camp in Hampshire. The scale of the dishonesty was such that sixty Scotland Yard officers were put on the case. One of them, Detective Constable Marchant, was an undercover officer, posing as a carpenter. Twenty-eight of Parkinson's employees at the camp were arrested. One man, another carpenter, Marchant had watched carefully and had never seen him do any work at all for the firm. Instead, he alleged, the man was stealing the firm's plywood and planks and making children's swings and gas-mask cases, for which there was a ready sale in the neighbourhood. 'The gas-mask cases were made from plywood obtained from stripping blackout boards and the swings from planks of various sizes.'[21]

The same philosophy of make-do-and-mend prevailed at Aberdeen crematorium from the outbreak of war until April 1944. The managing director and a helpful undertaker were then arrested for stealing 1,044 coffin lids, seven coffins and a number of shrouds. The Edinburgh courtroom was stacked high round the bench of the Lord Justice Clerk with coffins, coffin lids, shrouds and wooden name-plates, allegedly part of the booty. At the crematorium, when coffins were lowered to the vault, the lids were removed before they passed to the furnace. These lids, along with coffins and shrouds, were then sold. In a time of shortage, they were turned into desks, radio cabinets, rabbit hutches and seat-boxes. The undertaker alleged that some of those who worked at the crematorium also removed lids and handles from coffins before cremation, so that they might be sold back to funeral directors. The managing director of the crematorium told the police that this purloining of coffin lids and other items was what he called 'usual procedure' all over the country, including the prestigious crematorium at Woking. By disposing of the lids as he did, he was actually 'assisting cremation'.[22]

Most employees preferred to steal items which they could sell without the bother of making them into other articles. Some hauls were large but rare and others small but regular. A number of the biggest thefts were often the work of one individual and originated in unexpected quarters. So, for example, a man charged in 1943 with the steady theft of typewriters from the War Office had made the mistake of offering one to a senior army officer, for which he went to prison for six months. The number and size of the other stolen articles required steady pilfering of their components over a period of time. In 1943 a man was charged with stealing 1,196 motors, the property of the Ministry of Aircraft Production, from the Lancashire factory where he worked.[23]

As a rule, the items were more homely or immediately useful. In 1942, there was what could only be called mass pilfering of paint, distemper and varnish from Lewis Berger and Sons Ltd of Morning Lane, Hackney. This ended with fines and imprisonment for eleven ringleaders at North London magistrates court on 9 January 1943. Bergers had been at their wits' end to prevent stealing so widespread. 'In August, pilfering was getting so bad that the managing director spoke to the assembled employees and announced that pilfering had to stop, otherwise anyone caught would be prosecuted. A resumé of what he said was also put in their pay envelopes.'

Where the workforce was small, it was possible to search its members as they left. Elsewhere, thieves escaped because workers passed through the factory gates in thousands. It was impossible for police to stop and search more than a few suspects. Bergers had a thousand employees, too many to stop and search, but the disposal of the stolen paint was a far smoother operation.

> There is no doubt that over a considerable period of time paint has been taken by loaders and packers working under the direction of a foreman and passed over to the drivers who disposed of it. The proper price of the paint was thirty shillings a gallon. The people inside got four shillings a gallon which was split between two, and the drivers received fifteen shillings – exactly half the price – from the people who purchased it. Sometimes they had ten shillings.

A curiosity of the case was that all those fined and imprisoned were of previous good character and had worked for the firm for as long as twenty-two years. Before the war they might not have risked so much and would probably not have found a market to make it worthwhile. Times had changed, with a demand for black market paint stimulated by government restrictions. Indeed, the prosecutor made the breach of regulations sound almost as damaging as the theft itself.

> A firm is only allowed by the Ministry of Supply to have decorative paint on a government order, and on a government authorization, and that has to be used on authorized work within a month – and if there is any paint floating about and going to strangers who have no authorization, and it can be identified as Bergers' paint, Messrs Lewis Berger will get into serious trouble for having passed over paint irregularly to improper people. Paint is a controlled article.[24]

Bergers were not alone in their area of London, where heavy losses also occurred at such factories as Cossor Radios and Ever Ready Batteries. In the same court on the same day as the Berger case, a foreman and twelve other employees of Cossor Radios, Islington, appeared on charges of stealing and receiving radios and components. The foreman went to prison nine days later. At Cossor's, pilfering was more widespread than at Bergers. Some of the accused had simply hidden goods under their coats and made a bolt for the gates at knocking-off time, along with seven thousand others. They felt confident of avoiding search in a fast-moving crowd.

The Berger case was a parable of its kind. The prosecution called it pilfering, the magistrate did not. In passing sentence, he spoke of 'wholesale robbery'. Worse, it had been committed in a firm with a good record, by those of previous good character, incited by others who were ready purchasers of stolen goods. In this corruption of day-to-day life and of workers of habitual good character, black market-eers had much to answer for.[25]

During the war and the years of austerity, one black market relied on workers stealing food or cigarettes from their canteens. By January 1945, this form of pilfering reached such proportions that Superintendent Ivor Rees, one of the 'Big Five' superintendents at Scotland Yard, was appointed to tackle 'the works canteen racket'. Ministry of Food undercover inspectors had discovered a factory in the West of England where a van would drive up to the kitchens two or three times a week and drive away again, 'laden with food and sometimes cigarettes', its destination a hotel in a nearby town. In a similar case in 1944, at a factory in the Thames estuary, the food was being sold to various officers' messes in the area. 'It is known that all over the country thefts – not quite so bare-faced perhaps – are taking place in works canteens.'

Once lorry drivers were persuaded to cooperate, the size of such consignments was not an obstacle. In April 1943, Zinkin & Co., of Mare Street, Hackney, were 'pilfered' of bedroom suites and dining-room suites by their transport manager and his accessories. He had persuaded one of the firm's drivers to join him in a scheme, in which they 'worked out' impressive amounts of the firm's major items.

The rewards were substantial. In August 1942, licences for the manufacture of Utility furniture, the only type permitted, were restricted to twenty-two items. Those in greatest need were issued with priority dockets, entitling them to purchase what was essential to them. In such circumstances, the black market in furniture thrived, supplied by looters and thieves. Among these were the transport manager at Zinkin & Co., two drivers and three receivers. As the police inquiry began, however, the thieves and receivers fell out. One driver complained that he had made the deliveries – 'And all he ever gave me was a couple of quid'. The receivers swore they had bought the furniture from strangers in a pub 'in good faith'. The thieves and one receiver went to prison, the others being fined.[26]

Pilfered cargo of greater bulk than bedroom suites and dining suites was on the road. When meat was stolen, or 'diverted', from Avonmouth docks to a Home Counties' café, the total carried on a single journey amounted to sixty carcasses. In a further case from that source, seven men were sent to hard labour by Bristol magistrates for stealing large quantities of food from the railway sidings at the docks. The major items in this haul included half a ton of cheese and a similar quantity of jam.[27]

Those in positions of responsibility were not immune to temptation. As in the case of dishonest ship repairers, the docks offered promising opportunities to men in charge of the wharves. In January 1942, following the imprisonment of two officials entrusted with the supervision of a London wharf, those to whom they sold stolen molasses were convicted on forty charges of receiving, which carried fines of £3,978 (£160,000). In March, another wharf superintendent at London docks was found to be in league with two lorry drivers delivering consignments to a receiver. The load discovered by the police included 109 boxes of dried fruit, thirty containers of tinned meat and a variety of other goods. The accused man refused to name the receiver.[28]

In the same month, the suspicions of the CID were drawn to the house of another guardian of vital supplies in the East End. When raided, it appeared like a well-stocked grocer's shop. Much of the contents were traced to recent thefts. Among other items, the suspect was found in possession of twenty-two bottles of gin, fifty bottles of whisky and brandy, forty tins of milk and sixteen of cream, cigarettes, soap, chocolates, tinned salmon, tinned tomatoes, tinned sardines, tinned fruit, salt, meat, cakes and custard. He had been employed by Kearley & Tonge Ltd, of Durward Street, to combat pilfering.[29]

By no means all offenders in pilfering cases were career criminals. Three offenders were arrested after police descended on an air raid shelter in April 1942. The haul consisted of stolen biscuits, fish paste, scent, toffee and tinned salmon. There were five defendants in the case. The thieves were two boys, aged thirteen and eleven, and a girl of eleven. The receivers were a girl of thirteen and one of eleven. Their curiously assorted haul was the result of systematic raids on railway wagons in the goods sidings. Elsewhere, in January 1942, nine-year-old twins staged a smash and grab raid on a sweetshop in Brixton Road, Lambeth.[30]

Two major sources of pilfered goods throughout the war were the railways and the docks. In January 1942, the official view of railway pilfering was that many thefts carried out by porters and others were organized by outside gangs. The turnover of railway staff caused by the military call-up had facilitated the employment and activities of minor criminals, planted there by their mentors. Their preferred targets among goods in transit were silk stockings, cigarettes and whisky. Two months later, the chairman of the LMS railway company confirmed this general estimate when he warned of whole-sale robbery and pilferage now affecting the network, the thefts encouraged by receivers and black marketeers.

There was another factor in railway crime, omitted from such judgements. Railway pay had been poor in peacetime, something which the National Tribunal for Railway Staff had acknowledged in January 1939. It was a grievance which was to lead to widespread strike action when the war was over. In February 1942, the unions were still arguing for a basic £3 (£120) weekly wage. Not surprisingly, some of those caught pilfering in 1942 had begun stealing before the war and not because of it. Industrial relations were sufficiently poor by 1944, as men and material were being moved into place for the Normandy landings, for a group of disgruntled railwaymen at Leeds to sabotage points on the track so that they would have no work to do and could have 'a lazy time'. This sabotage was what the court called 'an almost incredible plan'. It had been carried out by fouling the points outside the engine sheds and came to light when a locomotive was derailed.[31]

Whether from the railways or the docks, the judges and magistrates were taken aback by the attitude of many of those brought before them as they 'put their hands up to it all'. A foreman cooper employed at a London wharf, where theft was running at record levels by 1943, was sixty years old with twenty-one years' service in his present job. When convicted of stealing a bottle of rum, he showed not the least regret. As he patiently informed the Thames magistrate, before being sentenced to two months' hard labour, 'It is one of those things that happen now and again.' It was hard for the judiciary or magistracy to understand that such 'extras' were as much a perk of the job as a businessman's expense-account lunch.

Despite the spectre of gangland penetration and organized railway thefts, relations between the railway companies and their employees were bad enough for much of the pilfering to be a matter of individual enterprise. Some did very well by it. A Manchester carriage-cleaner, for example, augmented his modest wages by glancing round Victoria station for available booty as he finished work at night. It was not uncommon for cartons of cigarettes to be waiting in transit on an unattended platform. When this happened, he commandeered the porters' trolley on which they were piled. Then, with a look of purposeful endeavour, he wheeled the trolley along the dimmed-out platform, and home through the blitzed and blacked-out streets. He was caught eventually in May 1941, not because of any vigilance at the station or in the streets but because he drew police attention to himself by disposing of so many wholesale cartons of cigarettes in the city.[32]

It required no enticement by black market gangs to corrupt a forty-two-year-old foreman with twenty-six years' service at Paddington GWR station, who worked quietly and alone to supplement his weekly wage. He had been stealing damaged parcels for years, before being caught in 1944. No one had seemed interested in these parcels and they were there for the taking. As he said before being sent to prison for six months, he had found the temptation too great. Long service was no guarantee of common sense in time of war. An engine driver who was fined and lost his job in 1942 for stealing tablets of soap, scent, rubber heels and similar articles from the locomotive sheds at Stewarts Lane, Battersea, was of previous good character and had been in his job for twenty-nine years.[33]

The way in which these stolen goods were put into general circulation was well illustrated by a case at Guildhall in July 1942. Four men and twenty-three women, employed at a large warehouse in Smithfield, had been running their own black market in rationed clothes stolen from goods in transit by a railway carman. The carman took his profit when he sold these to a warehouseman. The warehouseman then acted as retailer and sold the clothes coupon-free at a further profit to those who worked at the warehouse. Stolen clothes were not the only commodities sold or exchanged in this cooperative venture. 'Inquiries showed', said the Board of Trade solicitor, 'that among those employed at the premises all sorts of rationed goods were distributed and purchased.'

This scheme was discovered when the police stopped and searched a man leaving the warehouse. They suspected him of carrying concealed goods and naturally assumed that he had stolen them from his employers. Instead, they found his illegal purchases from the warehouseman. With that, the entire conspiracy began to unravel. The twenty-seven defendants pleaded that the railway carman had told them these were damaged goods and therefore no coupons were required. Unfortunately, this courtroom excuse had worn thin by 1942.[34]

The efforts of railway and civilian police failed to check the increase in wartime theft. The value of goods stolen from the railways reached an annual total of £1,000,000 (£40,000,000) for the first time in 1943. After that, it almost doubled in the first nine months of 1944 to £1,757,750 (£70,000,000). Indeed, this figure represented the sum paid by insurance companies, rather than the total value of goods stolen. The north–south lines were by far the worst, the LMS reporting £887,500 (£35,500,000) and LNER £526,000 (£21,040,000) worth of goods stolen, compared with £235,000 (£9,400,000) for the GWR and £109,250 (£4,370,000) for the Southern.

On 20 July 1942, the Chairman of the South-Western magistrates court concluded that 'railway yards are Augean stables of theft.' Railwaymen naturally resented such comments and when a motor driver was dismissed following allegations of theft at the Nine Elms depot on 5 October 1942, four hundred men ignored the war and came out on strike. Industrial relations on the railways retained their bitterness. In July 1946, when two men at the LNER Bishopsgate depot were dismissed for eating two tomatoes and thereby stealing them, 1,500 men struck.

Criminal charges frequently related to black spots on the Southern Railway lines out of Waterloo and South London. The Bricklayers Arms depot had a bad reputation for theft. For the six months to November 1941, the loss of cigarettes and beer totalled £10,200

(£408,000), according to evidence given on 26 November 1941 at Tower Bridge magistrates court, when two men from the depot were convicted of stealing silk stockings. At the trial of six women in July 1942, the value of all goods currently being stolen from the depot was said to be running at £1,000 (£40,000) a month, the equivalent for the whole of the Liverpool docks.[35]

Elsewhere, individual cases rivalled this. When two men were sent to prison in October 1941, it was revealed that silk stockings to the value of £1,000 (£40,000) a week had been lost in transit between Watford and St Albans. One of the thieves was a shunter and the goods yards had been his natural hunting ground. As the war went on and the goods yards were more closely guarded, some thieves either boarded goods trains halted by signals or else stopped them at the signals. In July 1942, Detective Ritson of the Southern Railway police admitted that 'There has been a considerable amount of theft recently. Trains have been stopped at signals and wagons ransacked while in transit.'[36]

Prison sentences were now regularly passed. It made no difference in one Bricklayers Arms case that the defendants were six married women, from Bermondsey, Camberwell and Clapham, five of them with children to care for. They were gaoled for two months each for what the magistrate called 'a form of petty treason in war-time'. The persistence of such thefts in the face of growing shortages had hardened the views of judges and magistrates since 1940, when Southern Railway employees had escaped with fines of £2 for handling stolen goods, the contents of stationary wagons robbed in the blackout.[37]

In response to what the police called 'very heavy thefts' from the railways in 1943 and 1944, more trials passed from the petty jurisdiction of the magistrates courts to the Old Bailey, where prison sentences were imposed ranging from one to four years. Yet not all criminals who stole from the railways were railway employees and by no means all were men. The conscription of women for work of national importance added to the number of female defendants. For example, when twenty-five accused appeared before the Guildhall magistrate on 8 July 1942, twenty-two were women and all were employees of a warehouse which handled clothes in transit, rather than employees of the railway itself.

Similarly, when members of a small all-female gang were sent to prison at the Old Bailey in December 1944 for 'wholesale theft of suitcases from Paddington, Waterloo, and other mainline stations', they were not railway employees but professional freelance thieves with a list of previous convictions. 'Thefts from the railways have got to be stopped,' said the Marylebone magistrate three weeks later in another 'suitcase-and-parcels' trial, this time gaoling an army private. It seemed unlikely that they would be.[38]

Security of access to the railways was difficult. The war had emphasized the problem but not created it. However, where the problem was at its worst, the police set up surveillance, as at Devons Road railway sidings in Bow. This was done in response to what Detective Sergeant Charman, at the trial of an engine fireman, described as 'enormous losses'. The defendant seemed to take it all in good part. 'I want to put my hands up to it all,' he said amiably, going to prison for six months for three robberies on the trucks. Security failed to improve as the war continued.[39]

Pilferers were augmented by those who came to rob with their own transport. When the West London magistrate, Sir Gervase Rentoul, demanded in February 1943, in a case of stolen wheat, how it was possible for two youths to be able 'to load their van with these heavy sacks and drive out without being challenged', it remained a rhetorical question. There was a further instruction to 'tighten up' the watch upon railway yards, for what good that would do.[40]

Threats, exhortations, exemplary sentences failed to coerce what the Old Street magistrate in 1944, in a case of batteries stolen from Spitalfields LNER depot, called 'this blackguardly minority who won't stop stealing'. Setting the total annual thefts against the number of prosecutions, the chance of being caught or punished was very remote. Given such opportunities and the low-wage economy of the railways, the criminality of the pilferers was perhaps much less remarkable than the honesty and patriotism of the great majority.[41]

7

Under the Counter

Until the end of rationing, there remained a universal belief that good things were available under the counter for the favoured few or for those willing to pay a little extra. The first scattered evidence of a black market was reported in the autumn of 1939. Yet from the spring of 1941 until the early months of 1942 'racketeering' was perceived by Parliament and public as so widespread and blatant that flogging, shooting and indefinite imprisonment were held to be the best response.

While black marketeers had been made liable to a maximum sentence of fourteen years in prison, rationing regulations had also proliferated since the beginning of 1941. The misery of shortages replaced the heroism of the blitz. Bacon, sugar and butter had been rationed since January 1940. Margarine, jam, syrup and treacle were rationed in March 1941, followed by a cheese ration of one ounce per week in May. Fresh meat had been rationed by price rather than weight and the least edible portions were not rationed at all. Under the Defence Regulations, the Ministry of Food retained the power to vary the size of these rations from time to time. Indeed, it was still doing so until the spring and summer of 1954. Similarly, in order to ration or de-ration items of food as quickly and as flexibly as possible, ration books in 1941 contained a number of 'points' coupons for less essential items. This form of rationing was also to last until 1950. 'Points' enabled a shopper to spend these coupons with some freedom of choice, provided the items were available. Throughout 1942, tinned food, biscuits, cereals and other foods were withdrawn from general sale and became available only 'on points'. Soap was also rationed.

Sweets were not rationed until 26 July 1942, when they were restricted to two ounces a week, while the manufacture of ice cream became illegal from 30 September that year. The government was content to allow tobacco and drink to be rationed by scarcity. Bread was not to be rationed until 21 July 1946, as the result of a world shortage of wheat, though the coveted 'white loaf' had turned grey long before the end of the war.

To the professional criminal, food by weight or bulk was not of great value. Moreover, the trade was undermined by an illegal market in ration books themselves. Food coupons were not worth forging when they could be easily stolen. A more promising development was clothes rationing which was introduced on 1 June 1941, accompanied by the restriction of all clothes to 'Utility' standard. Children received a separate ration, the number of coupons dependent on age, height and weight. In May 1943, the annual clothing coupon allowance was cut from forty-eight to thirty-six per adult, when a coat rated eighteen coupons and a pair of children's shoes two. Later the number of coupons was cut to twenty.[1]

The allowance of petrol for 'pleasure' motoring ended in the summer of 1942, following the Japanese occupation of Malaya and the success of U-boat attacks on Atlantic convoys. Only those who could prove a business need were allowed a 'supplementary' ration, with penalties for misuse. The loss of the Malayan rubber plantations also brought a crisis in the supply of tyres. From April 1942 these were available only for approved use, one tyre issued for each used tyre handed in. Most drivers lost the use of their vehicles for the rest of the war and petrol joined clothing as well worth the attention of the speculator.

Bitterness towards racketeers coincided with bad news round the world. Despite heroic resistance by the small Greek army, Yugoslavia, Greece and Crete were lost in the spring of 1941. The Eighth Army was in retreat before Rommel's North African offensive. Losses at sea included the aircraft carrier *Ark Royal*, the battleships *Barham*, *Prince of Wales* and *Repulse*, as well as the battlecruiser *Hood* in the action against *Bismarck*. Convoy losses threatened starvation. In March 1941 the Communist-led 'People's Convention' met in London to demand an ending of the war. The government chose not to ban the demonstration.

Though the Soviet Union became an ally following the German invasion of June 1941, it was not certain that Stalin's Russia would be an asset rather than a liability. Planes and armour were diverted to the Eastern Front as the enemy encircled Leningrad in September and German tanks were reported only sixty miles from Moscow in October. Even the American entry into the war in December 1941, after Pearl Harbor, was balanced by the loss of Malaya, Singapore and much of Burma to a semi-feudal Asian enemy. Imperial humiliation threatened strategic catastrophe. With this in mind, the black marketeer of 1941–2 was unlikely to be seen as a cheeky but amiable 'Jack the Lad'.

Such men were now denounced as 'traitors', 'saboteurs' or robbers of the nation's food, a single class for whom there could be no excuses. When two tins of pilchards were sold for five pence above the controlled price in May 1941 by Cohen's Cash Stores in Camden High Street, the Clerkenwell magistrate called it 'a treasonable act'. He regretted that as the law stood he could only fine the firm £20 (£800). Fines were not the answer. A month later Ministry of Food inspectors dismissed fines as 'ludicrous' and demanded the imprisoning of offenders.[2]

The Mayor of Stepney, George Chamberlain, went further. 'I would shoot profiteers against the wall for taking liberties with the food of the people,' he told his local Food Committee in June 1941, on the day that the Germans captured the city of Minsk, after less than a week of the Russian war. All black marketeers were now major criminals. In the following month the Secretary of the London Chamber of Commerce warned the government that food racketeers might become 'like USA gangsters', unless checked. In September 1943 the Old Bailey trial of a food supplier was held in camera, as though it were a case of espionage or treachery.[3]

The autumn and winter of 1941 brought scandal as well as complaint to the ears of a beleaguered government. On 11 October, news broke that a chief source of black market supplies was none other than the Ministry of Food. The goods in question had been 'salvaged' intact from docks and warehouses damaged in the blitz. They were requisitioned by the ministry, which then discovered that it had no organization to dispose of them. The racketeers were more adaptable and, while the NAAFI and government canteens waited, the entrepreneurs stepped in and bought the supplies. A ministry spokesman said defensively that it was natural that his colleagues should sell sal-vaged food to the sort of people 'who bought their goods in this way before the war'. He admitted that the sale had been ill-judged 'in the light of experience'.

No sooner was this embarrassment over than, in December, the press reported a meat racket scandal in a trial at Winchester. Ministry of Food officials had allegedly been involved in conspiring to divert meat supplies through illegal channels. This was confirmed by a series of Liverpool prosecutions in January, when the meat ration had been cut from 2s. 2d. (£4.40) to 1s. 10d. (£3.70) a week.

Because meat was rationed by price rather than by weight or quality, it was often the cause of customer protests. A number of complaints in Liverpool concerned a master butcher, William Alfred Eales, who was put under CID surveillance. He was arrested soon afterwards and at once informed on his accomplices. The conspir-ators had been caught in the middle of a major operation, one of its leaders being Donald Shaw, Ministry of Food supervisor for meat distribution at Warrington. He and Eales were sent to penal servitude for four years. A lorry driver and a docks checker were sent to penal servitude for three years, and two more men went to prison for eight-een months.

Their crimes involved major thefts as well as illegal trading. In this case alone, five refrigerated cargo ships docking at Liverpool had been robbed of 2,153 carcasses of beef and lamb valued at £5,070 (£202,800). The lorry driver would take a ten-ton van to the docks to load fifty carcasses for the Ministry of Food distribution centre. The driver carried £20 (£800) in banknotes, which he gave to the checker. The checker watched the carcasses being loaded but gave no order to the dockers to stop until there were seventy in the van. The driver took them to the distribution centre, where the quota of fifty car-casses was unloaded. The remaining twenty were then driven off and sold to black market wholesalers.[4]

Public disquiet at the conduct of the war on the home front as well as on the battlefields threatened national morale and the government sought to reassure its critics. In December 1941, black market fines were increased to three times the value of the goods or three times the price at which they were sold. In the opinion of most people, such fines were no deterrent to the racketeer, who was not being caught anyway. Even if caught, he would merely lose what he should not have had in the first place and would be back in business the same day. As the voices of vengeance grew harsher, black marketeers and hooch peddlers were the two groups nominated as candidates for capital punishment. The winter of 1941–2 settled down into what the *Manchester Guardian* called a season of 'widespread demands for floggings and firing parties'.[5]

As a more civilized deterrent, it was proposed in the House of Commons on 29 January 1942 to intern racketeers under Defence Regulation 18B, already used to detain enemy aliens, Fascists, and others who were regarded as a threat to the safety of the realm. This was dismissed as inadequate and three weeks later the first parliamentary proposal was made for flogging 'black market operators'. On the same day, in a parallel attack on those having too soft a war, Commander Stephen King-Hall MP advocated making anyone with an annual income of more than £1,000 wait for a year before receiving any clothing coupons.

At length, in March 1942, the War Cabinet ordered the Board of Trade, the Ministry of Food and the Home Office to take action. A department was to be set up to investigate thefts of food from docks and from dumps created for use in the event of a German invasion. The maximum penalty for black marketeering was also to be increased to imprisonment for fourteen years.

By the time the government acted to protect the invasion dumps, it was six months since the thefts had been headlined in the press, when tons of maple syrup from Canada were stolen. There were also allegations that racketeers had borrowed money from their banks to finance their operations. In the House of Commons' debate on 3 March 1942, the government was assured by its critics that public opinion would readily support the cat-o'-nine-tails and 'long terms of penal servitude' for what J. R. Clynes called 'treason of the very worst kind'.

The new powers were reinforced in June. Failure to pay a fine of £500 (£20,000) or more within seven days would lead to the bankruptcy and winding up of any firm, plus twelve months in prison for the defaulter. However, these threats were accompanied by a curious promise, reminiscent of the nursery and the schoolroom, to black marketeers who did the decent thing and 'owned up'. Those who surrendered their hoards or informed on others, within one month of a date to be announced, would be given a free pardon and protection against other gangs. Not a single racketeer appeared to respond to the offer.

The anomalies of food rationing were well known and intractable. Eggs, butter, even meat, were available to country dwellers as they could never be to the population of the cities. In July 1941, East End greengrocers were taking their lorries a relatively short distance into the country to buy vegetables direct from growers. Though they bought potatoes by the ton, there was little to stop them buying butter and eggs illegally from the same sources.

The Poultry Order as drafted in 1942 was routinely flouted, and there was little that could be done. Birds were brought to market, notably Romford which was convenient for the East End, where their sale was permitted only for breeding. After the sale, no one checked what happened to most of them. It was common knowledge, as one MP remarked in a debate on the Order, that birds for breeding were swiftly diverted to dining tables of hotels or restaurants and the West End generally. The Order had never worked and never would. Indeed, the Ministry of Food admitted that it had not the staff to enforce it.

The government's answer was to require all purchasers of poultry at market, or eggs for 'hatching', to sign a form identifying themselves as bona fide breeders, rather as officers and gentlemen could sign the bill when buying clothes without coupons. The marketeers were neither officers nor gentlemen. Many of the 'breeder's' forms scrutinized by ministry officials bore the signatures of 'Neville Chamberlain' or 'Winston Churchill' with the familiar Downing Street address. A similar attempt to curb a black market in Glasgow's stolen bicycles failed at the same time and for the same reason, when almost all the receipts for machines purchased proved to have been signed by 'Joseph Soap'.[6]

Anomalies in clothes rationing were another curiosity. Serving officers could buy without coupons, by signing the outfitter's receipt. When this concession was about to end, eight months after rationing began, tailors sent forms to military customers, inviting them to order without coupons before the loss of the privilege and pay for them later, when the clothes were required.

By contrast, the owner of a Croydon department store was arrested when he displayed a sign in his window, 'Coupons! Why wait? Why worry? Collect what you need here today. How to secure your merchandise now, without coupons.' He invited customers to pay for the clothes and take them away, lodging with the store their new issue of coupons which had not yet become valid. He was successfully prosecuted and fined in June 1943.[7]

Clothes and petrol rationing replaced food controls as a challenge to ingenuity. Yet the garment trade depended so much on outdoor workers in London and the northern cities that it was not easy to supervise. Nor was the work of individual tailors. In April 1943, at Old Street magistrates court, J. C. Marshall, solicitor to the Board of Trade, complained that after two years of clothes rationing most tailors were still disregarding 'with impunity' the cloth-saving provisions of the Making of Civilian Clothing (Restrictions) Order. This restricted the size and number of pockets and lapels, forbade turn-ups on men's trousers, and prohibited frills on women's knickers, among many other provisions. In May 1943, the Old Street magistrate threatened four more tailors from Whitechapel and Hackney with imprisonment if they repeated their offences. Each had made a pair of trousers in 'non-austerity style', two made a waistcoat each, one other had made a jacket. In wartime, the frivolities of fashion were a serious matter.[8]

Simple inspiration added to the supply of garments. As late as February 1944, the Board of Trade banned the manufacture of dust sheets which had not been included in earlier rationing orders. The reason was that the sheets were being used to make clothing. A restriction requiring coupons for curtain material had been added in June 1942, because women were buying the material and making dresses from it. Elsewhere, tailors were ordering cloth for women's dresses and invoicing it as material for making mattress covers. Some of the shrouds stolen from bodies in the furnace vault of Aberdeen crematorium had also provided shirts, blouses and female underwear.

In such areas of public life, the Chancellor of the Exchequer remarked pessimistically in the House of Commons on 24 February 1942, 'It is difficult to think of any arrangement which would not be open to evasion.' That, however, was not supposed to be the mood of the moment.

Many law-breakers were small fry who felt good and urgent reasons for behaving as they did. Looking back on six years of war and the two years of austerity which followed, *The Times* remarked in January 1948 that 'it is through Black Market offences that persons of hitherto irreproachable character graduate in crime.' At one extreme were criminal gangs and conspiracies, at the other was the small shopkeeper or market trader who bought goods for resale 'without asking questions'.[9]

By the end of 1941, small traders were getting the worst of it. Gang members or convicted criminals might install themselves in positions of trust at Admiralty stores or NAAFI warehouses. Yet a Brighton sweetshop owner was prosecuted and convicted on seven counts because an undercover officer of the Ministry of Food persuaded her to sell him four ounces of confectionery as a mixture, rather than as individual types of sweet – 'otherwise than under a Food Committee licence', as the law termed it. Though she had no idea that she had done wrong, the official charged her with the seven offences under the Defence Regulations for which she was tried and convicted.[10]

A similar case followed the ban on the manufacture of ice cream. Two women were convicted of making ice cream from alternative unrationed ingredients, a mixture they had thought entirely legal, for sale in their Notting Hill shops. In March 1943, two men were fined the large sum of £1,000 (£40,000) each for making chocolate couverture, used to decorate cakes, not in accordance with a Ministry of Food licence. The Brighton firm of Allen West & Co. was fined for failing to keep an accurate record of drinks and food used in its canteen, having allowed tea and sugar to be taken out of the canteen by carpenters working too far away to come back for their tea break.[11]

It was the individual trader whom officialdom had in its sights. From the first, the authorities had used their agents in a deliberate effort to see whether small shopkeepers and retailers could be persuaded to break the law. Too often there was an unwholesome enthusiasm among officials who, but for the provisions of wartime regulations, might have been regarded as accessories before the fact.

In November 1940, in an early case of its kind, a young woman went into the Hendon branch of Woolworths and asked for two ounces of tea, a week's ration. She also lamented to the assistant that she had missed the previous week's ration. When the assistant had almost finished serving her, the customer changed her mind and asked for four ounces. The assistant took the money but forgot that she had only cut out a two-ounce coupon from the ration book. The woman left, returning soon afterwards with a man whom most shopkeepers would have recognized as the area's Ministry of Food inspector. His system was to wait in a car round the corner while his team of fifteen presentable and plausible typists or clerks made 'test visits' to see if goods could be bought without coupons. Their target was twenty-five to thirty shops a day and fifty-nine Hendon shopkeepers were being successfully prosecuted.

This method of enforcing the law, or inviting the suspect to break it, was not popular. One butcher recalled the appealing smile of a well-dressed young woman and the question, 'I know I'm not registered here but do you think you could let me have a pound of steak?' Kindness of heart cost him a £20 (£800) fine. In the Woolworths case, the witness was asked in cross-examination, 'You went in there trying to get Woolworths to break the law?' She refused to answer and the court did not require her to do so.[12]

By September 1942, when rationing was at its strictest, undercover officials acting as *agents provocateurs* were more widely denounced. In Chelsea, a Ministry of Food inspector tried to get a restaurant proprietor to serve him with an extra course, so that the man should be prosecuted. In Stepney it was alleged that female undercover officers were deliberately targeting Jewish women who were small shopkeepers, believing them a 'soft touch'. 'Food officials, especially women, are calling on Jewish women and inducing them by hard luck stories to part with their rationed foods without coupons.'

Lord Woolton, as Minister of Food, piously reiterated to Parliament the official instructions on 1 September 1942. 'When test purchases are made, it is important not only that no persuasion of any kind should be used, but that nothing should be said for which it can be afterwards argued that persuasion has been used.' This was confirmed by Hugh Dalton, as President of the Board of Trade, on 8 September. Enforcement officers making test purchases 'should not hold any conversation with the trader about coupons, and should not say anything calculated to arouse the trader's sympathy. The officer should, as far as possible, avoid making purchases from young assistants.'[13]

Neither officialdom nor the courts took much notice of these injunctions as yet. Eighteen months after Mr Dalton's reassurance, an undercover officer of the Board of Trade went into Rales in Western Road, Brighton, to buy a coat. She pleaded with the proprietor that she had no coupons but was willing to pay extra. Eighteen coupons were needed for the coat, half a year's clothing allowance at the time. The price of the coat was £4 (£160), and the proprietor relented, selling it to her for £5 16s. (£232) without coupons. The shop owner was convicted and fined £100 (£4,000), while his unfortunate shop assistant was also fined £25 (£1,000). The court offered no criticism of the undercover officer's conduct. That was not always to be the case.[14]

The honesty of officials in the Food Offices was sometimes called into question more seriously. In April 1943, the Food Executive Officer of Barking Food Control Office had been writing out illegal permits. These allowed grocers to purchase excess sugar, in exchange for loans of money to the official, which he never felt a need to repay. 'Excess' sugar was perhaps an understatement, since he allowed them to buy ten times their allocation. It had started in a public house, when Leonard Blake was introduced to a grocer who complained of the difficulty in supplying the demands of his customers. Before long, Mr Blake was not only forging permits for this man but for four other grocers in the town.

These activities came to light when a clerk in the Barking Food Office noticed that forms which she processed appeared to have been altered by the addition of a nought to the amount allowed, giving the fortunate retailer a tenfold increase in the supply of sugar. Even when his customers were well provided for, there would be a substantial surplus to sell to black market traders. Sir Gerald Dodson, the Old Bailey recorder, sent the Food Executive Officer to penal servitude for three years and sentenced the grocers to lesser terms or fines, remarking with a grim judicial pleasantry that Barking 'must have been knee-deep in sugar with all these permits'.[15]

Sugar remained one of the greatest temptations, even to those in authority. When five receivers were sent to prison at Wealdstone in March 1942, for selling a ton of stolen sugar at three times the permitted price, one of them was a member of the Willesden Food Control Committee and was supposed to supervise the area's rationing system, while another was a War Reserve policeman. They loyally refused to name the thief who was their supplier.[16]

The crimes of most individual shopkeepers consisted either of selling rationed goods without coupons or selling them above the permitted price – often a combination of both. If they had committed these strict liability offences, their reasons for doing so were irrelevant. Yet in the armed struggle of 1941–2, it seemed incredible that even the smallest traders could bring themselves to take part deliberately in black market activities.

The reasons were not unimportant. Those small traders who dealt in rationed goods had naturally found their turnover and profits much reduced. For others, there was rationing by controls, quotas or sheer scarcity. Most household goods and most children's toys were not rationed as food and clothes had been, but were merely unobtainable. By selling them above the permitted price, the retailer was increasing his income when he had little to sell, and perhaps performing a service to a customer willing to pay extra for them.

Many people could afford extra. A persistent difficulty in combating the retail black market was the familiar wartime problem of too much money chasing too few goods. From 1938 to 1944 the cost of living rose by 50 per cent, whilst weekly earnings rose by just over 80 per cent. The government sought to attract this surplus into National Savings by celebrity events like 'Warship Week' or 'Wings for Victory', with targets to be reached and exceeded in every area of the country through sales of National Savings certificates. On 4 June 1941, according to the Chancellor of the Exchequer, Sir Kingsley Wood, the cost of the war had actually fallen by £250,000 a day, but it was still running at a daily total of £10,250,000 (£410,000,000). How much money escaped the war savings net was indicated, for example, by the record profits of greyhound stadiums and the unprecedented amounts staked on the tote, even when racing was restricted to one afternoon a week.

Though the increase in earnings was not evenly spread, many people were prepared to pay more for consumer goods. A scarce electric iron or radio set was not a necessity, but such comforts were worth a few shillings more if they made life easier. Food was not exempt from this calculation. On 20 March 1942, Francis W. Hirst, former editor of the *Economist*, opened a discussion at the Individualist Bookshop, London, with the claim that 'Most people would be glad to buy more sugar than they can get at a shilling a pound or fresh eggs at sixpence . . . orders and regulations produce crimes . . . many I believe are superfluous and mischievous.' If he was right, the campaign against the racketeers appeared ill-starred.

There was a more depressing explanation for the retail black market. The financial victims of war were often small traders and keepers of corner shops. In metropolitan boroughs like Wandsworth, 20 per cent of them had been forced out of business by 1942. The government advised them to 'concentrate', by closing some shops and keeping others open in partnership, but this had not proved workable. A business which could scarcely support one owner was unlikely to support two or three partners. In any case, the government was directly responsible for putting small shopkeepers out of business as what the *South London Press* called 'bothersome cogs in the war machine'.[17]

The powers of the Minister of Food enabled him to order that those retailers who had too few 'registered customers' should no longer be allowed to trade in controlled or rationed commodities. Without that trade, the great majority had no hope of survival. So, for example, on 6 August 1942 seventeen small traders in South London were summoned to appear at Camberwell Town Hall. They were to be informed by the local Food Control Committee, advised by its Enforcements Sub-Committee, which of them would be allowed to continue trading in these commodities and which would be put out of business. Some of those serving on such committees were themselves local retailers and therefore the competitors of those on whom they now sat in judgement.

A War Reserve policeman goes on duty on 8 September 1939 in civilian clothes, plus helmet, panniers and whistle, after finishing his day's work. The police notice warns, 'Air Raid Danger. Conceal Your Lights', with a reminder of the penalty for failing to do so

Above In the aftermath of air raids, furniture and household goods were at risk from organized looting, once their owners had been evacuated to reception centres

Opposite page 'The Bomb Lark.' The rent collector confirmed in evidence that no 'Arthur Victor Thompson' had ever lived at this address. Its ground floor had two rooms, not three. It was derelict long before the date when the fraudster claimed to be 'bombed out'

ASSISTANCE BOARD.
WAR DAMAGE TO PROPERTY.

C.P. No. ....3/13/W.D........

To the Area Officer of the ASSISTANCE BOARD.

Cross Ref. ....

I, THOMPSON, Arthur Victor.................at present living at 49, Lambeth Rd.....................
S.E.1
.... apply for a payment in respect of war damage sustained as a result of enemy action

on......Jan 11.................1941 at 154, Lambeth Bridge Rd, S.E.......

I. Circumstances of household at time of damage.

Members of household.	Age.	Relationship to claimant.	Income : Source and amount.
Thompson, A.V.	39		Pastrycook. 65/- wkly
" Ellen Eliz.	72	Mother	O.A.P. 10/- wkly

II. Extent of damage and immediate requirements.

All rooms demolished by fire

Total loss abt. £90/100

Self	Mother
Overcoat	Coat
Suit	Underwear
Underwear	Stockings
Socks	
Shirt	
Shoes	

III. In case of damage to furniture state number of rooms occupied, location (if necessary), and rent paid.

3 rooms   ground floor
16/6   front.

IV. I declare that to the best of my knowledge and belief the information given above (which has been read over to me) is correct, and that no other application has been made to the Board in respect of this damage.

Witnessed by   W.H. Steward

Signature of claimant   A.V. Thompson

Examined by

Date.....15. 1. 41.
(6464) Ws P1444—7088 80,000 11/40 T.S. 677
(6535—6466) WL P1816—7091 800m 12/40 T.S. 677

W.D. 71 (Dup.)

BRIXTON POLICE STATION,
"L" DIVISION.

27th January, 1941.

STATEMENT OF George W. SCRACE, Rent Collector, of
194, Walworth Road, S.E.

Who saith:

I am employed by Yates Estate Office,
194, Walworth Road, S.E.

I collect rents at 49, Lambeth Road, S.E.

This house has been vacated since 7th
December, 1940, due to enemy action. No person
has lived at that address since. There are only
two rooms on the ground floor. I have never
heard of Arthur Victor Thompson.

(signed)   G.W. Scrace

Statement taken and signature witnessed
by Herbert Fisk, Detective Sergeant, "P" Division.

Windmill Theatre showgirls (in their flimsy attire) wear their gas masks for fifteen minutes daily.

LITTLE MAN YOU'VE HAD A BUSY DAY, *by* **"MOUNTED MANNEQUIN."**

Fetishism goes to war. *London Life* frequently courted prosecution for obscenity but in May 1941 its cover, 'Windmill Theatre showgirls in their flimsy attire wear their gasmasks for fifteen minutes daily', was used to encourage ARP drill

Right Harry Dobkin murdered his estranged wife in 1941 and buried her under the ruin of Vauxhall Baptist Chapel, hoping she would be discovered as an air raid victim. He was hanged in 1943

The wrecked chapel, Kennington Lane, July 1942. Rachel Dobkin was found under floorboards by men clearing the site. Her lower jaw was missing and her skeleton showed evidence of strangulation and dismemberment

Organized thefts from rail depots fed the black market. Superintendent Robert Fabian, 'Fabian of the Yard', carries out an inspection

Some of the ingredients of a second IRA bomb, dismantled single-handedly by Fabian in Piccadilly Circus in 1939. The first had exploded a few minutes before. Fabian was presented with the King's Medal for Gallantry by George VI

Above NAAFI stores and US camps were a source of luxuries obtainable by hook or by crook. Here a Canadian airman sells cigarette lighters from a cigar box in 'Loot Alley', Houndsditch

Right Yardley's wartime labels were counterfeited for illegal and insanitary cosmetics sold to 'Black Market Beauties'. A batch of 6,788 bottles was traced in Cardiff, Swansea and Birmingham in 1944; 3,456 unsold bottles were also found at a Cardiff railway station

Put your best face forward...

To look lovely while you 'look lively' is a big help to good morale,
for good looks and a high heart go together.   Remember, though
Yardley beauty-things usually appear in wartime packings nowadays,
they still have all the qualities you know and trust.

BOND STREET COMPLEXION POWDER
BEAUTY CREAMS · HAND CREAMS
TOILET SOAP (Lavender & Rose Complexion)
LIPSTICK and Refill · ROUGE
TALCUM POWDER (Lavender and April Violets)
They may be difficult to obtain, but they are worth searching for.

Yardley

If you have any war-time beauty problems write to Mary Foster, the Yardley Beauty Consultant. She will be very glad to help you.
YARDLEY · 33 OLD BOND STREET · LONDON · W.1

A cigarette-girl offers 'Players Please' and other brands in a London club. The larger box on the near side of her tray suggests there is no cigarette shortage here

Two of the victims of this system, Arthur Telling and his wife, had traded from their corner shop in Consort Road, Peckham, for thirty years. They seemed to typify 'the backbone of the nation'. Their son was on active service, Mr Telling himself had served for fifteen years in the Army as a young man, and now he was in the Home Guard. 'Small shopkeepers are entitled to be treated like human beings,' he told the press. 'That's what this country is fighting for, isn't it? This is a far wider thing than the bounds of Camberwell.' Mr Telling was correct in his last comment, it was far wider. By August 1942, it had happened all over the country, since this power of putting traders out of business was taken by the minister a twelvemonth before.

In addition, as the General Secretary of the National Association of Outfitters complained in October 1942, small traders had become 'the most persecuted class in the whole of the country' and 'simply the servant of Lord Woolton'. If a small shopkeeper made an honest mistake over regulations and forms, which many lawyers could not decipher, he was 'hauled up before the courts as a profiteer sabotaging the war effort'. In three years of war, there had been 61,785 prosecutions for infringements of Food Regulations and 57,794 convictions so far, some of which had resulted in the licence to trade being withdrawn completely.[18]

It was hard to imagine circumstances under which Mr Telling and his kind were to be shot or flogged, as the hard-liners advocated, or even sent to prison for fourteen years, as the law now provided. Yet the pressure on small traders to save themselves by a little individual black marketeering was considerable and understandable. If they were to be criminalized anyway, some might feel they would take what profit they could. As one of them told J. L. Hodson in 1941, 'Men come to me offering "lines" at fabulous prices. One has been running his car and paying 7s. 6d. a gallon for petrol. Another boasts he makes £400 a week. They come and tempt you – and you know if you don't take the stuff, your competitor up the road will.'[19]

Retail black marketeering had settled down to a wartime routine by the end of the first year of rationing. On 29 May 1941, the Minister of Food, Lord Woolton, described to Parliament the regular deliveries of illegal goods to shops at about 4.30 a.m., the quiet hour of the blackout, between the blitz and the dawn, when cash-on-the-spot deals were done. Retailers placed their orders for the next deliveries and paid money in advance. Some, having parted with the money, never received the goods nor saw their helpful suppliers again. What could they do? Complain to the police or the food office?

Driven to extremes, they found ways of getting even. Leo Friedberg of Finsbury Park went to prison for a year in the month of Lord Woolton's speech for practising this fraud on twenty retail grocers whose premises ranged from Mile End to Maida Vale, and to Gloucester Place in the West End. No individual retailer might complain to the police, but Mr Friedberg dealt with a large number and had become too greedy. Someone had tipped off the law.[20]

By the summer of 1941, this form of black marketeering was persistent enough for courts to impose prison sentences. In June, the Thames magistrate sent a Stepney grocer to prison for two months, describing the offences of selling without coupons and above the permitted price as 'absolutely rampant'.

It was blatant as well as rampant, requiring little detection. In this case Mrs Weinberg, the 'customer' who entered the shop of Issy Marks in Wentworth Road, Stepney, was acting under instructions from the local Food Office, though not employed by it. She was chosen because she had known Marks for a long time and he would not be likely to suspect her. After making other purchases, she asked for butter without coupons. Marks said that he thought someone was watching the shop and told her to come back in a quarter of an hour. When she returned and received the butter, she noticed a female assistant selling rationed eggs from under the counter to customers who offered no coupons. Mrs Weinberg asked for some of these eggs, and was told they were four shillings a dozen – three pence, or 6 per cent, above the permitted price. Little care was taken at the shop to conceal what was going on.[21]

As a rule only the shopkeeper was prosecuted, though a customer might be convicted for making such purchases. When, in April 1941, John Garner Ltd, of Store Street, Bloomsbury, was fined £100 (£4,000) by the Clerkenwell magistrates for selling meat, bacon and butter to an unregistered customer without coupons, the customer was also fined £50 (£2,000) for buying them. In October, Woolworths and a number of hotels in Bloomsbury, including the Grand in

Southampton Row, were fined over £1,300 (£52,000) for buying eggs above the controlled price from a black marketeer who was sent to prison at the same trial.[22]

Even before the government strengthened the law in December 1941 and March 1942, prosecutions and convictions in the retail trade were running high. They seemed to make little impact. In April 1941, under the Food Control Order, 2,300 prosecutions were brought and there were 2,199 convictions, a success rate of 95.6 per cent. In March there had been 2,141 prosecutions and 1,994 convictions, at 93.13 per cent. Yet Mr Marks of Wentworth Road, Stepney, had racketeered happily, as though protected by magic.

An unexpected but natural development was the emergence of organized protests by housewives against the tactics of such retailers. On 10 June 1941, the first Langdale Street Housewives' Circle was formed in Stepney 'to see that working class families have an opportunity to have food at controlled and legitimate prices . . . The food racket is common to the whole country.' There had been some bad cases in the previous month, as the secretary of the circle explained, including the conviction of the London Tea Stores, Tower Bridge Road, whose proprietor was fined the substantial sum of £200 (£8,000) with twenty guineas costs at Tower Bridge court for selling jam, butter and eggs above prices allowed by the Maximum Prices Order.[23]

By the following month, two more housewives' circles had been organized in Stepney, where the problem was one of the worst. Elsewhere in London, street committees followed the Langdale example and concentrated on a boycott of shops which were found to be trading unfairly. The organizers had written letters to Lord Woolton, as Minister of Food, identifying the offenders. In themselves, these measures would not have brought an end to the black market or profiteering but they put further pressure on the government at a time when less temperate voices were advocating the execution or flogging of offenders.

Until the end of 1941, it was the courts rather than the government which seemed to represent the popular will. In July, Mr Justice Stable at Birmingham Assizes had sentenced four men to three years' penal servitude each, for stealing and receiving two tons of butter in 'a deliberately carefully planned robbery'. At last the headlines were able to report 'No Mercy For Food Racketeers'.[24]

During the black market scandals of 1941–2, the authorities again strove to promote the belief that keen-eyed men were on the heels of offenders. The worst of these culprits were businessmen who exceeded their quota of production, disposing of the surplus to illegal traders at a large profit. For 'quota offences' the penalties were severe after the measures of December 1941, increasing the fines and prison terms that might be imposed on defaulters. In March 1942 Isaac Isenberg of Houndsditch was convicted of supplying hosiery in excess of his legal quota. He had exceeded the quota by £2,507 (£100,280) and, as provided for, was fined three times this amount. He could not pay and went to prison.

The fine was just a beginning. On 29 April, Mr Isenberg was back in the dock, alongside the Houndsditch Warehouse Company, Burstins Ltd, S. Brown & Co. Ltd and six more directors, charged with conspiracy to effect black market sales to the tune of £120,000 (£4,800,000). The defendants were also accused, verbally rather than legally, of 'treachery', which had been made a capital offence by legislation two years before. The items sold included stocks of knitwear, trunks, haversacks, so that the quantities involved were as remarkable as their total value. At the end of April fines of £207,201 (£8,288,000) were imposed. Under the existing law, the fines might have been far more but there would have been no chance of collecting them from companies that were now bankrupt anyway.[25]

While illegal supplies might come from smuggling or quota offences, theft was a traditional and dependable means of acquiring goods for the retail black market. Receivers were the key to the trade, middlemen who put the goods into circulation. They proliferated and were caught in increasing numbers until 1944, by which time convictions for receiving were three times the number for 1938. However, before there could be receivers, there must first be robbery.

With the advent of rationing, clothing thieves showed an attention to detail which in peacetime might have been warranted by a jewel or bullion raid. Under cover of an air raid on the night of 11–12 January 1942, for example, a gang targeted the well-protected premises of

A. J. Izod in Hanover Square. With the finesse of a *Rififi* bank robbery, they had previously reconnoitred and identified all the burglar alarms on doors and windows, and the pressure pads. As the bombs fell, with the metal casings of anti-aircraft shells clattering on to the roofs and into the streets, the burglars broke through the ceiling of the show-rooms from premises above. Making a hole 2ft by 1ft, they spidered down into the fashion house, avoiding the alarms, and emptied it of all clothes which required coupons while ignoring the rest. Between the sirens of the 'all-clear' and the winter dawn, they left with their haul as silently and as anonymously as they had come.

Thefts of food had begun in earnest months before the first ration-ing of clothes. The first warning of a 'bootleg food racket' appeared in the press in February 1941 with the news that professional thieves were now specializing in stealing food. The police found it difficult to catch these 'professionals' but were trying to round up their receiv-ers instead.

Considerable quantities were needed to make a food robbery worthwhile. In an early case, four men were sent to prison at the Old Bailey in May 1941 for stealing from a Poplar garage a lorry laden with eight tons of sugar, a cargo that might have seemed unpromis-ing to hijackers in time of peace. Tons of meat were also being stolen by the autumn but these unfortunately carried few guarantees of their origin or freshness. The threats to health were more formidable than those from an elderly chicken, sold for 'breeding'. In North London during 1941, as the meat ration was cut to one shilling's worth a week, both tuberculous and dropsical meat was found to have been used in sausages and put on retail sale by black marketeers. Systematic thefts of liver, condemned as unfit for human consump-tion but kept for 'pharmaceutical purposes', were discovered at Brighton in December 1941. Those convicted of the thefts promised the court faithfully that they had only been supplying the contam-inated meat for feeding to cats and dogs. The evidence indicated otherwise, though how much had been consumed at the dinner table was not established.[26]

A little-known source of extra meat, exploited by Mr L. R. Brightwell, was the flesh of animals that had died at London Zoo, provided the post-mortem showed them to have been healthy. With the Zoo's permission, Mr Brightwell ate his way through wild cattle, deer, antelope, camel, giraffe, elephant (foot and trunk), coypu rat, porpoise and seal. Asked about a four-foot crocodile in 1942, he confided that when casseroled it was 'jolly good', looking and tasting rather like veal but perhaps a little stronger. 'What's more,' he added hungrily, 'it was off the ration.'[27]

Cases involving tons of stolen meat or sugar, or millions of cigarettes, were not uncommon and it was natural to wonder how so much contraband could be moved about cities or round the country without attracting attention. The problem of transport was frequently solved by using 'fake' vans and lorries, as in the looting of Dover. For smaller quantities of stolen goods, vehicles painted to look like newspaper vans were used. They could move quickly in any area without drawing attention. For larger hauls, the livery of Carter Paterson or another major transport firm might reassure the victims and the police.

The Carter Paterson impersonation was used in a major cigarette robbery when two men in a stolen lorry, disguised in the hauliers' livery, drove to the Carreras Arcadia factory in Hampstead Road in May 1944, equipped with false bills of lading. They had allowed the first of two genuine lorries to load up and leave, but arrived well before the second one. Because a second vehicle was expected, their bogus credentials received only routine scrutiny. Their lorry was loaded, while they waited in some apprehension, for fear that the arrival of the second genuine transport would trap them on the premises. Their timing was exact. Just before the second lorry appeared, they drove off with a load of 1,388,000 cigarettes, valued at £5,224 (£209,000). As a bonus, they had also acquired rationed groceries to the value of £1,400 (£56,000), belonging to Liss Brothers Ltd, which had been on the lorry when they stole it.

Even in the earlier years of the war tobacco thefts had shown a distinct professionalism. In April 1941, for example, 820,000 cigarettes disappeared in a well-organized blackout robbery at S. Goldsmith, a wholesale tobacconist at Kingston-on-Thames. Scotland Yard believed at first that the theft must have taken four men at least two hours. However, this robbery had involved breaking through the wall of the factory, and the owners thought it unlikely that any thieves could have remained undetected by guards or watchmen for long enough to accomplish it, or that it could have been done in silence. Time was important because even when the cigarettes were brought out, the eighty-two cartons had to be carried over three garden walls to the nearest side road, where a van or lorry was waiting. If a vehicle had been there for two hours, the warehouse guards would surely have noticed it. On inspecting the damage, however, the assessors realized that the gang had been to the site on previous nights. Under cover of the blackout and the detonations of the blitz, they had worked patiently at the factory wall, loosening bricks and preparing their entry, but always leaving the wall in such a condition that their handiwork was not evident. On the last night, the raid was carried out with speed and efficiency, before the guardians of the factory heard or saw anything.

Such elaborate planning and preparation were not always necessary. Two months later, an opportunist thief working alone in Peckham stole 1,489,000 cigarettes valued at £4,757 (£190,280). He used a less ambitious method in which he followed the van through the blackout as it delivered cigarettes to various dealers, waited until it was briefly unattended, then performed a split-second 'jump-up', making off with both the cigarettes and the vehicle.

Useful retail outlets for these black market thefts, notably clothes and accessories, were the London street markets or their country cousins. Traders who bought the goods would sell coupon-free, at a price. Berwick Street in Soho had the reputation of an open-air market where women's stockings were coupon-free and 'you can buy clothes coupons for 5s. [£10] a dozen'. For that reason, it was closely watched by undercover inspectors. Only customers known to the traders were likely to get the benefits of illegal coupons.

Berwick Street's best days came with the arrival of American troops in 1942 and the establishment of the American forces' YMCA social centre at 'Rainbow Corner' in Shaftesbury Avenue. Barter between Americans, over Rainbow Corner comforts unobtainable elsewhere, and local street traders produced a steady flow of rationed goods to the Soho markets.

By 1943, the value of trading in Berwick Street market had escalated considerably, as shown when Hyman Schnatz, a stallholder, was convicted of acquiring women's stockings and underwear without coupons. He was sent to hard labour for two months and fined £500 (£20,000) or two months further in prison. Detective Sergeant Grantford of the Flying Squad had searched Schnatz's flat and found cash which the trader used as his 'float' to purchase coupon-free luxuries. The wad amounted to almost £3,000 (£120,000).[28]

Not all markets were entirely open-air. Petticoat Lane offered a more sophisticated service for buying suits and overcoats without the need of coupons. A tout would accost a passer-by and say, 'We have got a nice suit to fit you', or 'What about a nice mackintosh or overcoat without coupons?' When the purchaser asked about the shop, he was told, 'You come with me and if you get fixed up, you give me five shillings [£10] when you come out.' A good many customers were 'fixed up' and a few shopkeepers were caught.[29]

Among open-air markets outside London, Romford still boasted the greatest notoriety. As in the East End, there was little subtlety in the methods. Traders relied on tic-tac men, whose usual occupation was in recession since the outbreak of war and the restrictions on horse racing. These men were to signal the approach of anyone who might be an undercover inspector. A consequent sense of security led to fast and unconcealed trading. When a stallholder at Romford was prosecuted in March 1942, it was because a female Board of Trade inspector had eluded the lookouts. She saw a crowd round a stall and joined it. When her turn came, she bought some underwear and was not asked for coupons. No one in sight was asked for coupons. 'An assistant was taking money as fast as she could', in the hope that before officialdom arrived, the stall and its staff would be long gone.[30]

The fate of this offender was no deterrent. Two weeks later, the *Romford Recorder* reported stalls in the market selling clothes without coupons and doing 'a roaring trade'. Even plain-clothes police made no attempt to interfere. In peace or war, they dealt with pickpockets or sneak thieves but regarded the regulation of the stalls as a matter for the Board of Trade alone.[31]

The markets began a chain of illegal trading. Those who bought clothes without coupons were not restricted in the amount they purchased. Some bought for themselves, others to sell again, coupon-free, at higher prices. In August 1943, the police on the gate of a war production factory stopped a young married woman on her way to work and searched the parcel she was carrying. She was surprised because, though the police on the gate might search workers as they left, they did not often stop them on the way in. The parcel contained a consignment of brand new underwear and stockings. Investigations showed that she was buying regular consignments at what the press was only permitted to describe as 'an East End market' and selling them at a profit to her fellow workers. The magistrate had no power to 'bind' the press, as he termed it, but asked them to 'oblige' him by not reporting the details of the case until the police had had time to investigate the source of this contraband.[32]

Even when market culprits were caught, they moved smartly to find a way out. In May 1942, two Romford stallholders were fined £50 (£2,000) each for selling goods without taking coupons, or taking too few coupons. The men had an immediate but unsuccessful explanation, insisting that the obviously new and unmarked pyjamas on sale did not require the regulation number of coupons, or any coupons at all, because they were 'shop-soiled'. In other cases, the defence was that the clothes were 'second-hand'. A Board of Trade regulation allowed a second-hand suit to be sold without coupons provided that its price was not more than £2 12s. (£104). As black marketeers invariably charged more than this for what was in reality a new suit, the defence seldom succeeded.[33]

Open-air traders cornered the market in small but useful accessories and then forced up prices well beyond the legal limit. Later in the war, razor blades, hair tonic, combs and similar items in short supply appeared at markets for at least double their retail price. The North Midland Price Regulation Committee was particularly plagued by this, with combs, hairgrips, elastic and pins offered at 'excessive prices'. The committee vowed to 'smash' the trade, though by the time the war ended it had not done so. There was a further cause for concern in this instance. Illegally sold cosmetics at the markets were not only expensive, they were of dubious origin and a downright danger to health.

Since 1941, cosmetics had been restricted by quota. The first prosecution under the new Soap Rationing Order was brought at Bethnal Green on 3 March 1942. At the same time, men were limited to the purchase of five razor blades each and razor blades became a natural commodity for racketeering. A major prosecution, at Liverpool Assizes in November 1943, revealed that, as one defendant put it, 'Before this case about 500 people used to be running around a West End hotel and in Piccadilly with samples in their hands.' These touts were offering middlemen 'sample' packets of razor blades in hotel lounges or bars at over three times the maximum permitted price, forty-two shillings (£84) instead of twelve shillings (£24) a gross. The retailer admitted his offence and the purchase of razor blades from the touts. As usual in such cases, he protected his suppliers. 'I cannot identify them. They gave no receipts.'[34]

By the beginning of 1943, there were stories of rackets and big contracts in Anglo-Irish smuggling, with penalties to match. In May 1943, the Belfast magistrates fined Thomas Stewart of Stewart Brothers, Belfast, £2,500 (£100,000) for being in possession of uncustomed razor blades and also fined him £170 (£6,800) for knowingly harbouring 570lb of tea.[35]

The greatest boost to the underground trade in cosmetics was the budget of April 1943 which increased prices by 50 per cent. Face powder was now twenty-five shillings a box (£50) and a tube of lipstick twelve shillings and sixpence (£25). Manufacturers were also restricted, under the Toilet Preparations Order, as to the amount they could produce. The cost of a box of face powder and a lipstick was now equivalent to half many women's weekly wage. Not surprisingly, professional gangs staged lipstick robberies. Also in 1943, a gang began the systematic theft of cosmetics in transit by rail between Somers Town goods station and the provinces.

The government behaved as though it could not have been expected to foresee such developments. At Bow Street, in May 1944, when a trader was convicted of selling lipstick and creams without invoices, the solicitor to the Board of Trade said innocently, 'The underground trade in cosmetics is perhaps the largest in the country, and the Board of Trade have been unable to get to the bottom of the matter.'[36]

Far more perilous than theft was the insanitary manufacture of illegal beauty preparations, complete with forged labels and fraudulent invoices for Yardley and other famous firms. With false invoices, the products could be distributed wholesale. The labels, like those for illegally produced wine and spirits, were run off by presses which otherwise printed counterfeit clothing or petrol coupons. However, the government's concern over the threat to health from illegal cosmetics was long-standing and, in October 1941, the Ministry of Information had released a short documentary film, *Black Market Beauties*, in which the swollen lips and disfigured faces of those women who had used these insanitary preparations were luridly depicted.

The distribution of unlicensed products was widespread. Sometimes they bore no manufacturers' names on their labels, as when a London trader in brilliantine and eau de Cologne was convicted in December 1944. More often, forged labels were used. In the spring of that year, Cardiff, Swansea and Birmingham had been 'flooded' with bottles of illegally labelled scent. Of these, 6,788 were traced. On one occasion two young men, perpetrators of the fraud, were said to have made £500 (£20,000) profit in two days. The trail led to the cloakroom of a Cardiff railway station, where they had deposited a number of cases. These contained 3,456 bottles of illegally produced perfume, with a market value of £700 (£28,000). Before they were sentenced to nine months' hard labour at Cardiff Quarter Sessions in April 1944, the defendants asked that other charges of conspiracy at Birmingham, Swansea, St Albans and Nottingham, involving an additional £780 (£31,200) profit from their home-made scent, should be taken into consideration.[37]

The conditions in which such products were manufactured were depicted at Marylebone magistrates court in January 1944, when Ibrahim Meah, a seaman from Mornington Crescent, Camden Town, was charged with contravening the Toilet Preparations Order by carrying on business as a manufacturer and packer of perfume without a licence from the Board of Trade. It seemed he was merely the hired labourer, 'engaged' at £1 a week by a man he could not identify to fill bottles with scent. He was fined £100 (£4,000) with 20 guineas (£840) costs. His common-law wife, Irene Doreen Julful, was bound over.

Detective Inspector Green of Scotland Yard described how he had found Meah at 'filthy premises' in a Paddington back street, 'filling bottles with perfume from a large crucible, while rain poured in through holes in the roof. Julful was also present.' Julful had explained that an Englishman delivered the materials in a van. She and her husband were paid to bottle five hundred gross in three weeks. She did not know that the value of the materials was £1,000 (£40,000) and, when made up, could be sold for £4,000 (£160,000). Unfortunately, by the time that Inspector Green and other officers arrived, the mysterious Englishman had got wind of the raid and was far away.[38]

The agents of justice too often seemed like agents of public relations. In February 1941, the nation was promised a 'Flying Squad' of six Ministry of Food officials who would tour London in search of 'meat ration dodgers'. The meat rationing scandals got worse. In September, the public was assured that twenty 'Coupon Scouts' were watching the shops. Three months later, illegal trading had increased to such an extent that the Wealdstone magistrate described it as 'the curse of Great Britain today'.

In a press release on 4 January 1945, Sir Norman Kendall, head of the CID, having conferred with Sir Charles Tegart, chief of the intelligence and investigation department of the Food Ministry, gave the public a thumbnail sketch of the black market as it had developed and of the men who now ran it. His evidence indicated about fifty leaders of the market, apart from small-time gangs, operating in the so-called 'L Triangle' of Liverpool, Leeds and London.

In reality, there had been few big cases involving so-called leaders. However, early in 1942, Scotland Yard and Sir Charles Tegart were informed of a major conspiracy involving up to a dozen men. They included the managing directors of two large wholesale grocery firms, a retail grocer from Clapton, and the managing director of a firm of wharfingers, who was involved in the conspiracy with some of his warehousemen. The prime mover appeared to be a 'general dealer' in the City of London, known as Sydney or Skylinski, working with a French-born owner of three West End restaurants, La Cigale, La Corvette and La Coquille. These premises were a convenient outlet for the goods.

The investigation was led by William Barker, a former Chief Inspector at Scotland Yard, seconded to the Ministry of Food as Chief Enforcement Officer for London and the South-East. Inspector Barker and Sergeant Henry Clarke began a surveillance operation on

Seymour Sydney and his premises, T. Sydney & Co., Philpot Lane, Eastcheap. On one of his busier mornings, 6 March 1942, they followed him to Stamford Hill, where he collected a hired van for his errands. Transport and petrol rationing appeared to present no problem to him.

Sydney left Stamford Hill and drove to J. Boxer & Co., wholesale grocers of Leytonstone. As Boxer was part of the conspiracy, it was no surprise to see the van being loaded with cases of tinned sardines. It returned to London, through the City to Arlington House, Mayfair, where the restaurateur, Pages, had his stores. Here the sardines were unloaded. It then drove through Victoria, over the Thames, to Lambeth and Horseshoe Wharf, on the Southwark riverside. There it was loaded with sacks marked 'Pearl Corn Starch', which contained black market sugar. Barker and Clarke followed it back across the river to the premises of another conspirator, a private warehouse in the unlikely surroundings of North Row, Mayfair. The remaining goods were unloaded.

Police raided Arlington House, North Row, and a larger store of contraband in Newport Place, near Leicester Square, described as 'absolutely stacked full of rationed foodstuffs'. The restaurateur was arrested. In a moment of dismay, he told the police that he had given Sydney £500 (£20,000) a few days before and, in return, Sydney had 'promised not to tell anyone about this place'. When Sydney was arrested, he was carrying £644 (£25,760) in his wallet.

On 18 April, managing directors, wholesale grocers, restaurateur, caterer and employees appeared at Bow Street. At the Old Bailey in July, it took an hour to read out the seventy-two charges. The Lord Chief Justice presided over the case in a courtroom crowded by solicitors and barristers, Ministry of Food officials and policemen. Sydney abandoned his defence and pleaded guilty to an impressive calendar of racketeering in sardines, sugar, cooking fats, ground nut oil, and canned goods, which included salmon, apples, peaches and pineapple.

The wholesale grocer of Leytonstone, for whom the whole thing had become too much, pleaded guilty and applied for bail and mitigation, on the grounds that 'this has got so extremely complicated because of all the restrictions'. Lord Chief Justice Caldecote informed him that this was no ground for bail.

Charles Topol pleaded guilty to supplying tinned salmon, tinned apples, three tins of rice to Sydney and obtaining rice from Richard James Hill. The goods were found behind Topol's premises in Upper Clapton Road. The plea of guilty meant that he could not be questioned about the source of the supplies, to determine whether they were the proceeds of theft or merely of dishonest trading.

Seymour Sydney had no licence whatever to deal in food. Sergeant Clarke explained that 'He was known to be dealing in foodstuffs, candles and footwear, and had been actively engaged in the "black market."' It was impossible to check his records. He had none beyond calculations which had been kept on hotel notepaper. 'It is impossible to say how much he has gained.'

Sydney drew the heaviest sentence, four years' penal servitude and a fine of £2,000 (£80,000), with the provision that he was to remain in prison after his sentence until that fine was paid. As the Lord Chief Justice told him, 'You have committed, in effect, acts of sabotage against this nation. You have played for high stakes and you have lost.' Pages, the restaurateur, was sent to prison for eighteen months with a fine of £2,000 (£80,000); he also was to remain in gaol until the fine was paid. Four others were sent to prison for shorter terms.[39]

In the week of the trial, eighty-six lesser prosecutions for coupon and ration offences were to be heard in London and the provinces. Indeed, those who wondered where Sydney had found so much sugar were to be regaled by another prosecution involving the theft of nine tons of the commodity at Acton.[40]

In the spring of 1942, three senior Scotland Yard officers were chosen to defeat the black market. One was Superintendent William Barker who had run to earth Seymour Sydney and his accomplices. Another was Superintendent Sands, and the third Superintendent George Yandell, who had publicly vowed to 'get' the racketeers. Yandell became Chief of the Board of Trade Investigation Department and directed a good deal of his attention to the North of England, the two points of the 'L' triangle represented by Leeds and Liverpool. Quite apart from bogus contracts and the defrauding of government agencies, there was serious theft and black market-eering in the North and North-West. Scotland Yard had intervened not long before Yandell's appointment in a case where a black market in stolen machine tools had developed during a crucial stage of the war.

There had been constant losses of 'highly important' machine tools from an engineering works on Merseyside. These thefts were of such importance that for some months two Scotland Yard detective sergeants, Glander and Ogden, worked undercover, posing as agents of men in the market for stolen equipment. A gang of one woman and eight men was soon identified. At length the policemen convinced the thieves that they were buyers of machine tools, stolen in Liverpool for sale in London. As the deal was coming to fruition, the woman and one of the men were in London, in possession of the latest batch of tools. In order not to be questioned too closely about the technical use of the tools, Sergeant Glander had posed as an insurance agent buying them on the instructions of a third party. When the deal had been done and the tools were being packed up, he revealed his police identity. The head of the little gang took it in remarkably good part. 'I was afraid of this,' he said genially, 'but I must hand it to you. You took us in properly.'[41]

Elsewhere in the North of England, to control the cloth trade was almost impossible. It was common to see workers in Leeds, in the course of their work, standing in bus queues with rolls of rationed cloth under their arms. The city inevitably became a centre of the black market in cloth which, in the later stages of the war, fostered a flourishing underground trade in cosmetics, silk stockings, shoes and underwear. If trafficking in coupons was not as extensive as in some other towns, that was because, it was said, 'you do not need coupons in Leeds if you are prepared to pay the price'.

When Yandell finished with Birmingham and turned his attention to Leeds, he promised that scores of millworkers, shopkeepers and tailors would be interviewed within the next few days. Unlike his more fastidious colleagues, he was not averse to using criminal informers and blackmailers. The underworld in Leeds had seemed to have an air of invulnerability, perhaps because it had never been under much threat. Under pressure, however, it proved less than comradely. Anonymous letters began to reach Yandell's officers and one or two individuals came forward to accuse 'big operators', not for money but in the hope of saving their own skins. In almost every case, Yandell believed that these informants had first tried to blackmail the racketeers and, when that failed, decided to secure their own immunity.

Chief Inspector McDonald and Detective Sergeant Hannan were also working in northern cities. Their aim was to unearth information about illicit traders in London by discovering their northern contacts. Those who were in prison for black market offences or for stealing goods which had found their way to the black market proved surprisingly cooperative.

A further attempt to clean up Leeds and Manchester came in the later stages of the war. At the end of 1944, a gang which had dealt in goods worth over £20,000 (£800,000) and almost 150,000 coupons was broken up and its members sent to prison. Its leader was George Wildey, who had been sentenced to death for murder but reprieved from the gallows in 1928.[42]

In a case soon afterwards, five men were charged with evading regulations by selling dress-making material without coupons as 'mattress covers', while charging four times the price permitted for such covers. This investigation linked three manufacturers in Leeds with tailors in Kensington. The London defendants were philosophical about the dresses made from material acquired by such means. 'I suppose there have been millions of these sold,' one man told the police candidly. 'We are doing the public a good turn and they don't mind paying the price. If our brains are clever enough to get round the Board of Trade and round these orders, do you blame us?'[43]

Yandell had warned the press that it would take a long time to break some of the rackets in the North. The war had ended by the time he brought forty-eight defendants to court in a major prosecution at Harrogate. A small boy at Drighlington in Yorkshire, the type of child who must have been the bane of any criminal's existence, collected car numbers as his hobby. He remembered the number of a car he had seen outside a warehouse in the town, when he went for a walk after dark. There had been four cases of warehouse breaking just before this, elsewhere at Drighlington, as well as in Morley and Leeds. When it was discovered that these premises had also been burgled, the boy was able to give the police the number of the car outside at the time.

As a result of the infant detective's information, forty-eight suspects were arrested and all were convicted. The driver of the car confessed and the stolen cloth was found at his house. When the thieves robbed the warehouse, the thirty rolls of cloth, worth £1,600 (£64,000), were cut up into convenient lengths by two of the conspirators and these were then sold to members of the public. These purchasers were now charged and convicted as receivers. They included a number of civil servants stationed at Harrogate, housewives, a dentist and a cook. Once again, the prosecution was forced to admit that these people 'may be described as being on the fringe, and they may be small fry involved in small transactions, but it is owing to the stupidity and antisocial activities of these small fry that this racket goes on at all'.[44]

The shadowy presence behind the rackets, the 'Mr Big' beloved of press reports and police appeals, was not caught. Yet a young man in Leeds was to be a 'Mr Big', better known than Billy Hill or those who made vacuous boasts of being 'Boss' or 'King' of the 1940s underworld. During the Fascists' attempts to march through the East End in 1936, he had fought them in the Battle of Cable Street and elsewhere. Though called up for the Army, he had been discharged in 1943 and made his way north. At the Regal Gaming Club in Chapeltown, he was now bodyguard to the owner. His name was Jack Comer, far better known by his nickname, Jack 'Spot'.

8

Hot Off the Press

With the abolition of the basic petrol allowance in the summer of 1942 and the reduction in the clothes ration, coupons became an alternative currency. To deal in tons of illegal meat or sugar was never easy, while the theft of petrol was confined to very small quantities. By contrast, the theft or forgery of coupons provided access to 750,000 gallons from a single weekend robbery at a Petroleum Office. Among deserters, there was a market for food ration books and for identity cards with forged entries, but it was not worth counterfeiting food coupons when they were so easy to steal. A helpful black market contact could supply these, while the deserter remained a grateful recruit to crime. Trained drivers from the forces were in particular demand.

The poorly guarded offices of the Ministry of Food, the Board of Trade or the Ministry of Labour were an easy target. Moreover, some thefts were carried out or facilitated by officials of these departments. Many of the food coupon robberies which resulted were so large that they spoilt the market. In 1944, at Ware and Romford, there were thefts totalling 14,000 and 100,000 complete ration books respectively.

The Romford haul was said to be worth half a million pounds in the underworld, though by 1944 £5 only would be paid for a ration book with a long period of validity. The theft at Ware was timed to ensure maximum use of newly-issued books, valid for a year, and showed how easy robberies were. It took place in the early hours of the morning on 30 May 1944. Two men with a lorry arrived at the premises and were seen by eyewitnesses, who assumed this was a delivery of the books for 1944–5. The entire stock was taken without difficulty. Those who went to collect new books in the morning were confronted by a notice in the glass panel of the locked door. 'The

160

issue of new ration books will not take place until this afternoon. Sorry! We have none.'

Thefts were normally carried out when premises were unoccupied but the Ministry of Food and the Board of Trade sometimes had offices guarded by a single watchman. This led to the first armed robbery of a food office, at Tulse Hill on the night of 18 May 1943, when two men armed with a revolver arrived during an air raid, held up the watchman, and broke into the office where 2,000 of the new issue of 1943–4 ration books had been stored. They drove off with these and were never caught.

By the beginning of 1944, the glut of stolen ration books and the approaching expiry date of the current issue drove down the price still further. When the Flying Squad raided a house in Norbury on 28 January 1944 and found 30,000 coupons in a bedroom, following a theft at Croydon, one of the two men arrested confessed that he had bought 210 ration books for no more than £1 (£40) each and was only hoping for resale at £2 (£80).[1]

Stolen ration books were never ten-a-penny but a case in July 1942 showed they could be bought for very little with small chance of being traced. Three men, including a butcher and a printer's 'taker off', were accused of trying to sell 1,858 stolen books at Smithfield Market. One was alleged to have shown a witness a box containing hundreds of new and unstamped books. 'I have got five hundred of these for sale at two shillings,' he said. The witness went to the police. When the men were arrested, the books could only be identified as printed by the Stationery Office and distributed to food offices. 'There was no serial number on them and it was difficult to trace them. There have been many reports of losses of these books in transit, but in this case the prosecution is unable to say where the books came from.' They were cheap because they were not stamped. However, stolen franking stamps were not hard to come by and forgery would be easy. A dishonest retailer could, in any case, cut the coupons from the books and use them. By black market prices, they were a bargain.[2]

Coupon theft was more common than counterfeiting and it took two forms. Coupons might be stolen when new, or stolen after they had been cut out and used, when they still had a value to the criminal. To prevent the fraudulent reuse of hundreds of millions of coupons after they had been cut out, regulations required their return to the offices which had issued them, where they could be checked. It was a Herculean labour and the system was unworkable from the start. The pretence of checking used coupons was nevertheless maintained. Not until much later, in November 1947 after two years of further post-war austerity, did the Ministry of Food admit what the underworld had noticed as soon as the scheme was introduced. 'Only a small percentage of the envelopes handed in can be checked because of staff shortages at the Ministry.' It was worse than that. The Post Office was responsible for the collection and shipment of all used coupons but the Post Office could not cope with such quantities. This part of the system had to be modified from the outset.[3]

The modification was bizarre. Traders would be permitted to take used coupons to a post office, usually in signed parcels of 500. They would hand in the parcel and receive a token for 500 coupons against their next wholesale purchases. The Post Office had declined to have anything to do with this scheme other than to collect the parcels and hand out the tokens. Some parcels which eventually reached the Board of Trade or Ministry of Food were found to contain nothing but torn-up newspapers or pages from telephone directories, with bogus names signed on the envelope. As a further protection of his own skin, a coupon racketeer might bribe a child or an 'assistant' to take the parcels to the post office and bring back the token, reducing his risk to an absolute minimum. The Post Office was not interested in the contents, being merely the point of receipt and issue of a token. It had never wanted the work and was certainly not prepared to open parcels nor to verify suspect signatures.

This form of fraud was impossible to control and difficult to conceal. Two men went to prison at the Old Bailey on 9 December 1941, convicted of obtaining 191,000 clothing coupons from the Board of Trade, through the Post Office, by false pretences. One had been 'educated at a well-known public school'. They were selling illegally obtained coupons at £1 a time, which promised to make them very rich. The press was prohibited by the court, 'in the public interest', from reporting the 'trick' the two men had used. Unfortunately, the 'trick' of handing in parcels of waste paper with false signatures and receiving vouchers for 500 coupons for each was already known to every rogue in the country and to much of the rest of the population as well.[4]

In case anyone should still be in doubt, a Doncaster court a month later imposed no ban on the reporting of a case in which two men were accused of substituting envelopes of blank paper, cut to coupon-size, for coupons being returned to the Board of Trade. This was done, the report added helpfully, with parcels at post offices, by the accused signing forms with fictitious names and firms.[5]

The authorities proved quite unprepared for the major thefts of new or used coupons, which increased with the full implementation of rationing in 1942. In an early case, 163,000 margarine coupons, together with clothing coupons and other documents, were stolen from Walthamstow Food Office. Three men were traced and arrested. 'You know that I did not take 167,000,' one of them said reproachfully to the police. 'You know I have only had some margarine coupons and also some clothing cards.' Only 30,000 coupons were traced to him but his co-defendants made up for the lack. All three men agreed that they had been caught fairly and squarely, and went to prison after pleading guilty.

A disturbing aspect of the case was the Ministry of Food's admission, for the first time, that it would not have known the number of coupons taken if the men had not confessed. According to H. A. K. Morgan, for the Crown, thousands of clothing coupons were 'lying around' in the office at Walthamstow, as they were in every similar office. There were millions arriving almost daily and ministries had no safes to contain them all. At the best, they were locked in a cupboard, childishly easy to open. 'I am sorry to admit the method of checking the coupons and arranging for their security is very far from satisfactory,' Mr Morgan added with careful understatement.[6]

Before the year's end, on 20 September 1942, the Ministry of Food admitted that, apart from organized robberies, thousands of coupons were being stolen daily in petty thefts, and these thefts were increasing. There were currently 8,000 coupons missing from Brighton Food Office and 5,000 ration books from a London paperboard mill. At the Old Bailey, three men had just been sent to prison, having been trapped by the police and the Food Office during the attempted sale of another 2,000 stolen books.[7]

By 1943, night coupon-robberies at poorly protected offices were hardly newsworthy. However, the increasing size of thefts made headlines until, one night in September that year, a record 5,000,000 coupons were stolen from an army store at Earlsfield, near Wandsworth. These were for civilian clothing issued to officers and men on discharge from the Army. They represented a clothing allowance for a quarter of a million people and had a black market value of some £15,000 (£600,000).

Given the scale of the theft, the Board of Trade invalidated until further notice all five-coupon vouchers for the entire nation. The board also summoned assistance from Chief Inspector Ted Greeno, who had penetrated the underworld perhaps more successfully than any of his Scotland Yard colleagues and who therefore had an unrivalled team of informants. As he began the Wandsworth investigation at the Army Forms Depot, these informants reported underworld gossip. A man was offering clothing coupons for sale in blocks of 150,000 at £500 (£20,000), touting them at dog tracks and in the bars of West End hotels. Divisional CID at Wandsworth still thought the coupons might have been mislaid. Greeno made a survey of the Earlsfield depot, then told the divisional CID to 'forget the mislaid part'.

The depot was a well-protected compound surrounded by a barbed-wire fence. The method used by the thieves was soon established. Car-tyre tracks led across allotments to the barbed wire. A railway sleeper had been laid against the wire to flatten it, so that the intruders could cross. On the ground, Greeno noticed a red security label, which had come from a parcel of coupons.

Despite evidence of a raid by outsiders, Greeno decided that a theft on this scale must involve someone who knew the depot. Coupling this with his informants' description of a tall, expensively dressed man offering coupons for sale, he was sure the thief was an insider. Of the personnel at Earlsfield who were kept under watch, one was shadowed while away from the depot, wearing his uniform with a major's single crown. Unfortunately, he was a 'one-pip' lieutenant with no right to the crown. Further shadowing revealed his addiction to dog racing and heavy betting, and his acquaintanceship with dubious friends at the tracks.

The suspect was arrested in the American Bar of the Charing Cross Hotel on the evening of Saturday 18 September 1943. He seemed unruffled by this 'mistaken identity' and maintained his pose of a War Office major carrying secret documents in his briefcase. He could not open it for the police or anyone else. He asked Greeno to telephone various fellow officers and a senior policeman who would vouch for him. Though the senior policeman and the others agreed they knew him, they did not know him well enough to vouch for him. When his contacts failed him, his briefcase was opened at City Road police station. It contained 'sheets and sheets' of clothing coupons.

The major was astonished. He admitted that he must have fallen for a trick at Harringay dog track that afternoon. A man had given him the case and arranged to meet him at the American Bar that evening. The major was then informed by Greeno that he had been under continuous surveillance by CID officers at Harringay from a range of ten or twenty feet. He was not carrying the case either at the track or when he left it. It was evident that he had brought it to the hotel in the hope of completing one of his deals.

With his bluff called, a version of the truth was the only defence.

> I didn't steal them myself, though I was the instigator. I took two other men, hired a car, and drove across the allotments to the Army Forms Depot at Earlsfield. I knew the windows would be open, they always were. I told the men how to get in and where the coupons were. I left the coupons in the garage overnight, and then I put them in the cloak-room at Euston station for a week. I sold one batch for £500.

Clothing coupons were not his only line. One accomplice was a deserter from the Royal Marines, to whom he sold a set of falsely completed discharge papers for £10 (£400). Next month, the lieutenant and an accessory were tried for the biggest theft of its kind during the war. He was sentenced to penal servitude for five years and leave to appeal was refused.[8]

In the latter half of 1943, as the demand for clothing and petrol overtook that for food, Board of Trade offices became an attractive target. During the weekend of 7–9 August, as if to show that nowhere was safe, thieves carried out a major robbery at the main Board of Trade offices in New Oxford House, Bloomsbury Way. Police investigations brought no results until December, when five men were arrested for the theft. During their appearance in court in January, there was small comfort in the claim that the current underworld demand was for 20,000,000 clothing coupons.[9]

As the war moved irreversibly in favour of the Allies, the grim resolve of 1941 and the demands for the flogging or shooting of racketeers fell silent. With the invasion of France in June 1944, only the date of ultimate victory was in doubt. Black marketeering no longer seemed the crime it had once been. Magistrates and judges talked less often of 'treason'.

In this climate, dealers worked quickly and often with impunity. In July, when 600,000 clothing coupons were stolen from a City of London employment exchange, it was estimated that the haul would bring £30,000 (£1,200,000). The touts were working hotel lounges, night clubs, city bars and public houses, offering them to individuals. Others were selling to wholesalers and retailers, enabling them to make coupon-free offers to customers at higher prices.

At the point of sale, clothing coupon thieves were at their most vulnerable. When the trade began in earnest, in February 1942, two Glaswegians in the lounge of a West End hotel were discussing 300,000 stolen coupons. 'You know how much a thousand we want for them?' 'Yes, £11 a thousand he asked me.' 'That's right – £10 a thousand they are, and he gets the odd £1 for the introduction. We can get half a million of them if you want them.'

It was unfortunate for the pair that they were Glaswegians. Many London criminals might have recognized the eavesdropper drinking on his own a little distance away. Detective Inspector John Capstick of Scotland Yard was not there by chance but because an informant had given him intelligence about the two men in the hotel lounge. They were arrested in possession of 305,000 coupons. 'They are ours,' said one of the men indignantly. His companion added, 'You will find they are straight up.' The coupons had been issued at Glasgow Post Office on 7–11 February. Within a week, hundreds of thousands were being 'worked' in the hotel bars and lounges of the capital.[10]

Some new coupons or ration books were put into circulation more efficiently by thieves than by the ministries. When the 1945–6 books and coupons were issued on 28 May, Thomas Wilkins was touting

100 clothing books, 6,400 coupons and 600 clothing coupon tokens within the first week. He then made a brief appearance at Clerkenwell magistrates court, on his way to the Old Bailey. Yet his efforts represented a small part of the total robberies. In that first week, 2,500 ration books had been stolen from five different distribution centres in the city.[11]

The speed of these operations made it difficult to catch the major thieves except by penetrating their organization, as Capstick, Greeno and John Gosling were to prove. In this undercover role, Scotland Yard also assisted Customs and Excise. Clothes rationing involved the enforcement of duty through purchase tax, administered by Customs and Excise. So, when 155,000 clothing coupons were stolen from a Customs and Excise office on 29 May 1943, the CID mounted an operation which ended in the arrest of the receivers by men whom they had thought were their accomplices.[12]

A good many gangs and receivers who traded coupons worked in small groups for safety. Even a major coupon-trafficking case, linking London and South Wales in 1944, resulted in only five men going to prison. The scheme depended on the regular theft by criminals in Cardiff of merchant navy clothing coupons from shipping offices in the docks. These were then brought to London and sold to tailors and rug manufacturers. The London 'merchants' were the aristocrats of the racket and regarded their South Wales suppliers as 'mugs', who had only to break a few panes of glass and force a cupboard lock.

These thieves were also less perceptive and more easily tricked by undercover police officers. Several 'mugs' were arrested and some talked. As a result, in July 1944, the investigation identified the first London contact, a rug manufacturer. Arrests followed, in Kensal Rise, Maida Vale, Hampstead and Knightsbridge. There was little honour among thieves, or in this case receivers. 'They have shopped me!' said the woollen merchant of Kensal Rise, in the moment before he began to implicate others. With the police already on his premises, the Knightsbridge tailor tried to flush 495 clothing coupons down the toilet, though they had nothing to do with the inquiry. 'I bought them crooked to keep by me,' he explained.

Some organizers of the London connection eluded arrest or identification at first. By the end of July, however, one of the lesser fry agreed to help the police, in exchange for a lighter sentence. On police instructions, he contacted a man he did business with and promised him a buyer for thousands of coupons, 'Mr Ferguson'. It was arranged that 'Mr Ferguson', *alias* Detective Sergeant Baker of Scotland Yard, should be introduced by the informant outside the Dominion cinema in Tottenham Court Road. They were watched from the far side of the street by Detective Sergeant Dawson.

The man assumed to be the leader of the gang appeared and was introduced to 'Mr Ferguson'. The leader, a government munitions inspector, said, 'You know what we are here for. I have got as many coupons as you want.' They drove to a house in Muswell Hill, followed at a short distance by Detective Sergeant Dawson. At the house, the seller of the coupons told Sergeant Baker to 'get rid of the mug', as the informer was now described.

They then drove to a house in Lanhill Road, Maida Vale. The government munitions inspector was not, after all, the kingpin of the conspiracy. At the second house a man arrived who described himself as a 'clerk'. He had brought 'Mr Ferguson' a parcel containing 10,000 merchant navy clothing coupons. Sergeant Baker checked these and made them 10,075. With Dawson waiting at the front door, he then arrested the man who had offered to sell the coupons and the 'clerk' who had just brought them. 'Fucking jack!' shouted the clerk, then swinging round on his accomplice angrily, 'What have you done to me?' Another 7,000 coupons were found in the room and also identified as 'part of a large consignment stolen from a shipping office at Cardiff'.[13]

The number of stolen ration books and coupons of all kinds in circulation during the war was beyond computation. By the closing months of hostilities it rated no more than an inch or two of newsprint. When, in January 1945, Kate Harris, of Westbury-on-Trym, was arrested for shoplifting in Bath, and the police found her in possession of thirty-five books of clothing coupons and nine ration books, all in different names, the story struggled to make the press.

It was a frequent claim by the defence in clothing coupon prosecutions that the thefts were wholly or partly 'an inside job'. In April 1942, when two men were fined and gaoled for using 891 coupons twice, the defence insisted that officials of the Food Office were involved. It was alleged, unavailingly, that the culprits had been getting their spare coupons 'from a friend holding a responsible position at the Hackney Town Hall'. The evidence suggested otherwise. In other cases, however, coupons were being stolen by officials, sometimes by an individual and sometimes collectively.[14]

The extent of complicity might be uncertain. In a major robbery on the night of 9 November 1943 at the Board of Trade offices at Grove Park, Camberwell, 40,000 coupons destined for the whole of the South London area were taken. There could be little doubt that someone had told the robbers where to look. The theft was carried out so silently and skilfully that the watchman and his wife, asleep on the floor below, heard nothing and the robbers escaped unchallenged.

One of the most fully documented 'inside' coupon robberies was committed by the 'Woman Enforcement Officer' at Brighton Food Office on the night of 5–6 August 1942. The Food Control Officer had the previous day discovered that a large number of ration books were missing, variously described as 'more than 250' and 'between 4,000 and 5,000'. The Ministry of Food admitted in September that there were coupons missing from the Brighton office but it could not explain how or why. After the discovery of the loss on 5 August, a more thorough check was to be made at the weekend. Before then, as the enforcement officer admitted, 'I decided that they should all be missing'.

The Brighton Food Office was in the Royal Pavilion where the enforcement officer was on duty as a fire-watcher in August. On the night of 5 August she entered the Food Control Officer's room, broke open a locked cupboard, and took a parcel containing 80,000 clothing coupons in 8,000 sheets. She maintained in her defence that this was done to save the Food Control Officer embarrassment at the weekend check-up. There could be no check-up or embarrassment if the coupons were stolen beforehand.

In the dance halls of Brighton, the thief was known as 'Tony Dawson'. Unfortunately for her defence of 'saving embarrassment', she now tried to sell the coupons to people she met at dances or to persuade them to act as intermediaries. In September, a woman at one dance hall, and a Royal Artillery gunner at another, refused to have anything to do with the proposal. 'Tony Dawson' told the gunner she had already sold 1,000 coupons in Brighton but had not been paid for them. 'She did not intend the same thing to happen again,' and was going to sell the rest in London.

She had no luck in finding an intermediary until the beginning of January 1943, when she met an electrical engineer from Worthing. There were still 70,000 of 80,000 coupons left. 'I told her I knew someone who could get rid of them for her,' the engineer said. He phoned a London contact, 'Barnes'. They agreed that the coupons should be brought to London, where the engineer would stay at the Regent Palace Hotel. When the deal was done, 'Tony Dawson' would get £750 (£30,000), the engineer £100 (£4,000), and Barnes £50 (£2,000) as contact man. On 23 January, Barnes brought two purchasers to the engineer's hotel room. As soon as the deal was done, the buyers identified themselves as Detective Sergeant Shepherd and Detective Constable Murray of Scotland Yard. The engineer denied all knowledge of the coupons, but when his room was searched a locked brown attaché case containing 69,000 coupons was found behind the blackout curtains. The Food Enforcement Officer went to penal servitude for three years and the engineer to prison for twelve months. The judge dismissed as 'ridiculous' the woman's plea that she had only taken the coupons to conceal the discrepancies at the Food Office.[15]

The theft at Brighton was the act of a single thief. Elsewhere, dishonesty was wholesale. As a safety measure the Walker Art Gallery, like the Royal Pavilion, was stripped of most of its art treasures for the duration of the war. It now housed the Liverpool Ministry of Fuel office. At the beginning of 1944, it was discovered that for the past nine months there had been what the Crown described as 'a big-scale traffic in clothing coupons . . . among women clerks and typists', though they were not the principals. Eleven were prosecuted and fined for aiding and abetting the transfer of coupons. At the start of the 'transfer', a book containing sixty-four clothing coupons was sold for twenty-five shillings (£50). The price when the book reached the Fuel Office was £3 (£120). As the Stipendiary Magistrate remarked: 'The public would be dismayed to know that such grave offences were going on in an establishment conducted by a Ministry.'[16]

Some thefts by officials were carried out with a modicum of criminal caution. In the month after the Liverpool trial, a case came to court which required some dexterity by the police. Coupons were missing from a Hertfordshire food office. It was not certain how many were involved or whether they had been stolen, because they were coupons returned after use. Even if they were checked, the system made it difficult to keep track of them. After checking, the practice was for the clerks to hand them to a storekeeper or put them in the waste-paper baskets, whose contents would be destroyed.

Information reached the police of a man offering first 1,200, then 2,500 coupons for sale in a local pub. It was necessary to search the desks of senior and junior staff without the suspects knowing. To ask for keys would alert senior officials. The search was therefore carried out when the office was unoccupied, with the aid of a mirror and a torch. The locked drawers of civil service desks were flush at the front. At the rear, there was a gap between the drawer aperture and the carcass of the desk. The rear wall of the drawer left a gap of an inch or more at the top of the drawer slot. By placing a mirror well behind the drawer and shining a torch into this gap, the CID officers made their unusual search. In the desk of the Deputy Food Officer they found the coupons which, according to the records, should already have gone to the furnace.[17]

The counterfeiting of coupons required rarer skills. Forgery by printing, as opposed to the alteration of genuine documents, was not common before the war. However, when the call to arms sounded, presses turned from pornography and tote tickets to war work: clothing coupons, petrol coupons and a modest number of identity cards.

Food coupons were not often worth counterfeiting, when they could so easily be stolen, but a racket in forged meat coupons was discovered in July 1942. However, both the investigation and the prosecution were frustrated when a key suspect, a butcher from New Cross, gassed himself shortly before his trial began. Investigators found the house in darkness and, not wishing to break blackout restrictions, looked for him with a lighted candle. The explosion and the blaze drew fire-appliances from a wide area.[18]

Counterfeit clothing coupons were, however, a major threat. They made headlines in July 1941, almost as soon as clothes rationing began, with news that London shops were 'flooded' by imitations.

These were sold by touts in the West End at ten shillings a sheet. It was possible to recognize the machines on which they were printed as having been used formerly to imitate tote tickets. Long before this, Scotland Yard had foreseen the likelihood of forgery replacing the theft of clothes coupons as the war went on. In January 1940, the police had warned counterfeiters that there was a 'magic eye' detector, whose 'black limelight' revealed fakes at once. Unfortunately, this proved no substitute for the intensive footwork of checking suppliers to see who might be buying unusual quantities of paper and the chemicals needed to carry out forgeries.

One attraction of counterfeit coupons was the simplicity of copying. Genuine clothing coupons, by their nature, were a primitive production. To forge them required nothing like the skill needed to copy a banknote. Moreover, few people through whose hands they passed were familiar with them, as they were familiar with Bank of England currency. If a coupon looked all right, most people assumed it must be genuine. A skilled detector of coupon forgeries was Stanley Bygate Gillespie, a Stationery Office expert. He agreed that genuine coupons were 'not difficult to imitate'. However, counterfeits were likely to be detected by the feel and character of the paper. 'The forgeries are more rigid to the feel, and the surface of the paper is smoother and more highly finished.'

Mr Gillespie confessed that many of the forgeries and forgers had been detected by such simple flaws as the 'awful spelling' on the back of the coupons. In one case he had noticed the word 'some' spelt as 'sum'. What he called 'the most obvious points of difference between the forgeries and the genuine coupons' also lay in the background designs, which were less likely to be inspected than the lettering. He confirmed that many forgers worked alone, without an accomplice to check their spelling or the details of the background.[19]

One independent craftsman was a fitter from Clapham, arrested in May 1944 for 'forging a document issued for purposes of the Consumer Rationing (Consolidation) Order, and unlawful possession of clothing coupons'. He had completed his photographic negatives of the coupons and was about to prepare a plate for printing. He was philosophical about his bad luck. 'You have stepped in a bit too quick,' he told the detective who arrested him, 'I was experimenting with photography and you can't touch me for that. Another week and things would have been different, because I should have had the plate done.'[20]

The first major clothing coupon forgery case began early in 1942, eight months after the introduction of rationing. It followed inquiries into the activities of a shadowy presence known as 'Mr Jackson of Birmingham'. There had been wholesale transactions in Manchester and London, during which Mr Jackson offered to cover large and illegal purchases of rationed goods, adding such homely assurances as, 'If you can get the hosiery, I can supply the coupons.' He could certainly supply coupons by the thousand, indeed in tens of thousands, because he was financing the underground press which printed them.

Unfortunately, Mr Jackson and his printer did too good a job. As their output of forgeries reached 100,000, the contents of an envelope containing some of these counterfeits was handled at the Board of Trade by an official who noticed that the paper felt 'funny'. It was smoother and of better quality than the government used. When this was reported, all the sheets of coupons in the batch were examined. Suspicion of forgery was confirmed by mistakes in the background of the design and by the odd appearance of the letter 'G'.

Once the alarm was raised, an examination was made of other parcels of coupons exchanged for 500-coupon vouchers in the Manchester area. Some retailers' signatures on the packages were obviously false. Casting the net wider, it seemed there was a double-headed conspiracy in Manchester and London, and that it had been flourishing ever since clothes rationing began.

In January 1942, the police were in a position to make their first arrests. The investigation had been a combined operation by Scotland Yard and the CID in Manchester and Salford. Detective Inspector William Salisbury led the Scotland Yard officers, while Detective Inspector Frank Stainton was in overall command in Manchester.

The conspirators first learnt of this at the beginning of February 1942 with the arrest of two men in Manchester and three more in Stepney. The Mancunians had been found in possession of 20,000 forged coupons and, on 3 February, Detective Inspector Stainton promised that 'vast inquiries have still to be made.' Three days later, these inquiries resulted in the arrest of two men in Stepney, in possession of 10,000 forged coupons. Next day, eight more men were arrested in Salford and remanded at Manchester. Before long, twenty-two men stood in the dock, ten of whom were later sent to prison.

Inspector Salisbury, Inspector Stainton and officers of the Manchester and Salford CID now raided a house in Salford. In the cellar and on the first floor they found, as well as paper and ink, a complete printing press on which 50,000–70,000 clothing coupons were being produced. It seemed that the forged coupons were mingled with genuine ones for return to the ministries who collected them. Had the 'feel' of the counterfeit coupons not betrayed them, the gang would have been in business a good deal longer. On 18 February, three men who had been arrested in London were formally discharged, only to be rearrested at once and taken to join those detained in Manchester. The total of forged coupons so far recovered was 97,000.

The London firms raided included Durabel (Patents) Elastics Ltd, at Buckle Street in the East End. One defendant, Jack Manches, was a director of the firm. He was described by police as 'of high reputation as a London merchant in a substantial way of business'. When the police arrived to question him, however, Manches said that he was busy but would see them in a moment. He went into his office and was observed, though he did not know it, in an undignified state of panic as he stuffed brown packages and a parcel into an attaché case. When the police entered, he produced some parcels of genuine coupons from his desk and claimed that they were all he had. Asked what was in the attaché case, he said sadly, 'Well, I suppose they are coupons as well.' He was, however, one of those acquitted.

The attaché case contained 5,000 forged coupons which Manches had bought from a man named Greenberg in Manchester. The buying and selling of genuine clothing coupons in large numbers seems to have been a general practice in the wholesale trade. A number of those accused of conspiracy to forge said that they thought buying and selling coupons, though illegal between members of the public, was entirely legitimate between businessmen. Meantime, in Manchester, a package of 8,000 forged coupons was traced to another director who admitted buying them from Joseph Levy of Medley Park. At the centre of the conspiracy was 'Mr Jackson's' printer, who had taken on the work to help his printing business in Salford.

Frederick Horne of the Stationery Office was an expert on typefaces. He had examined the press and type found in the police raid. Among the type, he could find no letter 'G'. The coupons had been printed using a 'C' that had been 'tampered with', instead of a 'G'. The defaced letter 'C' had disappeared since the case began. At length the printer admitted that he had destroyed it after the first reports of a police investigation appeared in the London press.

Of the twenty-two men charged, nineteen stood trial at Manchester Assizes in May 1942, variously accused of a conspiracy to produce the counterfeit clothing coupons and of forging signatures on the parcels of coupons handed into the post office. The shadowy 'Mr Jackson of Birmingham' went to penal servitude for four years, and nine other men, including the printer, to lesser terms of imprisonment. It was established that the going rate in the buying and selling of genuine clothing coupons was £11 (£440) per thousand. Sales were so common in the trade as hardly to cause comment. It was quite usual to have coupons on approval, presumably to see whether they were counterfeit or not.

The accused men repeated that they had no idea such buying and selling of coupons was illegal. Suppose a clothing retailer or wholesaler was called up for military service. Were not the coupons he held part of his stock? Was he not entitled to sell them along with everything else? The presiding judge, Mr Justice Asquith, cut swiftly through this argument. 'You have to consider how far you can believe anybody who, being a Manchester trader in clothing, says after the rationing scheme has been in operation for quite a long time that he had no idea it was wrong to buy or sell coupons.'[21]

Clothing coupon forgers proved elusive. There was no comparable prosecution until the years of post-war austerity. In August 1946, Scotland Yard admitted that the three master forgers of clothing coupons, whom they had been tracking for some time, had slipped through their fingers. Their counterfeit coupons were now said to be selling for £60 (£2,400) a thousand, produced by at least two different presses working somewhere in the provinces. The police claimed that they knew the 'Big Four' of the forged coupons racket. They were working in Leeds and Sheffield, from where many thousands of forged demob and industrial coupons had circulated in the past few months throughout the Midlands and the North of England, priced at 1s. 9d. to 3s. each. This was rather more than the £60 a thousand previously estimated.

In the following month, the government tried to reduce the value of forged coupons by releasing 2,200,000 army surplus garments for sale coupon-free, mainly shirts and underwear. Six months later, however, Scotland Yard reported that a gang with a mobile printing press was 'flooding' the country with new forgeries.

It was not until 7 August 1947 that Alfred Goldfine of Brixton and Jack Harris of Stepney were sent to prison for passing 12,000 of what were described as the 'best ever' fake coupons. The printing press itself remained undiscovered but there was an interesting development during the trial. The Old Street magistrate condemned Goldfine's 'appalling record' of theft, embezzlement, housebreaking, receiving and conspiracy to receive. The magistrate could only send him to prison for nine months. 'Why was he not sent for trial at the Old Bailey, where, if found guilty, he would have been liable to penal servitude for fourteen years?' J. M. Symons, prosecuting, said, 'There was a reason, but I can understand your feelings.' In other words, Mr Goldfine had given valuable information to the police in return for being dealt with by a magistrate, rather than at the Central Criminal Court, and going to prison for nine months instead of to penal servitude for fourteen years.

As a result, in the next few weeks Scotland Yard was able to break up a gang of Kensington coupon forgers who were brought to court in January 1948. The CID raided a house in Elgin Crescent, Notting Hill, where they found the printing press at last in a back room. Near by, in Arundel Gardens, a second house was raided and loose coupons found. Once again, the leader of the counterfeiters was philosophical when confronted with his work. 'You don't want me to tell you where they came from: they are not a bad job are they?' When told he would be arrested, he said, 'That is fair enough. Some of this gear could be used for perfectly innocent purposes. I hope I shall get it back.'

His defence was that he had printed the coupons from plates brought to him by the organizer of the conspiracy. The law decided that he himself was the organizer and sent him to penal servitude for seven years. Another man and two women were arrested. There was general agreement by prosecutors and defenders alike that these coupons had been 'beautifully forged'. However, one of the women said sadly, 'I must be mad to get mixed up with Watson round the corner. I know there are thousands of these coupons in Kensington.'[22]

Ironically, three months later the President of the Board of Trade, Harold Wilson, announced the relaxation of the clothes rationing system, while government and clothiers met to discuss the end of restrictions. The problem now, the clothiers insisted, was a glut of clothing, not a shortage.

By contrast with the illegal clothing trade, the demand for black market petrol was persistent and insatiable. Petrol was the major commodity which the country could not produce; even tyres might be recycled. It was also prohibited, for most people. In the summer of 1945, a basic ration was restored after the end of the war in Europe, only to be abolished in the fuel crisis of 1947. Motorists and garages were checked for evidence of the illegal transfer of coupons, the misuse of supplementary petrol for private motoring, and such uneconomic usage as allowing the engine to run while a vehicle was stationary, or driving 800 yards more than the shortest route, all of which were offences under wartime fuel regulations.

On such occasions as wartime Derby Day, thousands of racegoers were stopped and the source of their petrol checked. When 5,000 cars were counted at the race in 1941, anxious questions were asked in Parliament. With the end of the basic ration, anyone going to race meetings by car was likely to be met by civilian or military police, also present to check identity cards and military papers, as well as by officials from the Petroleum Department. In April 1945, when the war at sea was over, the opening of flat racing at Ascot saw the biggest check-up of all. Every driver at the course was questioned by the police. Other police stopped cars in the neighbourhood, and a ring of motorcycle police kept constant patrol some miles away. Drivers had to give details of their journey, their reason for coming by road, and explain how they obtained petrol. Hire car drivers were included in these interrogations.

Such was the culture of scarcity, austerity and enforcement. Prosecutions for the illegal sale or theft of petrol coupons began in 1940–41, before the ban on private motoring. The first major coupon theft was at the War Transport Office in Morden, in July 1941, when 500,000 coupons were stolen during the night by two men, using a tradesman's van, a skeleton key, and a jemmy to force the filing cabinets. Nine men were arrested and charged with stealing or receiving 43,436 of these coupons. In the end, the police were unable to prove the theft charges or catch all the thieves though they had 'a shrewd suspicion who they were'. The nine men prosecuted were convicted of receiving the coupons, which they had been selling at the equivalent of five gallons for £1 (£40). Three were described as 'wholesalers' for whom such robberies were 'a regular trade' and for which one had previous convictions. Indeed, he had worked for the Petroleum Board, gaining knowledge of rationing procedure and the use of franking stamps. He was sent to hard labour for three months.[23]

By 1942 thefts were more common. When coupons equivalent to 3,000 gallons of petrol were stolen from the Ministry of Transport Office in Gray's Inn Road, during February 1942, this was only one of 'several' similar cases which Scotland Yard was investigating. Even so, these thefts were still a modest beginning and no match for the subsequent weekend raid on 9–10 November 1947 at the Regional Petroleum Office in Churchill Way, Cardiff, when 175,000 coupons representing 750,000 gallons of petrol were stolen. By then, the black market price for such a haul was £45,000 (£1,800,000).

Despite the demand for petrol, counterfeit coupons were less readily marketed than those for clothing. The purchase of petrol was banned for the majority of the population and its use was likely to draw police attention. The counterfeit trade therefore looked for customers among those with fewer scruples about breaking the law than the purchasers of coupon-free stockings in Berwick Market. Indeed, the forgery of car logbooks was hardly less important than counterfeit coupons. Genuine logbooks of cars bought from scrap heaps or duplicates printed from these were in use to draw additional petrol rations on behalf of the criminal underworld. Billy Hill's printer,

'John the Tilter', had at one point run off more than 800 extra log-books, which were used to draw additional petrol rations. When the government attempted to check the circulation of counterfeit coupons by having new and differently designed sheets printed, Hill claimed that his counterfeits were in circulation even before the originals. If true, this was scarcely possible without the assistance of someone at the Board of Trade or the Petroleum Board.[24]

The underworld had as much need for petrol as those with other occupations. As a pimp, Gino Messina needed to drive round central London, through blitz and blackout, supervising the girls who were working for him. He could hardly apply to the Ministry of Fuel for a supplementary business allowance of petrol. Instead, it became an essential part of the girls' profession 'to cadge petrol coupons' from their clients by a selection of hard-luck stories.[25]

Forged coupons were seldom traced to their source. As Hill describes it, printers were better protected by the gangs than those who produced clothing coupons. Moreover, some dealers took the precaution of having counterfeit coupons printed in Ireland. As early as July 1940, the first importers of counterfeit petrol coupons from Eire were sent to prison. However, it was not easy to prevent something as light as a packet of coupons crossing the border between Eire and Northern Ireland.[26]

In the underworld of billiard hall and dog track, petrol coupons were easily traded. In July 1945, according to Detective Inspector Reid of Scotland Yard, the proceeds of petrol coupon robberies and forgeries were 'being sold in small quantities at dog tracks in various parts of the country'. As late as 1948, when petrol remained rationed, two forgers identifiable by the style of their coupons were still working in London. They had never been caught and never would be.[27]

The post-war basic ration was restored again on 1 June 1948, allowing motorists to travel about ninety miles a month. The urge to augment this with black market fuel remained strong. In August 1948, current counterfeits, described by the police as 'good forgeries', were still circulating in large numbers. In June and July that year, according to the Board of Trade, 200,000 gallons of petrol were lost through these imitations. 'There are people in practically every city and town throughout the country selling these things.' The police believed there were two forgers in London producing coupons independently, though it might be one forger with two presses. But the large number of counterfeits in circulation was spoiling the market. One of the traffickers' 'stooges' who sold the forged coupons to individuals 'to make a bob or two', as he put it, confirmed that there were so many that they could now be bought for three shillings and sold again at three shillings and sixpence.[28]

The forgeries were so good that defendants claimed to have used them innocently. In March 1947, the Earl of Carrick was fined £100 (£4,000) for using coupons he thought genuine. Two months earlier, Marjorie, Countess of Brecknock had been given coupons she thought were genuine and was not prepared to betray her benefactor. 'I don't want to give away the person from whom I got them.' She was fined the lesser sum of £40 (£1,600), possibly because the court approved of her ladyship's refusal to act as a grass.[29]

Clothing and petrol coupons were an obvious choice for forgery, theft and barter, but some minor criminals profited from other documents. As war became inevitable, the National Registration Act had passed into law on 1 September 1939. Registration began on 29 September, followed by the issue of individual identity cards – green for adults and brown for children under sixteen. By July 1941, one twenty-eight-year-old army deserter had not only printed his own but was running a press to provide them for those who followed in his path. In the same month, 700,000 identity cards were lost, apart from blank cards stolen from the local offices of National Registration officials. Moreover, it was impossible to authenticate identity cards by photographs, when there were 46,000,000 holders.[30]

It was important that an identity card, whether stolen or forged, should be blank when it was bought. The card could be easily 'read' by any civilian or military policeman. When filled in, it would have four letters of the alphabet followed by four numbers. The four letters would identify progressively the area in which the holder lived, to within a few streets. The first three numbers then identified the family or household in that area to which the holder belonged. The final number identified which member of the family the holder was.

In December 1942, the Ministry of Labour admitted that the selling of identity cards was 'particularly rife at the moment'. Combined action by ministry and police 'to round up persons evading military service' had been frustrated by this illegal trade. 'People are becoming aware from the press reports of police swoops on sports meetings, public dances and the like, that they cannot hope successfully to evade military service unless they are in possession of registration certificates.' In the previous month it had been revealed that an identity card could be bought in Lambeth for no more than £4 (£160).[31]

Again, it was hinted that thieves had inside help. In May 1943, a man was arrested in a taxi in Dorset Square, with 110 new identity cards only just issued. He had been under surveillance by CID officers but seemed surprised when they closed in upon the taxi from which another man had fled. Turning to Detective Inspector Powell, he said: 'I want you to help me. You have got me but there are more in it than me. I don't want the others to think that I have shopped them, but if you go to Brixton Town Hall you will get the rest.'[32]

Forgery was not always a matter of using a printing press but merely of altering genuine documents. Changes to service travel warrants, or immaculate imitations by hand to increase the balance in a Post Office Savings Bank book, or falsification of medical papers, were as remunerative as selling identity cards. Leonard Shaw, an army deserter, showed such skill at imitating post office date-stamps freehand that he had carried out 557 savings book forgeries before he was caught, earning himself a total of £1,500 (£60,000).[33]

Occasionally, such cases had greater significance. Elizabeth Ann Dryden was charged in Brighton under the Official Secrets Act with being in possession of Grade 4 medical cards and rubber stamps marked 'Horsham' and 'Horsham Medical Board'. With these she could produce certificates exempting men from call-up. She pleaded she was only looking after a briefcase containing them on behalf of Reg Lester, who had already been sentenced. In December 1942, Sir Charles Doughty, Recorder of Brighton, sent her to hard labour, remarking of her offence, 'It touches the fringe, but only the fringe of a very serious crime, the crime of using ingenuity, and probably money, to enable most undesirable people to avoid the obligations which fall on citizens of the state.'[34]

Peace brought no respite. In December 1946, 47,000,000 new ration books were distributed and guards rode with the lorries for the first time. On the night of 14 January, 280,000 coupons were stolen from the Ministry of Labour offices at Hendon. Two nights later, the same gang stole 30,000 from the offices in Chiswick. Coupon crime ended only with the end of rationing but the voice of authority sounded until the last. William Ross was a grocer of Windsor. As foods came off the ration, his customers had redundant coupons in their ration books. Some cut them out and gave them to him to get rid of. A man of complete honesty, Mr Ross sent them as used coupons to the Ministry of Food. He explained why, but heard to his astonishment that he was to be prosecuted. Others were prosecuted for returning too few coupons but Mr Ross was prosecuted for sending too many. Windsor magistrates agreed with the defending solicitor that this was an outrageous abuse of power by officials 'looking for something to do'. Mr Ross was set at liberty.[35]

9

'You're in the Army Now!'

On 1 December 1941, Mr Justice Charles opened Lewes Assizes with a warning to the military.

> Even in the midst of war one has to do something to keep law and order in the country. With the exception of about five cases, every one in this calendar is a soldier – bigamy, housebreaking, rape – and I shall be told in every case that he is an excellent soldier and that the Army cannot afford to lose him. That doesn't affect my mind in the least.

Bigamy was back in fashion. A soldier with two or three wives had two or three women drawing allowances for him. In the confusion and dispersal of wartime it was difficult to track offenders.

Yet crimes against civilians hardly matched those committed against the Army itself. In the autumn of 1939, the War Office was unprepared for the scale of internal theft from supplies of the British Expeditionary Force, in transit to the Western Front. Indeed, it was so unprepared for troop movements of any kind in mechanized warfare that it appealed for help to the Automobile Association, 850 of whose Scouts were sent to France to keep the Army on the right road.

The first recorded appointment of a King's Provost Marshal to keep military discipline is that of Henry Guylford in 1511, though such powers were exercised long before. Yet by 1939, in maintaining military law and order, the Corps of Military Police still represented little more than the equivalent of a uniformed civil constabulary. More specifically, it lacked the investigative role of a civilian CID. A small Field Security Wing, formed in 1937, was an intelligence unit and had been transferred to the Intelligence Corps. In the first months of war, the Corps of Military Police still remained the equivalent of a uniformed civil police. It enforced King's Regulations, arrested defaulters to be brought before their commanding officers, and exercised cautionary surveillance on brothels which might be patronized by the BEF in France.

The BEF began to land in France six days after war was declared. Though its destination was the Franco-German frontier, its reserve dumps and stores were in North-West France, supplied through the ports of Brest, St Nazaire, Nantes and Le Havre. Vehicles and equipment were carried by rail to forward depots.

Cheap drink and drunkenness among British troops led immediately to assaults, wounding and sexual crimes in the old-fashioned towns of Western France. Six thousand soldiers were in camp near Rennes. In seventeen days they staged a smash and grab raid on the main jeweller's shop; four cases of the novel crime of car theft, including the town's only police car; housebreaking; robberies with violence; six cases of larceny; fifteen serious cases of assault, damage and fraud. At Nantes, in the first half of December, British labour battalions were responsible for a suspicious death, three cases of breaking and entering, twenty robberies, five cases of car theft, five cases of stealing and eight cases of assault.

Professional thieves in the Army also made contact with local black market receivers. When two supply ships berthed at Brest, 24,000 cigarettes were promptly stolen from one and 14,000 from the other, as well as food, chocolate and shaving cream, in 'large quantities'. From another ship, berthed at Le Havre, more than half its cargo of 50,000 razor blades went missing, as well as 1,400 items of equipment, including clothing, uniforms, cutlery and toothbrushes. Cases of spirits were a favourite objective.

Other thefts in transit, as supplies were carried eastward by rail, proved more serious. Military vehicles arrived in forward areas stripped of batteries, tool kits and essential spares, making them useless in a military campaign. Most items were looted by convoy guards or the local population. NAAFI stores suffered badly. Although some thieves were caught and charged, the cases were prepared by officers with little knowledge of military law. Too often, the Judge Advocate-General's department was obliged to advise that proceedings be dropped.[1]

At the end of November 1939, there was sufficient alarm at the War Office for the Chief Commissioner of Metropolitan Police, Sir

Philip Game, to be consulted. A senior CID officer, Chief Inspector George Hatherill, was sent to France on a tour of inspection, accompanied by Colonel Kennedy, Provost Marshal BEF. Hatherill found the situation as bad as he had expected, at almost every port, railway siding and depot.

He was asked by the War Office to make proposals. His first was that Military Police must guard supplies throughout their journey and at the railheads. Experienced police officers were needed. He recommended that those who had volunteered for the Army should be withdrawn from their units to form this escort. Such was the concern at the War Office that, within a week of his report, 500 were withdrawn for this purpose.

Hatherill's second proposal was for a Special Investigation Branch within the Military Police, and similar units in the Royal Navy and the RAF. Routine investigating and questioning, equivalent to the role of civilian detective sergeants or detective inspectors, would be carried out by senior NCOs. By the end of the war, SIB had investigated tens of thousands of cases, arrested more than 50,000 soldiers and civilians, and recovered what Hatherill called 'vast amounts' of stolen War Department property.[2]

On 12 February 1940, Major C. E. Campion, until then a detective superintendent in charge of the Criminal Records Office, with fifty-eight officers and NCOs recruited from men released by Scotland Yard, arrived for military training at the Corps of Military Police depot at Aldershot. This first detachment of SIB was then posted to the Provost Service BEF. It disembarked at Le Havre on 29 February 1940 and was soon involved in stamping out 'a large-scale racket in connection with NAAFI stores'.

A month later, Colonel Seymour Mellor, Chief Constable of War Department Constabulary, inspected the arrangements in France and made further recommendations for an increase in the Ports Provost Companies, whose principal role was to prevent pilfering and smuggling at the docks, and to expand those units guarding entrance gates or examining passes. He also recommended an increase in the number of SIB sections.

There was an early setback for SIB when its commander, Major Campion, received a fatal head wound in a German attack on

Boulogne on 19 May 1940. By then, however, Military Police and SIB were on a wartime footing. It was thanks to the directions and organization of the uniformed branch that so many soldiers reached the embarkation beaches and the port of Dunkirk.

SIB's role expanded rapidly, to the extent that 925 of its officers were killed or wounded during the course of the war. It established itself in the Middle East in December 1940, when the existing Military Police were hard pressed to contain the illegal trade in drugs and weapons between Egypt and Palestine, as well as to combat wholesale thefts of military equipment.

It was sometimes necessary to impose order at the battlefront. When Australian troops led the capture of Benghazi on 6 February 1941, Military Police were unable to reach the town until next day. Despite the enemy withdrawal, they reported Benghazi in chaos. Looting and drunkenness were unchecked. The source of this disorder was a unit guarding a captured building which proved to be the brewery. The guards had broken in, removed the entire stock, and consumed it in a single night with the aid of friends. Some might be fighting drunk and some comatose but none of the revellers was in a condition to meet an enemy counter-attack.[3]

Egypt's population was less than wholehearted in its support of British military action. Army deserters slipped easily into the underworlds of Cairo, Port Said and Alexandria, with their lucrative trading in drugs and weapons. Deserters who called themselves the 'British Free Corps' and the 'Dead End Kids' became gangs in their own right. As at home, a majority of thefts occurred from railways and docks. A disgruntled Egyptian railway worker had only to mark a wagon containing valuable supplies and fail to lock it securely for the contents to be looted before it reached the railhead. NAAFI stores were looted at the railhead, and, in one case, buried in a rubbish dump for collection.

The British Army still held Egypt and Palestine. In July 1941, after a month of fighting, the Vichy French in the Levant states of Syria and Lebanon were defeated by the Allies and both countries were occupied against a possible German attack through neutral Turkey. The underworlds of Alexandria and Cairo at once engaged in a drugs trade with Beirut, since the growing of opium was tolerated in the Lebanon. Stolen army lorries would be driven to the docks at Alexandria and loaded with military supplies by virtue of forged documents and bribed dockers. These vehicles, immune from search by Egyptian police, were then driven to the Lebanon. With the assistance of a member of the Lebanese parliament, stolen goods were exchanged for hashish, to be smuggled back in four-gallon jerrycans. In the more rigorously policed culture of Cairo or Alexandria, the hashish could be sold at a very large profit.[4]

As a variant, the stolen lorries were sold in the Lebanon. Indeed, vehicles and tyres were the major thefts from the Army in the Levantine states. However, other vehicles which returned to Egypt with drugs also carried normal freight and passengers. On one return journey through Palestine, an innocent passenger was the comedian Tommy Cooper. Only when the lorry crashed and the wreckage was inspected by Military Police and SIB was hashish discovered, packed in the jerrycans. The passengers were not informed and it appears Cooper never guessed that he was travelling with a dozen kilos of drugs. The Alexandria gang was broken by SIB, after a raid on a villa at Sidi Bishr, the arrest of the dealers, and the discovery of cans of hashish buried in the garden.

More threatening than drug dealing was the wholesale theft of weapons and ammunition. Jewish settlers in Palestine and their Arab neighbours prepared for conflict, even with the German army on African soil. SIB began to investigate gun-running by British servicemen and Palestine civilians in 1942–3. After the German defeat at El Alamein in October 1942, and in the wake of the campaign, both sides left behind them the debris of battle. Arms dumps were created from abandoned weapons, notably on the field of El Alamein.

The prospect of the British Eighth Army having to deal with an internecine war in its rear, while still engaging the Germans in the Western Desert, remained a possibility. The purchasers of weapons, smuggled to Palestine by army and RAF lorries, included Abraham Rachlin and Lieb Sirkin, two leaders of Hagana, a clandestine organization for Jewish self-defence, set up in 1920. In 1937 Lord Peel, Chairman of the Royal Commission on Palestine, had described it as a 'para-military organization'. In 1943 the military court which tried the two men called it 'a widespread organization extending even into the army'.

On 12 August 1943, two British soldiers and the two leaders of Hagana went on trial for what the prosecution called 'the large-scale running of guns into Palestine'. A principal source was still the arms dumps at El Alamein. 'Soldiers armed with forged documents drove Service lorries on what were apparently legitimate convoy journeys from Egypt to Palestine.' Officials at the frontier posts let them pass without interference. Their destination was the port of Haifa, to which they brought Italian, German and American arms and ammunition, sufficient to equip a small army. On their last run, the cargo included 300 rifles and 105,000 rounds of small arms ammunition. For these rifles, the soldiers were paid £900 (£36,000).

The investigation and the trial, whose complexities occupied two months, removed the immediate threat of civil war in Palestine. The soldiers, from the Buffs and the Royal Sussex Regiment, were sent to prison for fifteen years. Abraham Rachlin, of the Palestine Police, was gaoled for seven years and Lieb Sirkin, a Lithuanian and a prominent member of the Seamen's Union, for ten years, as what the court president called members of 'a dangerous organization for arms smuggling throughout the Middle East'.

Egyptian dealers in illegal weapons targeted trains and army camps, as well as the ammunition dumps of the desert. Guarding the dumps and the camps was one of SIB's duties, at a time when the rules of engagement permitted its members to fire on those attempting to loot War Department property. It was one of the few occasions when SIB soldiers shot to kill.[5]

Military criminality was not confined to drugs and gun-running. In all theatres of war, civilian contractors and soldiers conspired to defraud the War Office. In the Levant states, an officer of the Royal Engineers was supervising the construction of a desert road by a local contractor. It was to be a hard core highway, enabling British armour to move rapidly against a German invasion of Turkey. The contractor and the RE officer came to an agreement, whereby the contractor made presents of jewellery and money to the officer, in exchange for being allowed to build the road more cheaply. Unfortunately, the officer had not realized how cheap it would be. It was described at his court martial as little more than a strip of tar sprayed on the desert sand, unable to sustain the weight of a car, much less of an armoured vehicle. A similar series of cases was running in India, where SIB arrested some 3,000 suspects and recovered over £750,000 (£30,000,000) of stolen property. In one instance, the defenders were contractors who had made bogus claims to the amount of £27,000,000 (£1,080,000,000) for roads built in Burma.[6]

The most famous of SIB's clients in the Middle East was Captain Neville Heath of the RASC, hanged in 1946 after two of the most lurid murders of young women in English criminal history. In 1941 his unit was guarding the oil pipeline from Baghdad to Haifa, and Heath was making frequent visits to the nightlife of Cairo, in particular its brothels. It was plain that he had no money to pay for these indulgences and his commanding officer grew uneasy. This fatherly colonel drew up a financial plan for the young acting-captain. Heath needed no plan. He had already stolen an extra pay-book and was drawing double pay. He was about to buy the colonel's car with a worthless cheque and sell it before the cheque was returned.

At his court martial, as in similar cases, no one inquired how this young confidence trickster and housebreaker, a pilot dismissed the service for embezzlement by the RAF in 1937, gaoled for theft and released in September 1939, was accepted by the Army, commissioned and promoted to the rank of acting-captain within eighteen months of leaving Borstal. Cashiered by the Jerusalem court martial, he jumped ship at Durban, joined the South African Air Force as 'Captain Jimmy Armstrong', and re-emerged in the dock of the Central Criminal Court in October 1946.[7]

If military justice was hard-pressed in North Africa, it was daunted by the Italian campaign. Civilian and military crime assumed such proportions that, by the end of the war, thirteen sections of SIB were needed in this theatre, with a fourteenth to cover railway theft. In Italy alone, the branch investigated 22,809 cases and arrested 38,257 soldiers and civilians.

To investigate crime near the Italian battlefront was not always possible. In the winter of 1944–5, 'Shifty' Burke, a pre-war safe-breaker, arrived with his unit in a ruined village just behind the battlefront, facing the Wehrmacht's 'Gothic Line', the last German defence line, running across Italy from south of La Spezia to Pesaro. The pay officer came weekly with the brigade pay, secured in a three-quarter hundredweight safe on a lorry with an armed escort. Overnight, the safe was left in a damaged house with a lone sentry on the door. Burke and two friends extracted gelignite from a pile of defused jumper mines. They also equipped themselves with detonating fuses and detonators, used to blow up suspected booby traps left by the Germans.

In the darkness, the sentry was overpowered and tied up. The sound of the safe being blown was covered by the din of an artillery bombardment a mile or two away. No one had yet been paid and the safe contained £4,000 (£160,000) in lire and sterling. Before leaving with their haul, the thieves stood where the trussed-up sentry could see them, counted out £250 (£10,000), and hid it under a floorboard, so that he would know where to find it. It seemed he was not able to remember anything of his ordeal, nor to offer useful information to those investigating the robbery. By the time the inquiry began, the robbers were among those sent up to the front line and no longer available. Unfortunately for Burke, this was his last 'really good tickle' of the war. Worse still, the lira had fallen against the pound before he could change his share.[8]

In North-West Europe, from D-Day on 6 June 1944 until 31 March 1945, 7,875 servicemen were arrested by eight SIB sections and 36,366 charged by the Military Police, 10,363 as deserters. Others arrested included French and Belgian civilians who tapped petrol pipelines or were in illegal possession of War Department property. From the start of the Normandy campaign, army thieves made contact with local receivers. As the front line rolled back to Belgium and Germany, opportunities for illegal trading became more attractive. The greater the military success, the worse the problem. As Belgium was liberated, opportunities developed to smuggle tobacco, cosmetics and liquor between Belgium and France, and to trade currency illegally between them.

Losses at ports and depots were described as huge. By the beginning of 1945, SIB was fully occupied with existing cases with no scope for crime prevention in the supply network. One section was then detached and used solely as a surveillance unit for goods in transit. Further SIB sections were sent from England, in response to the growing quantity of stolen equipment and stores being passed to the French and Belgian black markets. The Ports Provost Companies were outpaced by the scale of theft at the French and Belgian ports.

In Belgium, vehicle theft assumed such proportions that Military Police set up car parks in all towns, so that vehicles were held under surveillance. In general, the civilian population was eager for food, cigarettes, clothing and petrol. Even stolen army blankets could be transformed into women's overcoats. Troops willing to steal these commodities acquired the jewellery, watches and cameras offered in exchange.

Many arrests seemed pointless. Though civilian offenders were caught and handed to the civil authorities, it was difficult to punish them. Belgian prisons were full of racketeers, looters, war criminals and collaborators. When civilians were convicted of black market-eering, the appropriate prison sentence was passed. They were then sent home and told to wait there until informed of a vacancy in a prison where they could serve their sentences.[9]

Deserters merged easily into the underworld of the newly-liberated cities. In the turmoil of liberation, easily forged documents and passes were scarcely worth a glance. To counter this, in February 1945, a secret operation was planned. For a period of forty-eight hours all local leave was cancelled and all troops, with a few neces-sary exceptions, were confined to unit lines or billets. Even those required to go out on duty were obliged to carry a special order. Across North-East France and Belgium, road blocks were put in place. SIB and Military Police raided suspect locations, including cafés and hotels. It was a joint exercise with the civil police, and when it was over, 450 deserters had been arrested. Unfortunately these were not the criminal élite, nor were they a large proportion of the total number of men who were missing.

A regular cause of investigation was the robbery by troops of enemy aliens or prisoners of war. Among these cases was the infam-ous voyage of the troopship *Dunera* from England to Australia in 1940. The ship was carrying German and Italian civilians to an internment camp near Melbourne, under the guard of a company of the Pioneer Corps. Each detainee was allowed a suitcase and these cases were stacked on deck. After a few days, it was noticed that many of the suitcases were broken open and that articles from them were 'strewn about'. Members of the escort suggested that this was because they had come open or broken open when 'slung aboard'. Yet the number broken open increased as the days of the voyage passed. Articles lying on the deck which appeared to be of no great value were then 'dumped overboard' on the orders of one of the officers.

On 16 June, Colonel Scott, commanding the Pioneer Corps, paraded his men on deck and addressed them, almost with an understanding wink.

> I am only too well aware that were we in the position of our guests [meaning the internees] after being searched we should be lucky if we had our buttons left. So therefore I close an eye to any little petty offence of purloining articles. I am an old soldier, I know that the British Tommy looks upon a time like this to help himself to any unattended trifles.

The parade became relaxed and responsive. Colonel Scott reassured them further.

> When I inspected your company the other morning I could not help seeing little articles which I am sure did not come aboard with you, but it has reached my ears that a certain number of people have started to loot cases. This must immediately cease, but I'm damned if I'm going to punish any man unless this really ought to be.

Major Mothersole of the Suffolk Regiment, who told the colonel that the cases should be guarded or stowed away for safety, received the choleric reply, 'Are you telling me what to do?' Major Mothersole nonetheless ordered the damaged cases to be stored and put four soldiers on charges for stealing from them. He might have saved his energy, since Colonel Scott admonished them and let them go.

During the remainder of the voyage, the military escort exhibited a mixture of criminality and incompetence. The detainees were robbed of their money, which was shared out among the sergeants' mess in the cabin of Regimental Sergeant Major Bowles. Colonel Scott thought Bowles 'an invaluable warrant officer with a character beyond reproach'. He had served in the Royal Dragoons for twenty-six years, won the Military Medal, had carried the Royal Standard at the Royal Review in 1924, and was a member of the King's Bodyguard.

When arrested by the Military Police on his return to England, Bowles was found in possession of a large number of articles belonging to the internees, including pairs of shoes, a leather toilet set, an electric razor, a leather writing case, a slide rule, a travelling clock, a chromium clock and a brown leather holdall to carry his acquisitions. These were said to be merely items the internees had 'left behind' on the ship – 'enough to open a shop', as the sergeant major admitted, during questioning. His interrogators were reduced to cataloguing the items by holding them up, one at a time, so that RSM Bowles could say simply, 'Mine' or 'Internees'.

At the same time, security was so lax on the troopship that at Melbourne a German detainee escaped through a porthole disguised in the sergeant major's uniform. He slid down a steel hawser, jumped, and reached the quayside. He was seen there by Sergeant Arthur Helliwell, who raised the alarm and gave chase. The fugitive was recaptured. He was then taken down to the cells on the troopship and systematically beaten up by Sergeant Helliwell. Captain Magnus, the interpreter officer, was appalled to find the prisoner Eckart in 'a deplorable state', not least because Helliwell was now refusing him drinking water or blankets. When Magnus asked what had happened, Helliwell said reassuringly that Herr Eckart had fallen on the quayside and his face had 'hit the ground'.

When Sergeant Major Bowles was questioned about his 'larceny on the high seas', he replied that all the transactions had been legitimate. After all, he said, none of the detainees had complained, as they could have done to Colonel Scott. It was certainly true that none of their complaints had been recorded.

A court martial at the Duke of York's barracks sent Bowles to prison for a year and ordered him to be dismissed the service. Sergeant Helliwell, who had beaten up the fugitive, was more lightly dealt with by a severe reprimand, as was Colonel Scott. Perhaps the spring of 1941 was not a season for draconian sentences and public examples. It was certainly a sensitive time to hold trials of this sort.

Even while the court martial was being held, the Military Police were busy with cases involving their own members. Three military policemen were sent to prison in April for robbing internees and receiving stolen property from Canadian soldiers. Gold sovereigns to the amount of £100 (£4,000), as well as other currency and property, had also been found at the home of a major of the Military Police who was commandant of an internment camp. Moreover, despite assurances by Sergeant Major Bowles that acquisition of the internees' possessions must have been legitimate because there had been no complaints, complaints came loudly and in impressive numbers once he was safely in prison. When the matter reached the House of Commons in September, members were assured that the government was meeting all the victims' claims at once.[10]

There were few army scandals in which men dealing with criminals proved themselves to be criminals of the worst type. The most notable, so far as it reflected on military policing, was the conduct by members of the Military Provost Special Corps at Gillingham Detention Camp, which ended with the deliberate killing of a detainee. Forty-year-old Rifleman Clayton was in the advanced stages of pulmonary tuberculosis but that was not the cause of death. On 17 March 1943, the prisoner was brought to Regimental Sergeant Major James Culliney by Flight Sergeant Chapman of the Provost Special Corps, who said, 'This man refused to march and I think he is malingering.' The two sergeants tried to make Clayton pick up his rifle and march but he refused.

Quartermaster Sergeant Leslie Salter was told to take Clayton to a single cell and put him in solitary confinement. Half an hour later, Culliney said, he heard Clayton was dead. It was alleged that Salter struck the rifleman but Salter insisted that Clayton 'threw himself to the ground'. Other witnesses saw Salter 'bash the rifleman in the face', bend over him, and strike him as he lay on the ground.

Salter ordered Clayton to be put on a passing handcart used for collecting refuse. The rifleman was lying on his back, knees drawn up, head hanging back over the edge of the cart, his eyes open and staring. The witnesses added that Staff Sergeant Webber, in charge of the cell block, walked across, took Clayton's legs and rolled him off the cart so that he fell heavily into a drain, gashing the back of his head. Salter said, 'That's right. Push him off.' Webber said to Salter, 'I think this man is either dead or very near it.' 'Do you think so?' said

Salter. 'I think you're right.' By this time, Clayton's face had turned yellow and Webber said, 'We don't take dead ones here.' He threw some water in the man's face but there was no response. Both Culliney and Salter were convicted and gaoled for manslaughter.

The defendants in this case could only plead that the harm they did their prisoner was unintended and less than alleged. Yet the proceedings revealed a casual ill-treatment of military prisoners that was often suspected by the public but seldom substantiated. Some NCOs, unsuited to responsibility of any kind, had been permitted to serve in units like the Provost Special Corps, reflecting a lack of manpower and the virtual absence of adequate selection. In the light of this case, the government ordered a judicial inquiry into the whole system of military detention.[11]

The suppression of crime committed by soldiers, or by civilians against the War Department, attracted its most graphic headlines in the wake of battle. Yet the most persistent criminality, and the most easily concealed, was reserved for the home front. The criminal and civilian underworlds had good reason to refer to their dealings with the military as a 'pay parade'.

10

Pay Parade

To those who preyed upon the Army, the NAAFI and its comforts shone like sun on a promised land, while civilian contractors had seldom found fraudulent conversion more tempting. Even before Dunkirk, NAAFI goods in transit were watched and trailed. Security precautions remained so few that a loaded lorry might be parked and left in London, on its way to the Channel ports. In May 1940, one such lorry, containing eighteen large wooden packing cases of cigarettes destined for the NAAFIs of the BEF, was left briefly in Packington Street, Islington. Cigarettes valued at £1,700 (£68,000) vanished. One man who was arrested by Detective Sergeant McDonald of Scotland Yard denied any knowledge of the crime at first. 'Am I supposed to be mixed up in that job? I should think so! That's the work of an organized gang.' When the case against him was put, he said stoically, 'It looks as though I am the mug. I will tell you what happened,' and he proceeded to name the gang.[1]

Previously respectable shopkeepers participated in the robbery of NAAFI goods, particularly when this required only a truckload of supplies delivered to the wrong address. In April 1941, Arthur Cole, a Kemp Town grocer who was fifty-eight and had been in business for many years, made a simple and profitable deal with Wilfred Swan, a NAAFI storeman at Brighton. An army truck would be loaded with tins of syrup from the stores and cheeses from the catering depot, for delivery to individual canteens and cookhouses in the area. It would be driven instead to Cole's garage in Eastern Road, where cheeses and syrup would be unloaded, in exchange for money 'for the soldiers'. No one asked precisely which soldiers. Cole would transfer the goods, a little at a time, by handcart from the garage to his shop. His friend Henry Ashley, a coastguard, would help with the handcart.

The plan worked at first but depended on the soldiers covering the thefts. Bacon and sugar from the NAAFI stores were added to the consignments. When the storeman and the coastguard saw the amount of syrup in Cole's garage, Ashley said uneasily, 'We can't leave it here. We must take it to the shop.' A month later, discrepancies at the NAAFI stores and the army depot became evident. Swan, the storekeeper, came under suspicion. When questioned, he tried to save himself by saying he had no idea what was going on. The first thing he knew about the syrup on the back of the truck was when the RASC driver beside him said that 'we had to get rid of it'.

No one believed him and in the end Swan pleaded guilty. All three men went to prison, the storeman and the grocer for six months, the coastguard for five. Their faces were ashen as the recorder, Sir Charles Doughty, began sentencing. 'It may be that some of you have seen that a dealer in food was sentenced to seven years' penal servitude for receiving food which he knew to have been stolen from a Government store.' Fortunately, the recorder then added, 'But I shall treat you with very remarkable leniency.'[2]

These three were not the stuff of which successful robbers and racketeers were made. The grocer and the coastguard, both fifty-eight, had no criminal past, the storekeeper at thirty-two was out of his depth. Dealing in easily counted objects like cheeses and syrups, they would surely be caught sooner or later. The more astute traders swindled the Army by frauds harder to calculate. A supplier who agreed with a senior NCO to charge for more meat or fish than was supplied was better protected than the Kemp Town grocer. A continuing arrangement also brought substantial sums. A local fishmonger and a warrant officer accused of running such a swindle were allegedly able to make £44 (£1,760) in each two-week period.[3]

Frauds of this kind were perpetrated with the compliance of those in the NAAFI who acted like professional criminals, which was not surprising since some were professional criminals. Six months after Dunkirk, the district manager of nine NAAFI canteens went to prison for fifteen months at London Sessions for stealing 10,000 cigarettes, 144 boxes of chocolates and 24 light bulbs. He had made false entries in his accounts to suggest that the money was paid into other branches than the one he had robbed. It was admitted that black market dealers had been planting their own men in NAAFI jobs in the turmoil which followed defeat in France. 'Our difficulties arose after Dunkirk, when it was necessary to take on several thousand new employees. The black market people, no doubt, got their men in during this time, and it is taking time to sort them out. We believe now that we have almost got to the bottom of the scheme.'[4]

This was not quite true. Among NAAFI management was John Firth of Maida Vale, who had seven well-concealed convictions, one leading to five years' penal servitude, another to four years' penal servitude, and a third to simple imprisonment for two years. Indeed, he had been in prison until September 1941. Firth's speciality was to promise club owners and publicans that he could lay hands on supplies of whisky illegally, presumably from the NAAFI. He would take payment in advance from his customer and then fail to deliver the drink. To vanish with the money was less risky than robbing the services.

The customer had also broken the law and there were few complaints until May 1944, when the proprietress of the Windmill Club in Old Burlington Street and the owner of the Flower Pot Hotel, Macclesfield, went to the police. They had paid Firth £240 (£9,600) between them and never seen a bottle of whisky. With the nimbleness of an old lag, he insisted that he had been 'badly let down by his suppliers', and pointed out that the owner of the Windmill Club had 'tried to buy the whisky illegally'. He was sent back to prison.[5]

In sending comforts to troops overseas, the NAAFI faced such a rising incidence of theft, from the warehouses and in transit, that by the beginning of 1944 it was packing consignments of shoes in separate cases, one for the right foot and one for the left, the device used by the Commissariat Department in the Crimean War. 'The drawback to the division of pairs of boots is that if one case is stolen the other is useless to us,' a NAAFI official admitted on 13 January, 'but at least the thieves gain nothing and it may act as a deterrent.'

The most lucrative NAAFI commodity to thieves and servicemen alike remained cigarettes. Compared with organized robberies, thefts from camp stores were small-scale but steady, in the hope of averting any serious inquiry. Nonetheless, a soldier who used this method was sent to six months' hard labour at Aldershot in November 1942 for stealing 11,000 cigarettes and marketing them through two civilian receivers – the regimental barber and a forewoman at the army depot.[6]

Soldiers, sailors and airmen were allowed to buy NAAFI cigarettes at lower prices than those prevailing in civilian life. There was support for this in the country and even suggestions that the price should be further reduced. The government feared that lower prices would create a natural supply for the black market. In March 1942, it was decided that NAAFI cigarette prices would be cut no further, though the Chancellor of the Exchequer resisted demands that soldiers should pay the full civilian price. In any case, by May 1942, the shortage of imported tobacco led to unofficial rationing by the NAAFI which restricted each man to five cigarettes a day. Few were likely to reach black marketeers.

In the later stages of the war, as cigarettes became an unofficial currency in liberated Europe, tobacco was a main target of military and civilian thieves. Four days before the invasion of France in 1944, Ernest Lovell, Assistant Chief Controller of the NAAFI, giving evidence at the trial of the director of the Piccadilly Billiards Club, admitted that 'considerable quantities' of cigarettes were being, as he put it, 'lost'. The defendant in this case was charged with receiving stolen goods, having been found in possession of 3,000 cigarettes in packets marked 'NAAFI stores. For His Majesty's Forces'.[7]

Within twelve months of D-Day and the establishment of an Anglo-Continental black market, the scale of robberies from the NAAFI reached new proportions. On the night of 5 June 1945, 2,000,000 cigarettes were stolen from the Army's warehouse at Watford by an armed gang using unmarked lorries. The night watchman was attacked and a NAAFI driver beaten over the head by four of the intruders. Their haul was 250 cases, described as a year's supply for a West End firm. Scotland Yard believed the robbery was the work of a professional underworld gang, known to the police, whose organizers provided alibis for the robbers and arranged the sale of the cigarettes before the theft. The gang had regular customers among publicans, hotel proprietors, cinemas, theatres and clubs. 'Salesmen' liaised with buyers. Bombed-out houses and condemned warehouses served as stores for goods in transit.

Unlike cigarettes packed for the invasion forces in 1944, cigarettes for distribution at home did not have the 'NAAFI Stores' stamp, and were easily marketed. In the first five months of 1945, NAAFI home cigarette robberies totalled some £60,000 (£2,400,000) at retail prices. Their black market value was far higher since, although it fluctuated, they funded many of its deals. A cigarette bought three eggs in France during the invasion of June 1944 but only one egg a year later. Yet it was in Denmark in 1945 that 25,000 cigarettes bought a seven-ton yacht.

In parallel with NAAFI robberies was a steady, unspectacular traffic in stolen goods from soldiers to civilians. Each criminal partnership might count for little in itself but the collective loss to the services was serious and embarrassing. In January 1941, the theft of military food supplies had reached such proportions that the Military Police were instructed 'to keep a sharp lookout for Army ration thieves. Large quantities of food stolen in driblets from camps by soldiers are being passed on to civilians.'[8]

The problem was too widespread to be easily remedied. A sergeant, prosecuted for a theft of provisions on a relatively small scale in 1944, told his interrogators that what he heard was the situation in other cookhouses was certainly so in his own. 'I decided it was no use being conscientious any longer and I decided to do what the rest of them were doing by helping myself. The cookhouse has been nothing but a seething mass of corruption since I entered it.'[9]

Soldiers might steal food to sell to civilians or sometimes as a gesture of solidarity. A remarkable case occurred on a heavily laden troopship sailing out of Liverpool in the summer of 1943. The voyage was not a happy one. On 24 August, three assistant cooks in one mess decided to brighten the company's lives by taking axes and smashing their way into the ship's food stores. They looted food and drink, including 837 bottles of beer and forty-four bottles of whisky, as well as cigarettes. An officer who came to see the cause of the noise found an 'orgy' in progress. The food had been cooked and served to the troops, now milling about the galley in a large crowd, some fighting drunk. The cigarettes were being smoked, the beer and whisky had been consumed and empty bottles thrown out of the portholes, as if to provide a convenient track for an inquisitive U-boat. Order on the ship was not easily restored.[10]

Equipment stolen from the services covered a wide range of goods, from consignments of vests and pants to a precision lathe from RAF Debden and, in May 1944, eight RAF aero engines and the lorry that carried them. These engines were later found abandoned, perhaps because the thief was unable to find a ready purchaser. Once the war was over, buyers became more audacious, as when a number of RAF planes, including four of the latest Beaufighters and two Mosquito fighter-bombers, took off and were never seen again.[11]

In wartime, it was more homely items that the civilian black market welcomed. Billy Hill's claim to have found an army bedding store in the West Country from which he could steal sheets worth £5 a pair was given substance in January 1941 when two civilians and six soldiers were caught running a similar racket in Kent, involving stolen army blankets. The civilians were sent to hard labour for six months and the soldiers court-martialled for 'considerable stealing of army property'. An army or civilian storekeeper who had charge of such supplies was in a good position to run a racket of this kind, as appeared when it was discovered that the storekeeper of the main Ordnance Clothing Depot in Leatherhead had been stealing shirts, vests and pants systematically for civilian sale. He was sent to hard labour in October 1941.[12]

Such items, sold without coupons, were in greater demand after the introduction of clothes rationing. Even army trousers were bought for manual work by Billingsgate porters, among many others. In May 1943, Military Police checking identity cards near the market arrested two men partly dressed in army uniform, on suspicion of their being deserters. They were not deserters but had bought the stolen trousers and shirts which were being sold from the back of a lorry at Billingsgate, and at similar locations, as 'rejects'. Before the police could find the vehicle, it seemed the gang's lookouts recognized trouble and the lorry had moved on.[13]

The scale of individual thefts might remain modest but the pilfering of military clothing and equipment was unremitting. In most cities, the pages of the local press carried weekly stories of those prosecuted and convicted as receivers of property stolen from the armed forces, whether cigars and RAF gloves at Hackney in January 1943; a stock of canned food, blankets and tinned milk at Tooting in April 1942; clothing pilfered systematically from the RAF depot at

Kidbroke in the same month, or 7,500 razor blades from the Canadian Stores Depot at Lambeth in October. These were the minnows of wartime crime but, wherever the journalist's jamjar was lowered, it came up alive with them. With a balance of euphemism and irony, men now spoke of such goods being 'liberated', as if from official detention.[14]

It was rare but not unknown for military supplies to find their way to manufacturers. In the summer of 1942, very large quantities of plywood, otherwise unobtainable, and wire were being stolen from the Royal Engineers in Essex. The value of one consignment was £500 (£20,000). This had been bought by F. V. L. Syndicate Ltd, of Rayners Lane, Harrow. The timber went to the black market and, in this instance, to a cabinetmaker. Once it had been made into articles of furniture and sold, the conspirators felt sure no one could trace it. Before then, they were caught. The dealers went to prison and the cabinetmaker to hard labour.[15]

If cigarettes were the most coveted booty from NAAFI warehouses, the most precious military commodity was probably stolen petrol. There were numerous prosecutions of soldiers and civilians for stealing and receiving military supplies but detection was not always easy. SIB kept a watch on suspect vehicles which, until the abolition of the basic ration in the summer of 1942, were allowed to use undyed 'white' petrol but not dyed army petrol. An inspection of one petrol tank revealed only white petrol. However, closer examination showed that this motorcyclist had concealed his extra tank of stolen army petrol in a large gas-mask case, from which a concealed pipe ran directly to the carburettor. Car drivers would cut out the petrol pump and feed the carburettor by gravity from cans of stolen petrol hidden under the bonnets of their vehicles.

The problems for petrol thieves were transportation and storage, for which reason the amounts stolen were not large, even where thefts were continuous. When an ARP stretcher-bearer went to prison for six months in March 1941, he had managed to carry away fifty-three gallons in jerrycans. It was a modest haul compared with the later thefts of coupons for 500,000 and 750,000 gallons. All the same, offenders were severely dealt with. Sometimes the severity caused unease. In 1942 there were protests in Parliament when a Dunkirk veteran went to prison for three months for stealing two gallons of army petrol.[16]

By August 1941, losses of army petrol had increased to the point where Scotland Yard was asked to advise on the pilfering and wastage of fuel. Among those rounded up and prosecuted as a result were soldiers at Bromley who had been stealing petrol regularly from the quartermaster's stores, and others at Aldershot, including a provost sergeant, charged with stealing and receiving. The downfall of the soldiers in the Bromley case came through an ill-judged attempt to sell some of the petrol to a 'loyal citizen', who reported them.[17]

Petrol was a serious matter for officers and other ranks alike. In February 1942, Captain William James Clapcott of the Pioneer Corps was court-martialled at Aldershot for using in his car petrol intended for army cookers. He was found guilty and cashiered – more of a social embarrassment than it might have been, since Captain Clapcott was also a member of Bournemouth Town Council. At another court martial in the North-East of England on 12 December 1942, Lieutenant-Colonel A. E. Lawrence of the King's Royal Rifle Corps was dismissed the service for using army petrol when he went fishing, shooting and beagling.[18]

In 1942, car tyres became almost unobtainable by civilians. Some dance halls and other entertainments gave free admission to those who came 'wearing' a used tyre and left it for salvage. Scarcity bred a black market in tyres stolen from the services, almost the last source of supply. Even though military tyres bore identification, a War Department insignia and a large black arrow, criminals were prepared to risk using them in desperate times. In one case, the casual glance of a CID inspector at a suspect car led to the discovery of a London basement packed to the ceiling with RAF tyres, stolen from an airfield in Norfolk, and to a prison sentence at London Sessions.[19]

Even civilians who shrugged off such thefts from the services as the inevitable accompaniment of war were unnerved by the pilfering of weapons and ammunition. Guns became easy to buy. In October 1942 the going rate for a Smith & Wesson revolver from Canadian soldiers was £7 (£280). Still more alarming was the ease with which weapons fell into the hands of children. Home Guard stores were seldom guarded and easy to break into. In June 1943, two boys, the elder fifteen, broke into a store from which they stole live hand grenades, ammunition and detonators. They took a hand grenade to a Brighton cinema and sat through the performance, the pin at one point withdrawn, idly pressing and releasing the catch. Later they practised throwing hand grenades on a hillside, before fitting detonators to two bombs and hiding them in the bushes.[20]

Their rivals for attention were two boys of fourteen and fifteen who, during March 1942, escaped from a Wallington remand home in football shorts and barefoot. Better to equip themselves as adolescent gangsters, they broke into the Home Guard store at Upper Norwood, emerging with a tommy-gun, 400 rounds of ammunition, a bayonet and the contents of the cash box which they had forced with the bayonet. In December 1942 ten boys, aged between ten and fourteen, broke into the store at Brentford to see if they could make live ammunition explode by hitting it with a chopper. It was, as the court heard, a miracle that no one was killed. So it was when seven boys burgled a Home Guard store at Clapton in February 1943 and stole 2,000 rounds of sten-gun ammunition. In the face of an existing juvenile crime wave, it was no comfort to hear in February 1941 that the remand homes were full.[21]

In March 1942 it was suggested that regular troops might be moved from other duties to protect Home Guard stores from predators. With the arrival of the US Army, theft was not always necessary. Two brothers at Windsor, aged ten and fourteen, traded buns and cakes with US troops for sixty live shells, which they kept in a cupboard at home. An RAF munitions officer who handled the shells at their trial, told the chairman that if one of them was accidentally dropped during the proceedings, it would severely injure everyone in the courtroom and demolish half the building. On the assumption that they meant no real harm, the elder boy was fined £5 and the younger £1.[22]

Not all these adventures were good-natured. In January 1944, six Glasgow teenagers acquired thirty-two hand grenades and two boxes of detonators. On Friday night, in the blackout, they went to Blytheswood Square to see what they could do to the offices of ICI. With impressive accuracy they began lobbing grenades into the building. By the time the explosions brought the police they had, among other things, blown up the company's boardroom.[23]

Teenage bravado merged easily into teenage crime. In March 1943 three seventeen-year-olds and one eighteen-year-old held up the cashier at the Ambassador cinema in Hayes with three loaded sten-guns and a .22 rifle, all of which had been stolen from the Home Guard armaments store at Hayes. Before being sent to Borstal for three years, they asked for forty-three other cases to be taken into consideration. By contrast with such youthful endeavour, the mere pilfering of army rations and supplies seemed mundane.[24]

The safest schemes for dishonest servicemen and civilians were those which involved no goods at all. Overcharging by civilian contractors, with the assistance of army personnel, was an easier crime. Civilian haulage contractors were frequently called on by the services. In the circumstances, it was impossible to check every mile claimed or even the number of journeys and vehicles. Yet the sums of money involved were far larger than most deals in black market food. Frauds took many forms and might simply consist of lorry drivers booking out more fuel than was used and selling the surplus coupons. They might equally well involve a major swindle of the kind uncovered by SIB at Hove in 1942 and continued through courts martial and civilian trials.

The 'Brighton Transport Case' was a classic of its kind, illustrating a fraud which the recorder claimed was 'common in many towns in this country' as a means of defrauding the Army. The details came to light in the court martial at Preston Barracks in January 1942 of Lieutenant-Colonel John Sidwell, Officer Commanding RASC duties at Brighton, one of only six lieutenant-colonel quartermasters in the Army. Colonel Sidwell had a distinguished record, with forty-seven years' service. He was acquitted at the end of February 1942 on three charges of stealing War Department oil. However, he was convicted and reprimanded on a fourth charge of failing to investigate a report that 'large over-payments of public money were involved in persistent overcharges by a local firm of contractors', to whom nearly £10,000 (£400,000) had been paid in just over twelve months. The firm, Over Brothers of Brighton, was well known in the area.

Colonel Sidwell was spoken of by his superior, Colonel Fraser, as a man whose 'reputation was of the highest, and his word had never been questioned'. On the other hand, when a report of falsified transport accounts, including forged and inflated hauliers' bills, was presented to him, Colonel Sidwell had said there was 'no use in washing dirty linen when the ramp has been stopped'. It was also alleged that he had ordered the transport officer at Preston Barracks, Captain Kingsmill Brown, to destroy a number of transport forms which were 'material evidence in any inquiry'. He made

> no attempt to get into touch with the Special Investigation Branch, or to communicate with Colonel Fraser at the time . . . At least the word 'forgery' and the allegation that a sergeant and private were spending money at the rate of £20 [£800] a week (when the sergeant's pay was £2 and the private's £1), ought to have caused him to inquire into the conduct of his staff.

His transport officer was acquitted of stealing War Department oil but also convicted and reprimanded on the charge of failing to ensure that proper inquiries were made. He also lost two months' seniority.

Following the revelations of the courts martial, civil police arrested the two contractors as well as the sergeant and private who were spending many times their rate of pay every week. They were all charged with conspiracy to obtain money by false pretences. The civilian defendants were the owners of the firm. The basis of the fraud consisted in making claims for more lorries than were used. As a further precaution, the conspirators had signed some of the requisition forms in such names as 'J. Horley', although 'there had never been an officer of that name in the regiment'. Once, when they ran out of names, they used that of a well-known Brighton tailor. Still there was no suspicion. However, despite Colonel Sidwell's orders to his transport officer to destroy such forms, some survived and were presented in evidence, showing clearly that they were forgeries.

The scheme depended on forms being altered when returned to the transport office with the hauliers' claims for payment. It was the transport sergeant who supervised this. As the private, his senior clerk who stood trial with him, recalled,

> If when checking I found that Over's acceptance showed five lorries and the account only showed three lorries, I was told to alter the

figures to the numbers shown in the accounts. I have many times found an item in Over's account which was not covered by a form. In these cases I was instructed to make out a form and sign it in some name which Gosney would tell me.

Junior clerks were instructed that forms should be sent out 'as blank as possible'.

Sometimes a form had been made out but no one had signed it. The senior clerk would take it to the transport officer who would tell him to copy the signature of the officer who had asked for the transport. 'Now you can do a bit of forgery,' the transport officer would say jocularly.

The swindle had begun in May 1940 and had run for a twelve-month before there was any suspicion outside the transport office. Life had been good, the sergeant had taken his senior clerk out to lunch at the best restaurants in Brighton, telling him that he received money from the hauliers as 'commission'. It was arranged that some of this 'commission' found its way to the senior clerk. Sometimes the clerk was sent to the hauliers' office to collect a sealed envelope which contained the sergeant's share of the illegal receipts.

Nemesis arrived in 1941 in the shape of a chief clerk, Bertram Wye, who was to inspect the accounts. He saw that some of the forms were obviously forgeries with altered figures and the signatures of non-existent officers. Close on the heels of Bertram Wye came Sergeant Major Frank Howarth of SIB.

The chief clerk was the weak link. He broke under questioning and agreed to plead guilty in the hope of leniency, admitting to SIB that some two hundred requisition forms were forgeries. Sergeant Major Howarth was asked by the chief clerk's counsel to confirm that his client never had any contact with the hauliers. 'Only by calling at the office to collect the money,' said the SIB man dryly. For the first, but not the last time, there was laughter in court.

There was little defence. One haulier insisted that they had no knowledge of 'overcharging'. If it happened, it must have been the result of a chaotic system of army requisitioning and accounting, in which lorries were away for days at a time. On the pretext of secrecy, the firm was refused information as to where they had been and what they had done. Payments were made three or four months late, whereas the hauliers had to pay cash immediately. If they had gone on dealing with the military, the firm would have been 'in the workhouse'.

The jury found this Over brother guilty and he went to hard labour for fifteen months. The second brother was acquitted. By this time, the transport sergeant had already been sentenced to eighteen months' hard labour at a court martial for these offences and the head clerk to twelve months. These sentences were not effectively increased. The private was given a one-day sentence and the sergeant three months to run concurrently with the time he was already serving in a military prison. As a result of the fraud, extra petrol had been obtained for non-existent transport duties but this charge was not proceeded with.

In passing sentence the recorder described this type of fraud against the services and the government as common throughout the country. The problem was that such men as those now convicted saw 'how easy it was' and found the temptation irresistible. Not only was it easy but, in many cases, there was little risk of being caught. Even those who were caught might find they had an easygoing commander like Colonel Sidwell who saw no use in sullying the regiment's reputation by 'washing dirty linen' once the 'ramp' was stopped.

Nor was it always civilians who defrauded soldiers. In 1941, the elaborate swindle of a 'long firm fraud' was planned, whereby soldiers who had stolen War Office notepaper used it to purchase large quantities of whisky and gin, on official credit, for which it was never intended the suppliers should be paid. Though the scheme was nipped in the bud, the sum involved was already put at £450 (£18,000).[25]

Colonel Sidwell had the reputation of an honourable man. Other officers and gentlemen took to pilfering or the misuse of army funds and supplies with as little hesitation as other ranks. Some found that, in dealing with the underworld, the biter was bitten. An RAF officer in East Anglia was known among London criminals to be 'at it', supplying parachutes for sale as 'surplus parachute silk' to the clothing industry. His outlet was a South London contact, 'Slippery Sam', with a large transport lorry. On hearing of this, Billy Hill approached 'John the Tilter', who owned a sports car similar to a type used by East Anglia police for traffic patrols. Dressed in police uniforms, Hill and his companions chased the lorry one night after it had picked up its load, overtook it and stopped it. At the sight of police uniforms, those in the lorry set off at a run across the fields, pursued briefly by Hill's men for the sake of appearances. Hill's 'police' commandeered the lorry and 1,230 parachutes which he claimed brought him £9,225 (£369,000).[26]

The number of officers who converted military funds to their own purposes was few. Fewer could match the lieutenant, a solicitor in civilian life, who was cashiered and sent to penal servitude by a Chelsea court martial in August 1942, after converting £831 (£33,240) to his own uses. He had also stolen ration cards and other documents before going on the run as a deserter. His defence, which evoked no sympathy, was that he had 'borrowed this money from army funds and found himself unable to repay it'.[27]

Elsewhere, there was more sympathy. The commander of the Camberwell Company of the Home Guard in 1942 was a fifty-four-year-old 'trusted bank clerk', a veteran of the First World War. He had spent his own money on the company, believing the government would reimburse him. The government refused. The commander decided that he was 'morally justified' in reimbursing himself. He did this by adding to the roll of his company the names of 'people who did not exist', drawing pay for them and forging their signatures. For this he went to prison for the relatively short period of three months.[28]

Far more common were officers who overstepped the mark in using military supplies or personnel. At Aldershot in April 1942, a captain of the Pioneer Corps pleaded guilty to employing soldiers for nine months, with army equipment and transport, to build his bungalow. At the end of the war, a captain quartermaster of the Irish Guards enjoyed the distinction of being held in the Tower of London after his home was furnished with easy chairs, folding chairs, household utensils, food and ladders which were all army property.[29]

In Essex, in the summer of 1942, officers and men were involved in an inquiry and two courts martial which led to the Officer Commanding the Colchester District being dismissed the service. In August, a Colchester court martial began investigating 'irregularities' by RASC officers who were living in a country house near their camp. They were accused of using soldiers to act as private servants at the house, drawing rations illegally and improperly, and using army mechanics to service and repair their private cars.

A captain who denied using soldiers as civilian servants and improperly drawing rations was convicted by the court martial and cashiered. Next day, the colonel commanding the Colchester district appeared. The fact that he had been a solicitor in civilian life helped to undermine his plea of having no idea of doing anything amiss by ordering extra rations or the repair of private vehicles in army workshops. Both he and his major were dismissed the service.[30]

Conscription brought the other ranks of the services a share of professional criminals, some well known like 'Ruby' Sparks, who was a Dartmoor escapee and self-styled 'Burglar to the Nobility', others like the young Frankie Fraser with a reputation to make. Most agreed that crime in the services was easier than elsewhere. L. J. Cunliffe, a Royal Navy conscript, found robbery at Portsmouth Barracks unchallenging. A night-time visit to the Pay Office yielded 1,000 ration books and forty pay-books from an unlocked drawer. The safe proved resistant but the NAAFI manager was content to keep his takings in a tobacco tin in the top drawer of his desk. As an adjunct to the black market, the crew of Cunliffe's landing craft at Southampton not only drew their own stores but, using the stores books of half a dozen unmanned craft, drew stores for those as well, recycling them to civilian purchasers. The daily issue of navy rum to non-existent sailors was sold to local publicans, and mahogany wardroom fittings were stripped out to make saleable items of furniture.[31]

There was a casual racket in forging details on service travel-warrants. The experienced serviceman who knew his way found it simpler to travel without a ticket. At London's Southern Railway termini, while law-abiding passengers queued patiently for the night train at the ticket barrier, dim figures from unoccupied platforms negotiated live rails in the blackout to climb up and enter on the far side of the carriages. Slow trains were preferred to expresses because, given the manpower shortage, there were unlikely to be ticket collectors. It was also possible, at some stations in outer London, to cross a platform from the main line, get on to an underground train, and shoulder one's way past a tube station barrier in the crowd.

Stealing army property was not felt to be robbing anyone in particular. A more personalized crime was taking money from other soldiers by time-honoured but illegitimate means. After six weeks of war, civilian police were called in by commanding officers to stop old sweats enticing new recruits into games of crown and anchor, which was traditionally not so much a game as a licence to rob. It had been the bane of workshops and factories for years before the war.

The unwary conscript was also at risk from 'good turn bandits', who exploited the lack of taxis and transport when the West End was full of servicemen on weekend leave. Having stolen a service car and armed themselves, two or three soldiers would patrol the area around Piccadilly late on Saturday night and early on Sunday morning. Seeing British or American servicemen waiting for a taxi or a lift, they would stop and offer to take one or two of them. The sight of an army car reassured the victims. After a short distance the car would turn into a darkened side street, where the passengers would be robbed at gunpoint, then turned out and left stranded. The robbers were ready for their next dupe. A sample carload of 'good turn' thieves got away with five assaults, involving seven victims, on the night of 7 August 1943.

Civilian enterprises fell prey to soldiers who used the weapons provided for them to carry out armed raids. Cinema robbery, which had become a genre of its own before the war, was still more appealing in the blackout. As far back as 1935 the *Police Journal* warned of 'gangster-style' robberies at cinemas, and two years later the term 'cinema-breaking' was coined. The attraction of cinemas was that their safes or pay-box tills were full late at night and overflowing at weekends, when the money could not be banked until Monday morning. The ideal time to strike was in the small hours of Sunday or Monday, when the weekend takings were still on the premises.[32]

Pay-boxes at the front of a foyer or projecting from the main building were easy prey, if the timing was right. A soldier with an automatic pistol, who held up the pay-box of the Regal at Farnham on the night of 4 February 1941, arrived when most of the money was already locked in the manager's safe. He found only six shillings and elevenpence in the till. Better luck attended the unarmed robber who snatched £144 (£5,760) from the Regal at Norwood, after the last showing of *Dressed to Kill* on 23 January 1942, and vanished into the blackout. At the Hippodrome, Rotherhithe, on 9 December 1942, the robbery was carried out with army rifles and .303 ammunition and at the Ritz, Horsham, by two masked gunmen in the early hours of 27 December 1942. Remarkably, there were no fatalities until May 1946 when an unidentified robber, described as an 'ex-commando', shot dead the manager of the Odeon Cinema, Bristol, just after he had locked away the takings in his office safe.

The armed hold-up of public houses was rarer and widely publicized when it happened. There were more staff on the premises and the raid might end in a fight. The manager of the Coach and Horses near Covent Garden had been shot dead by a soldier in December 1940. On 29 January 1943, two men in battledress held up the manageress of the Masons Arms public house in Upper Berkeley Street, after all the customers had left. One man pressed a revolver into her side and said, 'This is a hold-up.' When the raiders went behind the bar and took banknotes from the till, the barman grabbed the gun as it was pushed against his chest. It went off, burning his hand. He struggled with the gunman, got him on the floor, and grabbed the gun again. The soldier fired and the barman's other hand was injured. The man on the floor rolled free and both robbers ran away. Even for a handful of banknotes, the risks of such a robbery in an age of the death penalty were not worth it.

Despite hold-up dramas, a more common and homely image was the appearance at midnight of two soldiers in battledress without their caps, in the doorway of a jeweller's shop in Preston Road, Brighton, followed by a cracking of plate glass. It was June 1941. They were arrested almost at once, long before they could break into the shop. The men had been drinking in the pubs of central Brighton from opening until closing time, they had lost their caps and were too drunk to care. In this state, they were taken with the romantic idea of becoming jewel thieves. When sober again, they were contrite and pleaded guilty without bother. Most offences by the troops were far closer to this episode than to the Berkeley Street hold-up or the robbery of cinema pay-boxes with an automatic pistol.[33]

The routine enforcement of law in the services was a matter for the uniform branch of the Military Police. Seen by the nation's leaders as guardians of law and by other ranks as 'absolute bastards', there were few more controversial presences in the armed forces than theirs. From the autumn of 1941, they included policewomen of the WAAFs and later the ATS, whose first duties were to ensure that members of the women's services did not appear on the streets like 'slackers' or with a 'slovenly' look, to detain those who had 'plastered on make-up', and to advise women stranded in London where they might find lodgings for the night. The introduction of military policewomen was in part a response to the whispering campaign against the morals of the ATS, which had become the subject of discussion in press and Parliament that autumn.

Service police of both sexes remained unpopular and came under attack for officiousness, not least on the left wing of the House of Commons. In February 1943, Walter Green denounced the RAF Police for 'snooping' in London to catch men not saluting officers. It seemed a scandalous and insensitive waste of manpower at a time when pro-Soviet graffiti on the walls of the capital proclaimed, 'Britain Blanco's While Russia Bleeds!'[34]

In June that year, Lewis Silkin, a prominent lawyer and Labour member for Peckham, told the house of a still more outrageous waste of resources. An army car was being driven round London with a Union Jack on its bonnet and no one but the driver inside. It was followed surreptitiously by service police, ready to arrest any soldier who failed to 'salute the flag'. A month earlier, left-wing MPs had raised the question of military policemen trying to prevent men in uniform from listening to a Communist speaker in Daventry. The Secretary of War described this as 'the result of an error of judgement'. It was certainly that. The Communist was speaking in support of the National Government candidate at a forthcoming by-election.[35]

In their dealings with civilians, the uniformed Military Police were associated with catching deserters and enforcing the exclusion zones along the South Coast. They worked with civil police, as in other criminal cases. In the Elephant and Castle murder of 1942, when a teenager was killed in the course of a street robbery, both CID and Military Police combed the pubs and cafés of the area in search of known criminals or deserters. Most cooperation in this case was in the routine checking of identity cards and leave passes at horse races, dog tracks, railway stations and dance halls.

Efforts to exclude non-residents from security zones were concentrated in the months before D-Day, when Southern England resembled a military camp. Enforcement began in August 1943 with a purge described as the 'greatest-ever check-up'. Uniformed MPs set up barriers across the highway to isolate centres of population. Civilians and soldiers were stopped. Within the towns a similar process was enforced for pedestrians in main streets and shopping centres. Even workers who previously had passes admitting them to government property now required an additional permit to admit them to banned areas.

By the spring of 1944, checks were stricter. On 3–4 March, Brighton was sealed off with no specific reason given, while Military Police and officers of Brighton special police intelligence stopped all traffic and questioned drivers. Among other checks in the 'front-line' towns was the quarantine of Brighton on 12 May 1944, an operation which cordoned pedestrians into shopping centres and the railway station until their documents had been examined, while vehicles were halted and their occupants made to account for themselves. A week later, Military Police with the assistance of civil police officers launched a similar operation in Chatham, Gravesend and Gillingham. A fortnight before the invasion of France, it was not surprising that such measures were taken.

Some issues were less openly discussed. If Southern England was a vast camp of hundreds of thousands of British, Canadian and US troops, it might become an equally vast open brothel. Venereal disease shadowed the liberators of Europe.

Military policing included rounding up young women whose usual plea was that they had only entered a banned area to see their 'boyfriends'. Two such victims of the crackdown in August 1943 were a young married woman from Porthcawl and her younger companion from Exeter. They were arrested and handed to civil police after being found soliciting soldiers in the station approach at Brighton just after midnight on 26 August. The married woman, who was twenty-three, had been 'leading an immoral life for a long time'. She was 'known to the police of fifteen towns' and had nine previous convictions. Her unmarried companion was twenty-one and recently released from Borstal. She had made for Aldershot, and had been 'mixing with soldiers'.

One attraction of Brighton, they admitted, was 'the Canadians', whose army was there in large numbers. Despite this, the younger had no money in her purse, the elder had two shillings and three farthings. Their arrest seemed like an act of charity. Neither had an identity card, nor a ration book, nor any papers. They were not charged with soliciting but with 'being found in a regulated area without written authority and failing to carry identity cards' and 'unlawfully using the railway approach'.

When brought before the magistrates in September, the younger woman could only say that she had lost her identity card in London, while the elder claimed that her identity card and ration book had been stolen from her handbag at a dance hall. They went to prison for six months and four months respectively. Though scarcely a match for *Mother Courage*, their story was one which typified hundreds of others on the fringe of army life. Indeed, the chairman of the Brighton bench issued a warning that 'women like this can wander about from place to place without identity or ration cards.' As for venereal disease, 'They are not only a menace to themselves but to other people.'[36]

Throughout the country, Military Police, RAF Special Police and Naval Pickets were occupied in tracking down deserters, referred to euphemistically as 'absentees'. The less adaptable deserter was most at risk from systematic examination of identity cards and registration certificates. At Newmarket races in September 1942, every entrance was covered and every man and woman of military age required to produce these documents to Military or RAF Police. It was one of the biggest checks of the war. In November, there was a similar spot check of Canadian and British servicemen in Brighton and Hove, covering football grounds, dance halls, restaurants and the greyhound stadium. In October 1943, RAF police combed football grounds in search of what was admitted by the Secretary for Air to be 'an unusual number of absentees'.

On the afternoon and evening of Friday 21 May 1944, the biggest West End check-up to date was carried out by Naval Pickets, Military Police and US Military Police. Amusement arcades, restaurants and hotels were raided first. The size of the establishment was no deterrent.

At the Coventry Street Corner House, every customer at every table was checked. The main venue in the evening was the Astoria dance hall in Charing Cross Road. Service police spread out round the entire gallery. The band stopped playing and a civilian police inspector informed the dancers that all civilian identity cards and all armed forces leave passes would be inspected. As in the afternoon, all those failing to produce a leave pass or an identity card which showed them to be civilians were arrested.

On 16 May 1944, Military Police cooperated with uniformed and plain-clothes civilian police, Naval Pickets and US Military Police for a more intensive 'bayonet swoop' on the West End, during which the Military Police carried rifles with fixed bayonets. Checks and arrests on this scale were intended to curb the number of deserters, which had passed 20,000 by the end of the war, but particularly to catch those absentees who had found their way into the criminal underworld.

Though these swoops had a modest success, there were still 18,000 deserters on the loose some two years later, according to the figures for June 1946. Even a three-month period of leniency, during which they were offered clemency if they surrendered, brought in only a small percentage.

Deserters divided into two groups: those who sought refuge with family or friends, and those who took to crime, through force of habit or desperation. Defendants who had sheltered deserters were on the whole lightly dealt with. In January 1941, a man and woman harboured an absentee who was once their lodger. They were fined £3 (£120)and £7 (£280) respectively. In evidence, they pleaded that they thought the man had gone to the army camp every day but was allowed to come home at night. Unfortunately, when the police called, the woman first assured them that the deserter was her husband.[37]

Many deserters endured privations worse than life in the services. One was caught in 1941 hiding in a coal box less than half his height. Another spent four months under the floor of his home in Brighton, where his mother and wife were each fined £21 (£840) or twenty-one days in prison for harbouring him. On the other hand, when a naval deserter hid under the floor of his home, his mother and wife were fined only £5 (£200) each in 1942. A man at Biggin Hill made a trap-door in the floor of his home, disappearing when strangers came. He was sent to prison for a month and was then handed over to a military escort. A woman in Sussex hid her Canadian army lover in a wall-cupboard for a month. The civil police failed to find him but the Military Police were more successful. The woman was sent to prison for a month, which was the tariff by 1943. At Lambeth in November 1942, the sentence in a case where a man had helped to hide his friend had been six weeks' hard labour.[38]

Public reactions to deserters and those who harboured them lacked the high moral indignation which the authorities encouraged. At Bethnal Green, in January 1943, a woman who was in poor health and partially sighted had given refuge to various members of her family when they deserted and was now charged with harbouring her son, caught hiding on the roof in vest and pants on a bitter winter day. The police insisted that this was 'a family where there has been a good deal of encouraging and assisting of desertion'. When it was suggested that the woman might be sent to prison, which would have been usual in such a case, there were protests from all over the neighbourhood. The magistrate confessed himself 'staggered' by the amount of sympathy she had received and fined her £5 instead.[39]

Deserters did not always come quietly. They fought the police at the Elephant and Castle tube station, or at least sounded the alarm to others by shouting 'Look out! Bogies!' as the police closed in on a household of deserters and receivers of stolen property. Another used a butcher's knife to fight a policeman at the Cosmopolitan Club in Stepney in October 1942. In December that year, an army deserter in Dalston simply kicked a policeman's legs from under him and ran.

Police who arrived to make a routine arrest of two brothers in Balham got a rough reception. Detective Sergeant Layfield and his men were greeted by two brothers, both deserters, and their fifty-six-year-old mother. The elder brother snatched up a hammer and shouted, 'Don't come forward another step, and get out, or else I will have the satisfaction of killing one of you rats before you take me.' The younger brother, bottle in hand, added, 'I will split your fucking head open.' The mother then pushed protectively in front of her sons and shouted, 'You are two of Churchill's bastards. You are like the rest of your Home Secretary's clique of conchies! When Germany wins, you will all be out of a job.' The two brothers were held for fourteen days and then put under military escort, their mother being fined £2 (£80).[40]

An alternative to concealment at home was to find someone prepared to harbour deserters on a long-term basis. An Italian café proprietor in the Commercial Road was sent to prison for four months in July 1942 for harbouring a deserter, who committed ration offences on his behalf for two years, and also for harbouring a girl who had run away from an approved school. In June 1942, another deserter turned King's Evidence against two caterers, alleging that they had given him identity papers and civilian clothes in exchange for his labour at their café.[41]

Deserters who took to crime without becoming members of a criminal organization were usually content with shopbreaking, burglary or street and shelter robbery. Some, like a soldier arrested while selling flowers from a stall, simply went back to their civilian occupations and were not troubled. Those with a little more talent became moderately successful as criminals. Three deserters were sent to prison in separate cases in July 1942 for Post Office forgeries. The first was one of several counterfeiters who had sufficient skill to reproduce Post Office endorsements freehand. He admitted making £1,500 (£60,000) by this so far and asked for 557 other cases to be taken into consideration. A fortnight later, two deserters and a young woman appeared before the court, also charged with Post Office Savings Bank forgeries. They were convicted on four charges and, more modestly, asked for 171 other offences to be taken into consideration. The brains went to penal servitude for three years and his accomplice to prison for eighteen months.

In the following month another deserter was sent to hard labour for six months for forgery and receiving forty-two sheets of clothing coupons, part of a consignment of 20,000 coupons stolen while in transit from Brixton to the Stationery Office. In a curious case, during March 1942, a fugitive from the Military Police had organized his own shopbreaking gang of children between the ages of fourteen and sixteen to rob shops in the Elephant and Castle area. This modern Fagin prospered for some time until his youthful accomplices informed on him after being caught breaking into a shoeshop in the Old Kent Road.[42]

One advantage of deserters, in the eyes of the underworld, was that most had no criminal records in civilian life and no files in the Criminal Records Office. The police could not readily identify them and, armed with forged driving licences and references, they were sent to haulage firms as drivers. The firms chosen were those delivering silks, tobacco, whisky or clothing to the docks. After a few weeks, a lorry would leave the warehouse and never arrive at the docks. Neither it nor its driver would ever be seen again.

Such thefts were the web of everyday criminality. In 1942, however, the nature of the war at home and the appetites of its underworld were to be changed for ever. There were new sounds in the air and new excitements in London after dark. Luxuries which had ceased to exist after 1939 were there for the taking. From being a struggle for survival, the conflict was now a war that could not be lost. In January 1942, the first American troops landed in Belfast. They came ashore to a ceremonial welcome and brought with them the good things of life, extravagances unknown to most people in England even in peacetime. It remained to be seen whether they would prove to be the predators or the prey.

11

The Yanks Are Coming

Black marketeering by United States servicemen seemed no more common than among their allies until in 1944–5 its increase among fighting men in the European theatre of operations made headlines. In January 1945, the US Provost Marshal announced that there were between 18,000 and 19,000 deserters from the US Army, the equivalent of an entire division. 'The total is increasing daily,' Brigadier-General Rogers added. 'Being off the payroll they are driven to rob their "buddies" or hold up somebody else in order to live.' Deserters were being arrested by the hundred every day and 850 were awaiting trial in Paris alone.

The total of deserters was quickly corrected to 8,000, some mingling in London with men from Britain, Canada and other nations. By the winter of 1944–5 gangs of deserters, close behind the front line in Italy, threatened a breakdown of order. In the first week of November, British and American military police responded by combing the cities of Southern Italy house by house for members of two organizations.

One of these was the 'Lane' gang, whose leader went by the pseudonym of 'Robert Lane'. The first success in the investigation came in Rome, when a jeep driven by a Canadian soldier collided with a truck. The soldier driving the jeep was found in possession of a revolver stolen from an American military policeman in a Naples hold-up. SIB and the American military CID kept watch until a Canadian private in the uniform of a US officer and an American in a staff sergeant's uniform came to collect the jeep. An exchange of small-arms fire ended with the arrest of the two wounded suspects. They were taken to hospital and admitted being members of the gang. More Military Police with Thompson sub-machine guns came for them. When someone had the wit to check the 'policemen's' papers, it was discovered that these were also 'Robert Lane' gangsters, sent to rescue their comrades.

Most members of this and the other principal gang were American, working with Canadian and British deserters, joined by Italians, Corsicans and Yugoslavs. Their stolen transport included jeeps, weapon-carriers and the staff car of General Anders, commanding Polish troops in Italy. The staff car was stolen at gunpoint late at night, its chauffeur put against a tree to be shot. The chauffeur ran for his life and the bullets missed him. However, an unhelpful café owner was shot dead and a carload of the Lane gang was surrounded while taking another terrified Italian to a quiet place to be executed. He was a receiver who kept back more than his agreed share of proceeds from stolen goods.[1]

In France the situation was little better. At the end of December 1944, the American authorities arrested over 200 suppliers of the tobacco market, many described as 'Chicago gangsters'. Three weeks later, four officers of 'The Millionaires' Battalion' were arrested on the orders of General Eisenhower for their part in the racket. Two officers and 182 men of the unit had already been charged, some sentenced to long terms of imprisonment. Their trade was in cigarettes and other army supplies sold to Parisian receivers. The battalion commander was relieved of his post and sent to active duty in Belgium. This fraud was discovered after complaints by soldiers that officers had withheld many rations for months after D-Day, condoning and participating in thefts.

By contrast, the first American servicemen setting foot in Britain in the early months of 1942 were unblemished saviours of the Old World.

'So we had won after all.' Churchill's comment was a reassuring echo of Pearl Harbor and Hitler's declaration of war in support of Japan. The spectre of defeat in Europe faded with the old year. As a bonus, Germany still dragged the millstone of Italy and was failing to hold her own in a winter war with the Soviet Union. With the build-up of American arms and air power in Europe it was inconceivable that the common enemy could again threaten invasion or annihilation from the air. But the war that would be won was no longer the heroic struggle of Britain alone in 1940–41. The spirit of Dunkirk and the elation of the finest hour were engulfed in the loud and confident participation by American troops. Ultimate victory would be claimed by Washington and Hollywood. A sense of relief was sometimes tempered by resentment.

It became a commentator's cliché that the soldiers of the new ally appeared fitter and better-looking than their British counterparts. Individually, they were remarkable for courtesy and generosity. Collectively, they were apt to riot. Their home life was known to most people only from cinema portrayal, as being wholesome, friendly and affluent. They were certainly affluent. The difference between the pay of British and United States officers was less marked but, among other ranks, the Americans were paid between three and four times as much as their British equivalents. In their clubs and canteens, they enjoyed food and comforts unobtainable by their hosts since 1940. Professional criminals regarded them as innocents abroad.

However, the newcomers came from a nation which already had its own black market. Rationing in the United States was more selective. Clothes were not rationed, though shoes were. Some foods were rationed, notably red meat. Butter, sugar and a selection of canned goods were restricted, though allowances were more generous. More strictly controlled were petrol, fuel oils and rubber tyres. Yet even these rations allowed several gallons of petrol a week for private motoring.

The US black market followed the British example, being a partnership of professional criminals and opportunists who thought of themselves in peacetime as law-abiding. To combat both groups and to curb wartime inflation in the event of US involvement, on 11 April 1941 the Roosevelt administration created an Office of Price Administration. The OPA was to bring 170,708 prosecutions, winning 130,774 cases and sending 2,970 offenders to prison.

The term 'black market' caught on in America in the months after Pearl Harbor. It was made the title of an article in *Collier's*, on 6 June 1942, echoed by Leo M. Cherne in 'America's Black Market', an article published in the *Saturday Evening Post* on 25 July. The great fear was of strong demand for illegal supplies of petrol. Professional criminals worked easily with traders, creating what Chester Bowles of the OPA, in the *New York Times Magazine* of 30 July 1944, called

'The Deadly Menace of Black Gasoline'. Bowles estimated this black market at 2,500,000 gallons a day, equal to 10 per cent of all petrol used by the United States armed forces.

Coupon robbery and forgery proved even more lucrative than in Britain. In two and a half years of war, coupons worth $300,000,000 were stolen from government offices. Thirteen printing presses of counterfeit coupons were also tracked down. More than a hundred different types of counterfeit petrol coupons were in circulation. In an article in *Newsweek*, 'Theft by Counterfeiting', Chester Bowles claimed that by 1944 the profits from counterfeit petrol coupons were $1,000,000,000 a month. In the face of this, *Time* magazine concluded that the OPA's record was 'not such as to inspire confidence', though its enforcers grew from a staff of 200 to 4,400, including 800 lawyers.[2]

What was true of petrol seemed no less true of meat. 'Meatleggers' were in evidence within two months of Pearl Harbor. By March 1943, the National Independent Meat Packers Association, in evidence to a congressional committee, warned that the meat-rationing system was making the United States as corrupt as Britain. But it seemed that the trade, rather than gangsters, formed the basis of such meat-legging as went on.

No doubt racketeers who might have dealt in bootleg drink during prohibition had a part in providing black market supplies in wartime. But when Leon Henderson wrote in *Atlantic Monthly* of the wholesale 'chiseling' now going on, he added that current racketeering was largely in the hands of men and women with whom 'we have always done business'. So it was to be until American rationing ended in November 1945.[3]

In the week before D-Day, the total of American servicemen in Britain reached a peak of 1,526,965. The first set foot on the quayside in Belfast only seven weeks after Pearl Harbor. Next day, the Irish Republic protested at the presence of a foreign army in the 'Six Counties', to which it maintained a territorial claim. The first underworld to be encountered by the newcomers was the political presence of the IRA. In May 1942, two nationalists stood trial in a treason felony case in Belfast for 'conspiring to levy war against His Majesty and promote by force of arms an Irish Republic in Northern Ireland

and to advance the activities of the IRA'. They were alleged to have circulated pamphlets to American troops in Northern Ireland, urging them to mutiny and 'fight for Irish freedom'.[4]

Far more unsettling were reports in September 1942 of workers and women who formed 'spy rings' round US bases in Northern Ireland, gathering military intelligence for delivery to the German Legation in Dublin. One of them told the press, 'If it weren't for Hitler, we wouldn't have jobs.' By 1944, the United States added its protests to Britain's in an attempt to persuade the Irish government to close down the German and Italian legations, but to no avail.

As more troops arrived, they spread through the British Isles, until the GI became a familiar figure in pubs, dance halls and cinemas. When on leave, those who could do so made their way to London. They arrived in such numbers that at Christmas 1943 the capital was put out of bounds to American personnel unless they were serving within twenty miles of it. At other times, arrangements were made for them to sleep in the 'deep shelters', not much used between the failure of the German blitz after 1941 and the first rocket attacks by V-1 'flying bombs' in 1944. Deep shelters had bunks at a shilling (£2) a night, canteens, medical posts, air conditioning and communications. There were cheap meals and hot drinks.

A natural rendezvous for Americans on leave was 'Rainbow Corner', built on the bomb-site of the Café Monico in Shaftesbury Avenue. Open day and night from the end of 1942, it provided American food and drink, dancing, a library and writing room, a bed for the night, and entertainment by visiting stars. Rainbow Corner also attracted market traders from Berwick Street and Denman Street. Its supply of ration-free goods led to a nightly spectacle of US servicemen being jostled as they left, with invitations of 'Anything to sell? Anything to sell?' until the club was finally closed in January 1946.

By no means all pleasures were as wholesome. A million and a half men, who knew they could be dead in a few months, were 3,000 miles from home without female company. The appeal of London included the hope of picking up a girl. Despite the Provost Marshal's helpful brochure on *How to Stay Out of Trouble*, the girl might well be a prostitute. Rainbow Corner added a 'prophylactic centre', where the risk of having caught VD was minimized by preventive hygiene.

There were now more prostitutes in London, working longer hours. Marthe Watts recalled that when the US forces arrived, she began working a fourteen-hour day. The girls were known variously as 'Hyde Park Rangers' or 'Piccadilly Commandos'. The recommended reply to any whose prices seemed exorbitant was, 'Honey, I want to rent it, not buy it.'

In the House of Commons on 25 May 1944, Herbert Morrison insisted that the behaviour of American troops had been good. 'In particular, the innuendo that the United States authorities are failing to assist to the utmost in disciplining their troops and checking misbehaviour is quite unjustified. They have at all times cooperated to the fullest possible extent with our police.'

British civilians found American servicemen amiable and easy to deal with. Fighting on any scale was apt to be between servicemen of the two countries, as in Northern Ireland in 1942, or between black and white Americans. On 5 October 1944, for example, ten black soldiers left their camp and went to a nearby pub, the Crown at Kingsclere, near Basingstoke. They were met by US Military Police, who discovered that the soldiers had no passes and ordered them back to camp. The blacks went back, collected carbines, returned to the pub and lay in wait for the policemen. As one MP appeared they opened fire at random, killing him. Those in the bar threw themselves flat but concentrated bursts hit another of the military policemen and the publican's wife. There had been a not dissimilar incident in September 1943, in the town square of Launceston in Cornwall, when black soldiers who had refused to disperse opened fire with their rifles on US Military Police, wounding two of them.

Violence was not the prerogative of any one group. Seven months later, there was a riot at a famous East End pub, 'Charlie Brown's', otherwise known as the Railway Arms in Limehouse. It started when local customers threw glasses and bottles at a packed crowd of drunken and noisy US sailors watching a fight between a white and a black American. The landlord, with the aid of his truncheon and the police, cleared the pub. This might have remained a rowdy incident but for the US sailor who returned later, smashed a panel of the door and thrust a knife through, fatally wounding Charles Gilbey, a lorry driver from Bethnal Green who was helping the landlord to clear up.

The sailor was condemned to death by an American court martial but subsequently reprieved.[5]

Such incidents seemed inevitable among a million and a half servicemen. Yet their behaviour was generally good and Londoners had particular reason to be grateful to them. With the onset of winter in 1944 a housing crisis followed the flying-bomb attacks, 719,000 houses needed repairs and by 20 December only 258,849 had been completed. The rate accelerated when 3,000 American servicemen with housebuilding skills were diverted to these repairs. Not only was their labour more efficient but they won much goodwill.

By 1942, Londoners had already become familiar with 'Snowdrops'. Each morning, in Green Park, two hundred of them paraded. These were the white-helmeted 787th Military Police, their headquarters being with the 8th Military Police Investigation Section in the US Provost Marshal's headquarters at 96 Piccadilly. In Tottenham Court Road there was a Central District Guard House, where US servicemen arrested by their own police were held until they had been processed.

The US Military Police were a revelation to Scotland Yard officers like Chief Inspector Greeno, whose work included a murder inquiry conducted with a dapper Texan, Colonel Morony. Morony's men used large De Soto cars equipped with 'wailers', turned on as they raced through central London, in this case along Coventry Street and down the Haymarket. When the cars stopped, the doors opened and the seats swivelled round. Unlike British police who clambered out of cars, Snowdrops sprang out and straightened up, pistols drawn, in a continuous movement. In this case, they raided the Captain's Cabin in search of a fugitive, at gunpoint as a matter of routine. When dealing with their own troops, they also used their two-foot batons on troublemakers with a casual energy which would have caused dismay in a British court.

The sight of US Military Police was soon familiar in cities like Liverpool, Glasgow and Belfast, but most conspicuously in London. In November 1942, Major-General Key arrived as US Provost Marshal General in the European Theatre of Operations. He was heralded as a no-nonsense figure who 'cuts red tape to tatters'. His assistants included 'G-men', as FBI agents were still called, and he proposed a partnership with Scotland Yard. His philosophy was that if more men could be kept out of prison, 'the more we will have ready to carry a rifle'. In case his benevolent despotism failed, there was another soldier whose arrival received no publicity whatever. His name was Master-Sergeant John C. Woods. He was the US military hangman.

Until the American entry into the war, little thought was given to how law and order might be preserved, and justice done, among expatriate servicemen. Some would be victims of crime: others its perpetrators. Like the Canadians, these Americans were affluent enough to buy whatever the black market had. Their camps and canteens were soon a coveted source of supply. A realist would also expect that among so many single men, sexual offences might run high.

British courts might have dealt with violations of the civil law by US servicemen but the American government had two objections. The first was that domestic opinion would resent its troops being tried and punished by a foreign power. This was reinforced in 1942 when two US volunteers in the Canadian army were convicted of armed robbery under English law. The judge sent both to prison and ordered one to be flogged. After private protests from the American ambassador, John Winant, the Home Secretary, Herbert Morrison, countermanded the flogging.

The second American objection to British jurisdiction ran contrary to such protests. It was a fear, perhaps based on the dealings of British courts with Canadian servicemen, that 'undue leniency' would be shown to Americans who had come to fight for the common cause.

In the event, when US Military Police arrested British citizens, they handed them over to their British counterparts. This was reciprocated as when, for example, a US soldier stabbed to death an American waiter at Mac's Dance Hall in Windmill Street in September 1945, while the band played 'Don't Fence Me In'. The suspect was arrested by Scotland Yard who established his identity and handed him over to the US Provost Marshal without further inquiry.

American courts martial imposed draconian sentences on their own men, only to commute some of them subsequently. Victor Meek, a London policeman, arrested two USAAF deserters from 415 Squadron who were using forged Canadian Air Force leave passes. They might have escaped detection had it not been that the airmen's application for leave and the officer's counter-signature were in the same hand. Meek was a witness at the court martial in Grosvenor Square and was horrified when the two were found guilty and sentenced to life imprisonment. He asked a military guard how long they would actually serve, and was told about eighteen months. Even so, it was a deterrent sentence compared with the six months or a year that a British soldier might receive.[6]

Severity was encouraged. Following the murder trial of a US Navy rating, the US Naval Command in the United Kingdom, which had convened the court martial, publicly criticized the sentence of fifty years' hard labour as 'inadequate'. The twenty-year-old rating had shot dead two British marines in a quarrel at the American Red Cross Services Club at Greenock in June 1944. At his court martial in Greenock, psychiatric evidence was given that he was on the borderline of mental deficiency but knew the difference between right and wrong. In that case, by United States and English law, he was responsible for his actions. Yet the court martial convicted him of 'voluntary manslaughter', saving him from the gallows, and sent him to prison for fifty years. The US Naval Command ordered that the sentence should be reviewed. However, the review had only the power of reducing the term, which it did, sending him to forty years' hard labour in July 1946.[7]

The technical difficulty of jurisdiction was overcome by the British Parliament passing the United States of America (Visiting Forces) Act 1942, which became law on 6 August that year. It set up a state within a state. American servicemen might be arrested by their own police, interrogated by their own Criminal Investigation Division, tried in their own courts, imprisoned and in some cases executed in their own prisons, known as United States Army Disciplinary Training Centres.

Some centres were detention camps, others like Shepton Mallet were British prisons loaned to the Americans for the duration of the war. It was at Shepton Mallet, on 16 May 1944, that the US Army hanged a private for the widely publicized 'Colchester Taxi-Cab Murder', when two American soldiers killed their driver in the course of petty theft. Taximen were targets for late-night aggression and three more arrivals at Shepton Mallet had been convicted by court martial after an incident in the Welsh steel town of Port Talbot. They hired a taxi and, at their destination, crowded round the driver, telling him to 'Stick 'em up. We want all you've got.' There was no violence as they went through his pockets, bundled him into his cab and told him to 'beat it'. They were sent to hard labour for five years in November 1943.[8]

An American courtroom for military trials was created in Grosvenor Square, near the US Embassy. Elsewhere, old world accommodation was used if possible – Wycombe Abbey chapel for a murder trial and the panelled library of a Welsh castle for the taxi robbery. Another venue in Southern England, where large numbers of US servicemen were camped before D-Day, was the ballroom of Southampton's Polygon Hotel.

A Grosvenor Square court martial was embellished by the Stars and Stripes stretched behind the chair of the President of the Court, a belt with a revolver in its holster on the Judge Advocate's desk, two lanky marines with guns at their sides, nursing their batons. No oath was taken and counsel questioned witnesses while sitting with arms folded. In a court martial over brutality at a Disciplinary Training Centre near Litchfield, a colonel who was a chief witness was described as strolling into the courtroom smoking a cigar, which he placed in the defence counsel's ashtray, freeing that hand temporarily to give the President of the Court a leisurely salute.

In a high proportion of trials, the victim and many witnesses were British. British lawyers also appeared for the defence, when the accused requested them. G. D. Roberts KC, as 'Khaki' Roberts a famous defender of his day, appeared at a court martial in Grosvenor Square, defending a sailor charged with the murder of a British civilian. Junior counsel was a lieutenant-commander of the US Navy but the accused wanted a leader who was 'the best guy in the British legal business'.

Roberts was unsure what to wear, since everyone else would be in uniform. He consulted the Lord Chief Justice who told him without hesitation to wear the wig and gown and the court dress of a King's or Queen's Counsel at the English Bar. If the buckles and knee-breeches seemed bizarre to the American military, there was much that was odd to their visitor. Counsel for the prosecution walked 'miles' to and fro across the courtroom while addressing the court. At every recess, the courtroom air became blue with cigarette smoke, while tea and coffee were served to accused and officers alike. The 'Law Officer' overruled one of Roberts' objections saying casually, 'If I'm wrong, sure as hell Washington will put me right.' Yet Victorian legal precedents were quoted freely because much of the British legal code had been adopted in America. Once again, Roberts secured the acquittal of his client.[9]

A further curiosity to British observers was the length of court-martial sessions. At the Colchester Taxi-Cab Murder trials in January 1944, two defendants were tried simultaneously by separate tribunals in Ipswich Town Hall. Defendants, medical witnesses and officers were taken from one courtroom to the other to give evidence. The first trial adjourned at 9.30 p.m., after the court had sat for thirteen hours. The other was still in progress after midnight, the defendant being found guilty of murder at 1.30 a.m.

US prosecutors frequently called British expert witnesses. When two drunken US soldiers had a row with the doorman of Frascati's Restaurant in Oxford Street, one punched him and he fell into the gutter. That night, he died of a cerebral haemorrhage. Detective Superintendent Robert Higgins of Scotland Yard worked on the case with Agent Walter J. Riddle, seconded to the CID of the US Military Police by the FBI. The soldier was traced to a camp in Wiltshire, arrested and charged with murder. At the court martial Sir Bernard Spilsbury, who had conducted the autopsy, was called as the prosecution's key witness. He testified that the blood vessels in the doorman's brain were so fragile that they might well have burst had he stepped suddenly off a bus. The blow struck by the soldier would not have been fatal to a man in normal health. The defendant was acquitted of murder and sent to prison for assault. An Icelandic seaman, attached to the US Navy, escaped the death penalty for murdering a young ATS woman at Bournemouth in March 1945, when it was proved that her skull was exceptionally thin.[10]

Forensic evidence was all the more important in the rather perfunctory proceedings which characterized some US military trials. One of these, a classic of forensic pathology, involved a corporal charged with murdering an English girl of seventeen during a sexual act. It was not clear how he had killed her, though suffocation seemed a possibility. The incongruous setting of his trial was the chapel of Wycombe Abbey in Buckinghamshire. The court martial sat at a long table on a dais behind the Communion rails. A cinema screen was placed in front of the altar, while the Stars and Stripes hung before the hymn board. It proved to be a death by misadventure. The defendant had unknowingly induced an embolism from which his partner died. Even so, his freedom was not a foregone conclusion. At the end of what the press nicknamed 'the bubble trial' he was only acquitted after a secret ballot.[11]

Sex and violence, separately or together, occupied much of the tribunals' time. The first court martial under the Visiting Forces Act was held by the USAAF to try Private Travis Hammond four days after the statute became law in August 1942. The defendant was accused of committing a sexual offence against a British girl of sixteen, a shop assistant, in an air raid shelter. Two couples had gone into the shelter. The girl had allowed the defendant to kiss her. When the other two left, he lifted her up and she struggled. It sounded like horseplay. However, given the age of the girl and the fact that the Visiting Forces Act as well as the defendant was on trial, this was not an occasion for leniency. The defendant predicted that he would be 'shot at sunrise', but his sentence was commuted. In any case, most American servicemen executed in Britain were hanged. The inhabitants of Shepton Mallet, living near the prison, were said to have protested at sounds of dawn firing parties from within the walls. The truth was that convicted men were almost always hanged, executions taking place at 1 a.m., rather than first light.

The first murder trial by court martial took place at the end of August 1942. The scene of the killing was Belfast, where a fight had broken out between British and American soldiers after a dance. Private William G. Davis inflicted fatal stab wounds on a British private, Owen McLoughlan. Davis had seen McLoughlan and another British soldier at the dance, holding an American and punching him. Davis pulled one attacker off. After the dance, he saw two soldiers outside holding an American while McLoughlan was 'whamming' away at the victim with a stick. Davis was stabbed in the back while following McLoughlan with the intention of taking the stick away from him. His assailant was a Glaswegian, Private John Stevenson of the Pioneer Corps. Davis claimed that he was only aware of McLoughlan's death when he heard someone shouting that a British soldier had been stabbed.

The defence argued that the incidents 'justified Davis morally to enter a fray in defence of his "buddies" whom he had reason to believe were in danger of bodily harm'. The court found him not guilty of murder but guilty of the manslaughter of McLoughlan. He was gaoled for eight years. At a British court martial, Stevenson was acquitted of wounding Davis with intent to murder but found guilty of wounding with intent to maim Davis and another American.[12]

The US authorities were willing to encourage severity but uneasy over the reaction at home to the first execution of a serviceman in Britain. With the bulk of their forces still in Northern Ireland, in October 1942, a corporal and a private charged with the murder of a publican's son in County Antrim were acquitted of murder and sent to hard labour for ten years on a conviction for manslaughter. Not until January 1943 was the first capital sentence passed, on a black soldier from Alabama, who was condemned by a Glasgow court martial to be hanged for murdering a Polish seaman in a fight over two girls.[13]

This was not to be the first execution. The case was overtaken by the trial of another soldier before a court martial in East Anglia for shooting dead one of his officers. Private David Cobb had been on guard duty and the lieutenant was officer of the day. Outside the guardhouse, Cobb told Lieutenant Cobner that he was 'not staying at my post no longer'. Cobner ordered a member of the guard to arrest Cobb but the private pointed his rifle and told the man to halt. Cobner then told the sergeant of the guard to arrest Cobb, with the same result. Finally, Cobner tried to grab the rifle, at which Cobb pulled the trigger and shot him dead. Cobb was convicted and, three months later, was the first US serviceman to be executed, at Shepton Mallet by the military hangman.[14]

It was almost a year before a comparable case was tried. In October 1943, Private Lee A. Davis appeared before a court martial at Marlborough, charged with shooting dead one young woman who worked at Savernake Hospital and attacking another who was not in a mental condition to give evidence. They were attacked after leaving a cinema at Marlborough. One was found dead by the roadside, the other in a dazed condition at the edge of a wood. Medical evidence was once again given by British witnesses. Davis was convicted of murder and was hanged in December at an unnamed 'United States Army Disciplinary Training Centre in England'.[15]

Among those imprisoned for their crimes, some US servicemen found escape easy and British criminals hospitable. 'Armed and dangerous' was the usual description of fugitives. It was not surprising that they should be armed. Americans carried guns most of the time and were apt to draw them if there was trouble. But not all armed and dangerous men were what they seemed. One of the most intense manhunts came in the first days of peace. Private Ben Sutherland had been sentenced to life imprisonment by a US court martial on 6 July 1945 for the attempted murder of a City of London policeman on London Bridge. 'Life' in his case was intended to be thirty years.

Sutherland was also sentenced for jewel robbery. In August, he escaped from custody in France, while on his way from a detention centre in England to serve his time in America. It was thought that he would make for London. This proved true two days after his escape when, unknown to the British public, US Military Police fired on Sutherland in Park Lane.

Before his arrest for attempted murder, Sutherland had criminal contacts in Brighton and was running a number of rackets in the Victoria district of London. He was hunted by both US and Metropolitan police, using jeeps and foot patrols. Having escaped on 21 August, he was thought to be the man who paid £2 (£80) for a German automatic pistol in London on the following night. He had travelled to the city with remarkable speed and ease. FBI agents who had been brought from America to hunt black market gangs of US deserters were told to suspend that operation and find Sutherland instead. A few days later, the FBI and Scotland Yard decided that he must by now have been smuggled aboard a troopship at Southampton, among thousands of homeward-bound GIs, hoping to lose himself in post-war America.

There was still what Scotland Yard called a 'nationwide call' for the fugitive. A glimmer of hope came when one of his friends was seen making for the railway station at Clapham Junction in company with an unidentified US soldier. The mystery man vanished. The police seized Sutherland's friend who got away after a brief struggle, only to be arrested by CID officers that evening while having a quiet meal in a Brixton café. He was taken to Marlborough Street police station, its cells currently on loan to US Military Police. The man arrested confirmed that it was Sutherland who had been fired on in Park Lane.

There were no sightings for three weeks. Then Sutherland was caught in Portsmouth. His month of liberty had been dramatic but scarcely criminal. After escaping in France, he made his way to London. He had not planned a great criminal enterprise but had escaped for a most natural reason. He wanted to get married. He and his bride were married at Finsbury Registry Office on 22 August, attracting neither attention nor suspicion, while the newspaper placards warned the public of the 'Stop-At-Nothing-Gunman', with pictures of the wanted man. When arrested, he was on his way to America to begin a new life.

Other Americans escaped with extraordinary ease. In February 1946, eight 'most wanted' criminals under sentence at Chelsea Barracks simply left by way of the kitchen window. In July, two 'desperate' men quietly disarmed their guards on the way from Southampton to the American Army Police Camp at Tidworth in Wiltshire. Armed themselves, they drove off towards London. Next day, the US Navy sent its 'Shoot-It-Out' shore patrols after them.

Such men disappeared into the world of racketeering and crime. Those subsequently caught were harshly dealt with. In March 1944, two US privates were tried by a court martial which moved about the country to gather witnesses to their numerous crimes, sitting in Glasgow, Liverpool and Warrington. They were convicted of larceny and housebreaking, but also of breaking out of American military detention barracks at Glasgow in the first place. Before leaving Glasgow, they celebrated their liberty by breaking into four premises and stealing property including fur coats, women's costumes and drink worth £2,000 (£80,000). Each now received a sentence of sixty years' hard labour, which would leave them breaking rocks in their eighties, compared to forty years awarded to their comrade for the killing of two British marines in the case at Greenock three months later.[16]

Despite such cases, US servicemen and their supplies were far more likely to be the victims than the perpetrators of robbery. As the build-up of troops continued in 1942, accompanying thefts of their supplies increased. As usual, a valuable and easily portable commodity was cigarettes. In December 1942, a major prosecution involved the theft from the US Army of what was first thought to be 1,200,000 cigarettes in store at Liverpool docks, whose value was put at £7,500 (£300,000). There was no suggestion in this case that US personnel were involved.

The gang had been caught when a suspect lorry carrying 120 cases of Lucky Strike was trailed from the docks to a garage by CID officers, where the cigarettes were found. The police admitted that 'thefts of cigarettes brought to this country for the USA Expeditionary Force have been carried on for some months on a colossal scale'. In this case, the theft proved to be a little more colossal than first thought. Long after the robbery, goods stolen from US troops by the same gang were still being found, including a further batch of cigarettes to the value of £4,960 (£198,400).[17]

Sometimes it was not known whether the robbers were British, American or a partnership. In January 1945 when 50,000 dollar bills, issued in Britain for use in the Far East, disappeared while in transit from London to Glasgow, it seemed probable that these were taken by Americans. When a large proportion of them was later found in sacks abandoned on a river bank, it appeared more likely that British thieves had stolen them, believing them to be sterling, and then decided that the risk of trying to exchange them was too great.

Most British thefts from the US Army were small-scale but persistent, and they were dealt with sharply from the bench, which saw them as a betrayal of the grand alliance. At Stepney, Peckham and Shoreditch in November 1942, for example, there was a series of such crimes. All four thieves were described as having excellent characters. Three had each stolen one pair of US Army boots. Two of these men were convicted and sent to prison, the other being a man of sixty-seven who was fined £10. The fourth was stopped while on his bike and his

saddlebag was searched. It contained four US Army sheets. For stealing these, as well as two tins of pears and a tin of meat, from American
stores he was sent to prison for four months. British courts were as
determined as US courts martial not to be accused of leniency.[18]

In January 1945, a later case at Liverpool involved a conspiracy
between three British civilians and US servicemen 'to steal and
dispose of vast quantities of goods belonging to the American
Armed Forces'. The specimen charges related to 500 cigarette lighters, 500 powder compacts, 200 watches and 1,000 fountain pens,
valued at £2,450 (£98,000). The three civilians had approached a
British driver for the American forces, asking if he would join their
plan. He refused. They then showed him £3,000 (£120,000) in £1
banknotes and said, 'Don't be a fool. Take it while you can. The war
may be over at any time.' The driver's reluctance vanished at the sight
of the banknotes. He suggested two American soldiers who would be
willing to take part in the thefts. The soldiers would steal the goods
and bring them to the British driver's house in a jeep. The three civilians could meet them there. The plan seemed safe, even foolproof.
There was a preliminary meeting at the house with the American
soldiers. The two sides agreed that goods to the value of £2,450
should be brought by jeep in four packing cases and be paid for in £1
notes, except for £500 which would be brought in £5 notes.

Negotiations went well. At the next meeting, one civilian carried
£1,964 in £1 notes and £500 in £5 notes. A second brought £887 in
£1 notes, the third £332 in £1 notes. The cases were brought in from
the jeep and the soldiers opened them to show the dealers what they
were buying. It was then that two more men walked in and joined the
party, Detective Inspector Gardner and Detective Sergeant Balmer of
Liverpool CID. The helpful American soldiers proved to be officers
of the US Army Criminal Investigation Division. The two detective
forces got their men. On most occasions they did not.[19]

In London, when the war was over, there was only one end for
Rainbow Corner, to the disappointment of street traders who had
jostled outside it, night after night. In November 1945, it was already
an embarrassment to the American authorities as an easy supply
source for the British trade. The US Army asked Scotland Yard to
stop the bartering that went on outside it. Within two months this

was irrelevant. Of the 1,500,000 American servicemen in Britain in May 1944, only about 25,000 remained. On 8 January 1946, Rainbow Corner closed for ever.

The usual crowd of about a hundred men loitering outside varied their chant for the occasion. 'Anything to sell? Last night tonight.' Along the pavements of Shaftesbury Avenue, Great Windmill Street and Denman Street, their overcoat pockets and bags bulged with cameras, watches and fountain pens. From the far side of the street, Scotland Yard officers and CID from Savile Row police station watched the finale. A month later, the same traders had moved to the corner of Dean Street and Old Compton Street, offering 'precious' stones and 'foreign exchange'.

A prime cause of hostility between British and American servicemen was sexual jealousy. German aerial propaganda scattered leaflets over the Eighth Army, inviting its soldiers to remember that while they were fighting, their wives and girlfriends at home were at the mercy of American wealth and wiles. It was not merely propaganda. In October 1942, the Deputy Chief Constable of Bristol was appalled at the way girls between the ages of thirteen and sixteen were prepared to 'throw themselves' at what he called obliquely 'overseas troops'. In the House of Commons on 25 May 1944, the member for Grantham described what he called the situation in towns everywhere.

> It is unfit for a woman to walk unescorted through the town at night or in the daytime, due to the ineffectiveness of the American military authorities to deal with the improper behaviour of the American forces and the complete failure to prevent unconcealed immorality and give proper protection to women.

It was hard to agree a standard for 'unconcealed immorality' but no one could dispute that the areas round American camps were littered with discarded contraceptives. These mute witnesses to collective passion hung upon hedgerows or lay strewn in fields, at roadsides or in shop doorways. There was also felt to be a truth in the accusation that young girls 'are being accosted by members of the American forces, many of them being incited to alcoholic excesses, which is tending to undermine the morality of these young persons who, having been directed away from home, do not have the benefit of parental control'. A further complaint was that wives with husbands on active service were now neglecting young children, abandoning them at night to go out drinking and copulating with American servicemen.

American military justice took these matters very seriously. In August 1944, two US soldiers were hanged, after a West Country court martial in April. A girl of sixteen had been returning from a dance with another soldier at Bishop's Cleeve in Gloucestershire on 4 March when both were attacked by the two accused. It was snowing at the time and the British police took plaster casts of footprints at the scene. The casts, exhibited in evidence, had been compared with the prints of US soldiers at a nearby camp. Both defendants, who were black, were sentenced to death. Despite parliamentary protests at the severity of the sentence and the frequent use of such severity against black defendants, the men were hanged on 8 August. Rape was not a capital offence under English or Scottish law. However, the Visiting Forces Act had given the United States power to punish its servicemen by its own military code. Not all those convicted of rape were executed but eight American servicemen were hanged in Britain for the offence during the course of the war.[20]

Soon after Bishop's Cleeve there was a more contentious West Country court martial, when Leroy Henry, a black American truck driver from St Louis, Missouri, was sentenced to death for raping a thirty-three-year-old housewife on 5 May 1944 in the village of Combe Down, on the southern fringe of Bath. The woman claimed that the man knocked on her window late at night. When she looked out, he inquired the way to Bath Spa railway station. She gave directions, but he asked if she would come and write them down. She told her husband, put a coat over her nightdress, her knickers under it, and went downstairs. She claimed that Henry had persuaded her to come with him down The Avenue. Then he drew a knife, threatened her, made her climb a wall into a field, and raped her. Her husband came to look for her. 'He wanted to chase the coloured soldier but I told him about the knife . . . My husband took me to an ARP first aid post. One leg of my knickers was torn; I had never seen that tear before.' She saw and identified Henry, while she was in a police car being driven to Dr Charles Gibson, a Bath police surgeon. Dr Gibson found her very distressed, with a pulse rate of 112 rather than 70 or 72. There were scratches below her knees, probably from climbing the wall, but no other injury.

The court martial at Knook Camp in Wiltshire consisted of a president and eight other members, one of them black, as was customary when the defendant was black. The proceedings were perfunctory and, after a short recess, Henry was told by the president, 'We find you guilty and sentence you by the unanimous vote of every member present to be hanged by the neck till dead.'

The court dismissed Leroy Henry's evidence, which told a conflicting story. It was true he had signed a confession next day. But he and the woman were not strangers. He had met her eight days earlier in the Cross Keys public house.

> I said: 'I have been told there is a very nice place to spend money.' I asked her if she knew a nice girl. Finally I popped the question to her and she said, 'Why not?' She asked me for one pound and I gave it to her. When they picked me up was the third time I had been with her.

On this third occasion, they had met at the King William public house. She told him to knock at her window later and had come willingly to the field with him. 'She laid down and unbuttoned her coat . . . She asked for two pounds. I didn't have two pounds. I told her I had well over one pound. She walked off and said, "I will get you into trouble." I just laughed and walked off.'

Henry was arrested by Constable Temlett of the Somerset Constabulary but handed over to US Military Police, who took him by jeep to Bath police station, where they had an office and cells. His evidence of treatment after arrest was also ignored. From just after midnight until five the next evening, during which time he was vigorously interrogated, he was allowed nothing to eat or drink except a cup of tea. He was confined in a cell so cold that he had to wear his greatcoat. At 10 a.m. he was taken to the US Military Police office.

> After a few minutes, the American police brought me two long sheets of paper. They had me standing up to attention and asked me a few questions. I answered some and some I did not, as all they asked me

was not the truth. A police investigator wrote down just what he wanted to write down. I was trying to give a statement when I just had one blind flash as if someone had hit or kicked me from behind. They picked me up and shook me, and tried to make me stand to attention again. They filled a long thing out and asked me to sign. One said, 'God damn! You will sign!' I was almost out on my heels. He called a captain and said I must stand to attention. The captain was standing some distance away. I put my name to one or two sheets, but I don't know what was on the sheets.

The press had attended the court martial. On 30 May, the *Daily Mirror* led the protests under a banner headline: 'US Soldier Is Sentenced to Death'. On 8 June, General Eisenhower received a petition for Henry's reprieve signed by 33,000 citizens of Bath, headed by the mayor. Whether they had been moved by shock at the court martial proceedings or by the woman's conduct seemed immaterial. For example, she had described a knife and the feel of it pressing into her back. But the accused was still close to the scene when arrested. He was not carrying a knife and a scrupulous search of the fairly small area on Combe Down failed to find one.

By the end of June, the verdict was set aside on Eisenhower's instructions and Leroy Henry was released. *Tribune*, which campaigned on his behalf, pointed out that if the verdict was unsatisfactory, so was the statement on which it was based. The newspaper urged Eisenhower to consider a reform of 'the method by which statements are extracted from accused persons'.[21]

In relations between the sexes, American soldiers were at risk from prostitutes as decoys. A familiar city trap was for a woman to pick up a GI in a crowded pub and lead him to a surface air raid shelter with a promise of intercourse. During preliminary embraces, his wallet passed into her hands, the empty wallet was replaced, and the wad of notes slipped into the top of her stocking. He got no more for his money and, if he found his wallet empty before she left, she was usually safe in betting he would be too inhibited to demand that she prove her innocence. Sometimes she lost the bet, her court appearance accompanied by such descriptions of her profession as 'occupation not tendered'.

A more ambitious trick played on unsuspecting doughboys was for two women to allow themselves to be picked up. They would agree a sum to be paid by the Americans for an all-night 'entertainment', including drink and the hire of a room. There was a promise of luxury and the price was several times that charged by a professional prostitute. The money was payable in advance, since the room must be hired and the drink bought. The group would set off in a taxi for a destination and the cab would stop outside a block of flats. The women would then explain that they must sign for a room and would be back in a few minutes. They entered the flats and were, of course, never seen again.[22]

Americans were welcome in the West London brothels of Marylebone, Paddington and Kensington. At the height of the war, police and courts turned a blind eye to this inevitable accompaniment of the world struggle. There were exceptions over a brothel in Gloucester Place, Marylebone, where very young girls not known as prostitutes were 'passed from soldier to soldier'. Another in Norfolk Mews, Paddington, its clients mostly American, was raided in 1944 and the proprietress sent to prison, as if to mark exceptional depravity. 'More degraded and disgusting behaviour I have seldom listened to in this court,' the magistrate concluded.[23]

As hostilities in Europe ended, brothels used by Americans were more generally prosecuted. When a house in Bridport Mews, Marylebone, was raided in January 1945, US officers who patronized it and five ladies working there were caught. A further raid in the same month closed down a US soldiers' brothel run as a 'hotel' in Norfolk Square, Paddington. When two 'dance hostesses' were raided on 11 March and subsequently fined for allowing flats in West Kensington to be used as brothels, American servicemen were the only customers found. In the same week, the police were watching another 'hotel' in Warrington Crescent, Maida Vale, its clients described as 'mostly members of the American forces'. Similar premises were raided in Craven Hill Gardens and Hereford Road, Bayswater.[24]

A higher-class brothel at Herbert Crescent, Chelsea, was kept occupied by 'American officers and ladies who were not their wives'. The proprietress was known as 'Madame' in the social and sexual sense. She claimed that her premises were 'as well conducted as a church'. As for the form of worship, 'My butler and secretary were responsible for the letting of the rooms and it was with horror that I learned of the charge against me.' The hero of the raid, however, was a gallant American officer who refused to allow the woman with him to give her name and address. 'He is a man of honour in protecting his lady friend,' said Madame firmly, before going to prison for two months.[25]

The more stalwart women plied their transatlantic trade on the pavement with panache and aggression. One, describing herself as a Paddington 'hairdresser', was found by a War Reserve constable at 1.15 a.m. in the Edgware Road, surrounded by American soldiers. When told to move on, she refused. 'I am not going to move. Why should I?' Then noticing his War Reserve insignia, she added derisively, 'You're only a Utility copper!' To the cheering Americans, she shouted, 'Don't move for him!' She was arrested, and fined £2 (£80).[26]

The United States had an absolute right to try its own servicemen but no provision existed where a major crime was committed jointly by British and American defendants. What would happen if a Briton and an American planned a robbery, and one of them shot dead the victim or a policeman?

This was not an academic question, given the regularity with which off-duty US servicemen carried firearms and the ease with which they resorted to their use. In September 1944, a forty-six-year-old paint sprayer from Tottenham and an American soldier in civilian clothes robbed Camberwell post office at gunpoint. They escaped with the money, only to be cornered by two unarmed policemen at a tram stop. The soldier tried to draw the gun from a holster under his overcoat, but was clumsy enough to be overpowered. He was handed over to the US Army while the paint sprayer appeared before Lambeth magistrates. In January 1945 there was a near-tragedy at a pub in Seven Sisters Road, Holloway. Metropolitan police officers tried to question a woman about a false identity card. While she struggled to get free, the American soldier with whom she had lived for a year drew a revolver and was only prevented from using it by US Military Police, who were more persuasively armed than he was.[27]

Of all such crimes committed by Americans in England during the war, none was to rival in notoriety the armed robberies and murder known variously as 'The Inky Fingers Case', 'The Cleft Chin Murder' or simply 'Chicago Joe and Blondie.' It was a West London story of milk bars and super cinemas, street robbery and stolen guns, with a dash of Chicago and clubland striptease, the whole overlaid by the tawdriness of blackout and austerity.

On the afternoon of 3 October 1944, at the Black and White Café near Hampstead tube station, the protagonists were introduced by a mutual friend. A twenty-two-year-old American deserter, Private Karl Hulten of the 501st Airborne Division, masquerading as 'Lieutenant Ricky Allen', met an eighteen-year-old Welsh 'striptease dancer', Elizabeth Maud Jones, masquerading as 'Georgina Grayson'. Elizabeth Jones had not stripped nor teased for several months. Before that, however, she had appeared at the Panama Club in South Kensington and the Blue Lagoon behind Regent Street.

They were unlikely perpetrators of a major crime. Elizabeth Jones came from Neath. She was a runaway at thirteen, first sent to an approved school in need of care and protection, then as being beyond parental control. At sixteen, she married an army corporal, ten years her elder. She claimed he had hit her on their wedding night and she left him forthwith. Having had dancing lessons as a child and shown some aptitude, she set out from South Wales to London. She danced as 'Georgina Grayson', though her main income was a weekly 32s. marriage allowance from the Army. She denied being a prostitute and admitted only one lover, a Canadian bomber-pilot killed in action. Those who observed her on trial described her as a graceless blonde waif of little appeal or presence.

Karl Hulten, known to her only as 'Ricky', played the role of army paratroop officer and Chicago gunman in civilian life, but was equally nondescript. Born in Stockholm, he grew up in Massachusetts, becoming a grocery clerk, driver and mechanic. He had married, before sailing for England early in 1944, and a child had since been born. He deserted about six weeks before meeting Elizabeth, taking with him a two-and-a-half-ton military truck.

There was little romance between this odd couple. Six days after they met, Hulten was under arrest for murder, so, two days later, was

Elizabeth. Though he slept in her room on three nights of their six-day partnership, she insisted that there was no 'intimacy' between them. 'There was nothing of that,' she said firmly, in the accents of Welsh Nonconformity rather than of striptease. The press found it easy to dismiss them as 'losers', yet it was their consciousness of failure, even as criminals, that made them dangerous. They embarked on a career of armed robbery, petty in its rewards but savage in its methods. Their ineptitude made them likely to be caught at any moment. The murder gained them nothing they could not have had without it, yet for this they seemed certain to be tried and hanged.

At their introduction, they arranged to meet again outside the Broadway cinema in Hammersmith at 6.30. Elizabeth waited until she decided she had been 'stood up', but as she walked away a ten-wheeled US truck passed and 'Ricky' called her by the only name he knew, 'Georgina'. He explained that he had been a Chicago gunman, and was now leader of a London gang. He showed her his stolen automatic pistol, to be used in holding up a hotel near Maidenhead. As they drove west, 'Georgina Grayson' warmed to the idea of 'doing something dangerous' and becoming a 'gunman's moll'. They overtook a girl on a bicycle. Hulten stopped the truck and got down. As the cyclist passed, he knocked her off her bike, grabbed her handbag, tossed it up to Elizabeth Jones, and threw the bicycle over a hedge. They drove on, his companion rifling the victim's purse. But 'Ricky' decided there would be no hold-up that night. He thought they were being watched.

Back in Hammersmith, Hulten parked the truck and went on his way. It was two days later, at 5 p.m. on Thursday 5 October, when he called for Elizabeth at her rooms in King Street, Hammersmith. This time, they would rob a taxi driver. He drove the truck into London and followed a taxi heading north on the Edgware Road. A female passenger got out at Cricklewood. As the cab turned back, Hulten blocked its path with the truck, jumped out, and pointed his gun at the driver. Only then did he see that there was another passenger in the back, an American officer with his own gun drawn. Hulten ran for his truck and the couple drove off.

Returning through blacked-out streets to the Edgware Road, they noticed a girl carrying two suitcases towards Paddington station and the Bristol train. Hulten offered her a lift to Reading. After twenty miles, he stopped and got out, on the pretext that something was wrong with the back axle. As their passenger followed, Elizabeth offered her a cigarette, and Hulten hit the stranger on the head with an iron bar. Between them, they dumped her out of sight by the river and drove off with her cases. Though the victim was not dead, her assailants had good reason to suppose she might be. They returned to an all-night café in Fulham Palace Road, then retired to Elizabeth's room.

Next night, as Hulten stood in a shop doorway, Elizabeth hailed a hire car on Hammersmith Broadway. Though not licensed to ply as a taxi, George Heath agreed to take them to their destination for ten shillings. They drove out of London on a deserted stretch of road with factories at a little distance, to a roundabout on the Great West Road. Hulten said this would do. The driver turned and reached back to open the door from the inside for Elizabeth to get out. As he did this, Hulten, who was sitting behind him, shot George Heath with a single bullet from his automatic. It was a futile brutality. The body would be found at daylight. The search for the car would be a police priority.

Heath's death was not instantaneous but in the last moments of the driver's life Hulten pushed him aside, saying, 'Move over or I will give you another dose of the same', then drove the taxi himself. Elizabeth went through Heath's pockets as he died, taking the cash from his wallet, his fountain pen, propelling pencil, cigarette lighter and the watch from his wrist. She threw his photographs and papers from the window of the taxi, so that they were easily found. At length the couple stopped, dragged the body to a roadside ditch, and tumbled it in.

Next morning they slept late, went to the Saturday afternoon races at the White City dog track, had a meal in a milk bar, and spent the evening at a cinema in Victoria, watching Deanna Durbin in *Christmas Holiday*. They sat arm in arm, Elizabeth's head on Hulten's shoulder, a spray of flowers he had bought pinned to her coat. This was their nearest approach to happiness.

On the evening of their last day, Sunday 8 October, they drove to the West End in the hire car, parking just off Piccadilly near the side entrance of the Berkeley Hotel. Elizabeth wanted a fur coat, which was to be stolen from one of the women leaving the foyer. She chose a white ermine worn by a woman just coming down the steps. Hulten left the car, seized the startled wearer and began to strip the coat from her. A policeman on his beat came round the corner. Hulten abandoned the coat, ran back to the car, and drove off. Next day he was arrested when about to get into the car, parked in Fulham. George Heath's body had long since been found and the number of his car circulated. When it was seen parked in Fulham, the police set a trap and sprang it at the thief's return.

Such were the events leading to a public drama at the Central Criminal Court. The US Army was entitled to try Hulten but not Elizabeth Jones. At first, it was announced that Hulten's court martial would be postponed until the girl's trial was over. Unfortunately, this might have resulted in her being hanged before she could be called as a key witness in the later case. In these circumstances, the United States asked the British government to try both accused. It was the first time that America had handed over one of its citizens for trial in this way.

There was little hope for either defendant. The only chance for Hulten was that the firing of the automatic might be proved accidental, reducing his crime to manslaughter. Mr Justice Charles told the jury that the facts admitted made this impossible. Elizabeth pleaded her terror of the 'Chicago gunman'. The judge also disposed of this. She had admitted going to collect Hulten's bag from the left luggage office at Hammersmith underground station, which he had used as a place to keep his possessions while on the run. She had passed hundreds of people in the centre of Hammersmith, any one of whom might have listened to her plea for rescue from the killer waiting in her room.

Both were convicted and sentenced to death. On 7 March 1945, Hulten was driven from Wandsworth to Pentonville, where he was hanged the next morning. Pleas from his wife and mother, as well as his Massachusetts senator, had left the Home Secretary, Herbert Morrison, unmoved. Elizabeth Jones was reprieved, perhaps for her youth and despite a letter from Bernard Shaw to *The Times*, advocating her execution but suggesting that hanging should be replaced by making the death cell a secret lethal chamber, where she could be painlessly destroyed in her sleep without even knowing on which night it would happen. Supporters and opponents of capital punishment denounced this as grotesque.

It was hard to see what had given such glamour and drama to the trial of this dull-witted and ill-fated couple, who at length turned against one another at their trial. Yet at the Old Bailey and at their unsuccessful appeal hearing, the courtroom was filled by distinguished visitors, high-ranking officers and officials. The BBC so far forgot its political rectitude as to send a correspondent to cover proceedings, in company with the *News of the World*. In part, there was the novelty of a GI, a gangster at last, fighting for his life in the Old Bailey dock. There was the tabloid sensationalism of 'Chicago Joe' and his striptease dancer, a murder hunt accompanied by headline stories of film-famous American 'G-Men' joining forces with Scotland Yard. This was true, to the extent that FBI agent Walter J. Riddle and Lieutenant Robert De Mott of the US Army's 8th Military Police Criminal Investigation Section played their part. There was even a courtroom 'duel' between De Mott, a Colorado barrister in civilian life, and Hulten's counsel, John Maude KC.

De Mott had been the first to interrogate Hulten and had done so in a rather more robust manner than might have been permitted under Judges' Rules in England. Maude, the suave and practised English advocate, leaning towards his opponent hands on hips, confronted the plain-spoken Colorado lawyer whose hands gripped the edge of the witness box. At last, provoked too far by the subtle questioning, De Mott's voice rose and he shot out his arm, exclaiming, 'Sir, you are questioning my integrity!' Nor was the end of the trial easily forgotten, when the sentences were passed and Elizabeth Jones was led screaming from the dock to the cells below, followed by the stolid figure of her gunman, her shrill abuse of Hulten and cries of terror rising to fill the otherwise silent and motionless courtroom.[28]

The last test of law and order among the American forces came with the return of peace. With the great crusade over, tens of thousands of men waited to go home. A number of them were prepared to desert or try their hands at crime. The agitations were not widely advertised but, for example, on 11 January 1946, a column of 500 American soldiers, half of all those remaining in London, marched in protest from

Marble Arch to their country's embassy in Grosvenor Square, chanting 'We want to go home!' An officer at the embassy tried to address them and was so vigorously heckled that he could not make himself heard. The hecklers demanded to know where the US Navy and its ships were. 'They were disgustingly efficient getting us out from New York!' shouted one GI, while another added, 'I've never heard so many unmitigated liars in my life!' Major Campbell of the Redeployment Section then took over and told them that if they had no work to do he would find them some. 'You have no right to form mobs of this sort. You are not civilians yet.' That was as far as he got before his words were also drowned by the jeers of the crowd.

Some of them did indeed find things to do. Among others, a few weeks after the demonstration two American soldiers deserted and teamed up with a pair of Glasgow criminals to steal a US ambulance truck and use it in a series of armed robberies. Their activities became so troublesome that guns were issued to the British police and radio cars were used to track them. The four wanted men were 'shot to a halt' at Berwick-on-Tweed at 4 a.m. on 20 March. Armed police waited to ambush them at the north end of the Royal Tweed Bridge.

The truck approached Scotsgate, with its narrow arch over Berwick High Street. Ropes were stretched at windscreen height across the street, police positioned in doorways and on the arch. They signalled to the truck, in response to which it swerved and accelerated down the narrow street. Police marksmen opened fire, hitting it and bringing it to a halt. The four men leapt out, saw the police guns, and put up their hands. The excitement was over but such incidents persuaded both nations that the time had come to restore normality.

The number of American troops in Britain had fallen since the invasion of Europe in 1944 and was no more than a token 25,000 at the time of the Grosvenor Square demonstration. A month later it was said to be 10,000. American billets had been given up and, though many of the US camps were still occupied, they now contained 'squatters', British civilians and returning servicemen, who had nowhere else to live.

12

Clubland

As the first thousands of men were conscripted into the armed forces in 1939–40, the bishops, the service departments and the Public Morality Council campaigned to control the moral underclass of the nation's cities. In January 1940, the bishops formed a committee to keep watch on the welfare of the troops. As the number of troops grew, Scotland Yard came under pressure to deal specifically with clubs which existed to 'fleece men on leave'.

West End clubs in the phoney peace of 1939–40 operated as they had done for twenty years. In an age of cumbersome licensing laws, 'bottle parties' offered all-night semi-legal drinking. Customers at a Berkeley Square night club or a shabby basement in Soho could drink after hours by signing order forms which were sent to all-night wine retailers. Drink was bought in the customer's name and in theory never belonged to the club. An attempt was made to suggest that an Act of Parliament of 1867 made it an offence for all-night wine retailers to solicit orders. Was not that what they did in giving blank forms to the clubs? With some reluctance, the courts thought not.

When the war began, there were between 200 and 300 'bottle party' clubs open every night in the West End. Their status was succinctly described in 1937 by Lord Hilbery, when the proprietor of the Chez Nous Bottle Party sued the *Daily Telegraph* for damaging his reputation. Hilbery informed him briskly that he and his club had no reputation to damage, dismissed his appeal, and left him in prison for debt over the costs of the case.[1]

By the New Year of 1940, the Public Morality Council and its allies scarcely lacked ammunition. At one club, a 'dance hostess' was found to be Belgian, an unregistered alien, and fourteen years old. She shared the publicity that day with Sir Ronald Gunter who was knocked down during a fist fight at the Kit-Kat Club, Regent Street, at 4.45 a.m. The magistrate warned him that if he went to 'such places' he must expect to meet 'such people'. In another Bow Street case, a 'bottle party hostess' was revealed as an approved school runaway of seventeen.[2]

By March 1940, details of a new abuse reached Sir Philip Game, Commissioner of the Metropolitan Police, from the service departments. Touts on the streets of the West End as theatres, cinemas and pubs closed handed out cards for 'entertainments' at particular addresses. A soldier would be charged 3s. (£6) for admission and for leaving his greatcoat. He was charged only 1s. (£2) for a bottle of beer that was no more than near-beer, but required to buy a 'liqueur', costing 2s. 6d. (£5) and consisting of watered fruit juice, for a youthful hostess. In a few minutes he had spent half his week's pay. When his companion finished her drink, he was invited to buy another 'liqueur'. Within half an hour he was penniless. There was no music, no dancing, no kind of entertainment. When the man's money was gone, the hostess was under instructions to move on to another customer.

The service chiefs wrote to Sir Philip Game who replied regretfully that he could do nothing about it. The fact that soldiers were being charged many times the normal price for beer that was near-beer or cocktails that were fruit juice and water was not in itself illegal.

Apart from its inability to deal with the near-beer and fruit juice racket, in March and April 1940 the success of police action against the worst clubs of Soho or Mayfair declined unaccountably. Raiding parties operated out of Vine Street police station. How was it that in the few minutes it took to reach Soho or Mayfair, drinks had been removed from tables and cards or roulette wheels had vanished? Sir Philip Game demanded an explanation and was told that men were employed by club proprietors to watch Vine Street and telephone warnings. It was not expensive. One tout could act for several clubs. If a club was prosecuted despite this system, the touts went to court, in order to recognize next time the officers who gave evidence. Sir Philip ordered the entire squad to be relocated within Scotland Yard.

The results were mixed. A year later, Herbert Morrison assured Parliament that the clubs were under control. Between the outbreak of war and 30 April 1941, 854 new clubs were registered in the Metropolitan Police District, but 1,194 had closed or had been struck off. In the previous twelve months 133 clubs in London had been raided. This, however, still left far too many in business.

The Metropolitan Police had revived its 'Bottle Party Squad' in January 1940, under Divisional Inspector Mulveney. The squad chose a variety of targets. It raided the prestigious El Morocco Restaurant Bottle Party in Albemarle Street, taking the names of sixty guests, including two peers of the realm. It raided the New Harlem Bottle Party in Old Compton Street, Soho, whose owner Max Fredericks was fined £150 (£6,000). Nor was the law afraid to send men to prison. In May 1940 Tony Phillips, owner of the Mother Hubbard Club, Ham Yard, was fined and gaoled for twenty-one days, after he had repeatedly offended by serving drinks out of hours.[3]

In the spring of 1940, alarm at the popularity of bottle parties ran in parallel with a rising threat of nudity on the stage. The two scourges were interwoven in April when the 'El Morocco Bottle Party' began to put on striptease contests, as if it were a theatre club. The idea was not slow to catch on. Meanwhile, drinking clubs appeared everywhere and in the most unlikely places. Sixteen under-cover policemen and policewomen put on their dancing clothes and attended the Condor Social Club, Dagenham, which was described as 'a reconditioned garage'.[4]

In April 1940, it was decided that if troops on leave were going to drink anyway, it was better for them to do so under supervision. As an experiment, a licence was given to the Piccadilly Corner House to sell drink until 2 a.m. The police were in favour of the scheme. Indeed, because all those who wanted to drink could hardly be crammed into even the largest Lyons Corner House, the police undertook to draw up a list of 'good' bottle parties.

The West End's 2 a.m. extension, which added four hours to drink-ing time, was a success. The Criterion and the Coventry Street Corner House were added to the list. The Hotels and Restaurants Association was in favour but did not regard these extensions as an alternative to the suppression of bottle parties.

As the number of soldiers, sailors and airmen on leave in London grew to many thousands, it was never likely that bottle parties would be stamped out. Indeed, on 24 November 1944 the Chief Magistrate at Bow Street, Sir Bertrand Watson, did something unthinkable four years earlier. He dismissed charges against the New Paradise Bottle Party in Regent Street, as well as the wine merchant who supplied the customers, and ruled that the supply was perfectly legal so long as the customer reserved drink with the wine merchant before going to the party. The practical effect of this was to make further prosecutions difficult to sustain. However, it was not until January 1947 that the post-war Labour government announced it had no plans to stop bottle parties.

By the beginning of 1942 the government faced a greater threat than drunkenness among servicemen on leave. The new threat to the nation was 'hooch'. With the arrival of so many servicemen in London and other cities, shortly followed by the Americans, the demand for drink rose as wartime supplies dwindled. Hooch was a simple remedy, often crippling, if not lethal.

The government's concern became public in January 1942, following a report of the conviction of Benjamin Bennett, who had operated an illicit still at his café in the aptly named Asylum Road, Peckham. Mr Bennett was no innocent civilian distilling a little spirit for his own use. Distilling apart, he was a criminal with convictions for robbery with violence. The still, discovered in a scullery washhouse during a police raid, showed that 'a high degree of engineering ability had been used'. The wash from which spirits were distilled filled a hundred-gallon tank. Undefeated by sugar rationing, Mr Bennett distilled pure 'crystal clear' alcohol from chemically treated sugar beet and water. Apart from the low cost of ingredients, Mr Bennett was defrauding the Revenue of almost £5 (£200) on every gallon that he produced.

When Customs and Excise raided the café, they found in a wardrobe fourteen quart bottles of cherry brandy, recently produced. They also found 'essences' to transform pure alcohol instantly into gin, whisky or rum. Mr Bennett's gin, for example, was a compound of pure alcohol and water with juniper and almond essences. 'With a still such as Bennett had, whisky, gin and rum could be made so apparently perfect that only an expert could detect that they were synthetic.' The profit on such a product was described by the police as 'enormous'.[5]

It did not follow that because spirits were illicit they were always lethal. A 1938 case involved a Camberwell motor-dealer, described by police as 'a plausible scoundrel' and counterfeiter, convicted of making and selling what he modestly called 'rot gut'. The offence, as in 1942, was defrauding the Revenue. An anxious magistrate asked what the effect of the Camberwell whisky would be. But it had been made, like Bennett's, in a high-quality still and the prosecuting solicitor was forced to admit, 'Experts tell me it is some of the finest spirits they have ever seen, the reason being that they were very efficient stills.' In that case, the culprit was fined £240 (£9,600). Mr Bennett was fined £320 (£12,800) with the alternative of five months in prison.[6]

Those who drank the spirits from Camberwell and Peckham were fortunate, as the deaths or insanity which resulted elsewhere indicated. Three days after Mr Bennett's case, the Air Ministry warned RAF pilots about the 'hooch racket' in London. All three services were alarmed at the increase in the West End trade. Even a small amount of hooch would cause gastritis and temporary blindness. Anyone getting drunk on it might be permanently blinded, deranged or killed.

The Air Ministry had most to fear. In the nature of aerial warfare, pilots might be over Germany on one night and drinking with their friends the next. A pilot who drank the 'poison' of hooch might never fly again. Britain was still guarded by the RAF alone. To imagine the outcome if hundreds of its pilots were unable to fly, or if planes fell from the sky before they could engage the enemy, might seem overdramatic. It was not, however, unrealistic.

Herbert Morrison ordered analyses of hooch that was seized. It proved even more injurious than the variety sold in America during prohibition. Mr Bennett of Peckham had treated his customers to pure alcohol. Other suppliers made gin from one part of industrial alcohol, two parts of water, and a flavouring of oil of juniper. Yet many racketeers were now content to doctor the colour and the flavour of methylated spirits.

In May 1943, Customs and Excise uncovered what it called 'a spider's web' with its centre at the Granville Club in Albemarle Street. The web consisted of six men and two women, one the club secretary, the other the barmaid. Drums of industrial spirit were stolen from a bonded warehouse in Hammersmith. The spirit was mixed with boiled water and burnt sugar as colouring. It was packaged in genuine, though used, bottles of leading distillers. To make such products plausible, underground presses now printed counterfeit labels for leading brands. As much as 2s. 6d. each (£5) was offered for empty bottles.

Members of the Granville Club were an unwitting captive market, unlikely to be reassured by learning that they had now drunk seven gallons of 65 over-proof industrial spirit. Where the products had to be marketed, a 'salesman' would visit 'low' bars, bottle parties and night clubs, offering a genuine sample bottle. Once that was approved, the main supply would be counterfeit.[7]

Legitimate manufacturers of methylated spirits made its colour and taste difficult to disguise. However, a skilled chemist could improve on this. In January 1942, Scotland Yard was said to be following up a job advertisement for an analytical chemist with a knowledge of alcoholic compounds.

A committee of inquiry into the sale of hooch in the West End had been urged on Herbert Morrison in January 1942. No action was taken. Those who thought such concerns were a fuss about nothing, thought again when eleven men and three women died in Glasgow during a single incident in May. There had been several deaths a month earlier and seven other victims of that tragedy were still being treated in the Western Infirmary. In Liverpool, two seamen lost consciousness and one of them died after a single drink from a stranger's bottle. The inquest jury returned a verdict of death from asphyxia, following acute alcoholic poisoning. Nor was it just a matter of feckless drinking among workers and servicemen. In mid-May, in the House of Lords, Lord Teriot had demanded that hooch peddlers should be shot, following an incident when four company directors were paralysed and took ten days to recover after a small whisky and soda at a major London hotel.[8]

As public anxiety increased, an able seaman in a widely reported case threw himself to his death from the window of a canteen at Waterloo station in March 1942. He had fought off the canteen manageress and the Naval Picket, after being roused with difficulty from a stupor, and then dived through the high window. The manageress reported a number of non-fatal incidents like this, 'and we are attributing them to a kind of doped drink the men get hold of'. In the same month, a man who stole fifteen ounces of methyl alcohol from the oil wharf where he worked had added it to his home-made elderberry wine. He gave some of the wine to two seamen, who drank it and died.[9]

Even those who survived hooch were little to be envied. In March, a Canadian airman went berserk in a hotel and fought with such energy that it took six guards to hold him down. When at last he was medically examined the conclusion was that such brain damage would make him an invalid for life. In the wake of this, a proposal was made in the House of Commons for medical officers to be attached to the Provost Marshal's department and for patrols of Military Police accompanied by doctors to check clubs and bars for hooch and, if necessary, put the premises out of bounds to officers and men.

Few peddlers were caught, let alone shot. It was uncertain what sentences would be passed during the current anxiety. However, in November two men were sent to prison for six months and fined £250 (£10,000) each for attempting to sell drink containing methylic alcohol to the secretary of a Forest Hill club.[10]

In 1942–3 Scotland Yard tracked down a number of stills and closed clubs found to be supplying the drink. The principal lead came from victims who had drunk the spirit, survived to report it, and could remember where they had been. When Captain Cody of the London Irish Rifles was court-martialled for being drunk in Coventry Street on 7 July 1942, he was acquitted on the grounds that he had unknowingly drunk hooch. Elsewhere, Captain Humphrey Platt had his sentence of five weeks' imprisonment reduced to a fine of £40. He had assaulted a policeman in Argyll Street, fought two US soldiers and a second policeman who came to their aid. The appeal court accepted that he knew nothing between drinking the doctored wine and finding himself at the police station. However, he remembered where he had been poisoned. A 'hooch defence' was not infallible. Lieutenant Moore of the London Irish Rifles was sentenced to be reprimanded for being absent without leave. He pleaded unsuccessfully that he had unknowingly drunk hooch at a club, in consequence of which his mind was a blank and he knew nothing for two or three days.[11]

In the House of Lords on 23 May 1944, Lord Strabolgi offered the government the names of three West End clubs principally responsible for putting hooch into circulation, as well as names of eleven victims in the armed forces and of medical officers who would give evidence as to the cause of their illness. In that month, the owner of a still who was marketing industrial spirit as whisky at Dagenham was caught and fined. Once again, however, he was charged and convicted of defrauding the Revenue rather than poisoning those to whom he sold the liquor. The fines and penalties amounted to £641 (£25,640) with an alternative of twelve months in prison.

The method used by this defendant was similar to that at the Granville Club. It was described by the police as 'breaking down' industrial spirit, 'sweetening it, colouring it, and selling it as whisky'. The quantity on the premises was 135 bottles, labelled 'Fine Old Scotch Whisky', containing twenty-two and a half gallons with thirty more bottles waiting to be filled. It was not a very large consignment, but enough to kill or cripple a hundred people or to make many hundreds extremely ill. The defendant protested that he had nothing to do with the liquor. He had 'most idiotically allowed another man to take possession of his house and break down this hooch'. He was not believed and was sentenced while protesting that he had been left 'to carry the can back' for the true villain. It seemed that the police had caught one of the small fry and missed the thread that might have led to the major operators.[12]

The success of Scotland Yard in tracking down London stills and suppliers was balanced by an increase in the hooch trade in provincial cities, in the Midlands and East Anglia, and near military installations or air bases. A new market had opened up by October 1942 with the arrival of American troops. As a result of damage to those who drank hooch, commanders of American camps began to issue a free bottle of gin or whisky from camp stores to each man going on leave as a precaution against the shadowy figures of the bar and the invitation of the blacked-out street.

It was as well for the peace of mind of Britain's military commanders that they knew nothing of illicit stills being run by their own men in German prison camps. At Stalag 383 near Moosberg, from which coded letters were successfully sent, liquor was distilled from prunes, raisins and sugar from food parcels. There was a 'distillery' in almost every hut and when one man's supply failed, another found his liquor just maturing. The process took ten days and delivered 'a real kick'. German guards were 'bewildered' by the cheerful behaviour of their charges. The coded letters directed that contributions from the men's pay, accumulating in England, should be used towards the purchase of a Spitfire, christened 'Unshackled Spirit'.[13]

As whisky grew scarcer and the price accelerated, stealing and swindling proliferated. Among exports, there were extensive thefts at the docks. In one of these, seven containers of whisky arrived in Canada and, when opened, were found to contain only rubble from a dismantled Glasgow air raid shelter.

Scotland Yard officers were seldom able to catch tricksters at their trade. A rare exception was in July 1944. Captain Eric Westley of No. 3 Commando was approached in the bar of the Berkeley Hotel by a man who asked him if his father would like to buy a hundred cases of whisky for £1,700 (£68,000). With whisky selling at as much as £4 a bottle it might have seemed a bargain. Captain Westley recalled, 'This made me suspicious and I arranged to meet him the next day for lunch to discuss the matter further. I communicated with Scotland Yard and had an interview with two detective sergeants.'

With Detective Sergeant Collins in the battledress of an RAC captain, Westley met the man in a pub that night. They agreed to complete the deal three days later. When the time came, Westley and Collins went by appointment to a flat in Trevor Place, South Kensington. A sum of £1,700 was agreed for the whisky. At a sign from Sergeant Collins, Westley left the room and let in Detective Sergeant Wynn, who introduced himself and asked the dealer where the whisky was. After a pause, he replied, 'I haven't any whisky.' When such a case came to court, the defendant was liable to be recognized by others he had swindled. One of them in this instance, having parted with £437 (£17,480) for twenty-five mixed cases of whisky and gin, had seen neither the drink nor her money back.[14]

In a time of shortage, retailers were easily tempted by such offers. One swindler in January 1945 extracted a down-payment of £200 (£8,000) from the proprietress of an off-licence in Tottenham Court Road on a promise to supply 150 cases of whisky 'straight from the distillers'. In the same month, a defendant with fifteen previous convictions over deals worth up to £1,000 (£40,000) for such offences came up for sentencing. This time he had promised 200 bottles of whisky, twenty bottles of brandy and thirty bottles of port to an over-eager publican, taking £325 (£13,000) as a down-payment. He was sent to penal servitude for three years.[15]

When W. R. Inge, the 'Gloomy' Dean of St Paul's, asked a prison chaplain which class of offenders he considered to be incurable, the answer was not murderers, nor even criminals as such, but gamblers. Looking back on the war years, Dean Inge described betting as Britain's chief 'national vice', what Disraeli had called 'a vast engine of national demoralization'. Most of its activities were technically criminal, whether at roulette or chemin de fer parties in Mayfair and Belgravia, or in gangster-run clubs, or among workmen at the docks or in factories and those soldiers who cheated one another at crown and anchor or esmeralda.

Gambling was endemic in wartime. In one of his propaganda broadcasts from Berlin, William Joyce, 'Lord Haw-Haw', warned workers at the Bristol Aeroplane Company at Filton that after the Luftwaffe's forthcoming visit, the pontoon school in the canteen would have to find somewhere else to play. There was some consternation as to how he could know about the pontoon school in the canteen. The answer was that it would have been a remarkable factory, of such a size, which did not have a pontoon school or something like it in the canteen or elsewhere.[16]

The genteel swindles of illegal gaming-tables run by freelances at 'parties' in Lancaster Gate or Kensington, far removed from the gaming clubs of Soho or Whitechapel, flourished in war as in peace. It was, according to one's viewpoint, a gentlemanly relaxation or a means of enticing the unwary into a crooked game of cards among new-found 'friends'. In 1936, a man at such a 'party' who believed he had lost £10,000 (£400,000) by being cheated at cards had demanded his money back. The judge told him that those who went to such places knew the risks. He stopped the case and the press swore that no one would be so foolish in future as to join a private game among strangers. Dupes who knew the risk continued to gamble anyway.

They also knew, if they cared to remember, that anyone owing money could cite the Gaming Act 1845 which might make such debts legally unenforceable. That was why the underworld in Soho and elsewhere used brute force to collect its winnings.[17]

In war or peace, private gaming parties in Kensington or Lancaster Gate travelled from place to place. A more elusive quarry for the police than the clubs of Soho or Whitechapel, their atmosphere of polite confiscation was far removed from the sweltering animosity of two club minders like Edward Fleischer and Antonio Mancini in Wardour Street. In April 1940, police raided a private house in Roland Gardens, Kensington, at 1 a.m. on the night when its gaming party was presided over by one patrician lady as mistress of ceremonies and another as croupier. In October 1941, a 'miniature casino' was found in a flat at Prince of Wales Terrace, Kensington, where chips on the table for the game being played represented £1,160 (£46,400). It was not the top of the scale. Six months earlier, police had watched an apparently unoccupied flat in Gloucester Place. When raided in the course of a party, £3,712 (£148,480) in chips was found in a game of chemin de fer.[18]

There were bad losers among partygoers, as well as high court judges who heard their evidence sympathetically. A provincial solicitor, in April 1940, denounced the other players who had taken his money as 'swindlers'. In the most protracted case of the war, a Lancashire businessman refused to honour a cheque written to cover debts at a West End gaming party to which he had been taken by a 'friend' on 9 September 1940 and where he had lost £525 (£21,000) between midnight and 5.30 a.m. The host, Alec Taylor, was described by Mr Justice Hilbery as 'a notorious organizer of these parties . . . They are extremely profitable to the organizer.' The host ensured that 'plenty of food and drink was supplied'. Outside, the sirens had sounded and bombs were falling on what was the third night of the German blitz on London.

At 3.30 a.m. the Lancashire businessman was ahead by £300 at chemin de fer and wanted to go home. The host gave him a cheque for £300, but the others persuaded him to stay and continue playing to show what a good sport he could be. A lady called Bunty now sat beside him and placed bets with some of his chips. Two and a half hours later, he had drunk a lot more, his winnings had gone, and he was heavily in debt. 'What about my cut?' Bunty asked hastily. He had nothing like enough money on him. The host told him abruptly to hand back the cheque for his winnings and write two of his own, one of them to a woman he had never heard of, but who proved to be Bunty's sister. He had had 'too much to drink to understand properly what he was doing'. When sober, he stopped the cheque and Bunty's sister sued him. Mr Justice Hilbery described him as 'the pigeon to be plucked'.

In case anyone still thought such games honest, the judge explained how a flat or house was borrowed for the night and habitués were informed. Free liquor was provided. 'Not an unwise precaution because the more the habitués are in liquor the more reckless they are likely to become with their money.' The judge did not quite tell Bunty and her sister to whistle for their money but gave judgement for the businessman. 'Perhaps the less I say about the state of affairs shown to be existing in London as a result of this case the better.'[19]

Unfortunately, police resources available to control this form of gaming were severely limited. Once or twice an undercover operation was launched. In October 1942, police officers managed to infiltrate a chemin de fer party at Mount Row, Berkeley Square, where they arrested six other gamblers. The croupier was getting a cut of the stakes which earned him £22 (£880) an hour, reflecting the amount of money in the game. From time to time other private gaming parties were raided, though the premises and players lacked the social cachet of Bunty and Mr Taylor. They were often held in bookmakers' offices and, like illegal clubs, were easily located.[20]

Some wartime clubs sold liquor illegally, some offered illegal gaming, and some did both. The coming of war did nothing to check illegal gaming in the hard-faced clubs of Soho and the East End. On 27 December 1939, Scotland Yard announced that a £10,000 (£400,000) a day wartime 'gambling craze' had hit the capital. This was the sum changing hands every twenty-four hours. Some clubs were open night and day, while some made a point of not serving drink so that nothing should distract the dupes from the important business of emptying their wallets. There was never any doubt that they would lose. When the house was unlucky, a 'packet of strippers' or marked cards would be introduced, each club having in place its own card-sharps, who robbed the gamblers of their temporary winnings.

Scotland Yard's warning followed a raid on the Piccadilly Club in Denman Street and the convictions of those involved in running it. The club was what Superintendent Cole called 'an exclusive place', to which his raiding party had to gain entry 'by a subterfuge'. The Piccadilly Club's game was also faro, in which the possibilities for cheating were so notorious that it had at one time been made criminal by statute.[21]

Punters were not allowed to waste too much time in parting with their cash. Once the game had been in progress for about thirty minutes, the croupier would collect all silver, and paper money would be used exclusively. As servicemen and their pay reached the West End, faro was increasingly favoured by the clubs. Some had two faro tables going at once. Yet raids on these premises became fewer. The police, more concerned with enforcing the blackout than with illegal gaming, could do little more than warn the public. Law and order at the clubs was now provided at the doors by 'ex-boxers', who threw out non-members and undesirables.

The owners of the clubs usually kept out of sight. When the Forty Four Club in Gerrard Street was raided for the third time in May 1941, Superintendent Cole noted: 'Those really responsible kept in the background, and after each police visit others were placed in charge.' Even though not 'in charge', the proprietor made £170 (£6,800) a week by taking 5 per cent of the winnings. Unlike the polite ring at a doorbell in Gloucester Place or Roland Gardens, the police could only get into the Forty Four Club by forcing a padlock and chain which secured a steel lattice on the ground floor.[22]

When police infiltrated a club as members, the costs were modest compared with genteel gaming parties. Expenses for a night out in February 1942 amounted to £25 (£1,000), cheap at the price in Kensington, while the owner's fine was £100 (£4,000). At the Tower Bridge Social Club in Bermondsey or the Cleveland Club in Whitechapel Road, the costs were still less.[23]

By 1941, a simpler form of illegal gambling was making its mark. Fruit machines were being installed in clubs and other places of entertainment. In March 1941, in the case of an amusement arcade in Harringay, they were denounced as 'pure gaming'. Arcades had been spreading through the suburbs to which, it was said, servicemen were lured by women who promised cafés and small clubs with fruit machines and out-of-hours drinking.[24]

A principal objection to fruit machines was that they were crooked. In October 1941, the Tree Trunk Club in Albemarle Street was fined £40 (£1,600) for 'gaming with automatic machines', which had been rigged. In the case of the Mori Sini Club in Rupert Street, four months later, the proprietress was fined and the supplier of the machine was sent to prison. In March 1942, police cracked down on clubs of some respectability which had installed machines. Among those convicted were the Strangers Club in St James's Street; Tommy's Bar Club in Dover Street, which was part of the Green Park Hotel; the Esquire Club in Piccadilly, and the Miranda Club in Chesterfield Street.[25]

The social pretensions of most defendants fell short of St James's Street or the Esquire Club. Café pin-tables in the East End were deemed illegal in October 1942 by the Hendon magistrates. The sentence was £100 (£4,000) or six months in prison. Four defendants were convicted on similar charges involving a North London amusement arcade at Burnt Oak. The arcades increasingly attracted prosecutions. Six months after the war, there was an attempt to close down Brighton's largest arcade, the Happidrome, when twenty-eight machines were seized and ten convictions obtained. In the new clean-up even traditional fairground games were banned. The police decided that 'Wheel-'em-In' – the rolling of pennies down a board with numbered squares – was not a game of skill and prosecuted the stallholders who ran it.[26]

If gaming and betting were a national vice, it was not because of private parties in West London or Soho clubs. Across the country pontoon schools and poker schools were seldom 'rackets'. If a member was suspected of cheating, the others need only refuse to play with him. In military or civilian life, in the Army or the shipyards, games in which punters had no chance included esmeralda and, more often, crown and anchor. This game involved dice marked with crowns and anchors, a board or a crown and anchor cloth spread over a table on to which players threw coins.

Liverpool docks were to crown and anchor what Wembley Stadium was to Association Football. In February 1942, the ship's greaser who ran the gambling school at the docks went to prison. It made little difference. The wives of workers complained that their husbands were still losing their wages at these illegal games. Four more organizers were prosecuted and convicted two months later. In October, there were more complaints of dockers losing large amounts at crown and anchor and esmeralda. The rival to crown and anchor was not only esmeralda. When workmen were convicted of illegal gambling at Corsham a month later, two of them were running 'a greyhound race game' with £100, equal to several months' wages, as stakes.[27]

Crown and anchor games were played by large groups – a further reason for alarm among the authorities. During the flying-bomb attacks on London in the summer and autumn of 1944, workmen from all over the country were brought in to ensure that damaged housing stock was fit for habitation by the winter. Many were billeted in the terraces and squares of Kensington, from which soldiers had left to join the battle in France. Two thousand men were housed in Onslow Square and its immediate neighbourhood. On the last Sunday afternoon in August 1944, the Flying Squad swept into Onslow Gardens, which was filled by a crowd of participants and spectators gathered at a crown and anchor game being played at a central table with a crown and anchor cloth. As the police climbed from their cars, the crowd 'ran in all directions' but the three men thought to be ringleaders were arrested. Two of them were not ringleaders and only one was convicted of illegal gaming. The gamesters had fled leaving many onlookers trapped.[28]

Shed 101 at Southampton docks was another venue for illegal gaming. There were often 300 men playing at any one time. Because organizers had a nose for policemen, the Army Intelligence Corps cooperated with the CID. On one occasion they counted twelve games of crown and anchor in progress, on another fourteen. Men who could not get into a game had organized 'tossing rings', where they gambled on the toss of a pair of coins.

The police had no doubt that at the first sign of a raid the organizers would escape in the confusion, as at Onslow Gardens. Five members of the Intelligence Corps were therefore planted as workers and allowed to join the games. When the raid took place, these undercover men indicated the organizers to the police and, at a signal that the raid was beginning, each soldier seized and held one of the men until he was in custody. The men detained and convicted were three joiners, a labourer and a french polisher.[29]

When gaming cases of all kinds came to court, the penalties that could be imposed were trifling compared with the money to be made at private 'parties' or illegal gaming clubs. Stooges took the rap as club 'managers' in exchange for a generous weekly wage. By January 1942, Herbert Morrison had decided that hooch and illegal gaming were the two scourges of London night life. At the beginning of February he proposed a new Defence Regulation introducing sentences which, if they did not put an end to illegal gaming, at least made it less appealing. On the following day, Scotland Yard claimed to have a blacklist of gambling racketeers and even to know their car numbers.

By the beginning of March, Defence Regulation 42 CA was law and eleven men were prosecuted at Westminster police court under its provisions. The press celebrated the doom of illegal gaming and reported that party organizers were packing up in the face of the new penalties. For the time being, enforcement was a police priority. A month later, thirty-four Whitechapel gamesters appeared in court in a single case.[30]

The penalties were now a fine of £500 (£20,000) and three months' imprisonment. A stooge who came forward as manager of a club might have no objection to paying a fine on behalf of the owner. He was less sanguine at the prospect of going to prison for three months. In addition, he was always liable to be remanded in custody, awaiting his hearing or sentence, as had happened in the case of the New Club, Archer Street, in March 1941. On that occasion, the Bow Street magistrate offered the defendant the most useful gaming tip of all. 'The law always wins in the end. It is bound to do so.'[31]

The courts did not impose the new maximum penalties immediately. In June 1942, following a chemin de fer party in Frith Street, Soho, twenty-six men were convicted. The Marlborough Street magistrate, J. B. Sandbach, informed them that 'The government consider these gaming parties a danger, especially to troops on leave.'

One of the organizers was fined £180 (£7,200), the other, who was said to have a bad record in cases under the Gaming Act, was fined £150 (£6,000) and sent to prison for six weeks.[32]

Predictions that lawbreakers would be put out of business proved optimistic. Prison sentences were a deterrent but many wartime sentences were light because room in the prisons was scarce, as the underworld well knew. Not only had crime increased but by 1941 the country was suffering an influx of Italian prisoners of war. The Geneva Convention required that all should be housed and cared for. With the camps full, the authorities were obliged to commandeer civilian prisons to accommodate Italians, as they were obliged to provide others for the American armed forces.

Soon it was business as usual among the gamesters. In May 1943, in the course of a long-running prosecution brought against them, one group took the initiative by launching a legal move to have poker declared a game of skill. They won the point that the jury should have been allowed to decide whether poker involved skill but failed to get a declaration that poker was legal. Their further objection, in May 1944, was that the police knew perfectly well that poker was played in gentlemen's clubs in the West End, yet they did nothing to stop it. The police had infiltrated the less prestigious Lyndhurst Club at Finchley Road, Hampstead, had seen poker being played, and had brought the prosecution. They could not, of course, infiltrate White's or Brooks', where prospective members would have to be proposed and seconded, and might be blackballed. 'I intend to see this business through to the House of Lords,' said one defendant angrily, complaining at being 'sorted out' again. 'If we are not allowed to play, I'll see that Crockford's, Bates and the Hamiltons and all the other clubs in the West End are treated in the same way.' The case went to appeal, the convictions were upheld and the defendants were fined a 'nominal' thirty-five guineas each.[33]

The Defence Regulation of 1942 did little or nothing to stop illegal gaming, even though fines of £100 (£4,000) became common and £350 (£14,000) was not exceptional. At a time when the profits from poker at the Craven Club in Craven Hill, Paddington, were £500 (£20,000) a week, such fines were no more than an occupational hazard. It was only later, in August 1945, when wartime worldliness was set aside, that the two owners of the Empire Bridge Club in Kilburn High Road were sent to prison for four months and six months respectively for permitting all-night gaming at the premises.[34]

In July 1943, at a public meeting in London, the Archbishop of Canterbury, Dr Frederick Temple, described 'the alarming collapse of sexual morality' in wartime Britain. He commended the 'endurance, mutual helpfulness, and constancy, which during the "blitz" reached heroic proportions . . . but people are not conscious of injuring the war effort by dishonesty or by sexual indulgence . . . There is a danger that we may win the war and be unfit to use the victory.'[35]

At first, the authorities had seemed more alarmed at servicemen seeing too much female flesh than by any increase in prostitution, which received a high degree of toleration throughout most of the war. By March 1940, inspectors from the London County Council attended music halls, cabarets and stage shows at cinemas, watching for indecent jokes or nude scenes which might deprave impressionable soldiers. In April, the Lord Chamberlain, who exercised powers of pre-censorship over all public stage performances, summoned a conference at St James's Palace on 'the problem of nudity'.

On 16 April thirty-five people, including theatrical managers, attended the conference to draw up 'an undress line' for the stage. They agreed that the police should have more power over night clubs. The theatrical managers – including George Black, variety impresario, and Vivian Van Damm, whose Windmill Theatre was famous for its *Revuedeville*, with static nudes and lightly clad dancers – emerged to tell reporters piously that they thought nudity on the stage 'undesirable'. In reply to the question 'When is a nude girl not a nude girl?' P S. Le Poer Trench in the *Evening Standard* suggested that it was when she stood motionless on a half-lit stage with a wishing-well behind her.[36]

Nudity was usually synonymous with striptease and it was no joking matter. Prior to the war, it had often been a fairground 'fan dance', in which the dancer performed with two large ostrich fans so that she was never completely naked and never indecently so. The show usually moved on before trouble could reach it. John White toured the country in the last two summers of peace with his marquee and his dancing girl but was tactless enough to drum up custom through a hailer. 'Margot will now demonstrate her fan dance. What you see, keep to yourselves and tell nobody. If you don't see what you want to see, let me know and I will see what I can do for you.' His audience, at threepence (50p) a time, seemed to consist mainly of plain-clothes policemen. The local justices sometimes found the performances indecent.[37]

The Lord Chamberlain's conference seemed to make little difference. At the end of April, Middlesex County Council announced that it would send its officials to watch shows and put an end to striptease acts. Three days later Henry Lenet, a London producer, was fined for allowing a striptease in his touring revue, *Eve-Oh, The Naughty Gal Revue*, when it was performed at His Majesty's Theatre, Carlisle. A girl in a short frock sang at the back of the stage, while a curtain was drawn across her. It was opened at the end of the song with the lights dimmed to show her briefly nude and stationary.

As the war went on, official attitudes seemed ambivalent. In October 1942, the Ninety Club in Clapham High Street, frequented by 'men and women of the lowest order and troops of the Allied nations', was struck off and its licence withdrawn after evidence was given of 'women high-kicking in scanty clothing'. Two months earlier, on 31 July at the Trocadero, Elephant and Castle, an appreciative official party had watched the bathing beauties of the Stay-at-Home Holiday Week judged by Phyllis Dixie, 'strip-tease artiste and celebrated fan-dancer', a licensed favourite among entertainers of troops at Aldershot and in the West End.[38]

As opposed to live performances, books and magazines were little interfered with during the war. Successful obscenity prosecutions were brought in respect of James Hadley Chase, *Miss Callaghan Comes to Grief*, and Mae West, *She Done Him Wrong*, but a more curious development was pornography's place in the war effort. The dedicatedly fetishist magazine *London Life*, living close to prosecution much of the time, rallied the nation with its cover of 17 May 1941 on which it paraded semi-naked Windmill Girls in knickers and rubber gas masks. In Libya and Tunisia, the RAF dropped on the Afrika Korps wooden toys activated by a string, which caused a small figure of Haile Selassie to bugger another miniature figure of

Mussolini. On this front, where reluctant German troops had come to the rescue of the Italians, relations between the Axis allies were not good, and the toy proved extremely popular. The Luftwaffe later responded by scattering the Anzio beachhead with leaflets of a seductive English maiden stripping off in front of an eager American soldier. Since the American could be torn off the page and the stripping maiden retained, she proved a welcome boost to morale.[39]

If laws governing gaming and illegal drinking remained archaic, those which controlled prostitution were equally ineffective. It was not illegal for a woman to be a prostitute but a crime for her to solicit a man. It was criminal for a man to take money from a prostitute, living on her 'immoral earnings', and for a man or woman to take part in running a brothel.

The demand for prostitutes had increased long before the arrival of the first Americans in 1942, but to nothing like the extent that it increased thereafter. So far as the blitz had a beneficial effect on London, it seemed to the Public Morality Council that this had been in frightening prostitutes off the streets. Unfortunately, as their secretary complained, a lull in the bombing had seen the return to the West End of 'undesirable women', and an increase in 'daylight pestering'. He could only suggest to the Provost Marshal that 'the military police should be instructed to exercise greater vigilance.'

Types of prostitution remained what they had been in the late 1930s. Despite the stereotype of the razor-wielding Latin pimp, there were far more freelances than girls under the control of a ponce. The blackout might make arrests more difficult, but it did not inhibit the trade. A nominal attempt to suppress it, required of the police in peacetime, was quietly abandoned until most of the American troops had been sent to Europe in late 1944. Despite the blackout, lust found a way, as the girls stood in West End doorways, flashing a torch on themselves as potential clients passed. Those who worked in the parks communicated with servicemen in the darkness by directional whistles. Expert fingers could tell a man's rank, his likely wealth, even his nationality, by running over stripes or insignia on sleeve or epaulette.

At one remove from the freelances were those who solicited in the streets or the parks with a room near by and had the protection of a pimp. The pimps of Soho, despised by other professional criminals, were usually Italian or Maltese, the latter known as 'Malts' or 'Epsom Salts'. However, the intimidation of the girls and the unsolved murders of prostitutes remained features of the wartime underworld and of the first years of peace. In the immediate post-war crime wave, the shooting of Margaret Cook in 1946 was thought to be gang-related. So were the Soho deaths of Rita Barratt, 'Black Rita', shot in her room in Rupert Street in 1947, and Rachel Fennick, 'Ginger Rae', stabbed to death by a 'Mediterranean' knife in her Broadwick Street room in 1948.

Wartime protection passed into the hands of Soho families like the Messinas, whose rivals were the Vassalos. Marthe Watts left a graphic account of her life as a wartime prostitute run by Gino Messina. Far from the law cleaning up Soho or the West End in wartime, it was not until some years afterwards that the Messinas were finally brought to justice.

When confronted by the higher class of prostitution in the brothels of Mayfair or St James's, the authorities both in the period preceding and during the war had turned a blind eye. The reason for this tolerance was connected with an incident a year before the war. Inspector Ted Greeno of the Flying Squad was hailed on Lingfield racecourse by one of his regular informants who told him quietly of a brothel in Dover Street patronized by 'top-notch' people.

The Flying Squad did not as a rule raid brothels. Greeno passed the tip to Chief Inspector Bill Parker and was then summoned by the Assistant Commissioner at Scotland Yard, Sir Norman Kendall. Sir Norman ordered Greeno to be taken off all other cases and put full-time on observation in Dover Street. The observation was not so much to see who worked in this elegant bordello but who the clients might be. What would happen if the brothel was raided while 'top-notch' people were there? Sir Norman asked bluntly what would happen if the Flying Squad caught 'a cabinet minister or something like that'. Three days earlier, Anthony Eden had resigned as Foreign Secretary in disgust at Chamberlain's appeasement of Mussolini. Winston Churchill had launched an attack on the government in the House of Commons and twenty-five of its supporters had voted with him against their own government. This was no time for cabinet ministers to be caught without their trousers.

Greeno was equally blunt. Anyone on the premises, cabinet minister or not, would be taken to Cannon Row police station with everyone else. Somewhat uneasily, Sir Norman agreed. There were, however, to be precautions. Since the place was 'wide open' a Flying Squad sergeant would be infiltrated into one of the 'parties' held there, with instructions to appear tempted by the 'bait' but on no account to taste it. Until that was done there was to be no raid.

Greeno and his sergeant, Studdart, kept observation in Dover Street. Sergeant William Murray was accepted by the occupants as a client and attended two 'parties' without being suspected. As a further precaution, the raid was timed for just after 8 p.m., when any cabinet minister would be dining or taking his place in Parliament. At 8.40 Greeno, posing as a taxi driver calling at the wrong address, rang the bell. Before the door shut, he put his foot in the gap.

The premises were presided over by Carmen Rosena, a six-foot, forty-year-old Jamaican wearing thigh-boots and nothing else. Her staff were five daughters of the professional class and two unemployed men. The main bedroom was known as the 'theatre', its bed currently occupied by four of the cast. There were no clients at this hour. The drive to Cannon Row was accompanied by expressions of middle-class dismay, including 'What will my mother say when she knows?' and 'This seems to be serious. Can I explain my position to someone?'

As a safeguard against what might be blurted out in evidence, the public was banned from the so-called 'Vault of Vice' trial when it came on two months afterwards. Had the raid taken place several hours later in the evening, it might have provided Goebbels' propaganda ministry with useful copy. In wartime, the case was remembered as an object lesson. So long as hostilities lasted, it was best to let sleeping politicians lie.[40]

From his vantage point at Tottenham Court Road police station, Detective Inspector Robert Higgins watched thousands of troops on leave making for Soho, many of them in London for the first time in their lives. He noted that they were at the mercy of 'vultures' – male and female – as cases of assault and robbery rose. They rose faster with the arrival of Americans, who had an unfortunate habit of going into a bar and laying their wallets, cigarettes and lighters on

Illegal gaming was rife in wartime, from crown and anchor swindles in army camps or dock sheds to poker parties in Chelsea and Kensington and cellar clubs in Soho. W. R. Inge, the 'Gloomy Dean' of St Paul's, denounced gambling as Britain's greatest national vice

The White City Stadium, 1943. Dog tracks were a wartime success, though they were targets for dog doping and tote fraud. On 8 December 1945, £100,000 (£4,000,000 by modern values) was won by doping four of the five runners in the last race of the White City programme

Private Karl Gustav Hulten, alias 'Lieutenant Ricky Allen of the 501st Parachute Regiment', alias 'Chicago Joe'. A US deserter, his career of armed robbery led to an Old Bailey trial and a Pentonville execution for shooting taxi driver George Heath in 1944

Elizabeth 'Marina' Jones, alias Georgina Grayson, dancer at such wartime clubs as the Blue Lagoon near Regent Street and the Panama in South Kensington. British accomplice of Hulten, she was also convicted of the murder of George Heath but reprieved

The interior of 'The Murder Car', as the press called it, shows two dents made by the bullet that had passed through Heath's body. The first is on the trim below the glass of the side window. The bullet then ricocheted and dented the glove compartment

Deserters from the Free Polish Army, Henryk Malinowski and Marian Grondkowski, hanged for the 1945 Notting Hill shooting of rival racketeer, Reuben Martirosoff, alias 'Russian Robert'. They were also believed by Scotland Yard to have murdered taxi driver Frank 'The Duke' Everitt

A relaxation of the blackout to an end of war dim-out enabled participants in casual romances to see their partners more easily. In the blackout, the girls had stood in doorways and flashed pencil-torches on their faces

'Loot Alley', a Sunday morning market on the pavements of Exchange Buildings, Cutler Street, Houndsditch. A Voigtlander roll-film camera is examined. The brooches pinned on the trader's lapels are also for sale

The Oxford Street spiv who moved too slowly. His suitcase suggests a kerbside stock of nylons, watches and cosmetics

Osbert Lancaster, *Daily Express*, 24.6.47

"*Don't be so stuffy, Henry! I'm sure that if you asked him nicely the young man would be only too pleased to give you the name of a really* GOOD *tailor who doesn't worry about coupons!*"

'Bankrupt Britannia' faced five years of post-war austerity. Clothes rationing continued until March 1949

'Another day, another dollar.' In September 1945, a month after the war's end, money is fingered from a wad of notes to conclude one of the last of many millions of shady deals that ran in parallel with the world conflict

the counter as they drank. Street robberies in the Soho blackout were sufficient cause for MPs to suggest by 1942 that those convicted of them should be flogged or shot.[41]

Men who ran Soho had no objection to inflicting violence on its visitors and still less on one another, though to say that any gang 'ran' the chaos of Soho in wartime would be a simplification. Control of Soho was contested by those who called themselves the Whites of King's Cross, the Yiddishers and the remaining Italians. Early in 1941, hostilities were opened in Wardour Street by the Italians against the Yiddishers. At 3 a.m. one morning, Eddie Fleischer was attacked by two men with fists and life-preservers in the card room of the West End Bridge and Billiards Club. At the time, it was full of men playing cards. Two of his assailants were arrested, one on charges of grievous bodily harm and the other accused of malicious wounding.

Early on 1 May 1941, there was another disturbance at the club when the Italians started a fight. Antonio 'Babe' Mancini, doorman of the Palm Beach Bottle Party in the basement, had not been involved. Sometime later he claimed that he went upstairs merely to see what had happened and heard someone say, 'There's Babe. Let's knife him.' Mancini thought the voice was Fleischer's. There was renewed fighting within the club between the two factions. Mancini claimed that during this Fleischer came at him with a raised chair and that he took a knife to defend himself. Another man, Harry 'Scarface' Distleman, fell dying with a stab wound to his heart.

Mancini's defence was that in the circumstances he could not be convicted of more than manslaughter. A charge in a similar Soho case had been reduced to manslaughter only three months earlier. When the jury found him guilty of murder, it may be that his Italian nationality and underworld membership told against him. When he was hanged in October, he was the first gang-member to have been executed for many years. His fate was thought to have had a salutary effect on the petty tyrants of Soho, whose members had been ordered to 'protective duties' only.[42]

Despite the gang warfare which flickered in the area, members of the armed forces on leave were capable of adding a degree of violence which might have put an end to all contending factions. In 1943 a

French commando was committed for trial at the Old Bailey on charges of causing an explosion and endangering life in Dean Street. Having had a little to drink and in order to liven up the blackout, he had stolen some bombs from his unit. He met an RAF man, who was sympathetic to the idea. Standing in Dean Street, the commando took one of the bombs from his haversack, inserted the detonator, and threw it at a static water tank. It blew up part of the water tank, shattered the windows of the surrounding buildings, and rocked Soho's clubland.

An ARP warden soon afterwards found the commando and the RAF man lying in the roadway at the junction of Shaftesbury Avenue and New Oxford Street. They were not dead or injured, as he had feared, merely resting while they tried to prepare the next bomb. The RAF man asked the warden if he had a match and the commando added, 'We want to see if the match will set the bombs off.' The warden, deciding that it was best to humour the suggestion, offered to guide them to the YMCA where there would be plenty of matches. They seemed not to notice that he took them to a police station instead. When a police officer asked the commando what he had in his haversack, the prisoner said, 'Bombs. I am a commando and know the use of them.'[43]

In the blacked-out nights of war, populated by strangers and thousands of British or American servicemen in transit, it was not surprising that Soho and neighbouring areas were the territory of murder. The line between prostitution and respectability had shifted, at a time when, in Billy Hill's cynical phrase, 'good-time girls became brazen tarts' and 'ordinary wives became good-time girls'. The 'Vault of Vice' case or 'Sheila Cousins'' To Beg I Am Ashamed had shown that middle-class prostitution was no wartime novelty. However, the new amateurs, whatever their class, entered a dark world. Some died in unexplained circumstances, their killers never found. The word 'killer' was more accurate than 'murderer', where the reason for a death was questionable, even though the cause was established.[44]

When Agnes Stafford, who had come to London from Barnsley early in the war, was found dead in her flat in Holborn in May 1942 there was no immediate sign that she had met a violent end. Only the post-mortem by Sir Bernard Spilsbury established that a blow had fractured her jaw and that she had been strangled with a ligature. However, Spilsbury thought that she had struck first and that the blow to her jaw had been an instant, perhaps instinctive, response. She had died in 'an exchange of violence'. The questioning of suspects, including two Norwegian soldiers who boasted when drunk that they had known she was dead before the police did, proved only that they had alibis.

In some cases, the good-time girls lived more than one life. Evelyn Hatton, whose husband was a cinema usher, lived with him in Holland Park as 'Mrs Clayton' and in Bayswater as Evelyn Hatton. As 'Eve', she solicited in the Piccadilly blackout and had a thriving business with a flat in Duke Street, Mayfair. It was here she was found strangled in December 1944 on the sitting-room floor, naked but with a sheet tying her legs. The silk muffler with which she had been strangled three days earlier was still round her neck and her handbag had been rifled. She was thought to have had a large sum of money at the flat, now missing, and the police gave the probable motive for her death as robbery. They kept an open mind as to whether the murderer had been a man or a woman. The crime remained unsolved.

Sometimes suspicion was directed at Americans or Canadians. Audrey Stewart, who was found in her bed mortally injured by head wounds, catered for the American and Canadian trade. Though the murder weapon was never found, fingerprints were discovered on two whisky bottles. Scotland Yard had no match for them in its criminal records but they had an American suspect whom the American Provost Marshal's department said bluntly was quite capable of committing the crime. However, the fingerprints were not his and Audrey Stewart's death joined the series of unsolved murders.

A number of cases involved Soho prostitutes who were assumed to be victims of those controlling their profession. Just after the end of the war, in the case of Margaret Cook, a former policeman was walking down Carnaby Street, near Regent Street, when he saw a couple in an alleyway leading to the Blue Lagoon Club. The woman shouted, 'This man has got a gun!' The ex-policeman stopped and the man's voice said from the darkness, 'Get on your way, chum, this has nothing to do with you.' The witness walked on a little distance, then heard a shot and saw a man run to the further end of the street.

He chased him but failed to catch him. Robert Higgins, investigating the case, thought it was the crime of a man with a hatred of prostitutes. Most others, including the *Daily Telegraph* crime correspondent Stanley Firmin, believed it was the settling of a gangland score, 'murder for revenge'.[45]

Such acts were so repellent that it seemed remarkable for the culture they represented not to have been liquidated in the course of a great patriotic war. Yet for all its brutality, the hazards of the blitz, police raids and punitive legislation, clubland held a golden key to survival. It existed to purvey a gift of the gods at mid-century. That gift, worshipped weekly on shining screens and in crowded dance halls, was glamour – however tarnished by time or tawdry by association. A decade later the very notion of it would seem suspect to a post-war generation. Yet glamour in clubland offered its worshippers almost whatever they dreamed of, assuming that they dreamed of easy money, excitements that were wholly or partly illegal, and sex without the customary moral limits. The night club and the gaming table, the fan-dancer and the silk-stockinged legs of the revue stage or the pavement, the bubbles in the champagne glass and the cigarettes in their silver case: all these shone and glittered in the thoughts of millions who had never seen Soho or Mayfair, while the dance bands played from radios in bombed and rationed cities.

13

Going to the Dogs

While horse racing was severely restricted by wartime conditions, the accessible dog tracks of the inner cities and industrial towns survived and prospered. However, the tracks soon attracted far more criminality than horse racing, through doping or substitution at the kennels, forgery of tote tickets and even rigging of the tote. Apart from such crimes, bookmakers and the tote remained a handy means of laundering money that had been dishonestly acquired. Bookies and the tote at greyhound stadiums were among the first to be provided by the police with banknote serial numbers after any major robbery. Like the racecourse, the dog track had also acquired a pre-war reputation for gang violence, in consequence of such incidents as the so-called 'Wandsworth Stadium Murder' of 1936.

In wartime, the tracks became a natural venue for black market deals; for bartering stolen or forged petrol coupons, as well as for trading identity cards, ration books and coupon cards. They provided cover and even work for deserters and dodgers of conscription, so that US Military Police, as well as their British counterparts, watched them routinely. The tracks were popular with GIs, in whose country greyhound racing had originated.

So long as there were bookmakers at the dog tracks, there were likely to be protection rackets. In London, protection was currently disputed between the Whites of King's Cross and the 'Shepherd's Bush Boys'. However, the official tote was beyond the reach of such protection. From this 'automatic racecourse totalizator' punters bought tickets as if from a railway booking-office, and from it they claimed their winnings. The tote was the invention of a New Zealand consulting engineer, Sir George Alfred Julius, Chairman of the Commonwealth Council for Scientific and Industrial Research from 1926 until 1945. It had first been installed at Hialeah, Florida, in 1931.

'The dogs' were one of few financial successes in the pre-war recession. In three years of racing, annual attendance figures in London passed eight million. Wembley and White City, Walthamstow and Harringay, Wandsworth and Catford, were among the best known London tracks. Belle Vue at Manchester, Sheffield's Hyde Park, Brighton and Hove's Albion Stadium and Bristol's Eastville enjoyed local fame. Walthamstow, with grandstands, club rooms, dance hall, extensive car parks, was a complete 'pleasuredrome' of its day.

The outbreak of war might have been the ruin of dog racing. No track could be illuminated after dark, no meeting held with a threat of air raids. The stadiums seemed to the government a temptation to misuse petrol. On 22 May 1941, Herbert Morrison informed Parliament that Petroleum Department inspectors would watch stadiums in the next two months to prevent motorists using supplementary rations to take them to meetings. The onus would be on the motorist to prove that petrol in his tank was the basic allowance.

In July 1942, the basic allowance ended and mid-week dog racing was banned. Each stadium was permitted one afternoon meeting a week on Saturday or a public holiday. Horse racing was also reduced to 20 per cent of pre-war meetings. Even the consumption of petrol to take greyhounds from kennels to tracks had fallen to 164 gallons a week. There was little the stadiums could do to escape this straitjacket. In the winter months, stadiums must be cleared by dusk. Meetings were bound to conflict, further reducing the number of patrons. Catford began at 2 p.m. but New Cross had to follow shortly – 'Go Greyhound Racing Every Saturday 2.15 p.m. New Cross' – then Crayford at 2.30. It was not until May 1948 that 'dog days' were restored as Monday, Tuesday, Wednesday and Saturday.

In the event, applications were soon made for new tracks and betting facilities on such sites as Carlisle United Football Ground. Nonconformist England might hope that restrictions would deal a mortal blow to the sport. Yet incomes and inflation rose rapidly during the first years of the war. There was work to be done and men and women were paid for doing it, only to find that they had not much to spend their money on.

Dog racing was saved by betting, the revenues and profits of each stadium rising steadily, often spectacularly, in the hardest years of the war and during the period of austerity which followed. Some of the big increases were in the North-West. In 1942, the Albion Track, Salford, reported a 25 per cent annual increase in takings from betting, despite a reduction to one meeting a week. This revenue was £322,191 (£12,880,000) higher than 1937. Manchester tracks, at Belle Vue and White City, showed a similar increase. The 1940 takings at White City were £739,080 (£29,560,000), against £589,786 (£23,600,000) in 1938, the last full year of peace and unrestricted racing. Belle Vue was £308,713 (£12,350,000) higher in 1941 than in 1937.

Smaller tracks shared in the boom. At Watersheddings Stadium, Oldham, 1940 takings of £24,971 (£1,000,000) rose to £41,848 (£1,674,000) the following year. Albion Greyhounds (Salford) Ltd took £586,084 (£23,440,000) on the tote during the basic petrol allowance of 1941, dropping to £439,878 (£17,595,000) in 1942 when 'basic' was abolished, but rising to £711,279 (£28,451,000) in 1943, though private motoring remained illegal. In London, after the hardest year, the annual profit of South London Greyhound Racecourses Ltd, owners of Wimbledon Stadium, was still £94,000 (£3,760,000) in October 1943.

Restrictions were to be prolonged by the peacetime policy of austerity. In the winter of 1947 greyhound racing was banned during the government's State of Emergency from 10 February until 15 March because of the nation's near-bankruptcy and the consequent fuel crisis. Yet dog tracks returned such profits that many dividends for a single year almost equalled – and some exceeded – the entire value of the shares. The nation might be going bust but owners of stadium shares were not.

In September 1946, West Ham Stadium paid an 85 per cent dividend, while its capital shot from £25,000 (£1,000,000) to £45,000 (£1,800,000) and its shares jumped from one shilling to eighteen shillings. South London Greyhound Racecourses Ltd, which had weathered hostilities with a modest £94,000 profit, was now hinting at a final dividend for the year of 200 per cent. It had already paid an interim dividend of 75 per cent. Romford Stadium, which began as a modest £400 (£16,000) track, was suddenly a firm worth £500,000 (£20,000,000), a single promoter clearing £100,000 (£4,000,000). Among the more conservative companies, Wembley had paid a dividend of 40 per cent.

Clapton, which had paid a paltry 30 per cent in the previous year, consoled its investors with an interim dividend of 35 per cent. In the same month a Wembley dog, Yardley Whistler, changed hands for the record price of £3,350 (£134,000).

Alongside such success, dog tracks were among the first places visited by civil and military police rounding up deserters, conscription dodgers, black marketeers, petty gangsters, forgers of petrol and clothing coupons or traders in such currency. When Walthamstow was raided on 28 February 1942, the government reminded the press how easily those who lived by betting could evade military service. As for counterfeit currency, so many forged five-pound notes had been passed that by November 1945 four London tracks refused to take any more until they were issued with a silver anti-fraud strip.

Money on the scale of stadium profits attracted those with plans for getting their hands on it. There were minor thefts and, several years after the war at Catford, a robbery of the kind usually reserved for bank vaults. For most criminals, thieving related to the tote, and fraud to the doping of greyhounds.

The forgery of tote tickets, turning a losing number into a winning one or substituting a counterfeit ticket, was the commonest crime. In a pre-war case, for example, an attempt had been made to defraud White Temple Stadium, West Ham, with a tote ticket presented to the cashier with the winning combination number 3–2. The cashier saw that the '3' had been altered from a '5'. The forger's defence was flimsy but familiar. 'A man gave me the ticket and asked me to draw the money for him. I did not know that the ticket was forged and went to the tote with it.'[1]

A more ambitious scheme, described at West Ham on 8 June 1937, had involved tote frauds by the clerks. It was thought by the makers to be impossible but involved only an issue of surplus tickets, which the clerks used on their own behalf. A discrepancy appeared when the books were examined and, in retrospect, it seemed that the conspirators were bound to be caught.[2]

Presses existed to print counterfeit tickets but an individual trickster with a moderate amount of skill might prefer simpler techniques. In the spring of 1941, Adam Agar from Shoreditch was working the dog tracks in the North of England, customizing tickets for the tote and drawing relatively modest sums of money as his 'winnings' – £65 8s. 6d. (£2,617) was the amount drawn when he was caught at Belle Vue Stadium, Manchester, in May. He had been there previously on 5 April and then moved on to Bradford. In a Bradford pub before the races, he had got into conversation with Dennis Hirst, whose own previous court appearance was only two months earlier. Hirst said he had no money and Agar helpfully offered to get him some. At the races, 'I altered a ticket on the third and fourth races and obtained £2 [£80] place money. Dennis went to the paying-out booth and got the money.' This was the 'try-out' and it worked. Hirst had shown himself a man of trust. 'On Saturday 17 May, we came together to Manchester, where on a ticket I altered a "one" to a "two".'

Agar was an artist, in his way. His equipment was simple and his skill lay in his fingers. He carried a tin box containing razor blades, rubbers, coloured pencils and metal caps stained with ink. When the two men reached Belle Vue, he bought forecast tote tickets for each race of the afternoon. A counterfeiter's press would have turned out tickets in advance with every combination of numbers. Agar's forgery took place when the race was over and the result known. 'My way of doing it was to rub one of the figures out with a safety razor blade and insert a winning number, sometimes with a matchstick and ink and sometimes with a coloured pencil. It depends on the colour of the ink on the ticket.' It sounded simple but he had learnt the technique painstakingly from 'a man in London' who had been a master forger.

Once the forgery was completed, Hirst came into his own as the 'runner' who took the altered ticket to a paying-out booth of the tote. If the clerk behind the partition suspected a trick, the runner's defence was to say that he had been asked to collect the money or had found the ticket. He was not to betray the forger who would watch for the first sign of trouble and, if stopped as he made his escape, would deny ever having seen the runner before.

For the moment, Hirst was safe. Agar's forgeries passed for long enough to give both men a chance to get away. Inevitably, when the accounts failed to balance and all winning tickets were scrupulously examined, forgery came to light, as the Manchester CID explained.

After a race meeting at Belle Vue on 5 April, a forecast dividend ticket was found which showed that five units had been paid out in excess of the amount registered. Close inspection showed that there had been a clever substitution of figures on the ticket. One winning combination gained for the men £9 3s. od. [£366], another £5 3s. 6d. [£207], and in both cases the figure '6' had been removed and the figure '2' substituted.

From the April visit to Manchester, the police followed Agar's trail of forged tickets to Bradford on 10 May. The next racing day was 17 May at Belle Vue, by which time all tracks in the area were under surveillance. Hirst gave the game away, by being already known to Manchester CID. He and his companion were watched. Detective Inspector Lennox shadowed the pair until, after one of the races, he saw Agar hand a ticket to Hirst. At the paying-out window, with Lennox watching, Hirst collected £23 18s. 9d. (£960). As soon as he had gone, Lennox took the ticket from the clerk and saw the alteration. The men were allowed to incriminate themselves further, until they tried to leave after the seventh race, when the police moved in. Agar was carrying his equipment and nineteen more tote tickets whose numbers had made them difficult to alter.

At Manchester Assizes, Agar was sent to hard labour for eighteen months and Hirst for six months. In case their admirers should have any doubt as to the extreme penalty, Mr Justice Hallett said to the forger, 'I have seen a specimen of your work. It is quite obvious you were carrying out regularly, at this time, an extremely dangerous and cunning and persistent system of fraud. This can be punished by as much as fourteen years' penal servitude.' If the warning had any effect, it may not have been quite what the judge intended. In the same month, with the advent of clothes rationing, the police reported that the West End of London was 'flooded' with sheets of forged coupons and with the touts who sold them. A number of the presses on which they were produced had given up tote tickets for what appeared a safer and more lucrative product.[3]

Like most forms of fixing, tote fraud became more common towards the end of the war as stadiums grew more affluent, attendance figures swollen by American servicemen. Frauds were worked, for example, at the White City in 1944, at Walthamstow and Harringay in 1945, Oxford in 1946, and Crayford in 1947. At White City in December 1944, police caught what they described as a 'lesser light' of a gang of forgers passing 'a very good imitation' of winning tickets. Harringay suffered a long plague of forgeries in 1945, including a single loss in August of £1,250 (£50,000). Tote frauds at Harringay that month were running at £2,500 (£100,000), according to Mr Gentle of the National Greyhound Racing Association. Scotland Yard and special police of the NGRA were hunting the perpetrators of these 'really serious' losses, but not so far with great effect.

In response to growing fraud, it was announced in October 1946 that 'near-foolproof' paper was being used for tote forecast tickets, with special inks and the use of ultraviolet lamps, to catch the forgers. Unfortunately, there was then a successful and concerted coup at several London tracks, shortly before all greyhound racing was banned on 10 February 1947, during the fuel crisis. From inside information at printers or stadiums, this gang managed to discover what the colours of various tote tickets would be and what means were used to detect forgeries. They got away with 'many thousands of pounds' by changing numbers on tickets but more often by having tickets ready printed with a large combination of 'winning' numbers. Next month, the stadiums still boasted hopefully of infra-red lamps and 'secret devices'.

Not all assaults on the tote were forgeries. The neatest fraud of 1944 was performed at the White City by a tote mechanic, working alone. He rigged the totalizator recording mechanism, so that takings appeared less than they were, and pocketed the surplus. Though he only worked there on Saturday afternoons, the one meeting allowed each week, he had robbed the Greyhound Racing Association of £300 (£12,000) in nine months before being caught in March 1944 and sent to prison for four months. It was not encouraging to know that he was otherwise employed in an office of trust by the Fulham depot of the Petroleum Board.[4]

To some criminals, these methods seemed to show superfluous subtlety. On the evening of 30 May 1946, as 12,000 people struggled through the exit of Clapton Stadium at the end of the races, three men simply grabbed the tote supervisor and robbed him of £660 (£26,400) in a matter of seconds. The wedge of people pushing towards the gate made assistance or rescue impossible.

Most people who heard of dog races being fixed took this as a reference to ringing or doping. It is certainly true that greyhounds were more closely guarded than horses, whose 'lack of supervision' was deplored by the Annual Report of the Racehorse Owners Association in 1948. By contrast, in 1945 the National Greyhound Racing Association had a private police force, with over 300 retired Scotland Yard officers, including former Deputy CID Commander Percy Worth and ex-Chief Inspector White. Several days before a race, a dog was taken from its owner and kept in guarded kennels. Transport to the track was by yellow security van, described by Superintendent Robert Fabian as built like a Black Maria.

Ringing was sufficiently rare for a Clerkenwell magistrate on 2 November 1937 to ask 'What is a ringer?' and to be told that the word meant swapping a good dog for a bad, or vice versa, if the resemblance was 'near enough'. A dog might be stolen for the purpose, though often traded by amateur thieves for absurd prices. When Swashbuckler, second only to The Miller and valued at £2,000 (£80,000), disappeared before the war, the dog was said to have changed hands for only £7 10s. (£300). Another pre-war champion, Beau Sabre, was stolen from its owner but found by Chief Inspector Gooch of the Flying Squad at a track in the Midlands, its white coat so effectively dyed black that it could not be identified until the dyed fur had grown out.[5]

In general, ringing had given way to doping but stadiums still watched for substitute dogs. In March 1942, however, Eric Welsby won a case against Bolton Stadium, which had accused him of running a substitute. The stadium authorities had declared the race void and Mr Welsby had lost his bets. In August 1942 it was alleged that March Hare, the winner of the Red Cross Stakes at Wembley, was later raced as 'Breeze', an outsider, at Workington Stadium, where another dog was also swapped for the favourite, Outcast, in a hotel bedroom. As at White City in 1946, it was sometimes noticed that two dogs were wearing the wrong jackets, perhaps innocently, but this was put right before the race began.[6]

Ringing was often associated with so-called 'flapping tracks', which flourished at the end of the war. As the *Police Journal* remarked in 1947, virtually every police district in the country had its dog track. Some of these operated under NGRA rules. Others were 'flapping tracks', which did not. Though licensed by the local authority to operate on two days a week, they were usually 'run by one or two locals as a business venture'.

Most flapping tracks were ill-regulated, so that the only check on cheating was the track manager's handicap system, based on what a dog's previous performance appeared to be. The holding back of faster dogs in previous races and the substitution of 'ringers' were easy deceptions. There was no rule requiring an owner to have his dog in the kennels, and many dogs were brought straight from the car park to the track. The regulations were so ineffective that at Coalville, Leicestershire, in 1946, a winner namer 'Pretty' was borrowed from its owner by several conspirators and raced as 'Black Magic'. As an outsider, 'Black Magic' won at odds of 4–1. Fraud was suspected at once. Police detained the dog and the man who had it in his possession. By this time, almost all of those in the plot had collected their winnings and left the track. The man in charge of the dog had simply been paid to take it back to its owner. There was little that could be done beyond arresting the owner of the dog and fining him £20 (£800).[7]

A successful doper, like William Page of Brighton, could place bets calculated to bring him £1,000 (£40,000) a month. But doping was not for the amateur and difficult without the help of a kennel-maid or kennel-boy. The dogs were guarded in kennels at a little distance from the track by the stadium itself. Their food was checked, and tests were undertaken by vets.

Moreover, dope was no guarantee of winning. In a plot at Southend Stadium in December 1946, three accomplices doped every dog in a race but two, Safe Money and Rathgordon. They put £40 (£1,600) on the race to win £500 (£20,000) if the two dogs came first and second. To their chagrin, Safe Money put up such a poor performance that it was beaten by a doped dog. The three men were shortly afterwards arrested, and the ringleader went to prison for nine months.[8]

In other cases, so-called 'gangsters' had little idea of the amount needed to dope a dog. In a hurdle race at Crayford on 8 March 1941, three of the five dogs were 'in a dazed condition and practically paralysed'. They could hardly stand up, let alone race, and one subsequently died. The 'brains' of this conspiracy, fifty-four-year-old Louis Hoeltschi, pleaded not guilty but was convicted at the Old Bailey in May and sent to prison for eight months. Four youths, including the kennel-boy, also pleaded guilty. Hoeltschi's principal accomplice said philosophically when arrested, 'We all get caught sooner or later.'[9]

The preferred method was to bribe a kennel-boy or kennel-maid to doctor the dog's food. Sometimes an 'insider' might dope alone, as was the case at Manchester in September 1942, when a kennel-boy confessed that he had been doping successfully for some time before he made the mistake of taking up with a gang of incompetents.[10]

Even without inside help, it was still possible for an intruder to hide in the kennel yard while it was unoccupied and remain there long enough to add drugs to a dog's food. This was the method at White City Kennels before the last race on Saturday 8 December 1945, when the intruder arrived before the dogs and their escort. He nailed himself into a shed used for storing wood, making it seem the shed was locked, though he could come and go. His recipe was to put chloretone with fish into every food shutter of the separate kennels, except for that of the dog to be backed. The drug was more generally used to prevent travel-sickness in humans and very difficult for a vet to trace. Given to a racing dog, its effect was to make the animal's blood pressure rise rapidly at the first exertion, so that it soon 'faded' during the race.

At White City, in the last race on 8 December, four of the five dogs had been given chloretone. The race was won by the fifth dog, Bald Truth, at 8–1. It was rumoured that £100,000 (£4,000,000) had been scooped in a few minutes by the gang responsible, which had spread its bets through London to Birmingham, Manchester and Newcastle. Only when the remaining scraps of food were examined was the trick discovered.[11]

To make matters worse, a similar trick had worked at West Ham Stadium a week earlier. Before the month was out, an intruder was caught at Crayford Stadium kennels, where capsules in sausage meat were used. James King and George Porritt had also bribed a kennel-boy at Crayford to feed dogs with doped sausage meat on 18 December. Though the conspiracy got no further, both men were sent to prison for fourteen months in the following March. Porritt had gone on the run but gave himself up. 'I read in the paper that King had been caught, and I got frightened in case my name was dragged into it. I went down to the country to keep out of the way for a bit. I decided to give myself up when I read that King was trying to put all the blame on me.'[12]

At West Ham, a gang had used a different tactic to White City. Instead of doping all dogs but a comparative outsider, they had doped all of them except the favourite, Empor Feather, which came in at 7–4. It won by such a margin that the race was described as 'a farce'. The method of doping was discovered when the roof of the kennels was found loose on one side. The food had been pushed through the gap so that it fell into the kennels of the other five dogs.

Several weeks later, in January 1946, four London stadiums, at White City, Harringay, Stamford Bridge and New Cross, were able to announce that they had recruited extra guards for greyhounds, the new arrivals being men recently released from the services or the police. Tracks elsewhere continued to suffer. At Hendon on 11 March, the favourite, Good Host, came in last. Veterinary surgeons found traces of a sedative drug, though they could not tell whether it was chloretone, luminal or nembutal. The dog had been 'done' before leaving Hackney Wick kennels or while in the van. Hendon was followed by prosecutions of kennel-boys at Hackney Wick, where it was alleged that other dogs had been doped with aspirin.[13]

It was not always possible to be certain whether a dog's failure was a matter of drugs or natural causes. At White City again, Good Going, the favourite in the 9.30 race on Saturday 21 September 1946, faded badly after being bunched in the first bend and finished last. A vet examined her but found 'no suspicion of the dog having been tampered with'.

Doping was not, of course, a wartime novelty. In 1936, dogs at Rochdale Stadium were found to have been fed doped chocolates. A more curious method, used at Edinburgh in January 1939, was to slow down dogs by using gelignite. The unemployed miner who described this process explained that gelignite produces a headache if rubbed on the forehead, for which reason it was sometimes used on greyhounds.[14]

Paradoxically, gelignite in capsule form was also given to make a greyhound run, according to police evidence when members of 'London Joe's' gang were tried and sentenced in the spring of 1944. William Spicer had deserted from the Army three years earlier, his accomplice Charles Wells was an auxiliary fireman. On behalf of London Joe, they bribed kennel-boys at Hackney Wick to dope greyhounds entered at Hackney Wick and Hendon. In September 1943, one boy was promised a miraculous prize of £400 (£16,000) a week if he gave drugs to the dogs as instructed. However, miracles remained only promises and he never received more than £3 (£120) or £4 (£160) a week.

Unfortunately for London Joe's agents, another kennel-boy took fright and confessed to the police. The three lads were given the chance to turn King's Evidence in return for helping Detective Inspector Claud Smith's investigation. CID officers were thus able to witness a conversation in which Wells told one of the boys that Spicer's face was too well known and that Wells was going to take Spicer's place. Spicer, on the other hand, accused Wells of having taken on 'unreliable' accomplices. That certainly proved true in court, when Spicer was sent to prison for twenty-one months.[15]

During the hearing of the case, someone tried to tamper with the Crown's witnesses, the kennel-boys, threatening reprisals from the ghostly demon, 'London Joe'. The defendants received a warning from the bench on 11 January. According to Inspector Smith, Spicer was London Joe's 'right-hand man, the one who got at the kennel-boys', as well as a likely instrument in doping dogs at Coventry and Leicester stadiums during the previous months.

London Joe was little more than a name to the police but he became a myth taken up at once by the press, living in 'flash style' in the West End and making £1,000 (£40,000) a week by his activities. There were a number of these wraiths, many with similar names. Three months later the reality, 'Big Joe' Johnson, was one of three men sent to prison at Birmingham Quarter Sessions for doping dogs. He was not living in flash style in the West End but working as a coal miner in Sheffield. His co-defendants were a steel erector and a farmer, whose sole accomplishment in greyhound racing had been to spend £8,000 (£320,000) by backing losers.[16]

The two major wartime cases in which the police penetrated a conspiracy showed the reality on which the fantasy of London Joe had fed. On 1 June 1942, Alva Ashley was approached at the Studio Club in Knightsbridge by Solomon Gowers, a doorman. He knew that she had worked as a kennel-maid, though she was not doing so at the time. 'I can put you on to something with big money in it,' he said. Then he told her a story about a man who had girls working as kennel-maids all over the country and doping dogs for his 'syndicate'.

Two days later another man, Montague Kosky, called at her flat. He proposed that she should get a job as a kennel-maid at Wembley Stadium. As soon as she got it, he would pay her £50 (£2,000) down and later on £25 (£1,000) a week while she continued as a kennel-maid. She would be shown how to use the drugs and the first time she used a 'go slow' drug on a dog, she would be paid a further £400 (£16,000). 'I will give you plenty of capsules,' Kosky assured her. 'I have 101 places going like this and there are no failures.'

Before leaving, he presented her with ten £1 notes. He did not know, perhaps did not care, that she was married and had told her husband of the offer. He certainly did not know that her husband was a friend of Chief Superintendent Peter Beveridge of the Flying Squad. Beveridge listened to the story and suggested that she should act in future on police instructions.

Detective Inspector John Ball and Detective Sergeant John Gosling, the future commander of the 'Ghost Squad', were given the case. They went first to Wembley Stadium and asked for its cooperation from the security officer, Hector McPherson, a former Detective Chief Inspector at Scotland Yard. Through his employer, Sir Arthur Elvin, the cooperation was authorized. Alva Ashley was interviewed for a job as kennel-maid, which the staff manager gave her without knowing anything of the police investigation.

The second man in the syndicate, Kosky, made appointments by telephone with the kennel-maid but failed to keep them. She was later told that the syndicate was testing her, to make sure that she came to the rendezvous without a police shadow, and did not go to the police afterwards. After several tests, Kosky met her. A third member of the syndicate came to give instructions on how to dope a dog by wrapping meat round a capsule in such a way that the animal would eat it. Now she was also paid £25 a week for her services. At length she was invited to a fourth-floor flat in a modern block in Seymour Street, near Marble Arch. Here she met the three men as well as a woman who was tenant of the premises. It seemed the syndicate had accepted her.

Soon afterwards she was told to meet one of the men in the lounge of the nearby Cumberland Hotel, at Marble Arch, where she would be handed a package containing chloretone, to be given to the favourite running in a race at Wembley on the following Saturday. Miss Ashley received the package but, when the coast was clear, handed it to Detective Sergeant John Gosling. The drug was not used. Instead, the favourite was withdrawn from the race and the kennel-maid explained to the syndicate that the drug had made it ill. Her story was apparently accepted. A further rendezvous was arranged at the Cumberland Hotel for 7 p.m., when another package was handed over. This time, it was the club doorman who brought the consignment and then walked off into Hyde Park with the woman who was tenant of the Seymour Street flat. Presently he came back and demanded the return of the package from the kennel-maid. She had been on probation after her earlier failure and the box had been empty.

This 'dummy run', as he called it, was to ensure that the girl had not tipped off the police, who might be posing as guests and waiting in the lounge to arrest the courier. As it happened, at least two Flying Squad officers were there, Sergeants Gosling and Vesey, under orders not to make an arrest but to shadow the suspect. John Gosling was now able to follow him through the summer evening into Hyde Park, where he sat down next to another of the suspects, Kosky, who was waiting in a deckchair.

Alva Ashley was now invited to the flat in Seymour Street to receive the money due to her as a weekly retainer. It was still possible the syndicate had decided that she might have been planted by the police and was a danger to be eliminated. Chief Inspector Ball judged the time had come for the Flying Squad to move in. He and his sergeants kept the appointment. Kosky and Jones, better known to the Flying Squad as 'Owen', were in the flat and were arrested with the female tenant. The club doorman was arrested at the Studio Club in Knightsbridge. When told that they would be charged with conspiring to cheat and defraud those who backed greyhounds, Kosky said reproachfully, 'Conspiracy? When nothing happened?' He turned to the woman who was tenant of the flat and said consolingly, 'Don't upset yourself. We are only small fry. You have nothing to worry about.' In one sense, he was right. She had less to worry about because she was the only one acquitted at the Old Bailey. The two men found at the flat went to prison for two years and the third member of the conspiracy for nine months.[17]

Whether or not Kosky, 'Jones' and Gowers were small fry, they certainly had little to show for their conspiracy. A far more successful 'professional backer' was William Albert Page of Brighton, who won very large sums of money before he made headlines in the spring of 1944. Page had conspired with Victor Chapman, van driver at Brighton and Hove Stadium, to dope greyhounds entered there. He and Chapman had also tried to enlist Reginald Frost, a kennel-man at Trainer Smith's kennels at Aldbourne, which were used by the stadium. Chapman's daughter, who worked as a kennel-maid at a rival establishment, Birch's kennels, was a less enthusiastic assistant. She threw the first chloretone capsules into the incinerator instead of 'doing' a dog called Burning Hate because she did not like the idea of giving them to the animal. On further occasions, she sometimes obeyed her father and sometimes not.

Chapman admitted he was 'not long' in agreeing with Page to have the chosen dogs doped. Page was every punter's dream of a professional backer. By having dogs 'done', he had recently won £1,700 (£68,000) on a single race. His usual return was nothing like that but his quarterly income had been £3,000 (£120,000). Nor had he ever filled in an Inland Revenue tax return on his income. 'As a professional backer, I am not taxed,' he explained. He was plainly an example for men like Chapman to follow.

Page visited Frost at home in Brighton. He explained that Victor Chapman, and possibly his daughter, were working for him at Birch's kennels. Chapman had become grasping. In any case, Page needed someone at the rival kennels, Trainer Smith's, where dogs were also kept for Brighton and Hove. 'I have got the staff of one kennel working for me. I would like to give them a rest as the other chap is getting too greedy.' He had paid Chapman £100 (£4,000), £80 (£3,200) and £60 (£2,400) for his services. Frost was not to expect too much at first. 'Remember, this isn't Wimbledon, but leave it to me and I will be fair to you. Here's a tenner to be going on with.' He knew Frost had worked at Wimbledon, where he alleged that dogs had been 'stopped' by putting a straw under an animal's eyelid, causing it to blink throughout the race.

Frost's job would be simple and profitable. 'You work in the best kennels there. When you have the race to yourselves, I want you to stop as many as four dogs. When your kennels and Birch's have the race between you, we can work it so that we have a tenner up-and-down on the forecast, which we will share among us.' Page promised that if the forecast was '37s. 6d. [£75] at a hundred times', they could count on sharing £200 (£8,000) between three conspirators.

When the time came, Page produced a notebook and read out a list of dogs to be 'stopped'. Once he said cryptically, 'You can do the old lady for a start.' It was explained that the 'old lady' was a dog called British Housewife. Frost protested that British Housewife had no chance and did not need doping with the two pills. Page was unimpressed. 'You will have two pills left. You don't want to have to eat them, so you may as well give them to British Housewife.'

Unfortunately for Page, by the time he handed the pills to Frost the kennel-man was what he rather coyly called 'under police instructions'. He and the police were evasive as to when Frost saw a safer income as an informer than as a doper. Frost was indicted but then his accomplices were charged alone with attempting to corrupt him. The chloretone pills and £70 (£2,800) from Page had gone straight to Inspector Yates of Hove CID. Page's flat in Brighton was raided and a store of chloretone capsules found, which he insisted the police must have planted. At Sussex Assizes, in July 1944, he was convicted of conspiring with Chapman to incite Frost to dope greyhounds. He was fined £1,000 (£40,000) and sent to prison for fifteen months. The final indignity came when he explained his tax-exempt status to the judge. A fellow backer had established in court that winnings from gambling were beyond the reach of the Inland Revenue. 'If your friend comes before me he won't be so fortunate,' said Mr Justice MacNaghten dryly, 'as I am the Revenue Judge.'[18]

The lament of one of those convicted in the Crayford doping case of May 1941 was music in the ears of the authorities. 'We all get caught in the end.' It was, however, an unreliable estimate. There were certainly headline cases, including that of Walter Page and of those convicted of the Wembley conspiracy in 1942. However the journalist's spectre of 'London Joe' with his West End flat and 'flash style' concealed the reality of many humbler men and women who rigged, rang and doped with perhaps nothing more than Aspro in sausage meat but with a fair measure of impunity.

14

'Do Not Forget to Guard the Turkey in Your Car'

The surreal charm of a Christmas headline in December 1946 acknowledged the twin scourges of austerity and rising crime. Neither was uncommon at the ending of a great war, when the costs were to be paid and the soldiers brought home. The prime minister's son had written to a friend in Italy that in the post-war world there was 'little news from England but of robberies'. Returning servicemen brought such terror to the streets that 'people are almost afraid of stirring after it is dark.' He had watched an armed hold-up in Piccadilly, in which the criminals had brazenly fought off the forces of law and order.

It would have been small comfort to shopkeepers facing the automatic pistol of an armed thug, or beleaguered householders roused from sleep at the command of a masked intruder, to know that the letter was written by Horace Walpole to Sir Horace Mann in 1749, the year after the War of the Austrian Succession. If most other military crusades had ended in anarchy, there was less hope that the unwieldy war of millions in the 1940s would be an exception.

The war was not even over when public imagination was chilled by a single brief episode. There was little to distinguish this robbery from a dozen others in 1944. Incompetence and mischance played equal parts. To the press and public, it was an assault on society by anarchy and barbarism, as menacing in its way as the disintegrating spectre of the Third Reich. Worst of all, it was recognized instinctively as the way of the future.[1]

Birchin Lane, closely packed with shops and banks, lay in the financial centre of the City of London. Friday 8 December 1944 was a day of intense cold and winter fog, the war across the Channel halted by a three-foot snowfall in Holland. At 2.30 that afternoon, a black

Vauxhall saloon car turned from Cornhill into this narrow thorough-fare and stopped at a jeweller's shop, Frank Wordley Ltd. Three young men got out, one of them described as having hair so heavily greased that it shone like patent leather. The first swung a woodman's axe with a three-foot handle, shattering the display window of the jeweller's. In a few seconds, the other two raiders scooped up a pearl necklace valued at £2,000 (£80,000) and rings valued at £1,800 (£72,000).

While the passers-by watched, the robbers scrambled back into the car, which moved off towards Lombard Street at the far end of the lane. Several witnesses tried to stop it but jumped clear as the driver accelerated towards them. A Royal Navy officer, Captain Binney, was more resolute. Ralph Binney was fifty-six years old and at the point of retirement as Chief of Staff of the Flag Officer Commanding London. Without hesitation he stood in the path of the car, arms stretched out as it came towards him, perhaps intending to jump on the running board if it continued. The Vauxhall hit Captain Binney, throwing him on his back in the path of the vehicle so that the front wheels ran over him.

The lane was filled by office workers and shoppers who moved towards the place where Binney lay. With his escape to Lombard Street blocked, the driver reversed, as if to back out of the lane into Cornhill. But there was a crowd behind him as well. In panic, he went forward a second time, driving at those in his path, scattering them either side. As he ran over his victim again, the injured man's clothing caught in the suspension of the car, trapping him underneath it. Captain Binney was bounced and dragged along as the Vauxhall turned into Lombard Street, across London Bridge and into Tooley Street.

One motorist gave chase until, by the forecourt of London Bridge station, the thieves' car ran across a cobbled surface throwing the trapped man free against the kerb. The pursuer's car stopped to aid him, while the stolen Vauxhall disappeared down Tooley Street. It was found abandoned at the far end, near Tower Bridge. By coincidence, the forensic pathologist Keith Simpson became a witness of events. He was driving past at the moment when Captain Binney was thrown clear of the stolen car. Within a few minutes Binney was taken to Guy's Hospital, where he died three hours later from his injuries. Keith Simpson performed the autopsy that evening.

The Binney Medal, awarded annually for civilian bravery in assisting the police, was instituted in memory of the captain's courage. Some commentators thought him 'foolhardy' or 'almost stupid', but to many more he was a hero. He personified the millions who loathed and despised such thugs and bullies as the 'Elephant Boys' of Bermondsey rather more than they feared them.

Scotland Yard's first clue was the route of the fugitives, presumably to the safety of their homes and friends south of the river. The 'Elephant Boys' were not so much an organized gang as an association of friends and members of particular families. Behind the wharves and warehouses from London Bridge down to Greenwich lay a terrain of bomb-damaged streets and makeshift 'prefabs', the working-class housing of Bermondsey and Deptford, Lewisham and New Cross. Though this area was said to harbour more criminals to the square mile than any part of London, it was an insult to its population to suggest that the social fascism of the 'Elephant Boys' represented anything but a self-promoted handful of sullen and malevolent delinquents.

By next morning, CID teams had searched clubs in Soho and South-East London, as well as all-night cafés and tube shelters. Three men were arrested. At the Old Bailey in March 1945 the driver of the car, Ronald Hedley, twenty-six, was sentenced to death for the murder of Captain Binney. His appeal was dismissed but he was unexpectedly reprieved and sent to penal servitude for life. He was released nine years later and expressed his remorse for his victim's death. Thomas James Jenkins, the second man in the car, was convicted of manslaughter and sent to penal servitude for eight years.

The third man arrested was not brought to trial. Charles Henry 'Harry Boy' Jenkins, twenty years old, was the younger brother of Thomas Jenkins. Witnesses failed to identify him as the third man in the car. The reason suggested by Frankie Fraser was that Harry Jenkins, who had a record of violence, had deliberately 'chinned' a sergeant at the police station, in order to provoke as much damage to himself as possible. Insisting that his face needed sticking plaster to conceal his injuries, he was put on an identity parade with other men who were also obliged to cover their faces with sticking plaster. Unsurprisingly, no one among these masked figures was picked out.

Perhaps by quick thinking, 'Harry Boy' had got the better of the law. Ironically, had he gone to Borstal for several years it would probably have saved his life. Instead, he was given enough rope to hang himself, for his part in the shooting of another public hero, Alec D'Antiquis, after a bungled pawnshop robbery in 1947. 'All the persons concerned [in the Binney case] and in the subsequent case were associates and lived in the Bermondsey district,' said Sir Harold Scott, Metropolitan Police Commissioner, giving evidence before the Royal Commission on Capital Punishment. 'After the result of the case against Hedley and Thomas James Jenkins they . . . became actively engaged in crime. Some of them were arrested and sentenced to varying terms of imprisonment, but still they continued living their life of crime.' Such men as Ronald Hedley and Thomas Jenkins were cited as a standing argument for the maintenance of capital punishment.[2]

It was certainly true that the South London underworld had been in the news a good deal during 1944. In April, Scotland Yard warned the public that members of local gangs, which had for years been terrorizing Tooting, Brixton, the Elephant and Castle, and Bermondsey, had increased their activities considerably since the new year. There had been a number of cases of 'serious wounding', but so tight was the control of the gangs that 'Even men who have been seriously wounded will not give evidence.' One gang had been operating for eleven years. It had been broken up many times and members gaoled for smashing up cafés, assaults, wounding and theft, but each time it had recruited new members and regrouped.[3]

At the end of 1944, the murder of Captain Binney was an omen of post-war lawlessness. A new breed of criminal, the ruthless and resolute 'commando' of the underworld, had replaced the contented forger, coupon robber or dog doper of the recent past. Men and women feared for their security, in the belief that the incidence of crimes against person and property was spreading beyond control. Statistics seemed to prove them right.

Worse than statistics were the headline cases. Almost exactly two months before the death of Captain Binney, the papers were filled with a drama of Anglo-American robbery and murder in the so-called 'Cleft Chin' case. Indeed, 'Chicago Joe' and 'Blondie' were in their prison cells awaiting trial for their lives as the Birchin Lane robbery took place.

As if to confirm such predictions, in the autumn of 1945 the deaths of two contrasting victims, 'Russian Robert' and 'The Duke', revealed a peacetime world of professional black marketeers, in which murder was a casual expedient.

Early on the morning of 18 October, a policeman crossing London Bridge on his beat found a body, crammed through a narrow aperture into a National Fire Service pumping station, disused since the end of air raid precautions. The dead man was identified as a London taxi driver, Frank Everitt, known to other drivers as 'Honest John' or 'The Duke'. He had been killed by a single bullet, fired at very close range into his head, behind the left ear. Keith Simpson thought the muzzle of the gun might have been touching his skin.

There were no injuries to suggest a struggle but there was square-patterned bruising on his head. Though his pockets were empty, it seemed unlikely that the motive for murder was robbery. After the body had been taken to Southwark mortuary, Scotland Yard found Everitt's taxi abandoned on rubble at St Helen's Gardens, Notting Hill, and partially concealed by surrounding air raid shelters. The pattern of the carpet behind the front seats of the car exactly matched the bruising on his head. A .32 calibre bullet was found embedded in the framework of the vehicle, the calibre of the weapon with which Everitt had been killed. He had been shot in his taxi by someone in the back seat while he was in the driving seat. He had not died instantly but his body had been taken to London Bridge, slumped on the back seat, his head hanging down to the floor. Simpson suggested it would have taken two men to lift the heavy figure and force his body through the gap in the structure of the pumping station. The taxi had then been driven to Notting Hill and abandoned.

The dead man's acquaintances maintained that the title of 'The Duke' referred to Everitt's 'country estate', a bungalow in Gloucestershire which he had bought for £1,400 (£56,000) paid in cash. Where did he get such a sum? Separated from his wife, he rented a single room in South London, yet it emerged that he had three other addresses, including a Soho flat. Plain-clothes officers were sent to the haunts of the underworld to mingle and to listen.

They heard stories that Everitt had been involved with racketeers, that he had been known as a police informer. Other drivers recalled him saying that he knew the black market 'from the inside'. It was certainly true that he had once been a police sergeant. For the moment, the inquiry got no further.[4]

On another winter morning, a fortnight later, a pre-war Opel car was found abandoned in Chepstow Place, Notting Hill, about a mile to the east of St Helen's Gardens on the other side of Ladbroke Grove. Again, it was a policeman on the beat at 6.30 a.m. in thick fog who noticed blood oozing from under the nearside door. The body of a man lay spreadeagled on the back seat with his hat over his face. He had been shot at close range in the nape of the neck with a small calibre weapon. The bullet was lying by the driving seat, underneath which was a spent .32 cartridge case.

This investigation moved quickly. The dead man was a known black marketeer, a stateless Armenian and international criminal, Reuben Martirosoff, who went by the name of 'Russian Robert' but was also known in Soho as 'Marty'. The car was his. A signet ring, crocodile skin wallet, Ronson cigarette lighter, wristwatch and two other watches which he had been carrying were missing. Blood-smeared fingerprints on the steering column were not Martirosoff's.

The first rumours suggested that the police search in Soho as well as in the Notting Hill and Edgware Road areas was for a US Army deserter, posing as an officer, who had spent some years in Chicago. Chief Inspector George Somerset, heading the inquiry, also began to track the known acquaintances of Martirosoff and to infiltrate his officers into drinking clubs, restaurants, hotel hideouts and all-night cafés. Two days later, in the East India Dock Road, he arrested a deserter who was Polish rather than American, Marian Grondkowski. This man was a colourful and formidable black marketeer. He had fought for three years in the International Brigade during the Spanish Civil War, was taken prisoner, escaped to join the French army in 1939, escaped again after the capitulation of France, and joined the Foreign Legion in North Africa. In 1943, he volunteered for the Free Polish Army, came to England and trained in a Special Sabotage Unit, deserting two years later.

Grondkowski was in possession of 'Russian Robert's' wristwatch, lighter, wallet, signet ring and the other two missing watches. His were the fingerprints on the steering column of the Opel saloon. Sewn into his trousers was a holster which fitted a .32 revolver found at his Ilford flat. On the way to Ilford police station, he said helpfully to his escorts, 'I'll tell you everything. I no shoot Robert. Malinowski shoot him. He always carry a gun.'

Henryk Malinowski's history was a match for his fellow racketeer. In 1939, he had fought in the defence of Warsaw, been captured by the Germans and committed to a concentration camp. He escaped, made his way across Europe to North Africa, and joined the Foreign Legion, where he met Grondkowski. In 1943 both men had come to England, where Malinowski joined the Free Polish Armoured Division. He also deserted on the grounds that England and her allies had rid Poland of the Germans only to hand the country over to the tyranny of the Soviet Union. When arrested at his flat in Castellain Road, Maida Vale, Malinowski said, 'I was there but I do not shoot. Grondkowski kill him.' For good measure, he added that Grondkowski was one of those who had murdered the taxi driver, Frank Everitt.

On such evidence, the two men were tried, convicted after a futile 'cut-throat' defence in which they accused each other of the murder, and hanged. Scotland Yard dropped the Everitt inquiry.

The black market activities of the two Poles had extended from an entire lorryload of whisky stolen in the North of England, which they admitted they were awaiting when they shot Martirosoff, to the 'handbag game'. This was routine trickery and involved dressing a woman smartly and giving her an expensive new handbag, for export only and rarely obtainable by legitimate means. She would be positioned in a smart restaurant or club where other women would ask her where she had found such a treasure. She would explain that her escort was a well-known manufacturer of exclusive handbags. Orders would be placed, money would change hands, and the dupes would hear no more. The trick was simple but had proved effective.[5]

Of course there was nothing new in cargoes of stolen whisky or routine confidence tricks. The disturbing novelty was in the methods by which the new black market did business. These were not amiable rogues who signed 'Winston Churchill' or 'Neville Chamberlain' for their illegally purchased poultry. The shots that killed Everitt and

Martirosoff, as well as the cleft-chin taxi driver, George Heath, had more in common with Al Capone than with Billy Hill and his kind. Firearms, like cigarettes, were a currency of the new order. While it was true that Captain Binney had not been killed by a gunman, the 'Elephant Boys' were now ready customers for illegal weapons.

Few criminals in 1944–5 had fought in Spain or Warsaw, escaped from prison camps, joined the Foreign Legion, or learnt the arts of sabotage. Yet a good many were returning from long experience of armed combat, bearing with them thousands of abandoned American weapons or German 'souvenirs'. Tens of thousands of guns and tons of ammunition were available for the taking. Such cases as Captain Binney's or the black market murders by Grondkowski and Malinowski began to seem typical. Were they – or did they only seem to be?

During these last months of the European war and the first months of peace, the increase in violent crime was one which people felt they could see for themselves. Sometimes they saw as eyewitnesses or else in press photos, culminating in 1947 with the all too visible drama of Alec D'Antiquis dying on a West End pavement after attempting to intercept three young jewel thieves. As the number of robberies grew, even smash and grab raids returned to public view, having been infrequent since 1940. It remained a risky crime, as its practitioners insisted, some leaving impressive trails of blood from cuts sustained on the jagged fragments of shop windows.

A safer form of the crime was illustrated on 22 February 1944, when another jeweller, E. A. Baker, at the corner of Houndsditch and Stonehouse Court, was raided at 10.45 a.m. It was not the best time for a robbery, with the staff in place and on the alert. On this occasion, however, the thieves got out of their car and casually wedged iron bars through the handles of the shop's three double doors. Then, with time to take precautions for their own safety, they smashed the window with a 14lb hammer. Without interruption, apart from the unavailing efforts of the staff to open the doors, they collected the jewellery on display and drove off. Even this raid was said to have been over in 'a matter of seconds', but without the urgency of most smash and grab. A solitary passer-by threw the discarded hammer at the car, hitting it without effect. The stolen vehicle was found a few minutes later, abandoned in Billiter Street, a quarter of a mile away.

A blackout alternative to smash and grab, especially under cover of wartime darkness, had been the traditional 'run-out'. In one of the last cases, at J. W. Wise, jeweller of Mare Street, Hackney, a customer came in on 20 March 1945 and asked to see a tray of diamond rings. When this was shown him, he snatched the tray and ran. The shop assistant chased him, only to be stopped in the street doorway by a man whose bulk blocked the pursuit. The fugitives disappeared into an adjacent side street, where their car was waiting. The secrets of success were surprise and speed. The estimated time for this jewel raid was five seconds. Simple though it sounded, the precision and audacity relegated smash and grab to unskilled labour.

Such cases were a further reminder that the City of London was no less prone to be raided than the West End. However, when its police introduced a 'Flying Squad' of motorcyclists in 1945, it was responding to a new wave of jewel robbery. Smash and grab had been the trade of criminals who were content to be armed with a hammer, a brick or a carjack. As the war ended, a generation in its teens preferred to use guns. In November, five young men were convicted of a £6,000 (£240,000) armed hold-up at Catchpole & Williams in Grafton Street. Three were nineteen years old, one was eighteen and one seventeen. Three were soldiers, one a labourer and one a driver.

Their leader, Christopher Geraghty, though born in West London, was a member of the 'Elephant Boys' from Bermondsey and was currently on licence from Borstal. Two years later he was dead, hanged in Pentonville prison for murder. In the present case, one of the gang was left in the car as driver to ensure a quick getaway down Dover Street or Albemarle Street into the heavier traffic of Piccadilly, where pursuit would be more difficult. The other four robbers, three of them carrying guns and led by Geraghty, entered the showroom and held up the manager and manageress. When the manager raised his arm to protect the manageress from the three guns pointed at her, Geraghty beat him unconscious.

The five robbers were caught. They pleaded guilty and were sent to Borstal for three years. Geraghty and one of the other robbers, who was a soldier, were also charged with a second armed robbery of jewels worth £1,300 (£52,000) on 3 September 1945. The theft had taken place at H. & A. Kimball, jewellers and pawnbrokers, Aldersgate Street in the City of London. Six robbers had been involved: two approached the counter, two stood guard at the door and two went to empty the window of its jewels. Three of the men were armed with revolvers which they used to cover the staff. One of them shouted, 'Stand still!' at Mr William Everett, the manager, as he dived for the stairs to the basement, smashed a window down there, put his head out and shouted, 'Police!' He could hear the men rushing about in the shop above him. They ran out and jumped into a waiting car with the stolen jewels. Though the police spent that day and the following night searching hotels, lodging houses, all-night cafés and restaurants, Geraghty and the soldier were the only two found.[6]

Eighteen months after being sentenced in November 1945, Geraghty was free, carrying his gun and raiding jewellers. Whether, as Sir Harold Scott argued, the hanging of the men convicted in the case of Captain Binney's death would have deterred him was questionable. The ending of the war turned London and other British cities into a gunman's playground. A teenage amateur with an automatic pistol or revolver was a match for any policeman, householder, shopkeeper or bank manager.

It seemed that 1944 was to be the year of the gun. Early in January, an eighteen-year-old metal worker and a seventeen-year-old plumber were charged with the armed robbery of a Soho wine store and the attempted robbery of a nearby jeweller's. The Flying Squad alleged that both had been carrying fully loaded revolvers. They were also charged with breaking into two West End gunsmiths and stealing eleven revolvers and ammunition.

The response of shopkeepers to firearms was gratifying to the youths who carried them. In his statement, the plumber recalled that while they were robbing the wine merchant, with revolvers trained on the two men in the shop, the manager 'stood there praying with his hands in front of him'. The police alleged that the youths had then taken the contents of the till and run off. After this they admitted 'thinking of doing a jeweller's shop'. By the time of that attempted robbery, Detective Sergeant Compton and other squad officers had both under observation. Compton heard the metal worker say to the plumber outside the jeweller's shop, 'Grab some watches . . . Money in the till.' It was not the money or even the jewels that made headlines in such cases but, for example, Compton's report of having raided the address of the metal worker in Pimlico and found a cache of arms hidden under floorboards and in the chimney. His collection included a tommy-gun, 'a large quantity' of ammunition, three revolvers and two black masks.[7]

Even while the case of the metal worker and the plumber was heard, another court listened to the story of an armed hold-up by a deserter at Croxley Green station on the Metropolitan line. On the evening of Sergeant Compton's evidence in court, the Lorna Doone Café was also held up by a soldier in battledress, his face masked, carrying a tommy-gun. When the proprietor's wife managed to give the alarm, the soldier knocked her down and ran off empty-handed. She was more fortunate than others.[8]

The image of the pitiless bandit with his tommy-gun created a panic that was a weapon in itself. Four weeks later, on the evening of 4 February, three amateurs robbed the London Co-Operative Society's milk depot in North Kensington as the clerk and the manager were checking the day's takings. The men walked across the yard and entered the building, posing as milkmen who had returned from their rounds. They then forced the depot clerk under her desk and demanded the day's takings. They were not carrying guns. The manager hit one of them on the hand with a milk bottle and was then attacked with the chisel, which was the only weapon they had. Before leaving with £250 (£10,000), they ripped out the telephone wire and one of the robbers warned the clerk, 'We have another man outside with a tommy-gun. If you run after us, he will let you have it.' The manager was now lying on the floor with severe head injuries, inflicted by the chisel, but the depot clerk extricated herself from under the desk and ran across the yard to the fire-watchers at the post office to summon help. There was no rearguard with a tommy-gun.

A firearms panic among the law-abiding was a joke among robbers. In February 1945, five suspects from Southwark were arrested near Oxford Circus tube station and charged with loitering with intent to commit a felony. Revolvers, daggers and fourteen ignition keys were found in their possession. Initially, they were taken to a police phone-box near by. While they were there, a US Army automatic pistol was found on the floor, where one of the men had surreptitiously let it drop. They all denied possession of it. 'As for the gun, I didn't drop it,' said one man. 'Nor did I,' said a second. 'I don't know what it is all about,' said a third, 'I wonder if Father Christmas dropped it?'[9]

The fear of soldiers as armed robbers was strengthened by the number of deserters and the ease with which they took their weapons with them. On 4 December 1944, post offices at Great Easton and Thaxted were held up by gunmen in army uniform. The second raid, at Thaxted, was led by a man in a major's uniform, who told the postmaster's wife, 'We are desperate men. Give me the key to the safe or I'll blow your brains out.' Though a second man had dug a gun into her husband's ribs, the wife refused. One of the men grabbed £5 in coins and they drove off in a stolen army truck.

Worse than armed raids on shops or offices, where the robbers' bluff might be called, was the lonely terror by night, when the chosen victims were woken in their own homes to the threat of guns and bludgeons. This, too, seemed an accompaniment of the war's ending and a profession for deserters. Late at night on 5 March 1945, three armed men tricked their way into a house in Highfield Gardens, Golders Green. They used a revolver to hold up a couple and their daughter. The father and daughter called their bluff and tackled them. Though the daughter was injured, the thieves fled empty-handed, leaving behind a button from an army uniform.

Resistance to intruders was always a gamble. The Golders Green family fought off their three assailants but a few months later, in August 1945, Sir Sydney Jones, a former Mayor of Liverpool, was savagely beaten and left with severe head wounds by the burglars whom he had dared to defy.

Whether such criminals were caught was a matter of chance. At 4 a.m. on a January morning in 1945, two couples were woken at the Moat House, Walton-on-Thames, by two men wearing masks and carrying revolvers. The couples were made to lie face down on their beds while they were trussed with electric flex. The robbers tried without success to get the rings off the women's fingers, then allowed them to take them off themselves. In a curiously chivalrous gesture, they handed back a wedding ring. They then demanded the combination number of the safe and when the householder refused to give it, they began to beat him with a truncheon. He escaped the worst of this when the doorbell rang and two policemen were seen outside. The intruders fled and one got clear. Arthur Cox, the man arrested, was sent to penal servitude for eight years. The violation of a home was seen as infinitely more vicious than a comparable attack on a jeweller's shop or a post office but the length of such sentences was at best a partial reassurance to householders.[10]

The rational step was to cut the supply of firearms but this was impossible. Robert Churchill, owner of a famous gunsmiths in Orange Street, was the greatest ballistic expert of the day. He warned the Home Office that the law on the purchase of firearms 'hasn't affected the criminal at all'. American weapons and ammunition could be had almost for the asking a stone's throw from Piccadilly Circus, at Rainbow Corner. Almost any handgun was on offer for £25 (£1,000) and packets of ammunition were 'two a penny'.[11]

When Rainbow Corner closed, the 'arms racket' in Europe was well established as a source of supply. In the final stages of the war the price of a Luger semi-automatic pistol had risen to £60 (£2,400). Although other guns were available for much less, a Luger was preferred because it could fire sten-gun ammunition, which had been issued to British troops during the war in large quantities and was readily available. In the autumn of 1944, however, as the mass surrender of German troops began, the price of a Luger fell to £30 (£1,200) and by December was said to be as low as thirty shillings (£60).

Though the British Army's Special Investigation Branch, as well as the American Security Police and the French and Belgian authorities, were in active pursuit of gun-runners, the Continental trade was beyond control. In an effort to keep guns out of the hands of German dealers, deterrent sentences were passed. In August 1945, a British military court sent a Berliner to prison for life, after he had been found in possession of an automatic pistol. Yet dumps of abandoned arms and ammunition lay all over Germany, where returning soldiers of the Allied armies could help themselves to souvenirs. The weapons were contraband but as tens of thousands of troops returned from the war, searches of kit were minimal and a large number of stolen firearms was bound to get through. There were such soldiers' tricks as carrying a handgun in a now redundant army water-bottle. The metal bottle was cut in half, the dismantled gun parts were packed in oiled cloth inside it, and the two halves of the bottle rejoined. With its cloth cover in place, it showed nothing amiss.[12]

As the Jews and Arabs of Palestine began their own war, there was a profitable arms trade in the Middle East, where guns seemed worth their weight in gold and where soldiers found that very large sums were offered for rifles, revolvers and bullets. In Europe, the traffic in arms was such that one returning soldier wondered in Brussels if it was any longer safe to go out at night. It was common knowledge that British troops flew to Brussels or Paris on leave with weapons for sale that had been more easily acquired in Germany. The Belgian government was fearful that such arms might be used by supporters of the exiled King Leopold, now living in Austria, if he attempted to return to the country.[13]

In France, discontent among repatriated prisoners of war left the government fearful that demonstrations might become armed mutiny. Lawlessness in Paris during the autumn of 1945 made the post-war British crime wave seem a triviality. Gangsters, some in stolen American uniforms, were reported in stolen jeeps, staging a dozen armed hold-ups and a murder every night in the centre of the capital. The reality was not as bad, though in five days from 19 November there were five murders and thirty-seven armed hold-ups. Those arrested included thirteen French nationals and eleven US Army deserters. There were an estimated 12,000 American deserters in and around Paris.

Despite the example of France and the availability of guns, by no means all robbery with violence in England involved firearms. Some street crimes were as simple as the £250 (£10,000) wage snatch from a female cashier on 16 March 1945 as she returned from the bank to Addison & Co., Horsman Street, Walworth. A man jumped from a car, snatched the bag, jumped back into the car and drove off. More ambitiously, on 2 May, a gang targeted Lyons Corner House in Coventry Street. At about 9.30 in the morning £2,600 (£104,000) in takings was being wheeled to the bank on a trolley by three employees. The money was in fifteen pouches, notes, silver and copper, in a wire cage forming part of the trolley. The escort was attacked in Coventry Street by six men using a newspaper delivery van as their cover. The thieves defeated the burglar-proof wire cage by lifting the entire trolley into the van and driving off with it down Rupert Street and across Shaftesbury Avenue.

Even in the escalation of armed crime, no robber had yet shot a policeman. Such things had happened in the peacetime past, as in the famous case of the petty gangsters Browne and Kennedy in 1928. At the worst, there was now youthful bravado. When three youths were charged with office breaking at Berners Street in May 1945, evidence was given that PC Munn and others had cornered them in the building at 3.45 a.m. on 21 May. Two of the youths were caught after a chase over the roof of the building. An eighteen-year-old was found crouching in the corner of a room, pointing a .22 revolver loaded with five rounds, and clutching a bottle of pepper. 'Don't point that at me,' said PC Munn sternly, 'you are cornered.' He then jumped on the youth and took the gun from him. 'I could not shoot, there were too many of you,' said the teenage gangster feebly, 'I have lost my head.'[14]

At the end of 1945, Billy Hill and his rivals found a more peaceable method of jewel robbery. Simple and silent, it was effective and less dangerous to both sides than pulling out a Luger and telling a shopkeeper to 'stick 'em up'. On the evening of 4 December, Mrs Irene Coleman, manageress of Ingram Warwick, jewellers of South Molton Street, Mayfair, had almost arrived home. At 6.15 she walked past a large car, drawn up alongside the pavement in Napier Road, Tottenham. Four men emerged from the shadows, seized her, bundled her into the back of the car, tied her with ropes and gagged her. From her handbag, they took the keys of Ingram Warwick's front door and safe. The keys were handed to their accomplices and they drove Mrs Coleman round London until seven o'clock. Then they deposited her, still bound and gagged, on Hampstead Heath at a spot where she was likely to be found. Indeed, she was seen soon afterwards by three ATS girls. The police discovered that Ingram Warwick's safe was empty and the thieves had disappeared. The jewellery taken was valued at £18,000 (£720,000).

Hardly had this news reached Scotland Yard that evening when a second kidnapping case was reported. An employee of Fulham post office had been lured into a car and forced to give up her keys. The key to the safe was not among them and she had been pushed out of the car in Dawes Road, Fulham. Mrs Coleman was by then telling her story to Chief Inspector Bob Stevens at Savile Row police station. Stevens suspected that the robbers in the Warwick case might be those who had attacked the manager and night watchman of H. & A. Kimball the previous Monday, just as the shop was being locked up. Kimballs, of course, had been robbed by Geraghty and others in September. On this second occasion, the manager and watchman had been bound and gagged while the shop was ransacked of jewels and cash to the value of £5,000 (£200,000). The six assailants were described as 'young' and 'tough', wearing belted mackintoshes and slouch hats with the brims pulled over their eyes.[15]

As Mrs Coleman continued her story, the attempted post office robbery was followed by a report of another hold-up, at a turkey warehouse of the Upton Cold Storage Company and the Ministry of Food in South-East London. The object, ludicrous by comparison with the jewel haul, was 160 frozen turkeys. Nonetheless, masked men with guns held the watchman and two engineers in the cold chamber, while other masked figures loaded turkeys into a vehicle in the street. Morning brought news of a further attempted hold-up at Temple Hill on Dartford marshes, where a car carrying wages for Little Brook power station had found the road ahead blocked by another car and two men with revolvers. The driver of the wages car had reversed down the hill and escaped.

Before midnight, the Metropolitan Police had tried to seal off central London and prevent the escape of the evening's criminals. Scotland Yard had heard that jewellery stolen in City and West End raids would be smuggled out of the country and traded on an international underworld market in Germany. Later that night, a hundred CID and Flying Squad officers descended on the West End in a hunt for suspects. A watch was put on all main roads out of London to check suspect cars and their drivers. Savile Row was to be the headquarters of the operation, Detective Inspector Stevens its director. The Ingram Warwick jewel robbery was grudgingly acknowledged as 'Technique, 100 per cent.'

Roads to the north and the coast were cordoned off and patrolled. Throughout the night, cafés, pubs and clubs were searched. Further police reinforcements were brought from other areas and dozens of known criminals and two vanloads of 'loiterers' in Piccadilly Circus were detained. A West End address was raided and three men arrested. At Savile Row, questioning continued. The detainees overflowed the interview rooms and filled the main hall. Many of them were put on identity parades, so that detectives from all parts of London could memorize their faces. Savile Row was what Billy Hill called more like a railway station than a copper shop. Indeed, Hill himself was taken there some days later and put on an identity parade, but was not picked out.[16]

A similar 'swoop' had been staged by the Metropolitan Police in January 1944, though on a smaller scale and principally in a search for deserters and black marketeers. By December 1945, however, there was an air of desperation in Scotland Yard's activities. Its force was under strength at the very moment when post-war crime was at its worst.

On 8 December, following an armed robbery at the Elephant and Castle tube station the previous night, senior officers floated the suggestion that police manpower in the capital should be reinforced by drafting in men from country areas where crime was low, until enough men were released from the forces to balance the city's needs. Two days later there was more direct and immediate help when 'flying squads' of Military Police and RAF Police launched a round-up of deserters. Service police targeted mainline terminals, as well as suburban and underground stations. Leave passes and rail tickets were checked. Servicemen were required to produce their pay-books, to show that they were currently drawing pay at their units.

Deserters still offered a pool of labour to the underworld and Scotland Yard had asked for the assistance of service police in trying to track down those responsible for the current robberies. A further difficulty was that some were now disguising themselves in American uniforms, which were readily available, while the number of US Military Police in the country was dwindling.

On 11 December, Scotland Yard made an appeal for volunteers to enrol as special constables in London so that more full-time policemen could be released from routine duties to fight crime. Recruits were invited to apply at Bow Street, King's Cross Road or Gray's Inn Road police stations or their local station. That night another jeweller was injured in an armed attack at Leyton. However, one of his assailants was knocked down by a passer-by and another was arrested by the driver of a police car. In response to the surging crime wave, Dorset House announced that it was to be the first major block of flats in London to install electric burglar alarms. Alarms were needed because London County Council fire regulations required the management to leave open the roof doors, giving burglars access by way of the fire escapes.

Ten days after its earlier attempt to seal off London, Scotland Yard tried again on the night of Friday 14 December 1945. This was better planned. A total of 2,000 civilian police and several hundred service police hunted the 20,000 deserters and other wanted criminals. It was advertised as the first of a series of round-ups to be carried out unannounced in different areas of the capital. As if to show that this was a swoop in earnest, firearms had been issued to many of the CID officers.

A total of 15,161 people were questioned but the results were less than encouraging. Only fifty-three were arrested, only thirty-two deserters caught. Two men were arrested for housebreaking, four for larceny, nine for unlawful possession, one for breaking windows in Leicester Square. The greatest coup seemed to be the capture of three men driving over Westminster Bridge with a carload of furs. Even during the swoop, crime continued. Four men stole the safe from Pickford's in High Holborn and others helped themselves to the cash in a Lavender Hill off-licence. A second safe-gang robbed both the YMCA in Holborn and a firm in Harrow. The Clapham postmaster was attacked by three men who stole his keys.

It was not the decisive success hoped for, though Scotland Yard confirmed that a good deal of information had been gathered. When more snap raids were promised on 18 December, it was announced that the Military Police would play a bigger part. There were also suggestions that service police might be needed on a regular basis to supplement the undermanned civil power.

*

Though cigarette robberies provided the currency of liberation, an invasion of Europe was not needed for such booty to reach the Continent. In May 1944, Red Cross cigarettes intended for British prisoners of war were already on retail sale in Lisbon. However, robberies increased in size during the early months of 1945 with nine major raids, culminating in a theft of 2,000,000 cigarettes from a NAAFI warehouse in Watford on 6 June, as well as thefts of lorry-loads of cigarettes in transit and of the lorries carrying them.[17]

In a minority of cases in the summer of 1945, those who stole cigarette lorries in Holborn, Hendon and Chelmsford were caught and sentenced to six or twelve months in prison, which was scarcely a deterrent as the demand from Europe grew. By August, there was a severe shortage in Britain. 'Shop crawlers', as they were called, made their way from one tobacconist to another to build up their stock. 'Spivs', the post-war hucksters whose name originated among the race gangs of the 1890s, came into their own. Every evening in the West End they were offering twenty stolen cigarettes for three shillings, instead of the retail price of two shillings and fourpence. Bartering might sometimes bring the price down to two shillings and eightpence. The shortage was such that, by September, cigarettes destined for retail outlets in Armagh were brought from the railway goods yard to the shops under police escort.[18]

To explain this shortage, there were stories of smuggling, in which North Sea fishing boats carried illegal consignments to the Continent. But this was unnecessary. Allied soldiers in Europe, who discovered how much cigarettes could buy, particularly in Germany, were ordering them from home in large quantities and duty free. One man had a regular weekly order with a chain of West End tobacconists for 3,000 cigarettes. The Board of Trade admitted there was nothing illegal in this, as the law stood, but promised to look into the matter.

The mammoth British American Tobacco Company claimed to send 90 per cent of the cigarettes to Europe but admitted that many went to non-British soldiers. These black marketeers were Polish, Dutch and Belgian, serving with the British Liberation Army. Their orders would no longer be met. The service departments and the Tobacco Control Agency were monitoring the increase in demand from troops abroad. One small London firm was said to be sending cigarettes worth £500 (£20,000) every day. The protests of good intentions by those regulating the trade ignored the reality of a far greater supply to the black market from the US Army and a barter system in Europe now established so firmly that at the beginning of September the occupation authorities allowed the opening of a Berlin barter market in the Brunnenstrasse, to the north of the city centre.

As the war ended, some of those who robbed cigarette warehouses or hijacked lorries turned their attention to other luxuries. Cigarettes might be scarce but such items as a fur coat were virtually unobtainable. At the beginning of 1945, the Board of Trade announced that it would still not sanction the manufacture of fur coats, not even of the Utility kind, and that when they were permitted, they would probably be of mole or rabbit skin, in very limited numbers.

Fur coats of any type, new or second-hand, were so scarce that by January 1944 they merited a determination reserved several years earlier for a Bond Street jeweller's safe. They were also among luxury goods subject to purchase tax. Because they were too bulky for rapid smash and grab or armed hold-ups, night raids were organized in which security grilles were wrenched from windows by a chain attached to an accelerating vehicle and the glass then smashed.

Individual coats, seen on a woman in a public place, were noted by criminals with as much care as a diamond necklace. In the case of a first-rate coat, thieves would trace the address of the owner. One objective in December 1945 was a Russian sable worn by Mrs Wyndham of Caversfield House, Bicester. No Russian sable had been imported since the beginning of the war and its value was £4,000 (£160,000). Thieves watched Colonel and Mrs Wyndham until they went to London without the coat. When the couple returned, it had gone.

Even for less exclusive coats, the sums were impressive. In the autumn of 1945, Scotland Yard raided a clearing house in Paddington which contained the proceeds of fur robberies in Hampstead and Mill Hill, carried out by relative amateurs. Two Canadian soldiers were arrested as the burglars and three women as receivers. Five fur coats and a silver fox fur were valued at £800 (£32,000). Several more coats, including Indian and Persian lamb, increased the haul to £1,400 (£56,000).[19]

Unobtainable by most people, for love or money, the fur coat had a symbolic value by the war's end. In March 1945, thieves planning to rob warehouses and shops in the Hammersmith area cut the telephone wire at the nearby home of Chief Inspector John Scurr of Scotland Yard, so that the CID could not alert him. They also entered the house and stole his wife's fur coat, as if leaving a visiting card. By the time that the cut in the telephone wire was found and police cars converged on the district, the thieves had vanished.

The disposal of furs, whether stolen or free of purchase tax, was a sensitive business, as the fate of the Paddington five indicated. By the autumn of 1944, black market dealers were recruiting attractive young women from London night clubs. Each was hand-picked, dressed in one of the coats, and sent to a first-class hotel in a provincial town. She would then put 'Lady has good coat for sale' advertisements in the local papers. The coat would be sold for cash and the seller would return to London. She was paid a commission for her work, no money went through the dealer's bank account, and the sale appeared to be an innocent disposal from one woman to another.

For those who felt a growing alarm at the activities of the underworld at the war's end, crime statistics appeared to confirm their apprehension. Crime had increased moderately from 1939 to 1943. In 1944 and 1945, there had been a formidable growth. Cases of housebreaking, burglary and office-breaking in the Metropolitan Police district for 1936 had been just over 10,000. They rose by about a third to 1940, then fell back in 1943 to the 1936 figure and below the level for the early years of the war. But in 1944–5, the number of such crimes jumped from 10,000 to 24,000. Minor offences against property rose from 70,000 to 125,000 in the same two years.

Statistics were reinforced by the words and images of reported crime, not least those detailing the callousness of the perpetrators. Press stories depicted Captain Binney dragged to his death under the stolen Vauxhall; black market gunmen putting a revolver muzzle to the ear of Frank Everitt or the nape of Reuben Martirosoff; readers heard Chicago Joe warn his dying victim to 'Move over or I will give you another dose of the same.' Such words and images seemed more akin to the culture of the Nazi thug than to the brave good-humour of the men and women who had rid the world of him.

Some crimes of violence went unreported but the more serious woundings, like murder itself, were hard to conceal. How far was the alarm of newspaper readers justified? In 1940, there had been 1,776 cases of wounding in England and Wales of which 237 were felonious or grievous. In the next three years, to 1943, the figures rose by 28 per cent for wounding and 38 per cent for grievous wounding – an increase of 9 per cent and 13 per cent a year. They accelerated by 44 per cent in 1944 alone and 65 per cent in 1945.

How safe was the citizen who lay awake, listening for the footstep on the stair? Certainly no safer in mind for knowing that the nation's police manpower had fallen by 14,000 during the war. Yet the odds of any person being a victim of violence in 1945, including unintended grievous bodily harm, were more than 1,000 to 1. Murder was happily rare enough to make statistics inconclusive. However, the number of murders in England and Wales rose from 115 in 1940 to 120 in 1943. They fell back to 95 in 1944, contrary to the increase in other crimes, but rose to 141 in 1945. The odds against being murdered were thus about 300,000 to 1. The average citizen was 85 per cent more likely to be a victim of non-fatal violence in 1945 than in 1940, but only 22 per cent more likely to be murdered. But statistics did not tell the whole story. The actual number of murders in England and Wales had only gone up by six, from 135 to 141, between the last year of peace in 1939 and the height of the post-war crime wave in 1945.

A more general fear was that the war had promoted a culture in which readers and cinemagoers were so brainwashed by narratives of crime or gangsterdom that the last inhibitions of the violent young would be removed. There had always been an appetite for crime as entertainment, whether more or less violent, though many films dealing with violence were now a fictionalization of the war itself. Crime sold books, cinema tickets and newspapers but it had not needed a war to popularize such press dramas of the 1930s as the careers of high-risk thieves and cat burglars like 'Flannelfoot' or 'The Human Fly', and the white-slave murders of 1936. Fiction followed fact in a new style of crime writing seen in the success of Peter Cheyney, his private eye, Slim Callaghan, and American hero, Lemmy Caution. Such titles as *Dangerous Curves*, *I'll Say She Does* or *Your Deal, My Lovely* filled the front ranks of bookstalls, year after year. His rival, since the publication of *No Orchids for Miss Blandish* in 1939, was James Hadley Chase, an English writer and serving RAF pilot, the violence of whose Americanized prose made Cheyney seem genteel.

Cinema and radio rivalled the printed word. In war and peace, commuters hurried home to catch the beat of Vivian Ellis's *Coronation Scot*, introducing the week's episode of Francis Durbridge's latest 'Paul Temple' mystery, its suave hero moving deftly through a world of pretty women, murderous villains, expensive cars and Knightsbridge apartments. On Fridays, the *Evening Standard* supplemented this with a Paul Temple short story to ease the office worker's homeward journey. Yet, unshackled by BBC restrictions, it was Cheyney who dominated the middle market and for whom, as he entered a night club, the band would play the signature tune of his play, *Meet Mr Callaghan*.

In 1944, the *Police Journal* criticized the cinema for giving encouragement to potential delinquents and providing the final impetus to robbery or violence by illustrating the methods of committing them. These helpful examples on the screen showed how to avoid leaving fingerprints; methods of illegal entry and the instruments used; instructions in fraud and establishing false alibis; the use of guns, knives and knuckledusters. The audience was further instructed in the use of violence to intimidate witnesses, the falsification of evidence and the disposal of stolen property.

While it was true that crime films invariably had a 'moral ending', this was said to be undermined by making criminals appear as 'fascinating heroes' whose activities were principally 'a crusade against authority'. This argument against the crime film and, indeed, the cinema as a whole was encapsulated by the *Police Journal* in a quotation from A. E. Morgan's *The Needs of Youth* (1939), affirming that such screen entertainment was 'a school of false values and its scholars cannot escape unscathed'.[20]

By contrast, the Metropolitan Police Commissioner from 1945 to 1953, Sir Harold Scott, thought that the influence of crime fiction and the crime film on young male criminals at the end of the war was confined to what he called such 'externals' as the swaggering walk and the boastful manner. The moral influence went no deeper than 'imitations of Red Indians and pirates'.[21]

At one level, these arguments were irrelevant. Given the statistics of rising crime, the fearful citizen was apt to believe that what he or she saw on the screen was a reflection of established reality rather than a possible influence upon it. In reality, when an eight-year-old culprit volunteered to 'take the rap' for some infant venture, the world must be past saving. What was described as the 'worst gang' to appear before the courts in July 1945, at East London juvenile court, admitted twenty-six offences against the Larceny Acts. It consisted of 'gangsters' aged between twelve and fourteen.[22]

There was a good deal of truth in Sir Harold Scott's comment that the aspiring criminal sought to ape the style of screen heroes rather than their methods. A supreme example in 1944 was the scourge of dressing-table jewellery boxes in St John's Wood and Hyde Park Place, Eton Place and Hampstead, who called himself 'Tiptoes'. This elusive figure had more than a touch of Leslie Charteris' 'Saint', whose best-sellers featured Simon Templar as 'The Robin Hood of Modern Crime'. Tiptoes' first triumph was a theft of jewels in February 1944 from two women in Eton Place, where he left behind a saintly message in lipstick on the mirror. 'Sorry for the mess. Tiptoes.' Unusually, he returned less than a month later, leaving a message on the wall. 'Tiptoes again, gentle in manner, resolute in deed. You are still very beautiful, even asleep.' As an example of his audacity, he then put a letter through the flap of a house he had burgled, describing his career as jewel thief in swashbuckling style. It was a rare account of a burglar's life and state of mind in the blackout.

For nearly a month now I have staged a war against the police . . . It wasn't until 29 February that I met any serious opposition. Admitted the police gave me a good run, but I got away. My next serious encounter with the police was on 6 March. I had entered Eton College Road and was proceeding towards my selected target when I perceived a black form heading towards me. It was a police car with its engine off. Yet still I outwitted them.

On 9 March, with no moon and a slight fog, I glided silently through the night until I came to the danger area. Right before me loomed two dim forms of policemen. What shall I do? Run or hide? I hid 10ft above the ground and waited, not long enough, for no sooner had I got under cover than six other forms opened out of the nearby trees . . . Torches flashed, night became day. I was pinned in a cone of torchlight. My only chance was to create a diversion and so draw them all to one side of the shelter on which I was perched . . . My last card was a gun. I fired at one of them forcing them all to take cover, and before the vapour had drifted from the nozzle of the gun I had leapt and on impact with the ground broke my thumb and lost the revolver . . . and flew into the main road with the police in full pursuit. But what chance had they against Tiptoes? And so I am free to tell the true story.

Not surprisingly, Tiptoes already had a criminal record and was identified by the police as Claud Sweeney, nineteen years old, who had been sent to Borstal for attempted shop-breaking in October 1942 and was released in August 1943. He had then been called up by the Army and said openly that he regarded the Intelligence Corps as his enemy and would 'defeat' them. He claimed to have stolen maps and codes, cut telephone wires, and lighted flares to guide enemy planes. The Army discharged him as unfit for any form of military service. Tiptoes had found himself a one-room flat near Regent's Park, where his kit included three revolvers, two daggers and a cache of army socks. Like the famous 'Flannelfoot' of the 1930s, he burgled in stockinged feet.

As the police arrived to arrest him, Tiptoes quietly packed a case and disappeared by climbing down a stack pipe. Property valued at £461 was recovered from his room. The rest of the £5,500 (£220,000) he had stolen was not found. Having been in the Cheshire Regiment, he went to Chester, acquired an army uniform, and was shortly afterwards stopped by a military policeman who demanded his leave pass, which he did not have. His Chester lodgings were then searched and a revolver was found in the pocket of his civilian suit. On 4 May 1944, he was sentenced to four years' penal servitude at the Old Bailey, a young man said to be 'a good-looking youth with an attractive voice', and with a sense of style which made Billy Hill and other self-promoted 'bosses' of the underworld seem rather drab by comparison.[23]

The robber of Lloyds Bank, King's Road, Chelsea, in February 1945 was no less typical, in his undramatic way. Staff returning to the bank on the morning of Monday 21 February discovered that the night safe had been opened by false keys and emptied. The sum missing was £1,119 (£44,760) in notes and silver. Scotland Yard indicated that this was one of a series of bigger crimes. The gang was believed to have come from the King's Cross area, where cafés, pubs and clubs were raided by CID squads on the afternoon of 21 February and the numbers on the banknotes in the tills were checked. There was no progress in that direction. Fingerprint experts descended on the bank and police sifted the cinders in the furnace.

A bank cashier, not so far suspected, could stand the strain no longer. He was the 'gang'. He had spent six months making duplicate keys and arranged an accommodation address to which he would send the money. Even if he was suspected and searched, it would not be found on him or at his home. He had timed the robbery for a weekend when he was one of the fire-watchers. But having taken the money, he found he was not cut out for robbery. He burnt the leather money bags in the furnace and when the police sifted the cinders, he was convinced he would be caught. He owned up, returned the money, and went to prison for six months. Despite the armed robber of the headlines, his was a more typical face of crime at the war's end than Geraghty with his Luger.[24]

15

The Misfits

The frontiers of the wartime underworld extended beyond conventional crime or systematic racketeering. A political underworld was as prone to robbery and murder, avowal and betrayal, as its contemporaries in the gangs of Soho or South London. In its land of shadows, apostles of Nazism died on the same gallows as armed robbers. The blast of gelignite might equally be the work of jewel thieves or the IRA, whose bombs brought destruction to London and Coventry in 1939–40, long before those of the Luftwaffe.

Among the strange alliances, Herbert Vosch, an explosives expert who trained German saboteurs during the war, claimed to have been the man primarily responsible for the IRA attempt to blow up Hammersmith Bridge on 29 March 1939. Two IRA men went to penal servitude for ten and twenty years respectively as the perpetrators of the explosion. One of Vosch's most distinguished pupils in 1941–2 was also England's most accomplished safe-blower of the 1930s, Eddie Chapman, who passed most of his war in the hands of German intelligence, playing a deft but dangerous game.

Crime and politics proved easy bedfellows. As early as October 1936, the *Daily Sketch* had forwarded to Scotland Yard its photo coverage of the current Fascist meetings in London's East End. The editor drew the attention of the CID to the presence in Fascist uniforms of well-known professional criminals, mingling with Sir Oswald Mosley's Blackshirts. Prior to this, on 11 October, street fighting had spread to include the smashing of shop windows and the looting of the contents. Press photographs of such disturbances in the Mile End Road had shown individual criminals whose interest in politics was nil but who were identified as 'expert burglars and jewel thieves'.

According to journalists' reports, criminal gangs deliberately created pockets of disorder to cover their activities. Scotland Yard confirmed two days later that, quite apart from the shopbreakers, men known to have criminal records had bought Fascist uniforms 'with the main object of disguising themselves while canvassing houses in the search for a suitable place to burgle'. Their tactic had once again been to 'cause a disturbance in order to cover up stealing, pickpocketing and looting in the subsequent confusion'.[1]

The underworld of war, espionage and political subversion sometimes gave, to the criminal and the misfit, opportunities undreamt of in peacetime. Eddie Chapman was one of its most adroit agents. For some years before the war he had pioneered the use of gelignite, a weapon for which Scotland Yard was unprepared, as important in the science of safe-breaking as in any IRA 'mainland campaign'.

Chapman was born in Sunderland, a child of the inter-war depression. This 'prince of the underworld', as MI5 later described him, was tall and straight, with a close shave and clipped moustache. He remained in appearance the Coldstream Guardsman he had been briefly at seventeen, when he joined the Army to escape the Dole School for the youthful unemployed. He deserted after a period guarding the treasures of the Tower of London, a duty his superiors might have reconsidered had they known of his future proclivities. Sentenced to ninety days in a military prison, he was discharged in June 1933 with a civilian suit and a railway ticket back to Sunderland, which he never used.

Following a failed smash and grab raid, he first served a nine-month sentence imposed at Lewes Assizes. Then, having heard American criminals ridicule the antique British custom of picking locks, he put his faith in gelignite. Like his mentors, he used chewing gum to fix the wires. The press and the newly-formed 'Gelignite Squad' of Scotland Yard assumed for some time that an American gang was at work in England, since only Americans were thought to chew gum. Chapman's strength was in working alone, both in his robberies and in stealing gelignite from remote quarries in Wales. There were few people who could turn informer against him. When he agreed to work for MI5 in exchange for having previous offences pardoned, he admitted forty-five robberies by safe-blowing, thirty-eight carried out alone.

At twenty, the exercise of outdistancing Inspector Greeno and his officers was valuable training for a future saboteur. Chapman moved fast and unpredictably. As the Gelignite Squad closed on him, he blew the safe of the Odeon cinema at Swiss Cottage, carrying off the loot by underground train, then of the Odeon, Bournemouth. While the squad dashed from one to the other, he blew the Co-Operative Stores in Leicester four days later. With two companions he then drove to Scotland and blew both safes at the headquarters of the Edinburgh Co-Operative Society. It was a noisy job. At a signal, his 'chauffeur' raced the engine of the getaway car to drown the blast.

Unfortunately, when Chapman and his second accomplice tried the skylight through which they planned to escape, they found it jammed. In breaking out of the building, they made enough noise to attract a policeman on his beat. The policeman immediately 'played his flute', as Chapman called the whistle, and brought assistance. The two fugitives made a dash, climbed a high railway-wall and dropped into a marshalling yard, the accomplice breaking his ankle. Chapman sprang at a slow-moving goods train and clung to its buffers as it carried him to safety. His accomplice was arrested. Chapman and the other survivor were caught at Scotch Corner, driving home with assorted sticks of gelignite in the back of the car.

The worst sentence facing him was twelve years' penal servitude. Inexplicably, a Scottish court allowed him bail, pending his appearance at the Edinburgh High Court. He resumed work to gather funds for an escape to South America, though without a passport. A cinema safe was blown at York. This puzzled Greeno because his information put Chapman in Bournemouth again. Reassuringly, the Parkstone and Bournemouth Co-Operative Society safe went up five days later with unusual force.

Chapman needed no passport for the Channel Islands, from which he might easily get to France, and thence to South America. He caught a ferry for St Helier, where he survived on the proceeds of robbery until April 1939. Then, while he was eating his Sunday lunch in the ground-floor dining room of a hotel, the police arrived to arrest him. He had no idea which crime they had uncovered but managed to jump through a window and remain at large for a further twenty-four hours. Soon afterwards, he was serving a two-year sentence in the island's gaol for having burgled the safe of a local dance hall.

To escape from prison would mean getting clear of Jersey. He passed his time reading and memorizing Tennyson in the prison library. An airport timetable came into his possession. For his prison break, he chose an afternoon when he had been detailed to work in the governor's garden. The warder who watched him rather lazily knew that even if a convict escaped, he could not get far on the island. Taking his chance, Chapman disappeared into the house, where he found a suit and thirteen pounds in cash. To get beyond the prison boundary, he then climbed out on to the house roof, only to find the nurses in a nearby hospital pointing at him excitedly, ready to give the alarm. In a moment of inspiration, he took a piece of string from his pocket and began a pretence of measuring the length and breadth of the tiles. The nurses lost interest.

His plan was to reach Jersey airport, buy a ticket, and catch the 3.30 afternoon plane to London. He would be clear of the island, even in England, before the hunt began. By sheer bad luck, he got to the airport and found his timetable out of date. The last plane had left twenty minutes before. In a few hours, his stolen suit identified him and he was back in prison.

So long as he was serving a sentence on Jersey, he was unavailable to answer charges in the English courts. However, a Scotland Yard officer was sent to interview him. Chapman was still in the punishment cells. The governor led the Scotland Yard man to the block, assuring him that prison security on Jersey was quite good enough to hold the likes of Chapman. As the governor opened the cell door, the lock fell out.

Scotland Yard's interest was short-lived. By July 1940, France had surrendered and the German army was on Jersey. The governor of the island and many of the warders had left for England on the last boats. Chapman remained in his cell, where he now taught himself German. By the time he had completed his sentence, in October 1941, he was able to converse with the occupation forces. He went to the Kommandantur and applied to join the German Secret Service. This suggestion was received with amusement, until his interviewers checked his record. He was an expert safe-blower who faced many years in prison if England won the war. Better still, he appeared politically subversive and plainly had a grievance against the British system.

Chapman then disappeared into a lost world of German intelligence and sabotage training, from which he was to graduate more than a year later at the most remarkable stage of an unusual criminal career. He was first confined at Paris in the prison of St Denis, from whose inmates hostages were chosen to be shot in reprisal for the activities of the French underground. In February and March 1942, he was interviewed by German officials, who had been educated in America and England. On 10 April, he was escorted to the *château* of La Bretonnière, a German training school for spies and saboteurs on the outskirts of Nantes. For the next eight months, he underwent instruction in parachute jumping and sabotage.

In June 1942 he was required to sign a contract with his captors. He would be paid £10,000 (£400,000) for blowing up the workshops which produced the Mosquito fighter-bomber at the De Havilland aeroplane factory at Hatfield. A further act of sabotage against a second target would double the bounty. The Mosquito was produced in fighter, bomber, and photo-reconnaissance versions. Built largely of wood and with a speed of more than 400 miles an hour at 25,000 feet, it could reach Berlin from English airfields. Its speed and altitude gave it protection against any existing Messerschmitt or Focke-Wulf fighter by day or night. Its debut, a month before Chapman signed his contract, had been a high-speed daylight raid on Cologne at rooftop height.

In December 1942, Chapman was parachuted into East Anglia, landing near Littleport, about five miles north-east of Ely. His controllers had suggested he should remain in England for about four months. Then he would be picked up by U-boat off the English coast or a passage would be arranged for him on a neutral ship. For the time being, he was carrying a radio receiver and transmitter, explosives, detonators, £1,000 (£40,000) in sterling, a supply of chocolate, an automatic pistol and a brown suicide pill. The code in which he was to transmit had been derived from Lewis Carroll. Only when he landed did he realize that his English banknotes were done up in bands stamped with 'Deutsche Bank, Berlin', dated a few days earlier, and that the valves in the radio were also stamped as of recent German manufacture.

As in the case of many German agents, MI5 boasted that it was expecting him. Indeed, having caught the early train from Littleport to Liverpool Street, Chapman settled himself in London and made contact with British intelligence. His criminal career was investigated by its officers. Sex as well as safe-blowing had brought him before the courts. In one case, 'he behaved in Hyde Park in a manner likely to offend the virtuous public and was caught *in flagrante delicto*'. In its confidential report, the intelligence service alleged that Chapman had attracted women on the fringe of London society, indulged in violent affairs with them, and then proceeded to blackmail them by producing compromising photographs taken by an accomplice. In St Denis prison, he had made keys which would open almost every internal lock, giving him the run of the buildings at night and access to the women's quarters. He seemed more and more like a man who might be useful to his country's cause.[2]

His offences as a safe-blower were pardoned and, under instructions from his new controllers, he began to transmit messages. At first, Paris was unable to hear him but he made contact with Nantes. 'Well. Am with friends. Good landing. Fritz.' In the files of the Abwehr, he was known as 'Fritzchen'.[3]

The 'Twenty Committee' of MI5, so called because its Roman numerals 'XX' represented a double-cross, was chaired by John Masterman. It considered Chapman's case, recommended acceptance of him, and gave him the code name 'Zigzag'. The committee, officially known as B1A, included Foreign Office members as well as officers from the armed services. Its view of Chapman was that 'The subject is a crook, but as a crook he is by no means a failure . . . Of fear he knows nothing. Adventure to Chapman is the breath of life.' A more cynical appraisal suggested that Chapman loved himself, adventure, and his country – 'in that order'.

To use him as a double agent, it was first necessary to convince the Abwehr of his value by blowing up the Mosquito works at Hatfield, or at least to persuade German intelligence that its vital installations had been destroyed. His contract of June 1942 had been thorough and detailed. To qualify for the £10,000 bounty, he must blow up the boiler house or the electric plant. Either of these would effectively halt production of the plane.

MI5, using elaborate camouflage, reproduced the appearance of both power houses in ruins at De Havilland's works, and photographed the result. This had to be done with care and accuracy. As Chapman told his new masters, German intelligence had a complete set of photographs of the Hatfield works, which they had used at La Bretonnière to plan the operation. The pictures must also match the story Chapman would tell the Germans of an underworld accomplice, 'Freddie', whom he paid to assist him. According to this fable, using Freddie's car, they had stolen gelignite from a quarry near Sevenoaks. They then drove to Hatfield in the blackout and climbed a fence into the factory grounds. They spent the night in stockinged feet, locating the guards and timing their movements. In the blackout of 1943, this would not have been impossible. A few days later, according to this story, the saboteurs returned to Hatfield with two suitcases, each containing thirty pounds of gelignite activated by wristwatch and batteries. Wearing workers' overalls and carrying the cases, they climbed an unguarded and unlit fence at 6 p.m., when the shifts changed and they were less likely to be noticed in the movement of hundreds of workers. Chapman had hidden his suitcase under the transformers of one power house and Freddie had hidden his at the other. Shortly before seven o'clock, from a distance of two or three miles, they had heard what Chapman described to the Abwehr as 'a God-almighty explosion'.[4]

Such was the story. Having created the appearance of damage at De Havillands, British intelligence took aerial photographs, showing the power plants at the Mosquito works wrecked by a recent explosion. For the double-cross to work, it was essential to feed these photographs to the press, allowing German intelligence to see them in routine scanning of British newspapers in neutral capitals. John Masterman was deputed to approach Robert Barrington-Ward, editor of *The Times*. When he discovered the photographs were fakes, Barrington-Ward, to Masterman's dismay, declined to make *The Times* a party to untruth. It was contrary to the 'policy' of the paper. He suggested that Masterman should go to a less scrupulous publication. Masterman made his next call on Arthur Christiansen, editor of the *Daily Express*. Christiansen agreed to carry a photograph of the 'damaged' buildings on the back page of the final edition. Copies were sent for sale in Lisbon, in the sure knowledge that the Germans would acquire them.[5]

In April 1943, a somewhat reluctant hero of British intelligence,

Chapman was returned to the Abwehr. A passage to Lisbon was arranged as steward on the *City of Lancaster*, from which he would 'escape' when the ship docked in Portugal. The Germans had instructed him that if he could get to Lisbon, he was to go to the house of a man whom he would address as 'De Fronsenac', and to whom he would speak the code words, 'Joli Albert'. When he did this, the man had not the least idea what he was talking about. Someone had muddled the names and addresses. This house contained only puzzled German businessmen. The network for handling agents in Lisbon was nowhere to be found.

At length Chapman was flown to Madrid, then taken by car and train to Paris and Berlin. His story of sabotage was accepted, after he had been questioned and drawn maps to show the precise locations of the damage. Once his interrogators were satisfied, he was flown to Abwehr headquarters in Oslo to be greeted as a proven friend. He was told to take a long holiday and allowed the run of hotels and restaurants, as well as his Wehrmacht pay. His bounty was not £20,000 (£800,000) but £15,000 (£600,000). On the other hand, he was given German citizenship, promoted to Oberleutnant, and awarded the Iron Cross. Since his next posting was on the Baltic, they also gave him a yacht.

MI5 was cautiously jubilant over the success of 'Zigzag' and the way that the Germans had apparently accepted the evidence of sabotage. A few months later, on 17 August 1943, a headline in the *Evening Standard* announced, 'Sabotage at Works – Big Check-Up After Bomb Explosion'. Next morning, a *Daily Express* headline added superfluously, 'Police Hunt Saboteurs'. Masterman's friends had come to his aid again. A bomb placed by saboteurs was reported to have destroyed part of an unnamed and non-existent East Anglia factory. The photographs proved the 'truth'. A second unexploded bomb was found near by.

As it happened, a prime mover in this second case of 'sabotage' was Reginald Spooner, a young peacetime officer at Scotland Yard. In wartime, as Major Spooner, he was deputy commander of B57, under Superintendent Leonard Burt. B57 was the anti-sabotage section of MI5, housed in the cells of Wormwood Scrubs, which were proof against anything short of a direct hit. Following its success with Chapman, the Double Cross Committee had 'turned' a Dutchman sent to Britain by the Abwehr. In order to preserve his credibility it was again necessary for MI5 to carry out sabotage on his behalf, without informing the local police at any level.[6]

During these months, Chapman had become an instructor at a spy school in Oslo, where he remained until he was taken to Paris in the spring of 1944. His second mission to England had a number of objectives. He was to try to obtain plans or photographs of the new British Asdic detector used in anti-submarine warfare. He was also to get, by theft or bribery, a variation of a new radio-location device which was being used by the RAF to track German night fighters. The Abwehr thought the device was being made by Cossors Ltd at Hammersmith.

Chapman was also to locate USAAF airfields in East Anglia and identify which bases were used to attack specific targets. It was thought, for example, that those in Cambridgeshire targeted Hamburg, while those in Bedfordshire were used to bomb Berlin. No less important, he was to report on the accuracy of the new V-1 flying bomb which was launched a fortnight later, its destructive capacity, and rumours that the British had developed a 'valve' capable of throwing the successor V-2 rocket off course.

At the end of June, Chapman was flown from Holland and again parachuted into East Anglia. He made his way to London by train to Liverpool Street and reported to MI5. On the instructions of his controllers, he radioed information to his German spymaster which shifted the aim of the rocket bombs away from their target area of Britain's centre of government towards the streets of South-East London. Already the advance of the Allied armies had obliged his controllers to leave Paris for Hamburg. Soon afterwards, he received their final message. 'Regret delay in answering your messages but lost my house in bombing raid. Luck. Stephan.'[7]

It was too late for him to be sent back. In any case, his British controllers considered him indiscreet, unreliable, and further compromised by falling in love with a Norwegian girl to whom he had probably told too much. His previous offences had been pardoned but there was no doubt among his masters that he would return to crime. He was courting the company of beautiful women of apparent culture but was frequently in the company of known criminals, like Billy Hill.

The guardians of official secrecy were uneasy. The Double Cross Committee pondered such questions as, 'What will happen when Chapman, embroiled again in crime, as he inevitably will be, stands up in court and pleads leniency on grounds of highly secret wartime service?' In the hope of preventing this, he was given a payment of £6,000 (£240,000), and allowed to keep £1,000 (£40,000) of the money the Germans had given him. He bought a health farm, smuggled tobacco between Tangier and southern Europe, and was said to have committed other crimes carefully and unobtrusively for a while. He did nothing much to embarrass the security service, apart from getting himself prosecuted under the Official Secrets Acts in 1946, a case hastily dealt with at Bow Street, and being tried on a currency charge in 1948 and for assault in 1954. On the second occasion a senior officer from the War Office described him helpfully as 'one of the bravest men who served in the last war'. He died in his bed, in 1997, at the age of eighty-three.[8]

Chapman was not the only man of his type, though certainly the only one in his class. 'Gentle Johnny' Ramensky, the most famous of pre-war Glasgow safe-blowers, was a teetotaller, non-smoker, a cracksman who had never used violence in his robberies and, according to the policeman who caught him, would 'surrender to a child of three rather than upset the youngster'.

Soon after the outbreak of war, Ramensky was called to Scotland Yard and invited to put his talents at the service of the newly-formed Commandos, in exchange for having his slate wiped clean. His first duty was as an instructor in safe-blowing. After parachute training, he also became one of a commando group who operated behind enemy lines. He used his skill to blow open safes and remove documents in buildings that had been targeted in North Africa, Italy and Germany. With the main body of the Army, he retrieved papers undamaged when they had been left by the retreating enemy, blowing open four strongrooms and ten safes on the same day in Rome in 1944, and also the safes at Goering's Luftwaffe headquarters. Following the war, Johnny Ramensky returned to his profession. He was still in Peterhead prison shortly before his death in 1966.[9]

*

So far as the public knew, German espionage had been a failure. Sixteen enemy agents were executed in England during the war, all but one hanged in civil prisons after trials in camera. The sixteenth, Josef Jacobs, was convicted by a court martial and therefore shot by a firing squad on the miniature rifle range of the Tower of London in August 1941. He shook hands with each member of the firing party and was shot sitting in a kitchen chair. He had parachuted into the Home Counties and, like many of his fellow agents, was captured after a few hours, in his case by the Home Guard.

Most enemy agents were non-German nationals, though only three were British. The sharpest irony attended George John Armstrong, hanged after being convicted in May 1941 under the Treachery Act. He was a ship's engineer, not a Fascist but a loyal Communist. As such, his duty prior to the German invasion of the Soviet Union on 22 June was to work for the German-Soviet alliance of 1939. He was caught trying to communicate information to the German consul in Boston, Massachusetts. Seventeen days before his execution, Germany attacked the Soviet Union. All that Armstrong had worked for was now denounced by those who had encouraged his treason.

The great recruiting success in the Abwehr files was a rabid anti-English Welshman, an electrical engineer, Arthur Owens. He was code-named 'Johnny' and numbered 3504 by his Hamburg control, a skilful spymaster, Major Nikolaus Ritter, who passed as 'Dr Rantzau'. Some well-publicized acts of sabotage at an RAF base for which Saunders Lewis and other Welsh nationalists were sent to prison in January 1937 had been noted by German intelligence. A Welsh crowd had sung its defiance outside the Old Bailey, as Lewis was gaoled for two years and his co-defendants for nine months. It seemed to Ritter and his colleagues that it was worth putting 'sleepers' into Wales to recruit political dissidents. Sabotage and even a Welsh insurrection seemed possible.

A house in Marlborough Road, Cardiff, was the base of Hans Heinrich Kuenemann, managing director of a German engineering firm in South Wales, who escaped to Germany only twenty-four hours before Britain's declaration of war. Professor Friedrich Schoberth described himself as 'a visiting lecturer at Cardiff University'. Franz Richter, the manager of an enamel factory at Barry, and Dr Walter Reinhard, who covered North Wales from the German consulate at Liverpool, completed the quartet. From 1937, they lived and worked as professional men but with an eye to recruitment and intelligence gathering.

Owens, then selling electrical goods in Belgium, Switzerland and elsewhere on the Continent, was recruited by the Abwehr soon after the Saunders Lewis case. His name had come to German intelligence through a contact in the electrical engineering business. Arthur Owens corresponded briefly with Ritter through 'Postbox 629, Hamburg' and was then invited to meet the major in the summer of 1937. His Abwehr hosts dined him at the Vier Jahreszeiten Hotel, wined him at the Munchener Kindl, and let him think that he had been left to his own devices at the Valhalla Club on the Reeperbahn.

Of the four divisions of the Abwehr, Owens had fallen in with the section at Hamburg known as 'Luft', specialists in air warfare. He was paid cash on the spot for information about RAF electrical equipment and provisionally accepted as a 'passionate Welsh nationalist, bitterly opposed to everything English'. He was also offered payment in advance for information about Woolwich Arsenal. Owens took the money and sent the information. Unsurprisingly, the Woolwich Arsenal assignment was a trick. The Abwehr already had the information but were testing the sincerity and ability of their new friend. Owens, or 'Johnny' as he was now to be known, passed the test.

In the summer of 1939, Owens returned to Hamburg. A radio officer of the Abwehr, Major Werner Trautmann, taught him Morse code and how to build and conceal a radio transmitter. If the Abwehr were to be believed, Owens made an income from spying of £2,000 (£80,000) in each of the two pre-war years. Shortly before war was declared, he returned to England. From the cloakroom at Southampton station, he collected a radio transmitter and sent a successful test transmission in the words of German he remembered best, 'Ein glas bier.' Major Ritter's reply was businesslike and reproving. 'Must meet you in Holland at once. Bring weather code. Radio town and hotel Wales ready.' The spy was not to forget that the land of his fathers must rise on behalf of the Fatherland and that he was to find leaders of the rebellion among disaffected Welshmen. Indeed, he had now made a contact, identified only as 'G. W.'[10]

'Johnny's' true worth lay elsewhere. In the first ten months of war, he supplied the Abwehr with details of RAF airfields in England and France, descriptions of coastal defences and, most valuable of all, the locations and specifications of radar stations. As yet, the purpose of primitive Chain Home radar was unknown to most people. Mystified civilians swore that the engines of their cars had stopped dead as they passed the giant pylons. They guessed that an invisible ray would immobilize the vehicles of an invading army. In the spring of 1939, the German airship *Graf Zeppelin* had made a leisurely cruise up and down the East Coast of England, monitoring radar pulses. None of the data gathered on that occasion matched the fruits of Arthur Owens' treachery.[11]

So long as Belgium and Holland remained neutral, Owens the salesman could meet his contacts and, with some caution, slip into Germany itself. He met Ritter in Antwerp in October 1939 and in April 1940. After Dunkirk, Ritter suggested that Owens should buy a motor cruiser and keep it at an East Coast resort. He could then rendezvous in the North Sea with his control, who would requisition a submarine or a flying boat for their meetings. The German Naval Command refused to provide a U-boat and the slow-moving Dornier flying boat would have been an easy target for RAF patrols. In any case, as Owens explained, it was impossible to sail a private motor cruiser round the North Sea during wartime without being challenged. The same plan was tried with Owens aboard a trawler but the two men missed one another in the fog.

After this failure, Owens signalled Ritter that they might still meet, if he could get a permit from British Field Security to visit Lisbon. His pretext would be that Lisbon offered the only rendezvous with his clients from Switzerland, where most of his business was now done. There was still scepticism in Hamburg, not least when British Field Security granted the permit.

However, when he met Ritter, Owens produced sensational material. He had a technical report and plans for a new radar set, small enough to fit the cockpit of a night fighter. His German contacts remained uneasy. How could he have such documents unless British intelligence had given them to him? But there was an explanation. The papers came from a fellow Welshman, a squadron leader in the technical branch of the RAF, dismissed when his Communist sympathies were discovered. In his anger he had taken copies of the papers with him. There was no further proof of this, until Owens offered another meeting in Lisbon. He brought with him the embittered Squadron Leader Brown, who was hoping to reach Moscow via Berlin.[12]

The Abwehr had ceased to doubt 'Johnny' by then. Every item of his intelligence tallied with what they had gathered elsewhere. He soon became an organizer of the German espionage network in England. Most agents gave themselves away within days or hours of landing but Owens saved some of them. In the late summer of 1940, two men arrived by parachute, Hans Hansen and Goesta Caroli. They had intended to land near Salisbury. When they broke radio silence it was to warn Hamburg that the Heinkel bomber had dropped them sixty-five miles away, north of Oxford. Caroli's parachute had caught in a tree and he had broken his ankle. They were hiding in farm buildings, Caroli unable to move. By the next afternoon, a rendezvous had been made by Owens and kept at High Wycombe railway station. Caroli was taken away and nursed.

Hansen continued to transmit from a house north of London, at Barnet. He listed factories destroyed in the blitz of 1940–41, construction work at airfields, and the dispositions of the RAF. From Wye in Kent, he observed and reported the movements of Canadian and US troops before the invasion of Normandy in 1944.[13]

When money ran low in 1941, Hansen was told to board a number 16 bus from Victoria station at 4 p.m. on 26 October, wearing a red tie, carrying a newspaper and umbrella. He would see another man similarly equipped. Both would get off at the fifth stop. They would board the next bus and sit together. As instructed, Hansen then asked the stranger with *The Times*, 'Anything interesting in the paper today?' 'You may have it,' the man said, 'I'm getting off at the next stop.' The money was wrapped in the paper. The stranger was assistant military attaché at the Japanese embassy, with whose country England was not at war for a further six weeks.[14]

It seemed appropriate that an agent as skilled as Hansen should have been the last to receive a message from Hamburg on 2 May 1945, the day before the city surrendered to the British XII Corps of the Second Army. However, his grateful patrons never knew that Hansen, like Owens, had for years been under British control. The information in Hansen's messages, composed for him, was a skilful blend of what military intelligence judged the Germans already knew by such means as aerial reconnaissance and fresh items which would not add much of importance. Among all this, the 'news' of troop movements in Kent had been planted to reinforce German belief that the D-Day landing would be in the Pas de Calais, rather than Normandy. As for the rabidly anti-English Arthur Owens, he had a second code name, 'Snow', under which he first gathered intelligence for the British Admiralty, which had passed him on to MI6 at the beginning of 1936. Not a single German agent landing in England during the war remained at liberty. It was, in one view, the greatest triumph in the history of espionage since the exultant Trojans led the wooden horse into Troy.[15]

German agents who arrived by parachute or boat to work for Owens were arrested within days or hours. Their lives lay in the hands of the Double Cross Committee. Those who were useful and willing were turned and worked for their captors, as Hansen had done. Those, like Josef Jacobs, who loyally spurned the invitation or failed to be useful, stood their trial and went to execution. Their well-publicized fates assured the public of the sleepless vigilance of the nation's counter-espionage branch.

Trust did not exist in an underworld of this kind. For British military intelligence to work on the assumption that even Owens might be guilty of treachery was a natural precaution. When he first volunteered to collect pre-war intelligence, it was discovered that he was already in touch with Postbox 629 at Hamburg. He was able to persuade his MI6 mentors that he had done this to establish a channel of information for their use. Nonetheless, when he kept a rendezvous with a Special Branch contact at Waterloo station, the day after war was declared, the contact promptly arrested him. Owens had handed over his German transmitter for inspection by the branch, but his first messages to Ritter were sent under supervision from a cell in Wandsworth prison.

As for the treacherous RAF squadron leader who accompanied Owens to Lisbon, he was an Air Intelligence Officer from the previous war, now operating for MI5 under the code name 'Celery'. The

THE MISFITS

earlier fiasco with the trawler in the North Sea was caused by the presence of a second agent on board, a man with a record of petty larceny, drug smuggling and confidence tricks, but now adopted by the Double Cross Committee as a secret agent. This man, code-named 'Biscuit', and Owens each became convinced during the trawler's short voyage that the other was a genuine German spy. There was a confrontation, as a result of which Owens ordered the vessel back to England. As for the promise of sabotage and insurrection by Welsh nationalists, it was never anything more than German self-deception.

The reality of domestic sabotage and treachery ranged from the melodramatic to the absurd. Proceedings were routinely held in camera. Among the more sensitive revelations were those at the trial in November 1940 of Tyler Kent, a cipher clerk at the US Embassy, and Anna Wolkoff, a Russian émigrée, whose father had been naval attaché at the Imperial Russian Embassy before the Communist revolution. The family ran the Russian Tea-Rooms in Kensington. Kent had been a cipher clerk in Moscow, transferred in October 1939 to the staff of the ambassador in London, Joseph Kennedy. Both he and Anna Wolkoff were members of the so-called Right Club, founded before the war, as a Fascist pressure group, by the Member of Parliament for Peebles, Captain Archibald Ramsay, soon to be interned as a security risk under Section 18B of the Defence Regulations.

MI5 had placed its agents in the Right Club before the war and in 1940 a new operation was carried out, supervised by Captain Maxwell Knight in conjunction with the Special Branch. It was known that Anna Wolkoff was in touch, through a female courier, with neutral embassies sympathetic to Germany, and that she had socialized with the Italian assistant naval attaché immediately before his country's entry into the war.

In the spring of 1940 she was in contact with Germany through the Romanian Embassy in London. Her messages were carried there by a female courier, who was a fellow member of the Right Club and had been planted some years before by MI5. On 10 April, Miss Wolkoff handed a letter to this courier, addressed to Herr W. B. Joyce at the Rundfunkhaus, Berlin. The envelope was opened, the message read, and then allowed to continue on its way. It advised William Joyce of the effect in England of his broadcasts from Berlin. He should avoid praising the IRA or attacking the King. There was other news of which he might make better use.

> Churchill not popular – keep on at him as Baruch tool and war-theatre extender, sacrificer Gallipoli etc. Stress his repeated failures with expense lives and prestige . . . Butter ration doubled because poor can't buy . . . bacon same. Cost living steeply mounting. Shopkeepers suffering. Acknowledge this by Carlyle reference radio. Reply same channel, same cipher.

William Joyce, as an adult part-time student, had been awarded a first-class honours degree by London University in English language and literature. His literary hero was Thomas Carlyle. A few days after Anna Wolkoff sent her message, acknowledgement of safe receipt came over the airwaves from Berlin in the voice of Lord Haw-Haw. 'We thank the French for nothing. Where is their Shakespeare? Where is their Carlyle?'[16]

With proof that Anna Wolkoff had access to Berlin and that Tyler Kent had undoubted access to secret information sent to Washington through the US Embassy, Max Knight asked for an interview with Joseph Kennedy to explain that MI5 proposed to seek a warrant for the arrest of Tyler Kent. Kennedy, dismayed by this account of Kent's treachery, withdrew his cipher clerk's diplomatic immunity. When Kent was arrested, his flat in Gloucester Place was searched, and stolen copies of some 1,500 diplomatic telegrams were found, including those exchanged between President Roosevelt and Winston Churchill, still First Lord of the Admiralty. These were among the papers which Kent admitted lending to Anna Wolkoff. Any or all of them might now be in the possession of German intelligence. Cryptographers on both sides were puzzled by Churchill's habit of ending his messages with the letters 'KBO'. It seems likely that Roosevelt himself never recognized this Churchillian abbreviation for the encouragement to 'Keep buggering on'. At their trials, Tyler Kent was sent to prison for seven years and Anna Wolkoff for ten years. It was by far the worst breach of security of its kind.

Sabotage and treachery were never unimportant but there was a distinction to be made between Fascist zealots and crackpots or idlers. The zealous Anna Wolkoff had been busy organizing a Right Club 'sticky-back' campaign. Under cover of the blackout she and her supporters advertised their views by means of messages on adhesive labels and the use of grease paint to deface directions to ARP centres, medical posts or shelters. Sticky-backs were to be pasted on Belisha beacons, lamp-posts, phone kiosks, hoardings or bus stops – but not on walls because the glue was not strong enough for rough surfaces. The messages were predictable.

> This is a Jews' war . . . Lend to defend the rights of British manhood to die in a foreign war every twenty-five years . . . Don't be selfish. Save for shells and slaughter . . . Just remember your savings are much more wisely spent in the noble cause of death and destruction. Come on the first million pounds.[17]

Ironically, those who were closest to hand in the darkness were often the Communists, slapping their own anti-war propaganda on retentive surfaces. The messages might be few and far between but they had sufficient effect to frighten London Transport which, at the beginning of 1941, banned the distribution of all leaflets at tube shelters for fear of 'the passing on of subversive propaganda'. It was no secret that the Communist Party of Great Britain not only leafleted shelterers but aimed to get its members appointed as shelter marshals.

CID officers like Reginald Spooner, Major Spooner of MI5 for the rest of the war, confronted the more threatening cases of sabotage. In October 1940, at the end of one of his first investigations, a thirty-nine-year-old fitter was sent to penal servitude for four years for sabotage of planes at the Bristol Aeroplane Company. Spooner also investigated shipyard sabotage at Barrow-in-Furness in September 1940, followed by sabotage of the liner *Queen Elizabeth* in March 1941 and of warships in Scapa Flow soon after. It was thought significant that these incidents occurred at a time when the Communist as well as the Fascist party was in absolute opposition to the war. Despite the protests of one of its best-known leaders and MP for Stepney, Phil Piratin, the Communist Party of Great Britain had obediently decreed that this was an imperialist war whose victims were the working class of all nations.[18]

At another extreme, in February 1941 Dorothy Pamela O'Grady of Sandown, Isle of Wight, was sentenced to death under the Treachery Act 1940, which provided for the death penalty in cases of espionage or sabotage. The press seized on her as a 'traitress'. The acts she had committed were to draw a plan 'likely to assist enemy military operations' and to sabotage a telephone wire in the hope of impeding 'the operation of His Majesty's Forces', though there was no evidence that she had communicated with the enemy. Despite her treasonable activities, she showed a resolve similar to that of women who swore to resist Nazi storm troopers with hatpins and knitting needles. A traitress might also be mentally unbalanced. Her sentence on appeal was fourteen years' penal servitude for breaching Defence Regulations.[19]

At Manchester in May 1941, a man accused of sabotage by damaging parts of vehicles being assembled for the Ministry of Supply said to the police, 'I think the war is wrong and if I could do anything to stop it I would.' In the following month another man went to prison for three months and was fined £20 because he had tried to slow down production by making wage demands and attempting to organize a strike. The delay in work caused 'a violent explosion'. He proclaimed himself a socialist and anti-Fascist.[20]

A few instances were sabotage by any description. A young woman who worked at Imperial Metal Industries (Kynoch) Ltd was prosecuted under the Treachery Act at Birmingham in 1942. She was employed on the assembly line of a new and secret incendiary bullet for the RAF. Her acts of sabotage were to leave screws out of some of the bullets, risking an explosion in any plane that fired them. She was not unique. In 1943, a Lincolnshire woman was found to be deliberately assembling RAF shell fuses incorrectly so that they would blow out backwards in the breech block of a gun and wreck the aircraft. Resentment, rather than politics, was her motive and she was sent to prison for six months.

In the Birmingham case, however, the defendant had expressed pro-German views and her boyfriend had been detained for a while as a Fascist, under Regulation 18B. She had pilfered ammunition, supplied bullets to him, but was charged additionally and rather curiously with stealing a cup and saucer from Kynoch's. The couple were tried in camera, the press excluded, the frosted glass windows of

Birmingham Assize Court blacked out. However Mr Justice Croom-Johnson was unimpressed by the use of treachery legislation, which might carry the death penalty, in dealing with a pair of simple delinquents. He warned the prosecutor that he would 'make short work of it'. The only charge that could be sustained was the theft of Kynoch's cup and saucer.[21]

Other charges reflected little more than bloody-mindedness. Among these, in February 1942 a Berkshire man won his appeal against a conviction of sabotage. In a fit of temper, he had wrenched at an aluminium rail on an aircraft and damaged the wood to which it was attached. The court found the act 'grossly careless' but with 'no deliberate intent'. In December 1942, an NFS man at Oldham was charged with sabotage after breaking the gauges on a hot-water pipe and cutting a vehicle petrol pipe, when he was not allowed a clerical job. At Birmingham in March 1943, a jig-tool borer went to prison for three months for committing sabotage to have time off to play darts. He had cut the fuse wire and smoked the porcelain with his cigarette lighter to make it seem that the wire had fused. While this apparent fault was investigated, there was no work for him to do.[22]

Perhaps the most curious charge of wartime sabotage was committed to Hampshire Assizes in June 1943. Six Irish workmen were charged with conspiring 'to impair the efficiency of a concrete mixer' while on essential military repairs at Aldershot. They had thrown into the mixer a starting handle, a block of solid concrete, an unopened bag of cement and had then started the engine. The contractor's agent reported that 'the men have since worked 172 hours in cleaning out the mixer, which is still out of action.' The reason for their behaviour had been a dispute over the travel vouchers which they needed to visit their families in Ireland. As the nearest equipment to hand, the concrete mixer became the victim of their frustration. The Army's pristine concrete had been allowed to dry with boldly incised messages, 'Up the IRA!' and 'The Rebel Gang From Ireland Want Their Vouchers!'[23]

No wartime organization adopted the methods of criminal enterprise more readily than the IRA. Bank robbery, police murder, wage snatches, as well as a brisk trade in guns and explosives, were its hallmark. Operating against Britain from neutral territory, it courted Germany in the hope of dealing with Hitler as victor 'on equal terms'. Disowned by the Irish government, loathed in Britain, despised by the Germans, whose Abwehr called it 'a dead loss' and 'useless', the IRA combined occasional flair with chronic incompetence. The top secret 'S-Plan', outlining the entire strategy of a mainland campaign in 1939, was in the hands of Special Branch ten days after the first explosions. Another search yielded a coded message and the code book for deciphering it, kept conveniently together in an unlocked drawer. Yet the IRA in 1941–3 was to have an impact in Ireland disproportionate to its numerical strength or support.

Most galling to these guerrillas were the thousands of Irishmen who, with no call upon them to do so, served with the British armed forces. Indeed, those forces included one Irishman second only to Churchill in popularity as a war leader, Field Marshal Sir Bernard Montgomery. When invited to an England v. Scotland soccer international as guest of honour, he explained proudly that he could only come as a 'neutral'. In its dealings with belligerents, the refusal of the Dublin government to allow British access to bases on its territory was much publicized, while facilities for the Royal Observer Corps to be stationed on the Irish coast, and for British pilots to find their way home while German airmen were interned, were not.

The prelude to IRA wartime activities was an 'ultimatum' of 12 January 1939 to the British Prime Minister, with copies to the Foreign Secretary, the government of Northern Ireland, Hitler and Mussolini. The authors, describing themselves as 'The Government of the Irish Republic', stipulated that unless British troops were removed from Ireland within four days and an 'abdication' of power was promised by Britain, a state of war would exist.

The first explosions in mainland Britain occurred on 16 January 1939 and the last in March 1940. The campaign began badly. On the night of 16 January there were attempts to disrupt the electricity supply across the country and one man was killed in Manchester. By 18 January, the police had caught the guardians of the major arms dump in the city. Eight men were convicted in March and five went to penal servitude for twenty years, among shouts of 'God Save Ireland!'

Over a hundred mainland incidents involved explosions or arson, or attempts at these. There were devices intended to bring down the bridge carrying the Grand Junction Canal across the North Circular, to blow up Hammersmith Bridge, Mount Pleasant sorting office, the cloakrooms of Victoria and King's Cross stations, and failed plans to bomb the Bank of England and the Royal Exchange. Most explosions were on a smaller scale, intended to destroy telephone kiosks or unmanned electricity sub-stations, or to damage public lavatories and underground station cloakrooms. Gelignite was used but Hammersmith Bridge and other targets survived because those who planted the bombs had little knowledge of their structure.

Explosions at electricity sub-stations and the destruction of pylons had an immediate but temporary effect. So did the placing of bombs at ground level immediately above telephone cables. Elsewhere, despite the pledge of the S-Plan not to take innocent lives, there was injury and death. A passer-by lost an eye in the Piccadilly Circus explosion and a young doctor was killed by the bomb at King's Cross. A number of devices did not explode because their cheap alarm clocks failed before the time at which they were set. On the night of 24 June, when the bomb exploded in Piccadilly Circus, Robert Fabian was a Detective Inspector in the Vice Squad. The blast shook the windows of Vine Street police station and sent a gust of hot air through the building. Fabian snatched his gas mask, issued in the approach of war, and ran to the scene. He saw another brown paper parcel behind a traffic light and carefully unwrapped this second bomb. By laying out sticks of gelignite at intervals on the pavement, he reduced the risk that one might detonate the next. He slowly cut the fuse out of the gelignite with his penknife. Finally he separated the sticks, carried them to Vine Street and dropped each into a separate fire bucket.

No government responded to the IRA's January ultimatum, but in the summer of 1939 British and Irish parliaments turned from the imminent European war to deal with the crisis at home. The Irish parliament passed an Offences Against the State Act in June 1939. This made it punishable by ten years' penal servitude to attempt to usurp the functions of the elected government. It empowered that government to suppress illegal organizations and forbade the maintaining of any armed force. The British parliament's Prevention of

Violence (Temporary Provisions) Act, in July, gave the police powers to arrest and detain suspects for forty-eight hours, in special cases for five days, while seeking a deportation order. Previously, an arrest could not be made until a deportation order was granted.

The worst incident of the mainland campaign occurred in Coventry on 25 August 1939, though it was not the first explosion in the city. On 23 March, four bombs above GPO telephone cables had wrecked a thousand local lines, including many connected to armaments industries. Following this, two IRA men lodged at a house in Clara Street to make a bomb powerful enough to destroy an electricity sub-station. A third man was put in command. This man completed the bomb and collected it at lunchtime on Friday 25 August, market day in Coventry. The others were told it would be used at the electricity station that evening. The third man put the bomb in his bicycle carrier and pedalled to the shopping centre of Broadgate. He left the device in its carrier, the cycle resting on the kerb of a busy pavement in front of a parked car, a few feet from the plate-glass windows of Montague Burton, the tailors.

At 2.32 that afternoon, there was a flash of light followed by dense clouds of rolling black smoke and a thunderous explosion as the bomb went off with terrible effect. Five people were killed, including an old man of eighty-one, a schoolboy of fifteen and a young woman who was to have been married in a fortnight. More than fifty people were injured, twelve of them severely. It was only nine days before the outbreak of war with Germany and witnesses at first thought this was a sneak air raid because a bomber was flying overhead. The street was ankle-deep in lethal shards of glass, shopfronts had caved in, their contents blown into the roadway, and the injured lay where they had fallen.

The two men from Clara Street were arrested. Peter Barnes was found in London and Frank McCormack, who called himself 'Frank Richards', was detained in Coventry. They and the three occupants of the house were tried for murder at Birmingham Assizes in December. The others were acquitted but Barnes and Richards were found guilty. Their appeal against conviction was dismissed and they were hanged in Winson Green prison on 7 February 1940, despite a plea to the Prime Minister from his Irish counterpart, Eamon De

Valera. From the dock, Barnes and Richards made the speeches of Irish martyrs who had done their duty, but they were not the type of the ruthless bomber or gunman. They had thought the target was an electricity station with little risk of death or injury. They had been the dupes of the psychopathic 'stranger', still under psychiatric care in 1970, who committed the worst atrocity of the mainland campaign and left them to face the consequences.[24]

By July 1940, ninety-four IRA men and women had been convicted of possessing or using explosives or possessing firearms. Two had been convicted of murder. Eighty-three were sent to penal servitude, four were given prison terms, five were sent to Borstal, two were bound over, and the two men involved in the Coventry explosion were hanged. On 18 March 1940, an unexploded IRA bomb had been found in a Grosvenor Square litter bin and there was an explosion at a Westminster City refuse dump where litter was being dealt with. These were the last shots in the mainland campaign.

During this period the Chief of Staff of the IRA was Sean Russell, who had been appointed to its executive in March 1922, as the IRA and the first government of Eire parted company. Russell, frequently on the run, was imprisoned for three months in 1928 after an arms dump was found at his house in Dublin. In 1939, he had gone to the United States to justify the mainland campaign. He failed to win support. Indeed, the American government expelled him in September 1939. However, Russell delayed his departure until the spring of 1940 when, with the agreement of the German government, he sailed to Genoa and was taken by car to Berlin.

In the 1920s, there had been short-lived attempts to align the IRA with revolutionary Communism. By the end of the 1930s no one outside a lunatic asylum could believe that Hitler held dear the well-being and independence of small nations, but Russell saw no other ally. Having made his case in Berlin, he was to return to Ireland by U-boat. The U-boat sailed from Wilhelmshaven on 8 August 1940 with Russell and one other agent. On the voyage, Russell fell ill with acute stomach pains and the medical orderly could do nothing for him. A peptic ulcer had burst and he died at sea on 14 August, to be buried with full military honours, wrapped in a German flag.

At home, the IRA's finances were exhausted, if its morale was not.

Fund-raising became armed robbery. On 18 November 1939, the target was Amiens Street post office in Dublin, which yielded £5,000 (£200,000). On 22 November, the National Bank in Clonliffe Road was robbed, though only £200 (£8,000) was taken. The money was enough for the time being. A year later, following a Dublin gunfight between police and IRA, plans of the main Dublin banks were found, drawn as a preliminary to another series of raids.

As hope of a German victory withered, the IRA turned to Ulster, an easier target than the mainland. Members of the Dail had warned the De Valera government of a Fifth Column of IRA men, paid and organized by German intelligence. Now, it was said, these agents had penetrated Northern Ireland. By 29 January 1941, members of the Dublin government were certain that the aim of German policy was to cause a major rift in Anglo-Irish cooperation.

A new phase of armed robbery in Ulster began on 25 March 1942 with a raid on the Academy Civil Defence Headquarters in Belfast and the theft of a payroll worth some £4,200 (£168,000). These funds financed war on the streets of Belfast and in the towns of the North. Three days later, gunmen opened fire on the police and on a civilian crowd in West Belfast. On 4 April, in Dungannon, one policeman was shot dead and another wounded. On 5 April, another policeman was murdered on the street in Belfast and six teenage gunmen were arrested for the crime. They were convicted and were just old enough to be executed, but to hang all six seemed politically impossible. Only Thomas Williams was executed. His death provoked further disorder in which police patrols in the city were routinely fired on by 'IRA gunmen', some sixteen or seventeen years old and too young to be in danger of hanging.

On 5 September 1942, two more policemen were shot dead in County Tyrone, their killers escaping over the border into Eire, while police searching the Falls Road and Springfield Road area of Belfast came under concentrated fire from an air raid shelter. One of the gunmen, nineteen years old, was found wounded in the stomach, legs and wrist. On the same day another sixteen-year-old was arrested after a gunfight with police and yet another when an arms dump was raided. The only answer to the IRA, said the Londonderry magistrate, was 'straight shooting'. Demands were made for the gunmen to be tried by military tribunals, known as 'death courts' because the death sentence was the only one they were empowered to pass. Even as this suggestion was heard, three gunmen with revolvers and sub-machine guns shot dead one of the Dublin Castle guards. Violence knew no frontier between north and south.

The danger in Belfast was not only from gunfire on the streets or from armed robbery but from a general threat to public order. In October 1942, a night-time curfew was imposed in West Belfast. Headline stories of police murder and gangsters declined, only to be replaced in 1943 by dramatic escapes from prison. On 15 January, the IRA leader Hugh McAteer, serving a sentence of fifteen years, escaped with three others from Crumlin Road gaol. They climbed through a trapdoor in the ceiling of the latrines, broke out on to the roof, and scaled the prison wall with ropes made of sheets. Two fugitives were free for two years, one for two months, and McAteer for eight months.

McAteer next aided the escape of IRA men in Londonderry gaol in March. They had been digging a tunnel under the prison and the road outside. While McAteer provided transport, they escaped through the tunnel to the coal hole of a house on the far side of the road. To the astonishment of the family at breakfast on 21 March, twenty-one men appeared from the ground. Fifteen of them were taken by lorry to Eire, where they were interned.

A further IRA propaganda coup was planned for Easter weekend 1943. On Saturday 24 April, McAteer, with an accomplice and sixteen armed volunteers, commandeered the Broadway cinema near the Falls Road and kept its audience captive while a ceremony was held to commemorate the 1916 Easter Rising and its martyrs. It was McAteer's intention to let the press know that he was still active 'within a mile of the city centre'.

Prison breaks and anniversaries were no substitute for money and recruits. The IRA, characterized in the British press as Gestapo agents, was now irrelevant to the course of the war. Germany could do nothing and, anyway, the Abwehr thought Irish republicanism a waste of time. The last, most dramatic attack was a payroll robbery on 1 October 1943 at Clonhard Mill, Odessa Street, off the Falls Road. During this, another policeman was shot dead. It was a memorable tragedy, reflected by the human image of the IRA at war in F. L. Green's fine novel, *Odd Man Out*. As a drama of the last hours of a wounded Belfast gunman after a failed robbery, it was popularized in Carol Reed's screen version, hailed by the *New Statesman* in 1945 as the most imaginative film ever made in England. The film bore powerful witness to the idealism no less than to the duplicity of the armed struggle.

Once the war was over, the agents of the defeated powers became little more than a courtroom curiosity, whose activities had ranged from persistent subversion to self-righteous treason. Before the fall of France in 1940, however, it was felt better that Fascists in England should remain where they could be seen and heard. On 6 November 1939, for example, Mrs Margaret Griggs, Chairman of the Women's Organization of the British Union of Fascists, was merely bound over for twelve months after speaking in Limehouse from behind a police cordon. 'If ever a country wants a revolution now it is Great Britain,' she shouted, while the East End crowd jeered her party with cries of 'Dirty spies!' 'Dirty Germans!' and 'Go home to Hitler!'[25]

In another case, two girls of sixteen and seventeen, arrested while selling the Fascist paper *Action* in Shoreditch High Street on 4 January 1940, were charged with using insulting words. They too had been rescued by the police from 'a crowd of hostile men'. Though the younger girl shouted 'Hail Mosley!' at the magistrate and gave the Fascist salute, they were bound over for two years and released on condition that they ceased selling the paper.[26]

The situation was transformed by the Emergency Powers (Defence) Act, passed on 22 May 1940, the day that British troops evacuated Arras and the 1st and 2nd Armoured Divisions of the Wehrmacht advanced within striking distance of Calais and Boulogne. Next day, uniformed police, Special Branch and CID raided the headquarters of the BUF in Smith Street, Westminster. Seven officials were arrested and vanloads of documents were taken away.

Those arrested and interned without trial included Sir Oswald and Lady Mosley, and Captain Ramsay, the MP for Midlothian and Peebles, a founder with William Joyce and others of the pre-war Right Club. During the following weekend, as Boulogne and Calais fell and the Dunkirk evacuation began, the CID began to round up Fascist and Communist open-air activists. A man selling *Action* in Croydon town centre on Saturday was arrested after several people threatened him. A woman snatched the papers, tore them up, and threw them at him. He was carrying a revolver and seven rounds of ammunition. 'When the Germans get here, they will show you how to run Croydon,' he said.

At another open-air meeting, Inspector Carter arrested the speaker Douglas Hyde, also circulation manager of the *Daily Worker*, and was cheered by the crowd at Ealing. 'I have never been cheered before when making an arrest,' he said modestly. A Communist speaker at Edgware was rescued from angry servicemen and gaoled for three months. Another, at Hyde Park Corner, was led away among shouts of 'People like you are Quislings!'[27]

Fascist claims to have an effective 'underground' network were for the most part nonsense. However, the courts began to sentence them as if this were the truth. On 25 June 1941, Mr Justice Humphreys sent Elsie Orrin, a schoolteacher, to penal servitude for five years. She had said to soldiers in a Little Easton public house, 'Hitler is a good ruler, a better man than Mr Churchill.' She denounced the Jews, attacked the Churchill government, and criticized the soldiers for not being men enough to 'kick it out'. The soldiers reported her to the police. When they raided her home, they found a portrait of Sir Oswald Mosley. She said to them, 'I am proud to belong to the British Union.'[28]

Five years was not the longest sentence. In April 1943 a twenty-eight-year-old farm labourer from Gloucestershire, a member of the outlawed BUF, was accused of attempting to communicate with a person whom he had 'reasonable cause to believe was assisting the enemy'. As the 'person' was the German Minister in Dublin, it was hard to see how he could believe otherwise. The labourer had been twice interned but released in April 1941 on condition of good behaviour. In December 1942 he wrote to the Home Secretary that Mussolini's biography had reconverted him to Fascism. He also wrote to the German Minister in Dublin offering his services, a letter whose address absolutely guaranteed that it would be opened by the postal censorship. He had previously written to the War Ministry in Berlin in 1938 making the same offer to 'place my services and my life at the disposal of the Reich and to eventually earn the honour of becoming a German citizen'.

To complete his postal hat-trick, the defendant then added a crack-brained letter to Winston Churchill. 'I demand that you immediately make way for the one man who is really fit for the position you hold. Oswald Mosley can and will save the British Empire.' He might as well have named Adolf Hitler. For this bizarre round of correspondence, the young man was sentenced to penal servitude for life. His appeal against sentence was dismissed.[29]

In parallel with Fascist subversion lay the spreading of 'alarm and despondency', a criminal offence under the Defence Regulations. Even by 25 July 1940 almost a hundred people had been arrested for expressing defeatist views. They were matched by careless talkers, also subject to prosecution or reprimand. In February 1940, Ealing Studios were commissioned to make short 'anti-gossip' films, starring John Mills and other famous faces, under such titles as *Miss Nobody Spoke in a Café*. In April 1941, a government scientist, Dr Richard Beatty, was so efficiently advised about his careless talking by a sergeant of the Special Branch that he was found dead the next day.

Careless talk combined readily with 'despondency'. In May 1943 Edward Ryan, inventor of anti-submarine devices used by the Admiralty, was sent to prison for a month. He had told other firewatchers in Liverpool of his uncensored letters to the British Embassy in Madrid, revealing that the last five convoys from Liverpool had lost two hundred ships between them. To this he added, 'The last shots in this war will be fired in 1949. Germany will form a government similar to Russia and the two of them will overrun this country.' The statement was said to have caused great distress to those who heard it.[30]

Many offenders had no allegiance to Fascist or Communist politics. Mrs Dorothy Rycraft of Wood Green was accused in April 1941 of 'deliberately and persistently publishing statements with the object of stirring up trouble and causing despondency and alarm among women'. She had said to a Wood Green housewives' club, 'We will never win the war. We are going to be invaded. If the women meet a poor German they're not going to be hard on him. We are going to starve, not the Germans.' She added that food rations were insufficient and 'the poorer classes are going short while people with money can get what they want'. She urged the club to march on the town hall and demand better rations, then she incited further 'discontent' by asking why the government had not built deep shelters to protect the population.[31]

Truth or falsehood of opinion was not an issue in such cases. There was ample evidence of inequality of sacrifice between rich and poor. The belief that Britain was not going to win the war was widespread in the world at large. The growing success of the U-boat fleet, as *Bismarck* and *Prinz Eugen* prepared to enter the Atlantic in its support, justified a fear of starvation. That month, the Germans had occupied Yugoslavia and the British Army had evacuated the Greek mainland, fearful of 'another Dunkirk'. On the day Mrs Rycraft was fined £50 (£2,000), Rommel's Afrika Korps seized the Halfaya Pass and opened the way into Egypt. Yet such talk was resented and fists were apt to fly. One Londoner that month heard defeatism spoken behind him. He turned round and punched the culprit to the ground, only to find that he had hit the wrong man. He was fined ten shillings (£20) and ordered to pay £5 (£200) compensation.[32]

To judge public attitudes, Duff Cooper as Minister of Information sent out his pollsters to question the people, only to have these inquirers ungratefully dubbed 'Cooper's Snoopers'. Often the disaffected asserted that Germany rather than Britain told the truth. In March 1940, the BBC had published a report based on interviews with a random sample of 34,000 people. A quarter had listened to Lord Haw-Haw the day before and two-thirds listened to Radio Hamburg from time to time – 29 per cent in order to hear the German point of view and 26 per cent to hear the news their own side did not give them. Only 15 per cent thought the Hamburg broadcasts 'rubbish'.

On 20 November 1941 an American citizen once married to a German, Elizabeth Marion Hayward, went into a Brighton store. There she was guilty of 'publishing to Grace Richardson and Reginald Chapple a statement relating to matters . . . likely to cause despondency'. In conversation with a shop assistant, she said, 'We do not get true news in the newspapers because journalists are all crooks, whereas in Germany the press is under the control of one person, and the German press is always true. You always get true news from the German wireless.' She believed Germany would win and that Russia was finished. The German army could enter Moscow when it chose. The manager joined the discussion and she told him, 'You should listen to Lord Haw-Haw.'

When arrested, Mrs Hayward said, 'I am very sorry I allowed myself to be drawn into this little discussion with my friend here. Everybody talked about the war a little, but perhaps I talked a little more. Americans are apt to give their opinion more freely than English people. They consider themselves free, free country, free speech, and of course one forgets there's a war on.' Sitting at Hove on 14 January 1942, Brighton Borough Bench fined her £25 (£1,000) with the alternative of three months' imprisonment. The facts were to be placed before the Regional Commissioner.

On 23 March, she was in court again at Hove. Restrictions had been put on her movements after the previous conviction but on 21 February she had got into conversation with an army officer in a Hove café. She told him it was Britain's fault the country was at war. Then she expressed admiration for Hitler and his regime, adding that Germany would defeat Russia in the spring and would then invade England, which would have little chance of survival. She was fined £50 (£2,000) for her offence but also sent to hard labour for a month.[33]

There was continuing disaffection among those who, as late as 1943, wanted a negotiated peace. A middle-aged civil servant was fined in June that year after pleading guilty to chalking graffiti on the blinds of Southern Railway trains. 'Durable peace can be obtained only by negotiation,' he wrote. 'Ask the King to call an armistice now. W.C.M.G.' To readers of slogans W.C.M.G. was familiar shorthand for 'Winston Churchill Must Go'. By then, however, the great fear of 'despondency' had passed and Oliver Ward was merely fined £2 (£80) for defacing the property of the Southern Railway.[34]

The traitors' reckoning came in the aftermath of war. Justice was not done in every case, but it was not the Roman holiday of vengeance seen in many parts of occupied Europe, which some wished for in England. Thirty-one British defendants and three Canadian soldiers faced trial. Charges ranged from assisting the enemy to high treason. Most were prisoners of war who agreed to help Germany by broadcasting from Berlin, or were persuaded by John Amery to join the British unit of the SS, 'The Legion of St George', with its Union

Jack flashes and mess-hall portrait of the Duke of Windsor. Others were civilian broadcasters from Berlin who required no persuasion. Those assisting the enemy were charged under Section 2A of the Defence (General) Regulations 1939 and were liable to penal servitude for life. Others, tried for high treason or treachery, faced the death penalty. Sentences passed ranged from execution to discharge subject to being bound over for two years.

Four men were tried for treason, and one was court-martialled for treachery, all of them convicted and sentenced to death. Two of those convicted of treason were reprieved. Theodore Schurch, a regular British Army soldier of Swiss descent, who deserted at Tobruk and volunteered to assist enemy intelligence, was hanged after a court martial. John Amery, scapegrace son of a member of Churchill's War Cabinet, Leo Amery, was also hanged. Having fought for Franco, John Amery had made his way to Germany to persuade British prisoners to fight the Bolshevik menace on the Eastern Front, in his 'Legion of St George' or 'British Free Corps'. Neither unit ever saw action or was taken seriously by its German patrons.

The third man hanged was the most famous and his trial the most controversial. William Joyce was born in Brooklyn of American parents in 1906. His father, naturalized eight years earlier, and his mother on marriage in 1905, were born in Ireland but were American citizens under British and United States law. Though he lived in England most of his life, William Joyce never took British nationality. However, he fraudulently obtained a British passport in 1933, using it only to escape to Germany in 1939. It was argued that he had enjoyed the protection of the British Crown. He took German nationality on 26 September 1940, when the country of his birth was still neutral. By the Naturalization Act 1870 and the British Nationality and Status of Aliens Act 1914, Joyce in 1945 was a natural-born American citizen and a German citizen since September 1940. Under international law, an alien was regarded as owing allegiance to a country's laws while on its territory. That allegiance to Britain ceased for Joyce when he left for Berlin on 26 August 1939.

He appeared guilty of fraud rather than of the three counts of treason with which he was charged. On two of these, alleging that he was a British citizen, the judge directed the jury to acquit him. The third count alleged that Joyce committed treason by broadcasting from 18 September 1939 to 2 July 1940, while still owing 'allegiance' to George VI by virtue of a fraudulent passport. However, the BBC monitoring service could not identify any of his broadcasts before 2 August 1940. The sole evidence for that period came from Detective Inspector Albert Hunt of the Special Branch. He had heard Joyce speak before the war and had been monitoring broadcasts in the autumn of 1939. He could not say to what station he had been listening, nor which country, nor could he say when, except that it was September or early October 1939. No one else had been with him to corroborate the impression that this was Joyce speaking.

Until 1945, Inspector Hunt's evidence would have proved nothing. In so grave a crime, the Treason Act of 1697, amending the Statute of Treasons 1351, required two acts of treason witnessed by one person or one act witnessed by two people. Under these provisions, Joyce would have been acquitted. Yet in June 1945 a new Treason Act was passed, assimilating the procedure in treason cases to that in cases of murder. Joyce was kept in Germany until the Act was law and brought back to England next day to be charged under its new provisions.

Convicted on the third count, by virtue of Inspector Hunt's uncorroborated evidence, Joyce appealed unsuccessfully to the Court of Criminal Appeal and the House of Lords. He was hanged on 3 January 1946. To some, his broadcasts were a mockery of their suffering. Those who confessed to pollsters that they liked to hear their leaders satirized, found his performances one of the funniest things on radio. Joyce himself appeared a bully and a braggart. The uncomfortable truth was that he also faced death with great courage and became a martyr for white supremacist organizations in the United States. They reprinted his polemic, *Twilight Over England* by 'Lord Haw-Haw', as if under the impression that he was not just a British citizen but a peer of the realm.

William Joyce was hanged because politicians believed public opinion would accept nothing less. They were mistaken. To most people he had been a joke, represented in the title of the Western Brothers' music-hall patter song of 1940, 'Lord Haw-Haw, the Humbug of Hamburg, the Comic of Eau-de-Cologne'. In the year of his death, a *Notable British Trials* volume dealing with his case recorded a public feeling, not that Joyce should have been reprieved, but that he should never have been convicted in the first place. His conviction and execution had caused 'more disquiet than satisfaction'.[35]

In other allegations of treason, notably against P. G. Wodehouse, common sense prevailed. As a British detainee in Germany, Wodehouse had broadcast for CBS to the neutral United States in August 1941. He did not broadcast to Britain nor on behalf of Germany. This did not prevent him being denounced as a traitor. Malcolm Muggeridge, the intelligence officer who had later detained Wodehouse in Paris, described Duff Cooper as leader of the pack who sought vengeance for the 1941 talks. But Wodehouse was released in Paris and went directly to America in 1947. Muggeridge believed that in the desire for a few sacrificial victims, Wodehouse would have 'fared ill' in a British court.[36]

The excitement of hunting out traitors closed the nation's account with the political underworld. Public relief at deliverance from war was tempered by scepticism that the worst was over on the Home Front. Peace brought with it the Supplies and Services (Transitional Powers) Act 1945. As the sounds of battle died away, the physical control of resources was to be reimposed in the name of new household gods: 'Austerity', 'Utility' and 'The Dollar Gap'.

16

'Sacrifice Was No Longer in Fashion'

'After the war' had been spoken of as a future of democratic plenty to be enjoyed by the warriors of 1939–45 as a matter of right. Even in the depths of defeat, crooners had promised 'a lovely day tomorrow', while government and press promoted an auction of promises. A welfare state would create a nation where the sick were nursed in their own homes and the elderly lived at leisure in 'state hotels'. In July 1945, responding to the new vision, the people had turned their backs on a discredited past and returned the first majority Labour government.

There was no lovely day tomorrow. Far more apt was Noël Coward's assurance of bad times just around the corner. As the war ended, Maynard Keynes and the Treasury warned of a 'financial Dunkirk'. An American loan was negotiated with difficulty. A dollar gap brought shortages and restrictions to 'Bankrupt Britannia'. Government and press now warned the nation to 'export or starve'.

Wartime controls were continued and rationing was stricter. In 1946, the Old Street magistrate threatened heavier penalties for black marketeering. 'People should know that they can still be sent for trial and get two years and that, before me, they can get twelve months.' In May 1947, when the North London magistrate sent a stallholder to prison for being in possession of 500lb of pork 'not purchased by the Ministry of Food', he invoked the example of countries where controls had broken down. 'There is nothing worse than this black market business. You see its effects in other countries like France and Italy. It is literally killing those countries and it is in order to stop this country sharing in that situation that no leniency can be shown in these cases.'[1]

The new government might complain of bad luck. Its election was one of the few occasions when the British seemed to vote in favour of

352

a party, rather than merely to punish the previous incumbents. In six years of Labour office, a brave new world of socialism was equated with shortages, regulations, interference, arrogant bureaucracy. The humour, hope and buoyancy of Winston Churchill yielded to the unhappy features of Clement Attlee and Stafford Cripps. With more money and fewer goods, it was necessary to take cash from the people's pockets by what seemed like taxation for its own sake. Austerity became a cardinal virtue, symbolized by an 'Austerity Ascot' in 1946.

'After the war' proved to be a time when food office inspectors, accompanied by police, stopped and searched cars at random without a warrant. Lord Woolton, for the Conservatives, warned the government to feed and heat Britain first, not to be 'too internationally minded'. By February 1946, London had one week's supply of coal left. Herbert Morrison spoke of striving to avert famine caused by the shortage of wheat. Yet in April the government felt obliged to divert six grain ships from Britain to feed Italy, Poland, Greece and Austria. March 1946 brought food riots in Hamburg, while the press insisted that Germans under British occupation were not starving. They were suspected of holding hidden stores of food and their bread was whiter than in Britain.

The British 'extraction rate' from wheat was raised in April, making bread darker and rougher. The weight of the standard loaf was cut, the 4lb loaf to 3.5lb and the 1lb loaf to 14oz. In May, the cheese ration was cut to 2oz a week. Three food ships 'racing' for Liverpool from Canada and New Zealand made national headlines. By 3 July, the country had only eight weeks' supply of grain and bread was rationed at 9oz a day on 21 July. It was banned from restaurant tables at lunchtime and undercover officers were sent out to enforce this. A ration of dried egg powder was introduced to enrich the national diet.

When the official celebrations of victory took place belatedly in London, at Whitsun 1946, the beer supply had been halved. Queues for bread, potatoes, meat and fish formed at 4.30 a.m. By 8 a.m. many shops had closed again, displaying 'sold out' signs or 'More bread at 4 o'clock – perhaps'.

Shortages were evident elsewhere. In November 1946, Aneurin Bevan remarked with grim irony of the house-building programme that if it had been a military operation 'you could introduce discipline into the whole thing and shoot a few builders who did not toe the line'. As for cosmetic frivolities like lotions, creams, rouges and lipsticks, they were available only 'under the counter' in Bond Street and the West End. However, the Board of Trade announced in April 1946 that frills on knickers, illegal since 1942, would be permitted, but this was only on the luxury kind and not on the Utility issue. Shops themselves remained under a wartime ban on display lighting.

There was worse to come. In June 1946, Herbert Morrison promised a 'grim and rough' 1947. On 6 December, the Minister of Food, John Strachey, revealed that supplies of wheat were now half what they had been a year before. In November, the bread supply in the British-occupied Ruhr was enough for only three more days. Counterfeiters and coupon robbers flexed their muscles again and guards rode with the coupon lorries in December. Yet neither Strachey nor Morrison could have predicted for 1946–7 one of the most bitter and miserable winters on record.

A domestic fuel ration had been imposed: fifteen hundredweight of coal or coke per household for three months. Ministry of Fuel 'flying squads' toured the streets to ensure equal distribution. Freezing weather and fuel shortages hit the electricity supply before Christmas. On 9 December, an evening power cut in London put five busy tube stations out of action. A more severe cut two days later affected much of the country, and left cities like Leeds with no power at all for most of the day. Two days after that, in freezing fog, London traffic was led by men with flares. Snow fell on 19 December but the worst came after Christmas.

By 7 February 1947, when the fuel crisis had already led to a near-paralysis of business and industry, the dockers went on strike. Factories stopped and thousands were sent home. As fuel stocks declined, greyhound racing was banned, cinemas were restricted to one evening performance. Trains were snowed up by 10 February and two days later street lighting was cut to a level which people complained was as bad as wartime. Only in East London, at Stratford Stadium, did dog racing continue. The track was lit from a car engine, guarded by men with cudgels to prevent 'interference'. When Ministry of Fuel inspectors arrived to see how the 'electric' hare was powered, they found it was worked by two men on a tandem. A half-mile queue was waiting to get in.

On 5 March, 1,000 trains round London were halted in the worst conditions for twenty-five years. Women fainted in crowded carriages that were stuck for seventy-five minutes in Penge Tunnel, twenty-seven passengers crammed into one compartment designed for eight. Two days later, the AA reported 300 roads throughout the country closed, numerous lorries and other vehicles buried in twenty-foot drifts. Only one road remained open to connect London and the north, via Birmingham.

The winter was a symbol rather than a cause of resentment. Six years of war and sacrifice had led only to enforced self-denial and shortages. By 21 March, the government was planning for compulsory rationing of electricity based on the size of premises and the number of occupants. Those whose meters registered an excess use would be prosecuted. It was the only alternative to nationwide daytime blackouts for industry and the home.

Despite the miseries of 1946–7, disillusionment with the new government was not apparent in opinion polls or at by-elections. In December 1946, however, the Lord Chamberlain banned a song in a London revue, *Between Ourselves*, which opened at the Playhouse Theatre: 'Bevin, Bevan, Let's Call the Whole Thing Off'. In this the cast reminded the audience that they had put 'us' in and now, no doubt, wished that they could put 'us' out. The censor insisted that the song might offend cabinet ministers but it still did not appear to reflect the mood of the nation.

For those facing post-war deprivation more stoically, there was the easily drawn and glum graffiti figure of 'Chad'. Chad consisted of a horizontal line representing the top of a wall, a bald half-circle representing the head and eyes looking over it, nose and fingertips on the near side. Above the head was a question mark and underneath it the legend, 'Wot no . . .?' as in 'Wot no soap?' or 'Wot no snoek?' – a well-nigh inedible variety of canned fish acquired from the Soviet Union. If shortages had a human face, it was Chad's.

One street performer brightened the post-war gloom. The 'spiv' or 'drone' was as much a black marketeer as his wartime predecessor, a cross between a barrow boy and a racing tipster. He was familiar from the 'mock auctions' of Petticoat Lane, where an item was first offered at twice the market price and progressively reduced to persuade the audience that it was getting a bargain. 'Pitching', as it was called, broke every austerity regulation. 'The sooner it is stamped out the better,' said the Old Street magistrate firmly.[2]

With his trilby hat, loud racecourse clothes, padded shoulders and narrow waist, his quick-fire retailing of nylons from a cardboard suitcase at the kerbside, the spiv was a hero of austerity folklore. No one threatened to flog or shoot him. Instead, he was impersonated on the music-hall stage by such comedians as Frankie Howerd, Sid Field and Arthur English. Cartoonists relished his distinctive appearance. It had been possible to hate such a man while Germany was the enemy. As public antagonism turned against bureaucrats, snoops and politicians, the spiv was a licensed jester at the government's expense, 'Flash Harry' or 'Jack the Lad'.

There was even a so-called 'Spivs' Union' with a green membership card which entitled the holder to 'all the benefits, if any' of the organization. This was produced in court in June 1948. The Forum, Kentish Town, was a well-known meeting place for spivs. On this occasion, thirteen youths from Holloway had spilled out of the amusement arcade in Kentish Town Road, jostled and insulted passers-by, prevented them from boarding buses and pushed some of them off the pavement and into the road. When arrested, all were found to be carrying their union cards. The owner of the arcade agreed with the magistrate that it appeared to be 'the headquarters of the Spivs' Union'. 'Don't you think your premises are a curse in the district?' the magistrate asked. 'They keep the boys off the street,' said the funfair owner piously, though they had evidently not done so on this occasion.[3]

To most people, the spiv was the black market. The stern-faced men, relentless pursuers of illegal trading, carried out their last pre-Christmas swoop in 1947. The contraband was 'coupon-free' nylons, stolen or mysteriously 'imported' from Italy and Czechoslovakia. The criminals were said to be easily recognizable as men selling stockings from suitcases at the kerbside.

In November 1947 George Isaacs, Minister of Labour, took further powers to direct these drones, as he called them, to sign on for official employment. Men aged up to fifty-one and women to forty-one were liable for 'directed labour'. They would include barrow boys, workers in night clubs or football pools and at funfairs. All were required to register for essential work. The Supplies and Services: Registration for Employment Order came into effect on 8 December 1947, authorizing government inspectors to search funfairs, night clubs and football pool offices. Despite official rhetoric and threats, this was largely a waste of time. No responsible enterprise wanted to employ men and women who did not themselves want to be employed in the first place. Night clubs, funfairs and football pools remained little affected by the ministerial order.

Rationing, on which the black market depended, was not to end entirely until 1951. The 1947 crime statistics contained 18,363 offences against rationing or building regulations. In September that year, an anti-black market film, *Scotland Yard*, was re-released at the request of the police. It was still worth the while of professional criminals to steal lorryloads of commonplace food: fresh eggs and dried egg powder, butter and sugar; jam, sweets and meat. There was still a supply of helpers from men on the run. When an army corporal, a deserter from the East Kent Regiment, was sent to prison for four months in January 1946 for stealing a lorryload of sugar in Putney, the shadowy figures of the underworld were not far behind him. 'I took it because of what the other chap said he would do to me if I didn't.' Efforts to trace this 'minder' were unsuccessful.[4]

Food robberies were backed up, where necessary, by firearms. In June 1946, five men and three women were charged with the theft of crates of jam, corned beef and clothing coupons. For good measure, the leader of the raid had taken with him a revolver and thirty-six rounds of ammunition. In August 1948, police lay in wait for a gang who were hiding stolen food in disused army pillboxes. The trap was set near Cheshunt. When it was reported that the gang would be armed, the defenceless police had to beg shotguns from local farmers. There was no gunfight, however. The ambush was so disorganized that the suspects in their Ford V8 drove straight through it and escaped.[5]

Post-war black marketeering was often blatant but seldom as blatant as the fruiterer with a stall at Sevenoaks in May 1946. He opened for business, calling out encouragingly, 'Everything is black market today!' Though he ticketed the produce with the maximum legal price, the word 'from' in small letters preceded this. It was too good to last. After a few minutes one of his customers, who had bought tomatoes at two and a half times the maximum regulation price, introduced him to the town's Food Enforcement Officer. With misplaced self-confidence, the fruiterer had erected his black market stall immediately outside the door of the Sevenoaks food office.[6]

Elsewhere, 'flying squads' of retired policemen were enrolled to check serious pilfering of rations at London docks. As late as April 1947, a clothing manufacturer from Great Portland Street was sent to prison for six months for obtaining eggs illegally. Black market sweets were moved by the hundredweight in private cars and, in November 1947, a London gang managed to switch a consignment of cancelled sweet coupons for a million that were still valid. Again, the Board of Trade admitted that it had not the staff to scrutinize the flood of returning paper.[7]

Meat was one of the worst areas for racketeering. In June 1946 the Grand Hotel, Folkestone, and its suppliers were fined a total of £3,600 (£144,000) for illegal deals in poultry. Their defence was that after five years they did not really understand the regulations. By the end of December 1947, the Ministry of Food rated the black market in meat as worse than it had ever been. Curiously, in February 1945, almost three years earlier, the same ministry described the black market as unimportant and boasted that its own efforts had prevented an illegal trade from developing in Britain.[8]

An easy source of household goods were the building sites of new 'prefabs', prefabricated houses under construction to counter the housing shortage. A music-hall joke of the day advised tenants prone to mislay door keys to take a tin-opener out with them. Within forty-eight hours, at the end of May 1946, a dozen large and well-organized robberies from unfinished estates were reported. The biggest were in London, Margate, Bournemouth, Brighton and Harlesden. At Harlesden, the thieves carried off fifty refrigerators from one estate. Gas and electric cookers worth many thousands of pounds had also been stolen in the preceding month. Worse still, ungrateful tenants of some finished prefabs regarded all the fittings as their own property and were selling off cookers and refrigerators at £40 a time to black market touts who called at their doors. Local authorities issued reminders that this was a criminal offence.

Other gangs turned their attention to rationed clothing. A single night's work by one London gang, on 18 June 1946, brought £7,500 (£300,000) worth of goods. This consisted of Utility cloth to the value of £4,500 stolen by breaking through a wall into the warehouse of Lukin & Crook in Poplar, followed by clothing worth £3,000 from Thomas Matthews of Blackfriars. The scale of warehouse breaking was impressive. On a weekend in August 1947, for example, a gang hid in the warehouse of Rawlings & Son, at the approach to Waterloo station, from which they carried off in two lorries almost three thousand bottles of whisky and brandy with a black market value of £10,000 (£400,000).

Whether or not the peacetime black market was on such a scale as reports suggested, its profits were immense. Little of the money ever passed a bank counter but much of it was used to finance illegal gaming. In consequence, the illegal gaming-tables of London 'social clubs' were said to display as much money as the pre-war casinos of Cannes, Le Touquet and Monte Carlo.

The aftermath of war, as the military command relinquishes its control of men and materials, threatens any nation with disorder and escalating crime. The Allied victory of 1945 was no exception. A figure of 18,000 deserters in August 1946 seemed almost irreducible. In that month, a number of military police were put into plain clothes to search out and trap the fugitives. By the end of the year it had made very little difference.

On 22 January 1947, a period of 'leniency' was announced for any deserter surrendering before 31 March. Almost three thousand men surrendered and 767 were caught but, in the end, there were still 17,500 absentees. Though some had been reclaimed it seemed that almost as many had gone missing. These fugitives assumed, correctly, that the authorities would not go on looking for them much longer. Deserters need only disappear into the labyrinth of civilian life until the authorities grew weary. Some men had already been absent for years, simply returning to their civilian lives. No one had bothered to look for them. In April 1946 one of two brothers who owned Allied Chemical Products at Leyton was arrested and imprisoned as a deserter but only through bad luck after several years. He had absconded during the war in order to keep the business going when his brother was also called up. The firm had closed but he had opened it up again. It was not the vigilance of the military authorities which trapped him. His past came to light in 1946 when he was caught evading purchase tax on the firm's cosmetic products.[9]

By May 1947, the Ministry of Labour was also losing interest in those who had evaded conscription. At Clerkenwell magistrates court, a cook, aged thirty-four, was charged with having an identity card which did not relate to him. He had never registered for National Service but, because of his age, a further charge of being a suspect deserter could not be proceeded with. Though the magistrate accepted this advice, he was not impressed by it. 'It seems illogical that a person who has avoided responsibility in this unworthy manner cannot be punished or called up for service now.'[10]

Post-war disorder in the services increased in parallel with the frustration of men who felt they were being retained for no good reason. Naval deserters became armed robbers in Singapore within weeks of its liberation from the Japanese. There was defiance from men who were not demobbed as quickly as they thought was possible and at the conditions on the ships bringing them home. British and Canadian troops rioted at Aldershot. Men held in military prisons attempted mass escapes.

Disorder began, appropriately, on VE-Day when 1,400 men rioted for three days at the Headley detention barracks of the Canadian army in Hampshire. Their demands for an issue of cigarettes to celebrate victory were refused. They cut the fire hoses with razor blades and then burnt the prison watchtower to the ground. Windows were smashed, radiators and washbasins torn out, before the prisoners stormed the main gate and vanished through it, forty-seven of them getting away. A second Canadian riot, at Aldershot eight weeks later, led to three ringleaders being charged with mutiny. A crowd of 200 soldiers rioted in the town centre on successive nights, smashing plate-glass display windows and battering their way through the prudently locked door of an amusement arcade.

Unrest was not usually a matter for headlines. However, on Christmas Eve 1945, when military police tried to keep 3,000 troops on board the *Orion* at Liverpool for service in the Middle East, the sequel was a very public event. The men had no wish to remain in the Army, let alone to be posted to the Middle East, least of all on Christmas Eve, and certainly not on the *Orion*. Conditions on the ship were so bad that a detachment of 500 Australian airmen had walked off it a few weeks earlier. On Christmas Eve, several hundred men left the troopship and fought with baton-armed military police on the quayside until they were forced back on board. A number got off again and were arrested. At this, scramble nets were dropped over the ship's side and troops swarmed down to rescue the detainees, while sympathizers on board pelted the military police with petrol cans and fittings ripped out of the ship.

Two months later there was a riot at the Aldershot detention barracks. An RASC driver made a key from his mess tin to open his cell door. He managed to open a second cell, then rang for a guard whom he overpowered. After that, the guard's keys were used to unlock every door in the military prison, many of which were torn from their hinges for good measure. In the sequel, nineteen soldiers faced charges of mutiny. Three days later, 150 men rioted at another military prison, Fort Darland in Kent, and fifteen escaped in a snowstorm.

In the summer of 1946, there was greater trouble in the Far East when 243 men of the 13th Parachute Regiment, 6th Airborne Division, were convicted of mutiny at Kuala Lumpur after staging a 'strike' in protest at their conditions. Their mass court martial was held in an airfield hangar and they were sentenced to two years' imprisonment, not to be served 'at home', and to be discharged with ignominy. This had the makings of a major political scandal over the conditions in the camp and the failure of the demob system. Demands were made in Parliament for a judicial inquiry. The Secretary for War thereupon announced that there had been 'trial irregularities' at the court martial, whose members had been 'misdirected'. The paratroopers were freed and all their convictions quashed.[11]

In the sphere of military crime, a good deal of post-war racketeering by British servicemen occurred in mainland Europe rather than at home. In January 1946, Colonel T. 'Sherlock' Holmes, command-ing Scotland Yard and CID officers, was given headquarters in Berlin and the job of controlling a black market run by Allied deserters and 'displaced persons'. This followed the arrest of two captains and a lieutenant-colonel, charged with illegally shipping cars to New York via Rotterdam. Officers of more senior rank were suspended. Detective Inspector Vanstone, sent to investigate the 'war surplus' rackets on the Continent, had discovered that officials were being bribed in order that new and unused vehicles should be bought by entrepreneurs at scrap-metal prices.

There was naturally a black market trade between Britain and the occupied zone of Germany so that, for example, military smugglers in February 1946 were bringing into the country suits and leather goods bought wholesale from the underworld in Berlin and other German cities. Returning army and Royal Navy lorries were used as a means of transport. A made-to-measure suit of the best quality could be bought for £12 (£480) and no coupons. The smugglers would ask a customer for his measurements, show the patterns of cloth available, and bring the suit back in about a fortnight.

A further threat was the counterfeiting of both British and American currency in occupied Germany. One gang responsible for this was broken up in August 1946, at a time when the British zone of occupation faced rising crime. Those detained included three US ex-servicemen, employees of the US War Department, and twenty-two Germans, one of them wanted in France as a war criminal. The same gang was responsible for operating a black market in food and drugs, including consignments of morphine which it was about to distrib-ute. In June 1947, ten British soldiers also appeared before a court martial in Calais charged with selling tyres, sugar and other com-modities to the local population. Large numbers of British and American military tyres had come on to the market, at the improb-ably high price of £40 to £50 each set.[12]

The Continental black market was buoyed up by institutional dis-honesty. When 40,000 jeeps were bought from the US by the French government for the regeneration of French industry in 1946–7, some 20,000 of them went missing and there were resignations from the French Surplus Property Board.

Even such cases as this were small-scale compared to major robberies. In August 1946 the Director-General of UNRRA, Fiorella La Guardia, denounced massive theft and corruption in the UN relief agency. At the port of Trieste, food, clothing and medical supplies were being stolen on a scale that would have made Harry Lime seem a failure in his profession. Monthly supplies, landed at Trieste for Yugoslavia and Italy, were worth £10,000,000 (£400,000,000). Theft accounted for 20–25 per cent of the monthly total, that is £2,000,000–£2,500,000 (£80,000,000–£100,000,000 in modern terms), according to Dr Miles Vasic, a Yugoslav government spokesman. There was no reason to doubt him, since the method was all too familiar.

Truck drivers with false papers arrived at the port and loaded their vehicles with the connivance of some of those responsible for discharging the cargoes. The city and the port were policed by personnel of the Allied Military Government in Trieste, consisting of British and American troops and Venezia Giulia civil police. Slovene Communists in Trieste insisted that what they described as these Fascist terrorists were colluding with gangsters to sabotage the fledgling Communist republic of Marshal Tito's Yugoslavia by ambushing supply trains and trucks. The immediate cause of the August scandal was an entire cargo of penicillin which had found its way to the black market in Milan. It was no comfort that large quantities of food, including flour and sugar, had also been stolen from relief supplies arriving at Naples. La Guardia called the organization to account but not before the damage had been done.[13]

At home, though the dollar crisis had made currency smuggling by returning servicemen a concern for the Treasury, the most menacing import continued to be firearms. In May 1948, coffee from Britain was still being bartered for guns from Germany, exported through Hamburg to a ready market in such ports as London, Hull, Newcastle and Cardiff. In February 1946, Scotland Yard had offered an amnesty for the surrender of illegal arms in London. Three months later, they had collected 75,996 weapons, 5,873 bombs and shells, and 2,207,751 rounds of ammunition. Two years later, however, there was a busy trade in replenishing illegal stocks.

Anglo-Continental criminality in Europe was paralleled by a

murky domestic world of 'war surplus'. In May 1946, an armoured car could be bought from the government for just under £45 (£1,800). In the three years following the war, the government also sold off sixty operational bombers and a number of fighter-bombers. It was in 1947 that four Beaufighters and two Mosquito fighter-bombers took off from Thame in Oxfordshire and were never seen again. Special Branch eventually established that they had been sold to the Israelis. Two years later, four pilots were convicted of flying the planes out of the country. In a separate incident, it was thought that the black marketeer Stanley Setty was supplying aircraft to Jewish organizations in Palestine prior to the Arab-Israeli war. He was said to have double-crossed the purchasers, which was entirely possible, and that they had murdered him, cut up his body and dropped it in several parcels in the English Channel. As it happened, he was murdered by his partner in black market crime, Donald Hume.[14]

Thefts of war surplus material, either by servicemen or civilians, seemed childishly easy. The Report of the Comptroller and Auditor-General for 1945–6 listed thefts from the Army that year of vehicles valued at £263,000 (£10,520,000); thefts of stores £162,444 (£6,497,760); ammunition £1,862 (£74,480); petrol from pipelines overseas £58,475 (£2,339,000). These items alone gave a running total of thefts from the Army, in real terms, of some £20,000,000 annually. Quite apart from the vehicles, there was a healthy trade in stolen parts. When twenty-four men were charged with the theft of vehicle parts from a Ministry of Supply dump in September 1946, the court was described as looking like a huge motor store. Worse still, the ringleader, who was sent to prison, was the policeman in charge of guarding the vehicles.[15]

By no means all 'surplus' rackets were so blatant. Superintendent Vanstone patiently tracked down an illegal auction ring at Todmorden in Yorkshire and Weston-super-Mare, Somerset, which had quietly cheated the Ministry of Supply of £43,000 (£1,720,000) in ten days during 1949 by fixing the price of surplus copper, bronze and zinc. Though this was prevented for the future, the gang's past profits were safe.[16]

It was impossible to guard or even supervise adequately the stores or dumps which had become a legacy of war. By the autumn of 1947 a number of cases had come to court. There had also been a nation-wide inquiry into what Scotland Yard described as wholesale thefts from the Ministry of Supply in all parts of the country. In a barn at Cuddesdon, Oxfordshire, twelve lorryloads of goods stolen from the ministry were found by police at the end of September. The equipment included furniture, cooking utensils and typewriters, with a value of £20,000 (£800,000) from this single operation.

A week later, six men were sent to prison after the discovery of a racket run at the Ministry of Supply dump at Newbury racecourse. A dishonest purchaser would buy a few goods from the dump and then, in exchange for a worthwhile bribe, a dishonest foreman and his workers would load up the lorry with extra goods stolen from the war surplus. In November, four more defendants were charged after a further twenty-five lorryloads of equipment had been stolen from a Ministry of Supply dump near Oxford.[17]

A long-running case in the autumn of 1947 involved a depot described as a small town of huts handed over to the Ministry of Supply by the departing US forces early in 1946. The equipment included medical supplies but also refrigerators, washing machines, transformers, bedding and dressing gowns. It was alleged that lorry-loads of these goods were driven to South Wales for storage by dealers who had purchased them illegally from officers and men at the depot. From Wales they were later driven to purchasers in London. One driver recalled delivering sixteen refrigerators on each journey.

The most revealing evidence was given by a private of the Royal Army Ordnance Corps, who recalled getting £100 (£4,000) for loading the lorries. Seeing how easy it was to rob the depot, he and another soldier decided to 'do the same thing' themselves.

> We arranged over the phone for Mr Seal to send a wagon to the depot and we would supply him with things. I arranged to meet Mr Seal in Evesham at the roundabout at nine o'clock at night. With my assistance Mr Seal collected four loads and each time Ingham and myself were paid £100 between us. The loads consisted of dressing gowns, towels and transformers.

For these consignments, the private earned £300 (£12,000).

Asked if he realized he was doing wrong, the soldier said, 'No.

Everyone else was doing it.' His South Wales contacts assured him, 'We had no fear of being caught, because all the officers were in the swim as well.' He and his friend had then gone on leave, and crawled back through the wire to rob the depot. They were caught, held in the guardroom, and brought before a major next day. They asked to see the major in private and told him, 'If you say anything about this, you will all be involved.' Unfortunately for them, the Army had already sent an undercover investigator to the depot, posing as a replacement for a soldier posted out, to gather evidence. Compared with thefts on this scale, such rackets as buying surplus goods for export, when purchase tax was not paid, then selling them at home and pocketing the tax, seemed a modest accomplishment.[18]

The ease with which military property was stolen and traded made improbable defences plausible. Two Chevrolet engines were stolen from RAF Burnley on 6 November 1945 and found next day. The man in possession of them said, 'I bought them in the dark in Deansgate last night of a man who told me they were reconditioned Bedford engines. I paid him £100 [£4,000] for them. I don't know him. I paid him in £1 notes.' He was convicted. Yet in the culture of mass pilfering and casual deals, his story might almost have been true.[19]

Those who endured the shortages and frustrations of the post-war world were occasionally diverted by the spectacle of men and women living as if rationing and controls had never been thought of. Even the unpromising world of exchange control was invested with illicit glamour. Indeed, the first convictions of men and women who defied the Defence Regulations by purchasing and selling foreign currency occurred before the war was over.

On 7 December 1944, for example, an RAF flight lieutenant and his co-defendant were sent to prison and fined £1,000 (£40,000) for buying francs in Paris and selling them in London. The RAF officer had met an Englishman living in Paris who promised that he could get him francs below the price they would fetch in England. The flight lieutenant returned to England and went to a man who would finance the deal. He took back to Paris £1,450 (£58,000) in £1 notes and received 642,000 francs with a value in England of £3,210 (£128,400). It was an early but dramatic example of currency racketeering and the penalties of failure. By January 1946, customs officers had already targeted currency smuggling of this sort as the most dangerous activity of returning servicemen.[20]

Speculation in the German mark, which could be bought very cheaply for gold, commodities or Allied currency by soldiers of the occupation forces, was a variant form of racketeering. The result was a decline in its value to a level so dangerously low that British officers were warned, in 1945, that any officer dealing in the currency would be cashiered.

A principal concern of Scotland Yard was IGT (Illicit Gold Trading). During the summer of 1945, a good deal of intelligence was gathered on a network active in England and France. In September 1945, a French airman, Georges le Doduik, was convicted as the leader of a gold-smuggling operation. He bought gold and sovereigns in England, then handed them in a suitcase to a captain in the French Air Force. The captain gave the case to a girl named Paulette at an airport in France. She proved to be Doduik's sister. A consignment of gold worth £2,100 (£84,000) in England would be sold on the French black market for about £3,000 (£120,000). The first five trips were successful, the captain received £80–£100 (£3,200–£4,000) for each delivery and his aircrew £17 (£680) each. When the purchase of gold in England, which was illegal, was discovered, Doduik and another airman, as well as a Polish accomplice living in London, were arrested. The case in England was the thinner end of a wedge and in France sixty people were arrested. Doduik was sent to prison for six months and fined £8,200 (£328,000).[21]

To avoid national bankruptcy, an Exchange Control Bill was introduced in November 1946, stemming the outflow of gold and dollar reserves. Those travelling abroad, a particular drain on the reserves, would only be permitted to spend £75 (£3,000) during the following year, unless they could show reasons to justify more. The amount was subsequently cut to £25 (£1,000) and only raised to £50 (£2,000) in 1949. On the black market, of course, it was not necessary to travel abroad in order to spend sterling. In October 1945 there was a busy illegal exchange of pounds for French francs at Victoria station.

For the general public, as spectators of the conflict, the most entertaining melodrama came in the spring of 1947. Towards the end of

March, customs officers began to open all luggage after a tip-off about a currency smuggling gang led by a man in Belgium whose name they believed they knew. In April this rumour was eclipsed by banner headlines proclaiming the arrival of a sinister presence – Max Intrator. Known variously as 'Black' Max and by 17 April as 'The Spider Intrator', he was first said to be head of a Jewish underground currency racket in Palestine, fleecing travellers in Europe in order to finance paramilitary organizations. Then it appeared he was not Jewish at all but had lived in Egypt most of his life. One moment he was in prison in Paris, the next he seemed to be free. His web extended to Monte Carlo and Cairo, to Paris, Cannes and Brussels, even to a hotel in Torquay, where he rubbed shoulders with future murderer and present car-thief, Donald Hume.

Monte Carlo and its casino were a centre of his web. Max Intrator, sometimes passing as 'Prince Niki', waited for foolish Englishmen and Englishwomen to lose most of their £75 allowance at the tables or to run up unpayable hotel bills. Then his services were available to cash their cheques at a premium and sell them francs at a price well above the rate of exchange. To write cheques abroad was an offence under the currency regulations but, as one victim protested in court, she had only £1 of her travel allowance left. What else was she to do?

That spring and summer the press demanded excitedly, 'Who is Max Intrator – The Mystery Man of Monte Carlo?' It promised 'Max Intrator Speaks!' or 'Max Intrator Again!', revealing that Scotland Yard's new Currency Squad connected him with most of the 180 prosecutions now pending in England. In May, two cases brought prison sentences and fines of over £11,000 (£440,000). In June, a duke's daughter was fined £1,400 (£56,000) in a 'Max' case. At Bow Street, the prosecutor denounced 'the insidious way the agents of Max Intrator work on British subjects who go to the South of France, and how no opportunity is lost to force the British traveller to cash cheques'. Buying currency abroad, something perfectly legal at almost any other time, had become a focus of criminality.[22]

Intrator was said to have made £62,000 (£2,480,000) in the previous year by currency racketeering. Even when he disappeared after a few months, he was briefly revived in the person of another speculator, 'London Max', who actually lived in Paris or Brussels. This successor proved no substitute for the Spider of Monte Carlo. While the decent and gullible bourgeoisie queued up for the docks of the magistrates courts on their return home, the press and its readers were sad to see their international villain fade away. 'Black Max' Intrator, a rather solemn and dumpy little man in reality, had brought excitement and glamour to the drabbest and meanest season of their post-war world.

In other spheres, the ordinary commodities of peacetime remained unobtainable luxuries, for the most part subject to purchase tax to deter impulsive spenders or the profiteering of the smuggler and the spiv. In response, during November 1946, the 'Queen Elizabeth Gang' brought off their biggest coup yet when 5,000 pairs of nylons were successfully smuggled from New York, where they had been bought for fifteen shillings (£30) a pair, to be put on sale in Soho. The gang transported them to London in an American Buick, staging two 'dummy runs' in the previous week. They found it easy to leave Southampton docks without being challenged by police or customs. As it happened, they were already under surveillance by Scotland Yard and were allowed to get out, so that when the time came they could be arrested in London.

Unfortunately, the gang guessed someone had betrayed their plan. On 21 November, they left the docks with the nylons and, in an expected move, dodged through the back streets of Southampton to throw off the pursuit. Though Scotland Yard lay in wait, the Buick never entered the Metropolitan Police area. The powerful car was parked outside and the stockings were brought in by a slow and dilapidated Ford 8. At Southampton, it was still improbably easy for visitors to get on and off the great liners in dock. In this plan, one man had walked up the gangways of several ships with a suitcase, had a meal, and left again. This had been tried repeatedly with an empty case and no attempt was made to stop him. On the day, the cases were loaded in the Buick without interference and driven to London.

A steward on the Queen Mary was convicted in June 1946 of trying to smuggle a mere 186 pairs of nylons. By November, a warning was issued that smugglers were threatening the nation's finances by landing nylons secretly in the Thames estuary. A special watch was kept. Meanwhile, on the night of 1 December, a gang raided the warehouse of Wolsey's, in King Street, Leicester. They reached the third floor and silently threw down to accomplices below the entire consignments of nylons intended for London and Manchester.[23]

In the following January, an official of the Seamen's Union was caught trying to pass through customs with forty-two pairs of nylons, and in June a French waiter on the US liner *America* arrived without interception in Southampton with 144 pairs of nylons hidden in food tins, only to be arrested in London. As late as May 1949, when nylons were openly available in limited quantities, queues for a rumoured consignment began at 7 a.m. on 9 May, in what was called the biggest rush ever. Big stores were overwhelmed, a battle for the stockings ensued and extra police were called in.[24]

The frontier between luxuries and necessities was a shifting one. In 1946, when American comforts were promised at some unspecified date in the future, they included only cosmetics, vacuum cleaners and jelly powders. The undeniable luxuries of the day were furs, cosmetics, watches, jewellery and cigarettes. Carpets were necessities to those who had none, as was furniture whose manufacture was still subject to government licences and restricted to a few Utility patterns.

The illegal market in household goods was most evident in sales of second-hand furniture. In addition to central government regulations, twelve Regional Controllers had been appointed in 1940 to exercise delegated powers in their areas. As a result, rules were introduced in the Midlands in March 1944 to prevent profiteering at auction by unregistered furniture dealers. Buyers were required to sign an affidavit giving their name or the name of the firm for which they were acting. This was intended to prevent 'pirates' breaking the regulation which limited their profit to 50 per cent of the price first paid, or using false names, or buying cheap in one area to sell dear in another, or selling such furniture on the pretence that it was part of a house clearance or individual sale.

Prices at auction began to drop. In May 1944, the Parliamentary Secretary to the Board of Trade warned rogue dealers that the government was determined 'to prevent and check the present inflationary tendency'. They would be 'well advised to buy their new stocks with care'. In the same month, John Barker & Co. of

Kensington High Street were fined £1,025 (£41,000) on sixty-two summonses for selling second-hand furniture above the permitted price. By 1946, traders who were selling government surplus furniture had adopted a more open policy of putting a limit on the bids. If several bidders reached the limit, lots would be drawn to determine the successful purchaser. Here, at least, those who needed to furnish a post-war home could do so cheaply.[25]

The theft of carpets or linen was easier than that of furniture. Linen did not have to be new or clean. In June 1945, an Old Bailey trial revealed systematic thefts of laundry sent by US clubs and Red Cross units to contractors, Advance Linen Services Ltd. Losses were running at £250 (£10,000) a month in what was rather dramatically described as the heart of the linen black market.[26]

In the last months of the war and the first weeks of peace there was a demand which made even the theft of old carpets worthwhile. Vanloads returning from the cleaners were stolen, as at Acton in January 1945. Another thief's speciality was carpets from hotels. Stripping carpets from the Albemarle at Brighton earned him a six-month prison sentence in 1946. Similarly, thirteen new Wilton carpets were stolen from the *Queen Mary* during a post-war refit in July 1947.[27]

At the upper end of the market, a lorry driver and a labourer were accused of removing a carpet valued at £700 (£28,000) from Lord Grantley's home. In the following month, May 1946, others valued at £10,000 (£400,000) were stolen from an East Grinstead store by the so-called 'Magic Carpet Gang'. The police warned the public not to buy any carpet they suspected of being stolen. Though the gang soon turned its attention to more portable and more valuable items, quantity and value might still make carpets attractive, as when a gang jemmied the main double doors of the Fulham furniture depository of John Tucker & Sons in the small hours of 22 March 1947. They took fifty carpets with a value of £8,000 (£320,000). Scotland Yard claimed to be on the track of the man who financed and organized such raids but they had made the same boast the year before without tangible success.[28]

Cosmetics were among other vanished luxuries, strictly controlled by a quota system and restricted for the most part to an export trade.

When nail varnish became briefly available at an Oxford Street store at 1s. 3d. (£2.50) a bottle in May 1946, it was the first time for years that those who queued patiently had seen it on sale, apart from a small black market supply from the United States.

Lipstick was similarly restricted and well worth stealing. The Helena Rubinstein factory was robbed on the night of 10 June 1946 of over 10,000 lipsticks with a value put at some £7,000 (£280,000). It was thought that they might fetch £10,000 (£400,000) on the black market. Two men and a woman were arrested as receivers of 684 of the lipsticks in the following month. As scarcity eased, the values fell. In a similar robbery at the Colgate Palmolive warehouse, Shepherd's Bush, in February 1947, the value of 35,000 lipsticks was put at only £2,500 (£100,000). A number of these were recovered in a Flying Squad raid at Chiswick in the following month.[29]

The major cosmetics prosecution in 1947–8 was not for robbery but contravention of regulations in order to manufacture a surplus for the black market. David Weitzman, Labour MP for Stoke Newington, his three brothers and two other men were charged with conspiracy to contravene 'regulations on the manufacture and supply of toilet preparations'. The Newington Supply Co. was alleged to have been in difficulty before the war but appeared to prosper as restrictions increased. The charge was that the men had conspired to put in false returns, obtaining more controlled goods than they were entitled to. They were accused of making false entries and producing false documents from June 1940 to January 1946. The case began before magistrates in March 1947 and ended in the Court of Criminal Appeal in March 1948. The Old Bailey trial lasted twenty-five days before the jury retired.

The Court of Criminal Appeal was unimpressed by the argument that authentic documents unavailable at the trial had since been discovered in a cowshed. However, Lord Goddard ruled that David Weitzman, a barrister as well as an MP, took no part in running the firm and had no case to answer, though he had been in prison for a year. One of his brothers and the firm's accountant had been sent to penal servitude for three years, one other imprisoned for twelve months. The convictions of all defendants were quashed on the grounds that each indictment included three charges of conspiracy, whereas it was elementary law that only one charge might be included in each indictment.[30]

As cigarettes ceased to be the black market currency of Europe, major robberies became fewer. One of the last, in 1946, involved the familiar target of the NAAFI stores, this time at Fulford Barracks, York. Three men hired a van in Clapham and arrived at the barracks at 11.30 p.m. the same day, leaving seventy-five minutes later. By the next day 1,000,000 cigarettes were missing and the van had been returned to the hire firm. Because it had been hired for so short a time, during which it seemed the three suspects must have been at home in London, they had a chance of an alibi. Unfortunately, the van's milometer showed that it had driven almost the exact distance to Fulford Barracks and back. Seventy-five cases of cigarettes, valued at £5,993 (£239,720), were found in the attic of one of the suspects.[31]

Furs, watches and jewellery offered better prospects than cigarettes or even nylons in the new world of peace. With the opening up of Europe and a world market, professional thieves and smugglers needed little encouragement to join the export drive – or, indeed, the import drive. When ten men, including eight soldiers from the rank of major to private, were charged with trying to smuggle 10,000 necklaces and 27,000 brooches at Tilbury in 1946, the court was told that it would have needed a crane to lift the jewellery. By May 1946, fur thieves were stealing to order for markets at home and abroad. The monthly total in London was about £20,000 (£800,000), though a single theft from the Natural Fur Company of Newport, South Wales, by use of a master key yielded £11,000 (£440,000). A few days earlier, the furs were transported to Newport from a West End hotel, where they had been on show, and the gang had shadowed them. There were a hundred coats, including mink, ermine and musquash. In the same month there were three major Park Lane fur robberies in a week. Scotland Yard warned of a gang that was stealing fur coats to be remade so that they would be unidentifiable.[32]

Furs and jewels worth £72,000 (£2,880,000) were stolen in London in the first seventeen days of 1947. This was a prelude to an £18,000 (£720,000) raid on Dickins & Jones, Regent Street, in the small hours of 26 March, using a skeleton key. It was followed by another at Peter Vickery Ltd, Bond Street. The Dickens & Jones raiders unlocked a door in the darkness of Argyll Street at the rear of the store, forced a showroom door and removed the furs in a plain, fast van. This robbery was allegedly planned for a couple of months and financed by a wealthy receiver. Four men and a woman were charged. But the owner of the Bond Street shop was pessimistic. He had lost fifteen coats, Persian lamb and ermine, to thieves who tore off a wooden gate, smashed a plate-glass door and a steel-tube grille, set off the alarm, entered the showcases in full view of the street, and removed the coats. Mr Vickery concluded that there were not enough police-men about, those who were about were short-handed, and it was difficult to stop burglars of this violent kind.

A favourite choice for cat burglars was a house in an affluent dis-trict of London where a party was being held and where, as a matter of habit, the host or hostess deposited the guests' fur coats on a bed upstairs. In Fitzjohn's Avenue, Hampstead, a man saw a figure climb-ing down his neighbour's stackpipe. He shouted, 'Hi!' The man dropped what he was carrying and disappeared over the roof. Twenty fur coats, valued at £5,000 (£200,000), fell to earth. Perhaps, however, the prize should go to a waiter and waitress who had the acutely simple idea of burgling a police station. They broke into Harlesden police station at 4.15 a.m. on a March night and removed the fur coats that were being held as evidence in a case pending over a previous theft of those same coats. Their plan failed when they came under observation as behaving suspiciously. The waitress was more than snugly wrapped in the number of furs she was carrying and the waiter was found to be wearing a woman's fur under his own raincoat.[33]

Most families, given the choice of one post-war luxury, might have chosen a car and petrol to run it. A small basic ration was restored to celebrate victory in 1945. After the winter crises of 1947 and the increased dollar debt, the basic ration was abolished in September 1947, once again making private motoring – or 'pleasure' motoring as the government preferred to call it – illegal. War-time rules would apply again and it was promised that penalties for evasion would be severe. The basic ration was not restored until June 1948, when the private motorist might travel about ninety miles a month. It was almost two years before all petrol rationing was abolished in May 1950.

Those who could prove their need to use a car had always been eligible for a supplementary ration. In order that this fuel should not be misused or resold to basic users, it was dyed pink. After the restoration of a basic ration, a motorist using it for 'pleasure' motoring would still be guilty of a criminal offence. The police were empowered to make random checks on the petrol tanks of vehicles and to demand from drivers an account of the nature of their journey. On 25 August 1948, the first culprit to be sent to gaol for using 'red petrol' in his car was imprisoned for a month. In May 1949, there were warnings from magistrates that any conviction for stealing petrol coupons would carry a gaol sentence.[34]

For those facing a complete ban on the use of their cars, there was a temptation to acquire commercial petrol on the black market. Figures for the amount of the national supply of fuel used illegally ranged from more than 10 per cent estimated by the government on 3 May 1948 to 30 per cent estimated by the AA and RAC.

For a dishonest motorist to pass a spot check by the police it would be necessary to remove the red dye from commercial petrol. It was rumoured that this could be done by straining the fuel through the air filter in the base of a wartime gas mask. There was a pleasing irony in the suggestion that the government had freely provided the means by which its own measures could be defeated. It was certainly possible to remove the dye with a filter including charcoal, as court cases showed. However, colour was not everything. When chemically tested, the fuel would still react as the commercial brand and not as the basic ration of 'white' petrol.[35]

Counterfeiting or theft of petrol coupons remained common enough in 1949 for the coupons issued for the period beginning 9 May to carry a new design and a request that they be signed at once with the vehicle number. This was described as an 'anti-forgery measure'. However, even before the coupons came into use, there was a major robbery at the headquarters of the London Regional Petroleum Board in Bromyard Avenue, Acton. It took place with the simple aid of a ladder on the night of 1–2 May and coupons for 150,000 gallons of petrol were stolen. At a current black market price of twelve shillings a gallon, the potential value of these was £90,000 (£3,600,000). Black marketeers now used car dealing as a front for trading in stolen coupons, on the pavements of Warren Street and the Euston area.

Organized car theft included the stealing of brand new cars intended for the home market, so that they might be sold abroad, and the sale of cars at home which were intended for export. Two major car-theft conspiracies were broken up in 1946–7. The first was organized by a motor dealer and forged coupon trader, described at the Old Bailey as 'the centre of a serious conspiracy', in July 1946. He was assisted by two RAF deserters and two men who stole the cars for him to sell.

A second conspiracy, involving the theft of fifty-seven cars in London for sale in South Wales, ended in January 1947 with a sentence of five years' penal servitude. The value of the cars in this case was £10,000 (£400,000). The fifty-seven cars were a small part of the total haul. The leader of the gang had pioneered a 'ringer' system, whereby a car's identity was changed, using the index number, engine number and chassis number from a wrecked or scrapped vehicle. Detective Superintendent David Thomas of Monmouth CID saluted him as 'the first of the big operators'.[36]

A worse blow to the integrity of the Petroleum Board was the discovery that its office in Reading, to which applicants for a petrol allowance sent the logbooks of their cars, had been penetrated by a gang of professional car thieves. One gang member was working for the Ministry of Fuel in a capacity which gave him access to 'thousands of books that poured into the Southern Regional Petroleum Office'. He was purloining these to order so that they could be matched up with cars stolen across the South of England. By 1947 car theft was on the increase and the figure for London alone had risen to 9,872 in the previous year. At Berkshire Assizes on 21 March 1947, six members of what the judge called this 'most dangerous organization' were sent to penal servitude for terms of between two and seven years.[37]

The case was a further reminder that, in times of austerity, as in war itself, corruption might penetrate the very organizations which existed to prevent it.

17

'The Best Government that Money Can Buy'

On 23 January 1945, Hugh Dalton spoke in Parliament as President of the Board of Trade: 'I will do my best to prevent people who have been defending this country from being fleeced by people who have stayed at home.' It was an article of faith in the post-war creed. Because 'fleecing' had become increasingly sophisticated, Scotland Yard created a Fraud Squad in 1946.

Those who were entrusted with the implementation of Dalton's promise behaved honourably, with few but important exceptions. Both government and press insisted that the public in general trusted the system. In July 1946, when Mrs Violet Dean was appointed as what the headlines called 'Racket Buster No. 1', at the Ministry of Works, she received some 250 letters a day, most of them anonymous, reporting infringements of restrictions on building and repairs. Before long, an army of officials investigated 45,000 of these tip-offs. Mrs Dean and a former CID inspector assisting her radiated integrity and energy.

No case was too trivial for inquiry. A West End club decorating its interior without a licence was fined £70 (£2,800). Even a man who installed a new bath and towel rail at home without official permission was convicted and fined £25 (£1,000). More difficult was the fight against dishonest lorry drivers and their black market contacts. A firm supplying the government with baths for estates of prefabricated houses reported that half its June 1946 production had 'got lost' between leaving the factory and arriving at Ministry of Works distribution centres throughout the country. More disturbingly, Mrs Dean blamed the failure of 'untold' prosecutions on 'bribery and corruption' or the disappearance of her chief witnesses.[1]

Corruption came in many forms. In the month of Mrs Dean's statement, three clerks of works in South London went to prison for taking bribes from George Pierce, a Norwood builder who was repairing bomb damage. Mr Pierce had been told that unless he paid the bribes, he would get no more work from these local government officials. He alerted the police, so that when he handed over the money in the office of the first defendant, the room was under surveillance. The three officials protested in vain that the money was paid as 'a present for past services, not as a bribe for the future'.[2]

In November 1946 there was a good deal of amusement when the Stratford East magistrates were fined at Bow Street, following the discovery that they had been lunching on black market meat for years. The deputy chairman was arrested while carrying a parcel of lamb from the butchers to the court. However, Mrs Dean's worst fears were confirmed when two Board of Trade officials, a man and a woman, were sent to prison in May 1947 for accepting bribes from traders in order that their offences should not be reported. Corruption did not end with the two officials. They claimed to have inside help. 'We know the woman at the Board of Trade who keeps the letters. We can arrange that the letter should be lost.'[3]

A case of this kind was unwelcome in any department of government but it was particularly bad for the Board of Trade, the custodian of laws and regulations which were to ensure fair shares for all. Soon, however, this same government department was to provide banner headlines day after day for five weeks, in what was to be commemorated as 'The Lynskey Tribunal'. This was not a routine exposure of petty officialdom. Its terms of reference stipulated an inquiry into 'Allegations reflecting on the Official Conduct of Ministers of the Crown and other Public Servants'.

Rumour began to test its wings early in the autumn of 1948. On Monday 4 October a headline in the *Daily Graphic* reported a 'CID Inquiry on Controls'. By the weekend, rumour was flying high and with disconcerting speed. On 10 October, the *Sunday Pictorial* promised 'the biggest trade and political scandal this country has ever known'. A hitherto unknown figure of the post-war underworld, Sidney Stanley, had been arrested. He was to be released under detective guard on 21 October.

The sporadic hints in the press culminated in an announcement that the Fraud Squad of Scotland Yard, headed by Superintendent

Arthur Thorpe, had been at work for a month, examining serious allegations concerning the Board of Trade and the granting of permits to commercial organizations. The mud that was flying soon stuck, in passing, to the Ministry of Food and the Ministry of Health as well. The amount of dirty linen to be washed seemed prodigious. Twelve typists had been needed to compile the Scotland Yard report on Board of Trade 'irregularities', a pile of paper which stood a foot high. As a result of Superintendent Thorpe's findings, Lord Jowitt, Lord Chancellor in the post-war Labour government, sought a tribunal of inquiry, under the Tribunals Act 1921. The hearing would be held in public.

On 27 October the Prime Minister moved the setting up of the tribunal. The House of Commons sat subdued and silent as Clement Attlee recounted the story told by his young President of the Board of Trade, Harold Wilson, in August. Government ministers and senior officials had allegedly received bribes in exchange for dropping a prosecution against a well-known football pool promoter and for making extra allocations of paper to that firm.

But corruption in this case was a two-headed monster. The supply of paper in a time of austerity was, of course, controlled by government order. However, the import of steel, for which precious dollars must be paid, was far more strictly regulated. Like football pools, amusement parks with American-made dodgems or switchbacks – let alone gaming arcades – were not essential to the nation's survival. To the morality of the new Labour order, the arcades were downright distasteful. Two men who had felt the consequences were Jacob Harris, Vice-President of the Amusement Caterers Association, and Francis Price, managing director of Stagg & Russell, who dealt in 'amusement machinery'. Jacob 'Jack' Harris, owner of arcades in the Haymarket and of the Standard Restaurant in the West End, was described unkindly as having risen from jellied eels to oysters in Piccadilly.

Through his solicitor, Mr Harris heard of a man who held a government quota for £186,000 (£7,440,000) of imported steel. This man was prepared to transfer £150,000 (£6,000,000) of his quota for a consideration of £10,000 (£400,000). The philanthropist was Sidney Stanley, about whom little was known. Mr Harris certainly did not know that 'Stanley' was a stateless Pole against whom there had been a deportation order since 1933, nor that he was currently an undischarged bankrupt, nor that he had no steel quota now and never had, nor that such a transfer would have been invalid and illegal in any case. Stanley had soon convinced the solicitor, as well as Mr Harris, that he was a well-established steel importer in great favour with the government.

In consequence, Jacob Harris took his problems to Sidney Stanley's Park Lane apartment in Aldford House. The host was a short stocky man, impeccably shaved, manicured and brilliantined. He was genial, generous and flamboyant, with a way of speaking rapid but fluent broken English. Stanley confirmed that he was prepared to transfer £150,000 of his allocation for a 'consideration' of £10,000, which he pointed out was a modest premium of 7 per cent. To demonstrate his good faith, he then went into the next room, while Mr Harris listened to him through the open doorway. Stanley telephoned the Board of Trade. He asked for and spoke to a 'Mr Pearson', explaining the proposed transfer of the steel allocation and promising to bring the necessary forms for completion. In reality, of course, he did not speak to Mr Pearson and it seems most unlikely that the telephone was connected.

Stanley returned to his guest and chatted about his intimacy with members of the Labour government, 'from Mr Attlee downwards', as Jacob Harris recalled. He described the crucial part he had played in the negotiation of an 'American loan' for the nation, assisted by his brother Marcus Wulkan, who was prominent in the American trades unions and a friend to Britain. If Mr Harris wondered why a man called Stanley should have a brother called Wulkan, he kept the question to himself. As it happened, Sidney Stanley had been born Solomon Koszycky, but he also passed as Solomon Wulkan – and, indeed, as Solomon Hyman, Solomon Soachim and Solomon Rechtand, or Richtand.[4]

Stanley presented himself as a capitalist and entrepreneur who was nonetheless a supporter of the Labour government. It was true that he had wined and dined most of its leaders in the House of Commons and elsewhere, though they did not always know that he was the paymaster for such festivities. He had made gifts of cigars to Ernest Bevin, the Foreign Secretary, and whisky to Charles Key, the

Minister of Works. He was on close terms with George Gibson, former Chairman of the TUC and now a director of the recently nationalized Bank of England, as well as Chairman of the nationalized North-West Electricity Board. Stanley had a letter from this director of the Bank of England, who promised in writing that he would not 'readily forget' Stanley's generosity and hoped to assist his business ventures because 'I may be able to exercise a greater degree of influence in the future than perhaps I have in the past'.[5]

Stanley had also introduced Hugh Dalton, late Chancellor of the Exchequer, to Isaac Wolfson of Great Universal Stores as a possible employee. Even Dalton's ascetic successor, Sir Stafford Cripps, seemed to have acknowledged Stanley's role in the loan negotiations. Stanley claimed that he had urged the Americans to make a further advance to Britain, to be paid back eventually out of Marshall aid. As if in proof of this, he carried a letter about with him. 'Dear Stanley, we are pleased with the way you are helping us in the Government and with the work you have done for the party. Yours sincerely, Stafford Cripps.' Perhaps it was genuine, but it certainly had nothing to do with the American loan. Possibly it was the result of routine assistance to Cripps in financing election expenses in his Bristol constituency. To those who believed Stanley's story of the loan, however, the letter seemed conclusive proof of his standing with the government.

Stanley assured Jacob Harris that he was well in with the Board of Trade, particularly its Parliamentary Secretary, John Belcher. Until 1945, John Belcher had been a railway booking clerk, a loyal, hard-working member of the Labour party and the trade union movement. Like many of his intake, he had been swept into Parliament on the high tide of Labour victory. Having shown his worth, he was now a minister of the Crown. Unfortunately, before the scandal was over, Jacob Harris himself would be told by Francis Price, 'This is the sort of thing you get when the country is being run by thirty-bob-a-week railway clerks.'[6]

Stanley assured Harris that he had won Mr Belcher's friendship. He had given the minister expensive presents of food and wine, entertained him lavishly in Park Lane and elsewhere, taken him greyhound racing and with his wife to boxing matches, given him a gold cigarette case for Christmas 1947, showered presents on both husband and wife. He had paid for a tailor-made suit because he thought it unbecoming that a government minister should go about in patched trousers. He had tried to pay for another bespoke suit for the Minister of Works but Charles Key had managed to settle the bill himself. Stanley added that he had paid for a holiday in Margate for Mr Belcher and Mrs Belcher, their three children, and Mr Belcher's mother. All this was, unfortunately, true.

The 'holiday' resulted from Belcher's attendance at the Labour Party Conference at Margate in 1947. Stanley assured the minister that he had a house standing empty at Margate. It would be a pleasure if John Belcher and his family were to use it for a fortnight's holiday, including the period of the conference. Then there was a hitch and the house was unavailable. As a man of his word, Stanley booked the party into what he assured Belcher was an inexpensive hotel. It was not at all inexpensive. Belcher was dismayed by the size of the first week's bill and further dismayed to find that Stanley had paid it. Stanley had arranged with the hotel that the bill should be sent to him and on no account was it to be paid by the 'gentleman'. Though Belcher had intervened and managed to pay the bill for the second week, Stanley had in his hands the first week's bill receipted, proof that he had paid for a minister's holiday.

It was certainly true thereafter, as Belcher's private secretary later confirmed, that Stanley visited the minister almost every day at the Board of Trade. Hearing of Stanley's influence there, Jacob Harris and three others agreed to put up the money for the steel 'quota'. However, Francis Price was wiser than his colleagues in the amusement business. Having encountered Stanley, he described him as 'the biggest villain unhung'. Indeed, Mr Price was so troubled that he took his doubts to the former Conservative minister, Lord Woolton. Without hesitation, Woolton advised him to go to the police, and Francis Price went. The press now heard of corruption in high places.[7]

When the first rumours reached the youthful President of the Board of Trade, Harold Wilson, he took them to the Lord Chancellor, who in turn took them to the Prime Minister. Attlee and Wilson called in the police. Stanley, when confronted by the Fraud Squad, did not just mention John Belcher but talked of half the cabinet, including a handsome bribe to Sir Frank Soskice, the Solicitor-General, to drop a prosecution against Sherman's Pools. The impact of these allegations in the press was as if the Labour ship of state had taken a torpedo amidships.

The party had not merely come to power with a large majority in 1945. It brought with it a sense of the moral superiority and decency of socialism, for all its bureaucracy and regulations, as compared to the greedy and gobbling free-for-all represented by capitalism and Conservative politics. There was an earnestness, even a priggishness, attached to the new ethic but no one could doubt, for example, that Cripps sincerely regarded it as Christianity in action. To mock or subvert a commitment to national health, education and welfare was more than irresponsible criticism, it seemed almost a social blasphemy. Yet the party was about to suffer from an unforgiving rule of politics: the higher the moral pretensions, the more precipitous the fall.

But Stanley, in his genial dinner-throwing and present-giving way, had by no means done his worst. The monster's second head had stirred in Cardiff. Harry Sherman, of Sherman's Pools, was one of the richest men in the city and proprietor of one of the biggest football pools in the country. In essence, he had two grievances. Wholesale gambling was anathema to the socialist ethic and the Board of Trade frowned on his proposal to float Sherman's Pools as a public company. Second and more important, under the quota of paper allowed him, Sherman was hard-pressed to issue enough forecast coupons for each week's results. He and his competitors were left to divide the allocation among themselves but Sherman complained that he was not getting his fair share.

To protest against this, he made a very ill-advised visit to the Board of Trade. In the course of the conversation, John Belcher and other officials realized that Sherman had been infringing the regulations governing his paper allocation. They brought a prosecution against him in January 1948, involving 213 summonses. The hearing was abandoned when the Cardiff Stipendiary Magistrate died. Sherman's solicitor believed that the Board of Trade solicitor had behaved unfairly and suggested that a complaint should be made. However the prosecution was not dropped and in the summer of 1948 Harry Sherman was on bail and awaiting a new trial. A third grievance was born of this, to add to the difficulties of paper allocation and share flotation. He wanted the prosecution withdrawn.

That was how matters stood when Harry Sherman's brother, Abraham, 'Abe', Sherman, bookmaker of Merthyr Tydfil, took a trip to London, where he was talking with a rabbi in the lounge of Grosvenor House, Park Lane. A genial stranger came up and asked for a word. Abe Sherman said rather irritably that he was busy. The stranger said softly, 'It's all right. I know all about your case at Cardiff and the trouble you are having with your paper allocation. But I can help you. Mr Belcher is a particular friend of mine.'

So began a sequence of events in which Abe Sherman shortly afterwards paid Stanley a cheque for winnings of £715 (£28,600). Then Harry Sherman came to London and Stanley warned him that Belcher was 'very friendly' with Sherman's competitors. The paper allocation had been adjusted to 'put him out of business'. Stanley insisted he wanted nothing for himself, unless the Sherman brothers would care to join him in some property deals.

In the next weeks, Stanley journeyed regularly by rail between Paddington and Cardiff. Abe Sherman learnt with surprise that his brother had lent their genial benefactor £12,000 (£480,000), on the security of two cheques, one made out to Stanley by H. Lass & Co., the silk importers, but not yet due for payment. This loan appeared to be in exchange for the assistance Stanley was giving to Harry Sherman. Indeed, Stanley reported that he had used part of the loan to pay £2,500 (£100,000) each to John Belcher and Sir Frank Soskice, the Solicitor-General, to get the prosecution dropped. It was certainly true that the prosecution was dropped, though the other grievances remained. George Gibson, a director of the Bank of England, had promised to do whatever he could to help Stanley and was well placed to aid the flotation of Sherman's Pools. There was also the matter of the paper allocation. The Sherman brothers came to meet John Belcher in Harry Sherman's suite at the Savoy Hotel.

Belcher walked in saying abruptly that he could only give them a quarter of an hour. Annoyed by this brusqueness, Harry Sherman reminded him that this was no way for a man to talk who had been paid £2,500 (£100,000); a man who went dog-racing on Saturdays, lost all his money, came penniless to Stanley on Monday mornings and was sent away with £50 (£2,000) or £100 (£4,000) and whose wife was often given £100 by Stanley to tide her over.

Belcher looked thunderstruck and said, 'This is all Jack and the Beanstalk!' He paused and repeated helplessly, 'This is all Jack and the Beanstalk!' Then it seemed he heard the trap close on him and added, 'Stanley is a dirty lying little bastard!' During the row that followed in the hotel suite, Harry Sherman produced the two cheques given him by Stanley as security for the loan, out of which it was alleged Belcher had received his bribe. Belcher waved at the cheques and said, 'If I were you, I would put them in at once and get your money.' He made a phone call to tell someone he had been 'dealing with explosives', and then left. Both cheques subsequently proved to be invalid, indeed the £27,000 Lass & Co. cheque was a forgery.[8]

Yet the prosecution of Harry Sherman was certainly dropped. John Belcher protested that this had been done on advice from the Solicitor to the Board of Trade, Sir Stephen Low, and was no decision of his. The Board of Trade regulation broken by Sherman was abolished before he could be tried again. The first abortive prosecution was thought to have taught him a lesson. The solicitor saw little point in a retrial over a regulation that no longer existed.

On 29 October, it was announced that the tribunal of inquiry would be headed by Mr Justice Lynskey, a Liverpool-born Irishman, a devout Catholic, a firm but humane judge with long experience of both civil and criminal cases on the Northern Circuit. He was to be assisted by two King's Counsel, Russell Vick and Gerald Upjohn. There were no wigs nor gowns. The three members of the tribunal, convened in Church House, Westminster, sat in lounge suits. As Lynskey reminded his hearers, the tribunal was a court of law but not in the usual sense. 'You must appreciate that there is no defendant before the Tribunal. This is a Tribunal of Inquiry only.' A tribunal could subpoena witnesses but it could neither try nor punish them. Its sole duty was to issue a report on the matters before it. The witnesses were on oath but in giving their evidence they were less easy to control than they might have been in a civil or criminal court. It was this which turned Stanley into a popular entertainer and folk hero.[9]

A number of principal witnesses, including John Belcher, George Gibson, Harry Sherman and Stanley, were represented by counsel.

On behalf of the government, they were examined and, later, cross-examined by the Attorney-General, Sir Hartley Shawcross, known as 'The Noël Coward of the Law Courts'. Suave, good-looking and precise, he was a formidable courtroom presence and had led the British team at the Nuremberg war crimes trials. A certain lack of socialist passion spoilt his chances of leading the Labour party and he was soon to quit politics and the House of Commons.

Shawcross was well able to examine Belcher and Gibson, with whom he shared qualities of conscience or moral protocol. To examine or cross-examine Sidney Stanley and his associates was rather like trying to cross-examine the Marx Brothers. 'Please answer the question' became a refrain of counsel and members of the tribunal. At times, the hearing threatened to become a comic spectacle, interrupted by Mr Justice Lynskey's rebukes. 'There must be no laughter in court . . . This is a Court of Justice, not a place of amusement.' If rebukes failed, Lynskey proposed to clear the public from the gallery. Yet the issue could scarcely have been more grave: corruption and racketeering at the heart of government, black market and bribery among the nation's rulers.[10]

Nor was it corruption as a legal technicality but, as Shawcross said, 'corruption in the broader sense more generally understood by the public'. The questions to be asked of the witnesses were simple and comprehensible – 'When does a gift become a bribe?' – but the answers were not. When caught in a lie, witnesses would insist that the Attorney-General had been ambiguous or got his facts wrong and so had misled them by his questions.[11]

A fair sample of the difficulties facing counsel was Gilbert Paull's attempt to cross-examine Benjamin Pearlman, who had undertaken to buy 25,000 shares in Sherman's Pools if the company were floated, and who had to be traced by the police before he appeared.

> PAULL. Mr Stanley has said that you are an underwriter. Are you an underwriter?
> PEARLMAN. No.
> PAULL. What are you?
> PEARLMAN. I buy shares. I cannot be an underwriter. How can I be an underwriter?

THE CHAIRMAN. Keep your voice up.

PEARLMAN. I am not too well, that is why.

PAULL. It is not a question of 'How can I be an underwriter?' It is a perfectly simple question: Are you an underwriter?

PEARLMAN. What would you call an underwriter? I buy shares.

THE CHAIRMAN. Tell me what you are.

PEARLMAN. I buy shares.

THE CHAIRMAN. What is your occupation?

PEARLMAN. I am semi-retired.

THE CHAIRMAN. What were you when you were not retired?

PEARLMAN. A cigar merchant.

THE CHAIRMAN. You are a retired cigar merchant, are you?

PEARLMAN. Yes.

PAULL. What business do you carry on at 658 Salisbury House?

PEARLMAN. I do not carry on any business. I buy shares myself.

PAULL. What do you use the office for?

PEARLMAN. Just so as not to go about the street. You have got to have somewhere to go; that is all.[12]

Between the majesty of the law and the half-lit world of Stanley's commercial intricacies lay a defensive semantic labyrinth, hostile and impenetrable.

The Attorney-General tried in vain to cross-examine Stanley on his accounts. It seemed that he operated his bank account by cashing large cheques each week with the National Greyhound Racing Association at dog tracks on a Thursday, knowing that he would have the use of the money until Monday, when his bank would debit the sum. What happened to the money meanwhile was anyone's guess and Stanley could no longer remember. If he was running a bank account, however, where was his discharge from bankruptcy? 'I never asked for it,' he said simply. However irregular his conduct, that was another dead end. 'I asked you, have you *any* account books?' Shawcross inquired at last. 'None at all,' said Stanley amiably. 'Have you any documents whatever showing the state of your accounts?' 'Nothing at all.'[13]

Rebecca West, who watched Stanley give evidence – with his sudden expressions of pained astonishment at hostile questions or his habit of flinging his arms wide for emphasis – thought of him as a charmer from *The Arabian Nights* or, in his own financial jungle, swinging like a trapeze artist from cheque to cheque.

Sir Hartley Shawcross, on the other hand, suggested that the tribunal might think Stanley's mendacity and exhibitionism almost pathological. Yet there was to be at least one exchange between the man of law and the racketeer which surely deserved a place in any book of quotations.

After hours of lies and evasions, executed with good-humoured panache, Stanley was reminded by Shawcross that he had said that he met Hugh Dalton at a dinner party before Christmas 1947, when Dalton was still Chancellor of the Exchequer. With his habitual technique of trying to throw the questioner off balance, Stanley replied, 'I do not think I said that, I think you said that.' At the end of his patience, Shawcross demanded, 'Which do you say was the truth?' Stanley looked at him with momentary anger and replied, 'Do not try to trap me with the truth!'[14]

By the time that his cross-examination was adjourned for the weekend, Stanley emerged from Church House with his equilibrium and ebullience restored. As usual, he found the press waiting for their most rewarding interviewee. A reporter asked him how he was going to spend the weekend. Stanley was bright and smart again. 'You'll probably find me playing golf with the Attorney-General,' he said genially.

On the last afternoon of the tribunal, Shawcross wound up with a speech in which he castigated Stanley as 'The Spider of Park Lane'. When the Attorney-General had finished, the tribunal rose for the last time and gathered its papers. Stanley rushed across to Shawcross, who had just denounced him for the falsehoods and fantasies that he had built up around himself in the last thirty years or so. He tried to seize his adversary by the hand, and exclaimed, 'That was a fine speech! Thank you, Sir Hartley! I have been a fool, I admit it.' The Attorney-General retained his composure. 'If you say so, Mr Stanley, I'm sure it must be true.' But Stanley had not finished. Outside Westminster Hall, he appeared before the press with a large photograph of Shawcross and announced him as 'a very great man'. He sought out Superintendent Thorpe of the Fraud Squad and said, 'Thank you very much. You have played the game.' After which, he disappeared, almost with a puff of pantomime smoke.

Against such performances stood the ordeals of John Belcher and his wife, who was also summoned to give evidence, and George Gibson who would no longer be a director of the Bank of England nor Chairman of the North-West Electricity Board. Though the tribunal's report was not issued for a further month, their careers had already been destroyed. The inquiry had wound its way through the early winter, from 15 November 1948 until the afternoon of 21 December. Headlines trailed the names of the famous but innocent through the mud. To the public at large, these presented a potted history of the scandal and the proceedings.

Story Of American Car For 'A Lucky Blighter' . . . Stanley Told Me He Knew Attlee, Cripps, and Belcher . . . Belcher's £35 Suit – Stanley Paid For It . . . Cases Of Drink Sent To Mr Belcher . . . Sherry – Only Thing That Agreed With Him . . . Burgundy – Needed It For His Health . . . £1,000,000 Furs in Bond, Tribunal Told . . . Belcher's Patched Trousers . . . Story Of Cigars To Bevin . . . Stanley Promises Names of Firms Changing Import Licences Daily . . .

Day after day and week after week, members of the government were lampooned. In the dark December streets and the crowded saloon bars, jokes ricocheted around the Mother of Parliaments. 'What's the difference between Whitehall and the London Symphony Orchestra?' – 'None. They've both got fifty fiddlers.' 'If you want to retire from the Commons, old boy, the form is to apply for the Chiltern Hundreds.' – 'Make it thousands and I'll go.' 'What's the Whitehall pantomime this year?' – 'Ali Baba and the Board of Trade.' Remembering Belcher's tailor-made suit, the comedian Vic Oliver came on stage wearing what he called 'My Stanley suit. – It's the best that government money can buy.' The torchbearers of socialism could only keep their heads down and hope that the storm would pass.

John Belcher had resigned as President of the Board of Trade before giving evidence. He also resigned as an MP, returning to his job as a railway booking clerk at Paddington station, and he died in 1964. George Gibson resigned as a director of the Bank of England and as Chairman of the North-West Electricity Board. It had cost him

£2,000 (£80,000) in legal fees to be represented at the hearing and he confessed himself 'broke'.

Sidney Stanley was not so easily destroyed. The British tried to deport him to Poland but the Poles would not have him. In the end he slipped out of the country, where there was a warrant out for his arrest in the course of bankruptcy proceedings. Israel at first refused to accept him but relented and allowed him to settle in Tel Aviv, where he died in 1969.

In January 1949, with Sherman as its managing director, Harry Sherman Ltd was charged with keeping an office for illegal betting and fined £200, quashed on appeal. He was said not to have been well for some time and resigned from the firm. Abe Sherman was convicted in March that year after trying to bribe a Merthyr policeman. A bookie's runner had been arrested and Abe Sherman had handed the policeman £5 (£200), saying, 'See what you can do about it.'[15]

Even before the tribunal was over, the *People* promised on 19 December 1948 that there was 'a stinkeroo brewing at the Ministry of Food'. Scotland Yard had been called in and 'juicy disclosures' were promised, but never materialized. On 20 January 1949, Aneurin Bevan was obliged to deny in the House of Commons the truth of further rumours about a Fraud Squad inquiry at the Ministry of Health.

The report of the Lynskey Tribunal appeared on 22 January 1949. It cleared all those involved except John Belcher and George Gibson. The tribunal found that Belcher had behaved 'improperly', in that he had known the good things showered on him by Stanley were intended as a means of influencing him and that he had been so influenced in the matter of dropping the charge against Harry Sherman. As for Gibson, Stanley's promise of a directorship for Gibson in a retail company, in return for securing flotation of that company's shares, was recognized by Gibson as an improper approach, which he nonetheless accepted. The reaction of the press was less qualified and best summed up by a headline in the *Daily Graphic* on 26 January, which said simply, 'Belcher and Gibson Guilty'.

Racketeering and corruption appeared to have penetrated to the heart of government. As it happened, every member of that government and its appointees had been exonerated, except for Belcher and Gibson, both of whom were held guilty of errors of judgement rather than deliberate criminality. Yet disillusionment with the new order was sufficiently widespread for a Labour majority of almost 200 seats in the 1945 House of Commons to be very nearly wiped out a twelvemonth after the tribunal reported. The new majority of seven was unworkable. Eighteen months later, a further election in October 1951 returned a post-war Conservative government committed to the end of rationing and controls.

How far the collapse of Labour support in 1950 was a reflection of the revelations at the tribunal must be a matter of speculation. It was said that the party's parliamentary losses came as a surprise, not anticipated in opinion polls or by-election results, where it had not suffered a defeat in five years. However, a test of opinion at the ballot box came in London local government elections, ten weeks after the tribunal report was published. It was true that Labour was defending majorities won in 'good years'. However, in the London County Council elections of April 1949, the balance of seats changed from a Labour majority of 90–28 against the Conservatives to a dead heat of 64–64, the Liberals and Communists also losing seats. The Conservative lead in the popular vote increased again in the London borough elections in May. If such a movement of votes truly reflected a public mood, the damage had been done.

Sidney Stanley had been the super-spiv, an entertainer quite unlike the shoulder-padded, check-coated figure of the kerbside or the music-hall stage. Fluent, humorous, irrepressible, he was remembered long after most ministers of the current government had been forgotten. He was also a reminder to the nation that the world of rationing, shortages, controls, snoops and regulations had lasted for more than nine years by the time of the Lynskey Tribunal's report. The system was to survive for longer after the war than during it, and people were already sick of it. Its agents snooped to catch a man installing a new bath or putting up a towel rail, or spied into the plates of customers to ensure that they were not eating more than five shillings' worth of food. Worst of all, these restrictions had prolonged into peacetime the existence of black marketeers, petrol coupon forgers and criminal rackets. In one view, rationing and controls were the oxygen which allowed such creatures to live.

Reynolds News on 30 January 1949 came to the defence of the government, insisting that without controls and rationing, Britain would be 'a spiv's paradise'. But the *Sunday Times* regarded socialist restrictions as the 'foster-father' of Stanley and his kind. Sir John Anderson, a wartime Home Secretary, went further and denounced socialism as inconsistent with public morality. In similar tones, the *Evening Standard* of 26 January, on behalf of the Beaverbrook press, described Stanley's 'squirming underworld of dishonesty' as being created by the bogus assumption that a planned economy was morally superior to a free market.

The public argument was soon to be overtaken by a defeat of socialism, as represented by the Labour government, and by the end of all rationing in 1954. Petrol rationing was abolished in 1950, eleven years after its first introduction: some rationing lasted for fourteen years.

The world of the ration racketeers died with the restrictions they had exploited. Criminals who had perfected the skill of hijacking a lorryload of butter or warehouse-breaking in search of nylon stockings, were free to return to more ambitious pursuits. Those civilians who had merely ventured over the border of criminality, in order to keep their larders stocked or their cars running, became in the 1950s the respectable citizens of a 'home-owning democracy'.

A great majority of the nation had been brave, obedient, conscientious throughout the war. The criminal underworld and even the willing customers of the black market might be counted in tens of thousands but they were still a small proportion of the population. Similarly, the figure of 20,000 deserters and perhaps 50,000 more who fell foul of military justice, might be shocking as a statistic but meant that far more than 90 per cent of servicemen and women did their duty as and when called upon.

As Horace Walpole had noted two hundred years before, there was a price to pay for war, in the corruption of social morality. The gang leader Billy Hill and church leaders were united in observing the destruction of sexual fidelity. Elsewhere, a new culture of dishonesty was less immediately threatening but pervasive. When post-war British leaders deplored the shirking and indifference to be found in industry, the bloody-mindedness of strike action and trades unions, it was convenient to select left-wing or subversive influences for blame. Those who bore in mind that a generation had served in the armed forces during the war, and that another generation of young men had been conscripted for National Service until the 1960s, saw other influences. For every subversive schooled in Marxism-Leninism, there were a thousand more who had for years been exposed to the simpler dogmas of 'Never volunteer', or 'Make the job last because, if you finish it, they'll only find you another.'

In parallel with this was a concept of property which had had a marked effect on moral scruples during the war. Whatever belongs to everyone belongs to no one. Lead on the roof of a bombed building or a quarter of a bottle of gin on the floor of a wrecked public house hardly seemed to constitute looting. Who was hurt by trivial thefts of army rations or clothing? Who would be hurt if a military vehicle went missing? What effect, apart from fleeting inconvenience, would be caused by the theft of a few thousand cigarettes from the NAAFI stores? Even blowing open a safe for the brigade pay would really hurt no one, because it would mean only that more money must be brought and the troops would be paid anyway. It seemed scarcely more than an inconvenience. Ultimately the money belonged to the government but that was only to say that it belonged to no one who would be personally distressed by the theft. To think otherwise would mean that even the compiler of a tax return who understated income or overstated expenses would be on a par with the safe-blower, which seemed absurd.

Mean-minded crimes had always existed. So had crimes that were seen as necessary by their perpetrators. Yet perhaps there had never been such a time when it was possible to rob, cheat and racketeer in the most important areas of life with a sense that there was no victim, given that government and authority were insensitive to pain. The last word in this moral lesson, taught by the war but reflected alarmingly in the crime statistics of the peace that followed, was surely spoken in 1955 by Alec Guinness, playing Professor Marcus in the film *The Ladykillers*. Confronted with the criminality of stealing a vanload of banknotes, Professor Marcus justifies this as only a farthing on everybody's policy. It was a line that perhaps seemed funnier after the war than it would have done before.

Notes

CHAPTER 1: The Lost Peace

1. Sheila Cousins, *To Beg I Am Ashamed: The Autobiography of a London Prostitute*, Paris: The Obelisk Press, 1938, pp.168–76.
2. Bow Street Magistrates Court, 10 March 1938; Central Criminal Court, 5 April 1938.
3. Westminster Coroner's Court, 9 June 1936.
4. David Thomas, *Seek Out the Guilty*, London: John Long, 1969, pp.39–52; Paul Harrison, *South Wales Murder Casebook*, Newbury: Countryside Books, 1995, pp.72–5.
5. Graham Greene, *Brighton Rock*, London: William Heinemann and The Bodley Head, 1970, p.xi.
6. Lewes Assizes, 29 July 1936.
7. Central Criminal Court, 16 November 1936; 17 November 1936.
8. *Paddington News*, 19 February 1938.
9. Marylebone Magistrates Court, 16 October 1937; Marlborough Street Magistrates Court, 28 January 1938.
10. Billy Hill, *Boss of Britain's Underworld*, London: The Naldrett Press, 1955, pp.74–5.
11. RAF Court Martial, West Drayton, 13 February 1950; General Court Martial, 20 April 1950; Hastings Magistrates Court, 24 May 1950.
12. Southampton Magistrates Court, 10 August 1950.
13. S. F. Crozier, *The History of the Royal Corps of Military Police*, Aldershot: Gale & Polden, 1951, p.121.
14. Hampstead Magistrates Court, 30 May 1939.

CHAPTER 2: 'Don't You Know There's a War On?'

1. *East London Advertiser*, 13 June 1947; Sir Harold Scott, *Scotland Yard*, Harmondsworth: Penguin Books, 1957, p.68.

2. *Tribune*, 28 April 1944.

3. *Police Journal*, XV (1942), 165.

4. *The Times*, 23 May 1941.

5. *The Times*, 19 November 1942.

6. 60 *Times Law Reports* 82.

7. Bow Street Magistrates Court, 23 August 1941; 19 September 1941; 10 October 1941; Central Criminal Court, 9 December 1941.

8. Clerkenwell Magistrates Court, 3 January 1945.

9. *Evening Standard*, 12 November 1941.

10. *East London Advertiser*, 5 July 1941.

11. Bournemouth Magistrates Court, 26 August 1942.

12. Cf. *Evening Standard*, 5 June 1941.

13. Mansion House Court, 26 September 1941 [Arliss]; Bow Street Magistrates Court, 30 October 1941, Mansion House Court, 6 November 1941 [Coward]; Bow Street Magistrates Court, 13 July 1942 [Black]; Bow Street Magistrates Court, 29 March 1943, 3 April 1943, London Sessions, 18 May 1943 [Laurie]; Bow Street Magistrates Court, 24 April 1944, Central Criminal Court, 16 May 1944 [Novello]; *Kensington Post*, 16 September 1944 [Silvester].

14. James Langdale Hodson, *Home Front*, London: Victor Gollancz, 1944, p.25.

15. Ibid., p.163.

16. Croydon Magistrates Court, 25 May 1940.

17. Brighton Juvenile Court, 12 February 1941; North London Magistrates Court, 14 July 1942; Liverpool Magistrates Court, 21 February 1942.

18. Leeds Magistrates Court, 13 June 1944; Slough Magistrates Court, 11 January 1946; *Evening Standard*, 19 March 1946.

19. Brighton Magistrates Court, 18 June 1941; Lewes Assizes, 23 July 1941.

20. Brighton Magistrates Court, 6 April 1943.

21. Brighton Magistrates Court, 19 August 1943.

22. West London Magistrates Court, 19 June 1946.

23. Marylebone Magistrates Court, 18 February 1943.

24. Yarmouth Magistrates Court, 22 November 1940; Eastbourne Magistrates Court, 7 February 1941; Winston S. Churchill, *The Second World War: The Gathering Storm*, London: Cassell, 1948, p.560.

25. West London Magistrates Court, 4 December 1941.

26. Hastings Magistrates Court, 23 May 1944; Bournemouth Magistrates Court, 11 May 1944.

27. North London Magistrates Court, 6 November 1939.

28. Mansion House Court, 12 November 1940.

29. North London Magistrates Court, 12 November 1939; Hove Magistrates Court, 19 June 1944; Amersham Magistrates Court, 12 November 1939; Southall Magistrates Court, 12 November 1939.

30. Patrick Hamilton, *The Slaves of Solitude*, London: Constable, 1972, pp.100–101.

31. Hove Magistrates Court, 8 March 1944.

32. Thames Magistrates Court, 28 February 1941.

33. Lambeth Magistrates Court, 25 November 1942.

34. Manchester Magistrates Court, 1 July 1946.

35. Lambeth Magistrates Court, 15 November 1942.

36. Mansion House Court, 30 May 1945.

37. Croydon Magistrates Court, 16 March 1940.

38. Wilfred Trotter, 'Panic and its Consequences', *British Medical Journal*, 17 February 1940.

39. *South London Press*, 24 March 1942; 29 May 1942.

40. Ibid., 24 March 1942; 29 May 1942; Central Criminal Court, 17 May 1942.

41. Churchill, *The Gathering Storm*, pp.560–61.

CHAPTER 3: Running for Cover: The Dodgers and the Dealers

1. *The Trial of John George Haigh* [Notable British Trials], ed. Lord Dunboyne, London & Edinburgh: William Hodge, 1953, pp.59–60.

2. Brighton Quarter Sessions, 30 December 1942.

3. Bow Street Magistrates Court, 27 May 1940.

4. General Medical Council, 26 November 1942; 28 November 1942.

5. Thames Magistrates Court, 8 December 1942; Central Criminal Court, 13 January 1943.

6. Liverpool Assizes, 18 February 1942.

7. Old Street Magistrates Court, 10 January 1944.

8. Stratford East Magistrates Court, 6 November 1940.

9. Clerkenwell Magistrates Court, 29 December 1942.

10. North London Magistrates Court, 30 December 1942.

11. Brighton Quarter Sessions, April 1941.
12. Enfield Magistrates Court, 19 January 1942.
13. Lambeth Magistrates Court, 1 December 1942.
14. *Evening Standard*, 20 July 1942; Hill, *Boss of Britain's Underworld*, p.100.
15. Tower Bridge Magistrates Court, 26 January 1942.
16. Bow Street Magistrates Court, 13 March 1942.
17. King's Bench Division, 20 January 1941.
18. Hill, *Boss of Britain's Underworld*, p.71.
19. Ibid., pp.71–2.
20. Ibid., pp.86–7; Marlborough Street Magistrates Court, 26 June 1940.
21. Bow Street Magistrates Court, 25 July 1940.
22. Reading Magistrates Court, 10 November 1939.
23. Acton Magistrates Court, 8 March 1940.
24. Thames Magistrates Court, 18 March 1940.
25. Hendon Magistrates Court, 28 March 1940.
26. Hill, *Boss of Britain's Underworld*, p.73.

CHAPTER 4: The Bomb Lark

1. *Manchester Guardian*, 6 May 1941.
2. Marthe Watts, *The Men in My Life*, London: Christopher Johnson, p.189.
3. *Evening Standard*, 24 September 1940.
4. Hodson, *Home Front*, p.146.
5. *Tragedy at Bethnal Green: Report on an Inquiry into the Accident at Bethnal Green Tube Station Shelter*, London: The Stationery Office, 1999, *passim*; *Daily Herald*, 25 February 1944; ibid., 19 July 1944.
6. *East London Advertiser*, 28 June 1941.
7. Statement by Rural Deanery of Hammersmith, 28 November 1940; Wimbledon Magistrates Court, 19 December 1942.
8. *West London Chronicle*, 7 January 1944.
9. Central Criminal Court, 23 February 1944.
10. Thames Magistrates Court, 29 October 1940; 6 January 1941.
11. Thames Magistrates Court, 17 February 1941; 29 January 1941; Westminster Magistrates Court, 14 December 1940.
12. Old Street Magistrates Court, 9 November 1940.

13. Hammersmith Magistrates Court, 7 November 1940.
14. Thames Magistrates Court, 23 November 1940; Bromley Magistrates Court, 1 November 1940.
15. Thames Magistrates Court, 5 March 1941.
16. House of Commons, 25 October 1940.
17. Thames Magistrates Court, 24 October 1940; Guildhall Magistrates Court, 1 November 1940; Tottenham Magistrates Court, 28 November 1940; Thames Magistrates Court, 11 November 1940.
18. Clerkenwell Magistrates Court, 18 January 1941; East London Juvenile Court, 13 January 1941.
19. Clerkenwell Magistrates Court, 5 May 1941; 17 May 1941; *West London Chronicle*, 18 August 1944; Bow Street Magistrates Court, 23 December 1940.
20. East London Juvenile Court, 25 November 1940.
21. Southend Quarter Sessions, 17 July 1941.
22. Marlborough Street Magistrates Court, 16 October 1940.
23. Tower Bridge Magistrates Court, 12 March 1941; Central Criminal Court, 24–28 March 1941.
24. Bromley Magistrates Court, 21 April 1941.
25. Maidstone Assizes, 25 June 1942; Lewes Assizes, 4 December 1942.
26. Marylebone Magistrates Court, 16 November 1940.
27. Camberwell Magistrates Court, 6 January 1941.
28. Bow Street Magistrates Court, 25 September 1940.
29. Southend Magistrates Court, 27 August 1942.
30. Croydon Magistrates Court, 26 August 1940; Middlesex Appeals Committee, 14 January 1941; London Petty Sessions, 10 March 1941.
31. Manchester Crown Court, 7 July 1941; North London Magistrates Court, 9 January 1941.
32. East London Juvenile Court, 23 December 1940; Southwark Magistrates Court, 15 January 1941.
33. Clerkenwell Magistrates Court, 2 October 1940.
34. Old Street Magistrates Court, 22 October 1940.
35. Middlesex Sessions, 18 February 1941; London Petty Sessions, 23 January 1941; ibid., 29 January 1941.
36. Sutton Magistrates Court, 12 February 1941.
37. Central Criminal Court, 16 October 1940; West London Magistrates Court, 17 February 1941.

38. Mansion House Magistrates Court, 23 May 1941.

39. Central Criminal Court, 26 February 1941.

40. Central Criminal Court, 21 March 1941; Bromley Magistrates Court, 23 April 1942.

41. Central Criminal Court, 28 February 1941; Central Criminal Court, 16 November 1942.

42. Thames Magistrates Court, 3 October 1941; Thames Magistrates Court, 28 October 1941; Clerkenwell Magistrates Court, 21 March 1941.

43. *West London Chronicle*, 23 June 1944.

44. Central Criminal Court, 18 September 1944.

45. *Daily Herald*, 1 August 1944; Lewes Assizes, 24 July 1944.

46. *South London Press*, 15 August 1944; *Evening Standard*, 22 March 1945.

47. *West London Press*, 1 September 1944; ibid., 29 September 1944.

CHAPTER 5: Deeds of Darkness

1. Tower Bridge Magistrates Court, 13 July 1942.

2. Edward Greeno, *War on the Underworld*, London: John Long, 1960, pp.105–9; Robert Jackson, *Coroner: The Biography of Sir Bentley Purchase*, London: Harrap, 1963, pp.305–6; Norman Lucas, *The CID*, London: Arthur Barker, 1967, pp.62–4.

3. *Brighton and Hove Gazette*, 3 January 1942; 4 December 1943; Sussex Assizes, March 1943.

4. John Capstick, *Given in Evidence*, London: John Long, 1960, pp.46–52.

5. *Brighton and Hove Gazette*, 15 May 1943.

6. *The Trial of Harry Dobkin* [The Old Bailey Trials Series], ed. C. E. Bechhofer Roberts, London: Jarrolds, 1944, *passim*.

7. Bow Street Magistrates Court, 17 February 1942; Central Criminal Court, 27–28 April 1942; Fred Cherrill, *Cherrill of the Yard*, London: Harrap, 1954, pp.177–89; Douglas G. Browne and E. V. Tullett, *Bernard Spilsbury; His Life and Cases*, London: Harrap, 1951, pp.392–3.

CHAPTER 6: Opportunity Knocks: The Civilians

1. West London Magistrates Court, 27 May 1941; Allen Andrews, *The Prosecutor: The Life of M. P. Pugh*, London: Harrap, 1968, p.150; High Court, 18 July 1944.

2. Newton-le-Willows Magistrates Court, 7 March 1941; 10 March 1941; 17 March 1941; 18 March 1941; Liverpool Sessions, 26 May 1941.

3. Manchester Assizes, 17 December 1942.

4. Basil Cochrane, *An Inquiry into the Conduct of the Commissioners for Victualling His Majesty's Navy*, 1823, p.5.

5. Liverpool Magistrates Court, 31 August 1942; Liverpool Assizes, 4 November 1942, 9 November 1942, 13 November 1942, 19 November 1942.

6. Glamorgan Assizes, 22 July 1941; Thames Police Court, 13 March 1941; Bow Street Magistrates Court, 20 March 1941.

7. Liverpool Magistrates Court, 10 July 1943; Liverpool Assizes, 14 April 1944.

8. *Daily Herald*, 21 October 1944.

9. Watford Magistrates Court, 19 March 1940.

10. Mansion House Magistrates Court, 17 November 1941.

11. Marlborough Street Magistrates Court, 28 May 1943.

12. Clerkenwell Magistrates Court, 6 January 1941; Bromley Magistrates Court, 30 May 1941; West London Magistrates Court, 25 September 1941; *West London Chronicle*, 18 August 1944.

13. Central Criminal Court, 27 January 1944.

14. Mansion House Magistrates Court, 2 February 1944; Central Criminal Court, 15 January 1941; 22 January 1941; 29 January 1941.

15. Mansion House Court, 26 September 1941.

16. Bow Street Magistrates Court, 30 October 1941, Mansion House Court, 6 November 1941.

17. Bow Street Magistrates Court, 19 December 1941.

18. Bow Street Magistrates Court, 24 April 1944; Central Criminal Court, 16 May 1944.

19. Canterbury Magistrates Court, Special Sitting, 28 August 1942.

20. Bow Street Magistrates Court, 29 March 1943; 3 April 1943; Central Criminal Court, 18 May 1943.

21. Aldershot Magistrates Court, 1 November 1939.

22. Edinburgh High Court, 7 November 1944; 9 November 1944.

23. Bow Street Magistrates Court, 19 February 1943; Stourbridge Magistrates Court, 23 January 1943.

24. North London Magistrates Court, 9 January 1943; 11 January 1943; 27 January 1943.

25. North London Magistrates Court, 9 January 1943.

26. North London Magistrates Court, 12 April 1943.

27. Bristol Magistrates Court, 27 November 1941.

28. Southend Magistrates Court, 16 January 1942; Thames Magistrates Court, 1 April 1942.

29. Old Street Magistrates Court, 28 March 1942.

30. Romford Juvenile Court, 15 April 1942; Lambeth Juvenile Court, 30 January 1942.

31. Leeds Magistrates Court, 20 April 1944.

32. Salford Magistrates Court, 12 May 1941.

33. *West London Chronicle*, 17 March 1944; Lambeth Magistrates Court, 11 July 1942.

34. Guildhall Magistrates Court, 8 July 1942.

35. Tower Bridge Magistrates Court, 31 July 1942.

36. Watford Magistrates Court, 23 October 1941; Lambeth Magistrates Court, 11 July 1942.

37. Wimbledon Magistrates Court, 4 January 1940.

38. *Kensington Post*, 2 December 1944; ibid., 23 December 1944.

39. *East London Advertiser*, 9 January 1943.

40. West London Magistrates Court, 19 February 1943.

41. Old Street Magistrates Court, 31 December 1944.

CHAPTER 7: Under the Counter

1. Hill, *Boss of Britain's Underworld*, p.100.

2. Clerkenwell Magistrates Court, 29 May 1941.

3. *East London Advertiser*, 28 June 1941; Central Criminal Court, 30 September 1943.

4. Winchester Assizes, 19 December 1941; Liverpool City Quarter Sessions, 10 January 1942.

5. *Manchester Guardian*, 12 March 1942.

6. Robert Colquhoun, *Life Begins at Midnight*, London: John Long, 1962, p.96.

7. Croydon Magistrates Court, 4 June 1943.

8. *Hackney Gazette*, 14 April 1943; Old Street Magistrates Court, 20 May 1943.

9. *The Times*, 23 January 1948.

10. Hove Magistrates Court, 18 March 1942.

11. West London Magistrates Court, 17 November 1943; Central Criminal Court, 19 March 1943; Brighton Magistrates Court, 29 July 1941.

12. Hendon Magistrates Court, 11 November 1940.

13. Woolton, House of Lords, 1 September 1942; Dalton, House of Commons, 8 September 1942.

14. Brighton Magistrates Court, 7 February 1944.

15. Central Criminal Court, 8 April 1943; 9 April 1943.

16. Wealdstone Magistrates Court, 3 March 1942.

17. *South London Press*, 7 August 1942.

18. Ibid., 7 August 1942; 23 October 1942.

19. Hodson, *Home Front*, p.86.

20. Thames Magistrates Court, 2 May 1941.

21. Thames Magistrates Court, 27 June 1941.

22. Clerkenwell Magistrates Court, 18 April 1941.

23. *East London Advertiser*, 5 July 1941; Tower Bridge Magistrates Court, 22 May 1941.

24. Birmingham Assizes, 21 July 1941.

25. Guildhall Magistrates Court, 9 March 1942; 29 April 1942; 30 April 1942.

26. *East London Advertiser*, 17 May 1941; *Hackney Gazette*, 23 June 1941; Edward Smithies, *Crime in Wartime: A Social History of Crime in World War II*, London: George Allen & Unwin, 1982, p.66; Brighton Magistrates Court, 31 December 1941.

27. *Evening Standard*, 8 May 1942.

28. Marlborough Street Magistrates Court, 26 March 1943.

29. Mansion House Magistrates Court, 29 February 1944.

30. Romford Magistrates Court, 5 March 1942.

31. *Romford Recorder*, 20 March 1942.

32. Old Street Magistrates Court, 31 August 1943.

33. Romford Magistrates Court, 28 May 1942.

34. Liverpool Assizes, 13 November 1943.

35. Belfast Magistrates Court, 24 May 1943.

36. Old Street Magistrates Court, 30 May 1943; Bow Street Magistrates Court, 2 May 1944.

37. Bow Street Magistrates Court, 19 December 1944; Cardiff Quarter Sessions, 26 April 1944.

38. *West London Chronicle*, 7 January 1944.

39. Central Criminal Court, 3 July 1942; 10 July 1942.
40. Acton Magistrates Court, 16 April 1943.
41. Liverpool Magistrates Court, 19 January 1942.
42. Manchester Assizes, 9 March 1945.
43. West London Magistrates Court, 15 June 1945.
44. Harrogate Magistrates Court, 20 February 1946.

CHAPTER 8: Hot Off the Press

1. Croydon Magistrates Court, 28 January 1944.
2. Guildhall Magistrates Court, 21 July 1942.
3. *Evening Standard*, 24 November 1947.
4. Central Criminal Court, 9 December 1941.
5. Doncaster Magistrates Court, 10 January 1942.
6. Stratford Magistrates Court, 11 March 1942.
7. Central Criminal Court, 26 September 1942.
8. Central Criminal Court, 27 October 1943; Greeno, *War on the Underworld*, pp.152–6.
9. Clerkenwell Magistrates Court, 4 January 1944.
10. Bow Street Magistrates Court, 16 February 1942.
11. Clerkenwell Magistrates Court, 7 July 1945.
12. Central Criminal Court, 30 July 1943.
13. *Kensington Post*, 4 November 1944.
14. Bow Street Magistrates Court, 10 April 1942.
15. Lewes Assizes, 13 March 1943.
16. Liverpool Stipendiary Magistrates Court, 7 January 1944.
17. Central Criminal Court, 18 February 1944.
18. *South London Press*, 10 July 1942.
19. Manchester Magistrates Court, 27 March 1942.
20. Bow Street Magistrates Court, 6 May 1944.
21. Thames Police Court, 18 February 1942; Manchester Magistrates Court, 3 February 1942; 7 February 1942; 13 February 1942; 19 February 1942; 23 March 1942; 27 March 1942; 31 March 1942; 2 April 1942; 7 April 1942; 8 April 1942; Manchester Assizes, 29 April 1942; 5 May 1942; 6 May 1942; 7 May 1942; 8 May 1942; 11 May 1942; 12 May 1942; 13 May 1942; 14 May 1942; 15 May 1942.
22. Old Street Magistrates Court, 7 August 1947; West London Magistrates

Court, 7 January 1948; Bow Street Magistrates Court, 27 January 1948; Central Criminal Court, 20 February 1948.

23. Wimbledon Magistrates Court, 29 August 1941.
24. Hill, *Boss of Britain's Underworld*, pp.142–3.
25. Watts, *The Men in My Life*, p.186.
26. Bow Street Magistrates Court, 25 July 1940.
27. *West London Chronicle*, 20 July 1945.
28. Greenwich Magistrates Court, 25 August 1948.
29. Marylebone Magistrates Court, 21 March 1947; Petersfield Magistrates Court, 29 January 1947.
30. Central Criminal Court, 18 July 1941.
31. West London Magistrates Court, 9 December 1942.
32. Lambeth Magistrates Court, 29 May 1943.
33. Central Criminal Court, 1 July 1942.
34. Brighton Quarter Sessions, 31 December 1942.
35. Windsor Magistrates Court, 12 February 1946.

CHAPTER 9: 'You're in the Army Now!'

1. Crozier, *History of the Royal Corps of Military Police*, p.169.
2. George Hatherill, *A Detective's Story*, London: Andre Deutsch, 1971, pp.27–8.
3. Crozier, *History of the Royal Corps of Military Police*, p.67.
4. Hatherill, *A Detective's Story*, p.29.
5. Military Court (Emergency Regulations 1937), 12 August 1943; 28 September 1943.
6. Hatherill, *A Detective's Story*, p.29; Crozier, *History of the Royal Corps of Military Police*, p.180.
7. Paull Hill, *Portrait of a Sadist*, London: Neville Spearman, 1960, pp.70–82.
8. Shifty Burke, *Peterman: Memoirs of a Safebreaker*, London: Arthur Barker, 1966, pp.38–40.
9. Ibid., p.134.
10. General Court Martial, Duke of York's Headquarters, 20 May 1941; 21 May 1941; 26 May 1941; House of Commons, 9 and 30 September 1941.
11. Chatham Coroner's Court, 5 May 1943; 10 May 1943; Maidstone Assizes, 25 June 1943.

CHAPTER 10: Pay Parade

1. North London Magistrates Court, 6 May 1940.

2. Brighton Quarter Sessions, 30 July 1941.

3. Brighton Magistrates Court, 25 March 1943.

4. Central Criminal Court, 25 February 1942.

5. Marlborough Street Magistrates Court, 31 May 1944.

6. Aldershot Magistrates Court, 9 November 1942.

7. Bow Street Magistrates Court, 2 June 1944.

8. *Evening Standard*, 22 January 1941.

9. General Court Martial, Chelsea Barracks, 22 May 1944.

10. Liverpool Magistrates Court, 13 December 1943.

11. Princes Risborough Magistrates Court, 23 April 1949; George Wilkinson, *Special Branch Officer*, London: Odhams Press, 1956, pp.240–50.

12. Hill, *Boss of Britain's Underworld*, p.73; Bromley Magistrates Court, 30 January 1941; Epsom Magistrates Court, 10 October 1941.

13. Mansion House Magistrates Court, 5 August 1943.

14. North London Magistrates Court, 8 January 1943; Surrey Quarter Sessions, 1 April 1942; Woolwich Magistrates Court, 16 April 1942; Tower Bridge Magistrates Court, 20 October 1942.

15. Old Street Magistrates Court, 8 August 1942; 1 September 1942.

16. Bromley Magistrates Court, 21 March 1941; House of Commons, 9 July 1942.

17. Bromley Magistrates Court, 25 September 1941.

18. General Court Martial, Aldershot, 10 February 1942; 27 February 1942.

19. Victor Meek, *Cops and Robbers*, London: Gerald Duckworth, 1942, pp.110–12.

20. Brighton Magistrates Court, 19 October 1942; Brighton Juvenile Court, 2 June 1943.

21. Croydon Juvenile Court, 5 March 1942; Brentford Juvenile Court, 21 December 1942; Clapton Juvenile Court, 23 February 1943; *Brighton and Hove Gazette*, 22 February 1941.

22. Windsor Juvenile Court, 29 December 1944.

23. Glasgow Central Police Court, 11 January 1944.

24. Central Criminal Court, 2 April 1943.

25. General Court Martial, Preston Barracks, Brighton, 30 January 1942;

7 March 1942; Brighton Magistrates Court, 25 April 1942; 11 May 1942; 20 May 1942; 27 May 1942; 3 June 1942; 17 June 1942; Brighton Quarter Sessions, 6–10 August 1942; General Court Martial, Chelsea Barracks, 7 January 1941.

26. Hill, *Boss of Britain's Underworld*, pp.122–3.
27. General Court Martial, Chelsea Barracks, 1 August 1942.
28. Lambeth Magistrates Court, 18 July 1942.
29. General Court Martial, Aldershot, 28 April 1942.
30. General Court Martial, Colchester, 20 August 1942; 21 August 1942; 23 August 1942; 5 November 1942.
31. L. J. Cunliffe, *Having It Away: Thirteen Years of Crime*, London: Gerald Duckworth, 1965, pp.25–6, 32–3.
32. *Police Journal*, VIII (1935), p.1.
33. *Brighton and Hove Gazette*, 21 June 1941.
34. House of Commons, 17 February 1943.
35. House of Commons, 22 June 1943.
36. Brighton Magistrates Court, 24 August 1943; 1 September 1943.
37. Chertsey Magistrates Court, 16 January 1941.
38. Old Street Magistrates Court, 21 March 1941; Brighton Magistrates Court, 27 April 1942; Bromley Magistrates Court, 2 January 1943; *Brighton and Hove Gazette*, 1 May 1943; Lambeth Magistrates Court, 29 November 1942.
39. Old Street Magistrates Court, 11 January 1943.
40. Thames Magistrates Court, 30 September 1942; Lambeth Magistrates Court, 20 November 1942; South Western Magistrates Court, 3 August 1942.
41. Thames Magistrates Court, 13 July 1942; Lambeth Magistrates Court, 29 May 1942.
42. Central Criminal Court, 1 July 1942; Central Criminal Court, 14 July 1942; Lambeth Magistrates Court, 5 August 1942; *South London Press*, 3 March 1942.

CHAPTER 11: The Yanks Are Coming

1. *Daily Herald*, 10 November 1944.
2. *Newsweek*, 27 March 1944; *Time*, 30 April 1945.
3. *Atlantic Monthly*, July 1946.

4. Belfast Magistrates Court, 8 May 1942.

5. US Naval Command Court Martial, 6 May 1944; 8 May 1944; 9 May 1944.

6. Meek, *Cops and Robbers*, pp.113–16.

7. US Court Martial Convening Authority, US Naval Command, 1 December 1944; Court Martial Review, 5 July 1946.

8. US Army General Court Martial, [Ipswich], 19–20 January 1944; US Army General Court Martial, 24 November 1943.

9. G. D. Roberts, *Law and Life*, London: W. H. Allen, 1964, pp.110–13.

10. Robert Higgins, *In the Name of the Law*, London: John Long, 1958, pp.206–7; US Naval Command General Court Martial, [Southampton], 17 May 1945.

11. US Army General Court Martial, [Wycombe Abbey, Bucks], 11 October 1945; 13 October 1945.

12. US Army General Court Martial, [Belfast], 31 August 1942; 1 September 1942.

13. US Army General Court Martial, [Northern Ireland], 9 October 1942; US Army General Court Martial, [Glasgow], 4 January 1943.

14. US Army General Court Martial, 6 January 1943.

15. US Army General Court Martial, [Marlborough], 6 October 1943.

16. US Army General Court Martial, [Warrington], 31 March 1944.

17. Liverpool Stipendiary Magistrates Court, 18 December 1942.

18. Thames Magistrates Court, 4 November 1942.

19. Liverpool Stipendiary Magistrates Court, 18 January 1945.

20. US Army General Court Martial, 19 April 1944.

21. US Army General Court Martial, [Knook, Wiltshire], 25 May 1944; *Daily Mirror*, 30 May 1944; *Tribune*, 9 June 1944; ibid., 16 June 1944; ibid., 23 June 1944; ibid., 30 June 1944.

22. South Western Magistrates Court, 9 August 1944.

23. *West London Chronicle*, 18 January 1944; ibid., 23 June 1944.

24. *West London Chronicle*, 19 January 1945; ibid., 26 January 1945; ibid., 6 April 1945; ibid., 23 March 1945; ibid., 20 October 1944; ibid., 15 December 1944.

25. West London Magistrates Court, 2 April 1945.

26. *West London Chronicle*, 29 June 1945.

27. Lambeth Magistrates Court, 9 September 1944; North London Magistrates Court, 31 January 1945.

28. C. E. Bechhofer Roberts (ed.), *The Trial of Jones and Hulten* [The Old Bailey Trials Series], *passim*.

CHAPTER 12: Clubland

1. High Court, King's Bench Division, 3 November 1937.
2. Highgate Juvenile Court, 10 January 1940; Bow Street Magistrates Court, 17 January 1940; 3 February 1940.
3. Marlborough Street Magistrates Court, 24 January 1940; Bow Street Magistrates Court, 24 May 1940.
4. Stratford Magistrates Court, 29 April 1942.
5. Lambeth Magistrates Court, 3 January 1942.
6. Lambeth Magistrates Court, 12 February 1938.
7. Clerkenwell Magistrates Court, 24 May 1943.
8. Glasgow Coroner's Court, 23 May 1942; House of Lords, 13 May 1942.
9. Southwark Coroner's Court, 24 March 1942; Grays, Essex, Magistrates Court, 20 March 1942.
10. Greenwich Magistrates Court, 16 November 1942.
11. General Court Martial, Duke of York's Headquarters, Chelsea, 28 July 1942; ibid., 14 August 1942; Central Criminal Court, 11 January 1944.
12. Stratford Magistrates Court, 5 May 1944.
13. *Evening Standard*, 1 June 1945.
14. *West London Chronicle*, 21 July 1944.
15. Marlborough Street Magistrates Court, 16 January 1945; Central Criminal Court, 9 January 1945.
16. *Evening Standard*, 19 March 1947.
17. High Court, King's Bench Division, 31 January 1936.
18. West London Magistrates Court, 6 April 1940; ibid., 31 October 1941.
19. High Court, King's Bench Division, 7 November 1941.
20. Marlborough Street Magistrates Court, 12 October 1942.
21. Bow Street Magistrates Court, 22 December 1939.
22. Bow Street Magistrates Court, 29 May 1941.
23. Bow Street Magistrates Court, 2 February 1942.
24. Middlesex Sessions, 10 March 1941.
25. Bow Street Magistrates Court, 13 October 1941; ibid., 19 February 1942; ibid., 5 March 1942.

26. Hendon Magistrates Court, 26 October 1942; Brighton Magistrates Court, 28 January 1946.

27. Liverpool Magistrates Court, 21 February 1942; 23 April 1942.

28. *West London Chronicle*, 1 September 1944.

29. Southampton Magistrates Court, 28 May 1947.

30. Westminster Magistrates Court, 2 March 1942.

31. Bow Street Magistrates Court, 8 March 1941.

32. Marlborough Street Magistrates Court, 5 June 1942.

33. Court of Criminal Appeal, 4 May 1943; 25 May 1943; Central Criminal Court, 22 June 1944; Marylebone Magistrates Court, 31 May 1944.

34. Marylebone Magistrates Court, 16 July 1946; *West London Chronicle*, 17 August 1945.

35. *Evening Standard*, 10 July 1943.

36. *Evening Standard*, 15 April 1940.

37. Liverpool Magistrates Court, 27 May 1937.

38. South Western Magistrates Court, 14 October 1942.

39. Bow Street Magistrates Court, 22 April 1942; Chatham Magistrates Court, 5 August 1942.

40. Bow Street Magistrates Court, 10 March 1938; Central Criminal Court, 5 April 1938.

41. Higgins, *In the Name of the Law*, pp.71–4.

42. Bow Street Magistrates Court, 16 May 1941; Central Criminal Court, 4 July 1941; Jackson, *Coroner: The Biography of Sir Bentley Purchase*, London: Harrap, 1963, pp.111–13; Arthur Tietjen, *Soho: London's Vicious Circle*, London: Allan Wingate, 1956, pp.65–8.

43. Bow Street Magistrates Court, 24 June 1943.

44. Hill, *Boss of Britain's Underworld*, pp.75–6.

45. Stanley Firmin, *Murderers in Our Midst*, London: Hutchinson, 1955, p.51; Higgins, *In the Name of the Law*, pp.165–8; Jackson, *Coroner: The Biography of Sir Bentley Purchase*, pp.133–7.

CHAPTER 13: Going to the Dogs

1. West Ham Magistrates Court, 5 April 1938.

2. West Ham Magistrates Court, 8 June 1937.

3. Manchester Stipendiary Magistrates Court, 12 June 1941; Manchester Assizes, 1 July 1941.

4. *West London Chronicle*, 24 March 1944.

5. George 'Jack' Frost, *Flying Squad*, London: Rockcliff, pp.176–7.

6. Manchester Assizes (Civil Actions), 13 March 1942; 16 March 1942.

7. *Police Journal*, XX (1947), 223–8.

8. Southend Magistrates Court, 12 November 1946; ibid., 17 December 1946; Southend Quarter Sessions, 12 May 1947.

9. Dartford Magistrates Court, 21 March 1941; Central Criminal Court, 2 May 1941; ibid., 5 May 1941.

10. *Evening Standard*, 14 September 1942.

11. The doper was known to the police but, as he told the commander of the Flying Squad, 'You've got nothing on me.' Cf. Robert Fabian, *Fabian of the Yard*, London: The Naldrett Press, 1950, pp.50–54.

12. Dartford Magistrates Court, 28 February 1946; Central Criminal Court, 25 March 1946.

13. North London Magistrates Court, 17 August 1946.

14. Edinburgh Sheriff Court, 26 January 1939.

15. Clerkenwell Magistrates Court, 8 January 1944; Central Criminal Court, 14 February 1944; ibid., 16 February 1944.

16. Birmingham Magistrates Court, 12 May 1944; Birmingham Quarter Sessions, 3 July 1944.

17. Marylebone Magistrates Court, 21 July 1942; 29 July 1942; 19 August 1942; Peter Beveridge, *Inside the C.I.D.*, London: Evans Brothers, 1957, pp.103–7; John Gosling, *The Ghost Squad*, London: W. H. Allen, 1959, pp.190–93.

18. Hove Magistrates Court, 30 March 1944; 6 April 1944; Lewes Assizes, 14 July 1944.

CHAPTER 14: 'Do Not Forget to Guard the Turkey in Your Car'

1. *Letters of Horace Walpole, Earl of Orford, to Sir Horace Mann*, ed. Lord Drover, Second Edition, London: Richard Bentley, 1833, II, 336.

2. Robert Church, *Accidents of Murder*, London: Robert Hale, 1989, pp.141–9; Scott, *Scotland Yard*, pp.74–5.

3. *Daily Herald*, 17 April 1944.

4. *Evening Standard*, 20 October 1945.

5. Duncan Webb, *Crime Is My Business*, London: Frederick Muller, 1953,

pp.111–27; J. D. Caswell, *A Lance for Liberty*, London: Harrap, 1961, pp.223–36.

6. Central Criminal Court, 16 November 1945.

7. Bow Street Magistrates Court, 10 January 1944; 24 January 1944.

8. Watford Magistrates Court, 24 January 1944.

9. Marlborough Street Magistrates Court, 23 February 1945.

10. Chertsey Magistrates Court, 25 January 1945.

11. Macdonald Hastings, *The Other Mr Churchill: A Lifetime of Shooting and Murder*, London: Harrap, 1963, p.252.

12. British Army Summary Court Martial, Berlin, 27 August 1945.

13. *Evening Standard*, 19 June 1945.

14. Marlborough Magistrates Court, 22 May 1945.

15. Hill, *Boss of Britain's Underworld*, pp.107–10.

16. Ibid., p.108.

17. House of Commons, 9 May 1944.

18. Central Criminal Court, 5 March 1945; Chelmsford Assizes, 12 June 1945; Central Criminal Court, 5 September 1945.

19. Marylebone Magistrates Court, 1 November 1945.

20. *Police Journal*, XVII (1944), 62, 64–5.

21. Scott, *Scotland Yard*, p.74.

22. East London Juvenile Court, 16 July 1945.

23. Marylebone Magistrates Court, 11 April 1944; Central Criminal Court, 3–4 May 1944.

24. West London Magistrates Court, 3 March 1945.

CHAPTER 15: The Misfits

1. *Daily Sketch*, 14 October 1936; ibid., 16 October 1936.

2. J. C. Masterman, *The Double-Cross System in the War of 1939–1945*, New Haven: Yale University Press, 1972, p.122; *Daily Telegraph*, 5 July 2001.

3. Frank Owen, *The Eddie Chapman Story*, London: Allan Wingate, 1953, p.126.

4. Masterman, *The Double-Cross System*, p.131; *Daily Telegraph*, 5 July 2001.

5. Masterman, *The Double-Cross System*, p.131; *The Times*, 5 July 2001.

6. Iain Adamson, *The Great Detective: A Life of Deputy Commander*

Reginald Spooner of Scotland Yard, London: Frederick Muller, 1966, pp.118–19.

7. Masterman, *The Double-Cross System*, pp.171–3; Owen, *The Eddie Chapman Story*, p.258.

8. Owen, *The Eddie Chapman Story*, p.259.

9. Colquhoun, *Life Begins at Midnight*, pp.85–9.

10. David Kahn, *Hitler's Spies: German Military Intelligence in World War II*, New York: Collier Books, 1985, pp.305–6; Nikolaus Ritter, *Deckname Dr Rantzau: Die Aufzeichnungen des Nikolaus Ritter, Offizier im Geheimen Nachrichtendienst*, Hamburg: Hoffman und Campe, 1972, pp.148–50, 166–7, 198–216, 242–54; Charles Wighton and Gunter Peis, *They Spied on England: Based on the German Secret Service War Diary of General von Lahousen*, London: Odhams Press, 1958, pp.101–4.

11. Churchill, *The Gathering Storm*, p.122.

12. Kahn, *Hitler's Spies*, p.306; Ritter, *Deckname Dr Rantzau*, p.320; Wighton and Peis, *They Spied on England*, pp.108–24.

13. Kahn, *Hitler's Spies*, pp.349–50; Ritter, *Deckname Dr Rantzau*, pp.219–36; Masterman, *The Double-Cross System*, pp.49–51; Wighton and Peis, *They Spied on England*, p.125.

14. Masterman, *The Double-Cross System*, pp.93–4.

15. Ibid., pp.36–41.

16. The Earl Jowitt, *Some Were Spies*, London: Hodder and Stoughton, 1954, pp.70–73.

17. Ibid., pp.46–7, 67.

18. Adamson, *The Great Detective*, pp.117–18.

19. Central Criminal Court, 10 February 1941.

20. North-Western Magistrates Court, 2 May 1941; West Riding Magistrates Court, 29 June 1941.

21. Andrews, *The Prosecutor*, pp.149–50; Lincoln Magistrates Court, 16 February 1943.

22. Berkshire Quarter Sessions, 9 February 1942; Oldham Magistrates Court, 21 December 1942; Birmingham Magistrates Court, 23 March 1943.

23. Aldershot Magistrates Court, 28 June 1943.

24. *The Trial of Peter Barnes and Others (The I.R.A. Coventry Explosion of 1939)* [Notable British Trials], ed. Letitia Fairfield, London,

Edinburgh, Glasgow: William Hodge, 1953, *passim*; Tim Pat Coogan, *The IRA*, London: Fontana/Collins, 1987, p.167.

25. Thames Magistrates Court, 6 November 1939.

26. Old Street Magistrates Court, 5 January 1940.

27. Ealing Magistrates Court, 27 May 1940; Marlborough Street Magistrates Court, 27 May 1940; Hendon Magistrates Court, 27 May 1940.

28. Hertfordshire Assizes, 25 June 1941.

29. Central Criminal Court, 6–7 April 1943.

30. Liverpool Magistrates Court, 20 May 1943.

31. Wood Green Magistrates Court, 18 April 1941; 25 April 1941.

32. Clerkenwell Magistrates Court, 16 April 1941.

33. Hove Magistrates Court, 14 January 1942; ibid., 23 March 1942.

34. Croydon Magistrates Court, 25 June 1943.

35. *The Trial of William Joyce* [Notable British Trials], ed. J. W. Hall, London, Edinburgh, Glasgow: William Hodge, 1946, p.36.

36. Malcolm Muggeridge, *The Infernal Grove: Chronicles of Wasted Time*, London: Fontana/Collins, 1975, pp.252–3.

CHAPTER 16: 'Sacrifice Was No Longer in Fashion'

1. Old Street Magistrates Court, 5 January 1946; North London Magistrates Court, 24 May 1947.

2. Old Street Magistrates Court, 27 November 1944.

3. Clerkenwell Magistrates Court, 17 June 1948.

4. South-Western Magistrates Court, 26 January 1946.

5. Epsom Magistrates Court, 12 June 1946.

6. Sevenoaks Magistrates Court, 19 July 1946.

7. Old Street Magistrates Court, 4 April 1947; *Evening Standard*, 24 November 1947.

8. Folkestone Magistrates Court, 24 May 1946.

9. Stratford Magistrates Court, 24 April 1946.

10. Clerkenwell Magistrates Court, 2 May 1947.

11. House of Commons, 10 October 1946.

12. General Court Martial, Calais, 26 June 1947.

13. UNRRA Council Meeting, 5 August 1946.

14. Princes Risborough Magistrates Court, 23 April 1949.

15. Whitehill, Hampshire, Magistrates Court, 9 September 1946.
16. Charles Vanstone, *A Man in Plain Clothes*, London: John Long, 1961, pp.149–53.
17. Berkshire Quarter Sessions, 6 October 1947.
18. Honeybourne, Worcestershire, Magistrates Court, 8–10 October 1947; ibid., 13 October 1947.
19. *Police Journal*, XX (1947), 11–12.
20. Bow Street Magistrates Court, 7 December 1944.
21. Bow Street Magistrates Court, 21 September 1945.
22. Bow Street Magistrates Court, 9 May 1947; Bow Street Magistrates Court, 18 June 1947.
23. Southampton Magistrates Court, 29 June 1946.
24. Southampton Magistrates Court, 20 January 1947.
25. West London Magistrates Court, 24 May 1944.
26. Central Criminal Court, 21 June 1945.
27. Brighton Magistrates Court, 23 March 1946.
28. Buckinghamshire Quarter Sessions, 8 April 1946.
29. Clerkenwell Magistrates Court, 13 July 1946.
30. Court of Criminal Appeal, 9 March 1948; 16 March 1948.
31. Kingston-on-Thames Magistrates Court, 16 April 1946; York Magistrates Court, 24 April 1946.
32. Bow Street Magistrates Court, 3 July 1946.
33. Marlborough Street Magistrates Court, 15 April 1947; 2 May 1947; Willesden Magistrates Court, 26 March 1946.
34. Plymouth Magistrates Court, 25 August 1948; Marlborough Street Magistrates Court, 18 May 1949.
35. Uxbridge Magistrates Court, 24 January 1949.
36. Central Criminal Court, 23 July 1946; Central Criminal Court, 14 January 1947; David Thomas, *Seek Out the Guilty*, London: John Long, 1969, pp.63–73.
37. Reading Assizes, 21 March 1947.

CHAPTER 17: 'The Best Government that Money Can Buy'

1. *Evening Standard*, 9 July 1946.
2. Central Criminal Court, 25 July 1946.
3. Hampstead Magistrates Court, 7 May 1947.

4. *Proceedings of the Tribunal appointed to inquire into Allegations reflecting on the Official Conduct of Ministers of the Crown and other Public Servants* [The Lynskey Tribunal], London: HMSO, 1949, 17 November 1948 (evidence of Jacob Harris), p.53; *The Lynskey Tribunal*, ed. Henry T. F. Rhodes, Leigh-on-Sea: Thames Bank Publishing, 1949, p.10.

5. *Report of the Tribunal appointed to inquire into Allegations reflecting on the Official Conduct of Ministers of the Crown and other Public Servants*, London: HMSO, 1949, p.50 [para. 209]; Rhodes, *Lynskey Tribunal*, p.114.

6. *Proceedings of the Tribunal*, 17 November 1948 (evidence of Jacob Harris), p.54; Stanley Wade Baron, *The Contact Man*, London: Secker & Warburg, 1966, p.78.

7. *Proceedings of the Tribunal*, 17 November 1948 (evidence of Jacob Harris), p.51; Rhodes, *Lynskey Tribunal*, p.15.

8. *Proceedings of the Tribunal*, Affidavit of Abraham Sherman, pp.595–6; Ernie Millen, *Specialist in Crime*, London: George G. Harrap, 1972, p.147.

9. *Proceedings of the Tribunal*, 1 November 1948 (preliminary sitting), p.ix; *Evening Standard*, 1 November 1948.

10. *Proceedings of the Tribunal*, pp.336, 350.

11. *Proceedings of the Tribunal*, p.1; Rhodes, *Lynskey Tribunal*, p.3.

12. *Proceedings of the Tribunal*, 10 December 1948 (evidence of Robert Benjamin Pearlman), p.495; Rhodes, *Lynskey Tribunal*, p.88.

13. *Proceedings of the Tribunal*, 1 and 2 December 1948 (evidence of Sidney Stanley), pp.338, 347; Baron, *Contact Man*, pp.154–5.

14. *Proceedings of the Tribunal*, 7 December 1948 (evidence of Sidney Stanley), p.423; Baron, *Contact Man*, p.167.

15. Glamorgan Assizes, 14 March 1949; Court of Criminal Appeal, 20 June 1949; Tredegar Magistrates Court, 15 March 1949.

Index